THE BIG BOOK OF
CLASSIC
MONSTER
MOVIES

70 YEARS OF CLASSIC MONSTERS
(1910-1980)

By John LeMay

BICEP BOOKS
Roswell, New Mexico, U.S.A.

BICEP BOOKS
Roswell, New Mexico, U.S.A.

For Jason Jaconetti.

THIS BOOK HAS BEEN DISCARDED BY JONATHAN HARKER
FROM THE LIBRARY OF CASTLE DRACULA

TABLE OF CONTENTS

INTRODUCTION

A few years ago, I wrote a little book called *The Big Book of Japanese Giant Monster Movies* which reviewed, as the title suggests, Japan's kaiju movies. It was nothing special—just my own thoughts on the films mixed in with some trivia and production background. I didn't expect it to do much. I wrote it for fun more than anything else. To my shock, people actually liked it. My fellow fans enjoyed my takes on the films, just as I had enjoyed similar review books in the past. So, is it really any wonder that I endeavored to write a second?

There's plenty of film genres out there that I love, but second to the giant monsters of Japan, my other favorites are the good ol' human-sized monsters made popular by Universal and Hammer from the 1930s through the 1970s. On that note, if you're a Universal or Hammer scholar, I doubt you'll learn much. A few things maybe, but if you're looking for sheer, unadulterated information on production background, etc. I suggest *Universal Horrors*, *Hammer Complete*, and many other better books than this one. As stated earlier, I did this book because I enjoy reading similar books by fans like myself who tell me why they liked this or that film, what stood out to them, etc. Sometimes I'll read a review from a fellow fan who happens to love a movie that I completely disdain. Occasionally, that person's writing will encourage me to go back and watch the film again. Or, on the other end of the spectrum, sometimes they will point out flaws in my own favorite films that I never noticed. (My own sensibilities are quite different from the regular fan, I'd rather watch *Dracula A.D. 1972* over the 1931 *Dracula* any day, for instance. But that's just me.)

The main scope of this work is every Dracula, Frankenstein, Mummy, and werewolf movie from either Universal or Hammer between the years 1910 and 1980. In other words, this isn't a book about classic horror films in general, but movies starring the "Classic Monsters," which I define as such based upon their creation in literature before film. *The Invisible Man*, *The Strange Case of Dr. Jekyll and Mr. Hyde*, and even *The Jewel of the Seven Stars* (the inspiration for *Blood from the Mummy's Tomb*) all started out as books before they were transformed into movies. Even

4

Hammer's exploitive *The Vampire Lovers* was based upon a novella, *Carmilla*, that predated Bram Stoker's better-known *Dracula*. Anyhow, that's how I define "Classic Monster"—if they were birthed in a book and later adapted to film by either Hammer or Universal, they'll be in this book. After that, you're in the wild. What I'm trying to say is, while I do cover a lot of non-Universal and Hammer Frankenstein and Dracula movies—*Lady Frankenstein* and *Billy the Kid versus Dracula* to name only a few—you're not guaranteed to find every non-Universal/Hammer Frankenstein or Dracula movie out there in this book. Furthermore, a few movies I review here don't even have classic monsters in them, like Hammer's *Kiss of the Vampire*, for instance. (However, it did begin life as "Dracula 3" at Hammer.) *I Was a Teenage Werewolf* wasn't based on a book, but I included it too. Why? Because it would have been rather odd to include its sequels, *I Was a Teenage Frankenstein* and *Blood of Dracula,* without the film that kicked off that little teenage monster craze. Bottom line: There'll be plenty of things for nitpickers to complain about in terms of why I included this movie but not that one and so on. As I said, the only thing you're guaranteed is all the major Hammers and Universals that contained the signature monsters of Frankenstein, Dracula, a mummy, a werewolf, Dr. Jekyll and Mr. Hyde...heck, even Jack the Ripper snuck his way in via Hammer, even though the Ripper's not really a "classic monster".

And why the seemingly random Septuagennial celebration of 70 years between 1910 to 1980? Well, the first one is easy since 1910 is the year that the first "classic monster" movie came out in the form of *Frankenstein*. As to why I stopped at 1980, to be frank, I'm not a fan of a lot of the movies to come out after that. Granted, I think the Francis Ford Coppola *Dracula* is great, along with *Mary Shelley's Frankenstein*, Stephen Sommer's Mummy movies, and so on. While I love those films, I just didn't have it in me to cover the sheer magnitude of lesser movies to accompany them over the years. As it was, 1980 seemed like the right place to end it for me. Will I return one day to cover everything from 1980 on up? Time will tell, but for now, from one fan to another, I hope you enjoy this 400 page love letter to cinema's first seventy years of classic monster movies.

John LeMay
October 16, 2021

THE FILMS
1910-1980

FRANKENSTEIN

(EDISON STUDIOS)
Release Date: March 18, 1910

Directed by: J. Searle Dawley **Screenplay by:** J. Searle Dawley
Cast: Augustus Phillips (Frankenstein) Mary Fuller (Elizabeth)
Charles Stanton Ogle (the Monster)

Academy Ratio, Black & White, 13 Minutes

SYNOPSIS After only two years away at college, Victor
Frankenstein discovers the secret of life. However, instead of a
perfect being, due to the "evil in Frankenstein's mind," he creates
a monster. The creature is so terrifying that upon its emergence
from the lab, Victor faints. Victor returns home and puts the
experiment behind him, planning to wed his fiancé Elizabeth. On
their wedding night, the monster reappears to briefly menace the
couple. In the end, the monster disappears into a mirror and
ceases to exist.

COMMENTARY Mary Shelley's *Frankenstein; or, The Modern
Prometheus* was written in 1818 and was being performed in stage
plays by the 1820s. In 1910, it finally made it to the medium of
film, still very primitive at the time, courtesy of Edison Studios.
The picture was directed by J. Searle Dawley over the course of
five days in New York City from January 13th to the 17th of that
year. Because certain members of the populace feared
Frankenstein was taboo to adapt, Edison Kinetogram's staff
reassured patrons that their adaptation would de-emphasize the
horror aspects in favor of the "mystic and psychological".

This rings true in the film, as this version of Dr. Frankenstein is
more akin to a witch practicing magic than a scientist in a lab.
Said lab is decked out with various skeletons, and the doctor has
a huge cauldron out of which he somehow creates the monster.
For 1910 standards, the monster's creation is quite thrilling.
Unlike other iterations, where lightning is used to bring life to a
makeshift body sewn together out of corpses, this monster begins
to form within the cauldron. It's similar to Dracula's resurrection
in *Scars of Dracula* in that we see the monster slowly begin to take

shape through trick photography. At times the flaming skeleton looks like something out of the Terminator franchise. (This effect was created by burning an effigy of the monster, and the footage was run in reverse. *The Moving Picture World* called the scene "the most remarkable ever committed to a film".) When it becomes fully formed, the monster is a far cry from the more popular Boris Karloff/Jack Pierce version of the creature. If anything, it looks like a tamer version of the title creature of 1974's *Frankenstein and the Monster from Hell*. (Perhaps the Edison *Frankenstein* influenced that one's design?) The action is rudimentary, with the monster menacing his creator in a few scenes before being overcome. In keeping with the magical/whimsical tone, the monster meets its end at the sight of its own reflection. Upon seeing itself in the mirror, the monster suddenly becomes trapped in the mirror and slowly fades away. The allegory is apparently that since Victor Frankenstein has been married, the purity of his bride has overcome the evil in his mind, and thus also the monster.

Critics and audiences alike were impressed, but Edison's *Frankenstein* was soon forgotten and lost to the sands of time—literally, it was forgotten until an old issue of *The Edison Kinetogram* from March 15, 1910, was discovered in 1963. By 1980, the American Film Institute included it on their list of the ten most culturally and historically significant lost films. Fortunately, a collector had acquired a print of the film in the 1950s and in 1993 the film "premiered" again for a new generation in Milwaukee.

FINAL WORD Though it isn't likely to knock a viewer's socks off in the 21st Century, it should still be required viewing for horror fans for its historical significance. That creation scene truly is spectacular, and, after all, it's only ten minutes of your time.

DR. JEKYLL AND MR. HYDE

(THANHOUSER COMPANY)
Release Date: January 16, 1912

Directed by: Lucius Henderson **Screenplay by:** Thomas Sullivan based upon the novel by Robert Louis Stevenson **Cast:** James Cruze (Dr. Jekyll/Mr. Hyde) Florence La Badie (Jekyll's fiancé) Harry Benham (Mr. Hyde) *Additional scenes

Academy Ratio, Black & White, 13 Minutes

SYNOPSIS Shortly after creating an elixir that changes him into Mr. Hyde, Dr. Jekyll begins courting the daughter of a minister. Eventually, Jekyll begins to turn into Hyde at random times, wreaking havoc on his love life. One day he begins to transform in front of his fiancé in the park and runs away. Hyde soon returns to menace the girl and kills her father when he intervenes. A policeman chases Hyde back to Jekyll's residence but finds only the doctor. Knowing he can no longer control the transformations and that one day he will become Hyde permanently, Jekyll bids his fiancé goodbye and tells her that he is leaving, never to return. When Jekyll turns into Hyde for the final time, his butler reports it to the police. Before the police can break into the lab, Hyde drinks poison and kills himself.

COMMENTARY As it stands, this is not actually the first motion-picture adaptation of Robert Louis Stevenson's *Dr. Jekyll and Mr. Hyde*. The first, which is now lost, came about in 1908 and was essentially a filmed performance of the 1887 stage play upon which it was based. As to why the stage play was adapted over the book itself, that's because the book lacked the requisite love interest (or female characters of any kind, really) needed for most movies.

Even though it's about the same length, this film is a bit more involved than *Frankenstein*. That doesn't make it a better movie. All in all, it's not very memorable. It does hit the ground running at least, and in less than two minutes Dr. Jekyll has already turned into Mr. Hyde. (But then again, at only twelve minutes in length, I suppose that's actually about right.) Jekyll transforms into Hyde via a jump cut, and the makeup certainly isn't bad. (This transformation is nothing, of course, compared to the 1910 *Frankenstein* creation scene.) Though the transformation itself is well-handled enough for 1912, Hyde looks a little goofy in this go-around. However, that said, this Hyde is also fairly faithful to the one in Stevenson's novel, as Stevenson described Hyde as being somewhat "dwarfish" in appearance. The first transformation doesn't last long, and Hyde transitions back to Jekyll, which is achieved by having the actor look down at the floor as his brown hair returns to Jekyll's white.

Critiques of the time were fairly harsh, with Troy Howarth noting that he felt like Jekyll's lab looked like a cheap closet. He also said that in Hyde's rampages the character acted "like an unrestrained child who is allowed to run amok by a distracted parent... [rather] than a genuine menace."

FINAL WORD Though the 1910 *Frankenstein* is highly recommended, this one is not, and even at only 12 minutes is still a waste of time in my humble opinion.

DR. JEKYLL AND MR. HYDE

(IMP)
Release Date: 1913

Directed by: Herbert Brenon **Screenplay by:** Herbert Brenon based upon the novel by Robert Louis Stevenson **Cast:** King Baggot (Dr. Henry Jekyll/Mr. Hyde) Jane Gail (Alice) Matt B. Snyder (Alice's father) Howard Crampton (Dr. Lanyon)

Academy Ratio, Black & White, 26 Minutes

SYNOPSIS Despite having a good outer facade doing charity work, Dr. Jekyll has evil desires to unleash an alternate side of his personality: Mr. Hyde. He does so by means of a potion. After a night of terror as Hyde, Jekyll repents of his misdeeds the next morning and vows not to bring out Hyde ever again. However, Hyde returns without use of the potion. Hyde's reign of terror continues with him killing the father of Jekyll's fiancé. Eventually, Hyde plans to transform in front of Jekyll's disbelieving colleague, Dr. Lanyon. He does so, and Jekyll then faints from remorse. Soon after, he transforms back into Hyde. By then the townsfolk have had enough and chase Hyde down to Jekyll's lab. The stress of the dual persona has become too much for the shared body Jekyll and Hyde inhabit, and it perishes.

COMMENTARY Ironically enough, though Universal never produced a classical adaptation of *The Strange Case of Dr. Jekyll and Mr. Hyde* during their horror heyday of the 1930s/1940s, one of the very first horror pictures they ever produced was an adaptation of said novel. (If one wants to be technical, at the time the company was called IMP but later changed to Universal. As a further aside, that same year had also seen the release of *The Werewolf* from the studio, which is sadly lost today.)

Like the last two adaptations, this one was again based upon the play and as such includes the fiancé character. It's also silent like the last version and you've got to love the text cards, one of which reads, "In the dead silence of the night Dr. Jekyll plans to set free his evil self." Whereas in the last adaptation it took two minutes to get to Mr. Hyde, this one takes about five. This iteration of Hyde is dwarfish like the last one and is made so via the hunched over stature of the actor (the others did this via the shorter double playing Hyde). The makeup is also sadly less elaborate, though possibly less goofy looking. (King Bagot applied his own makeup, which comprised of greasepaint and a wig and transforms via a camera dissolve.) That said, this version of the character is still comical more than anything else. Case in point, in one scene Hyde randomly walks into a bar, waltzes around to frighten the patrons, and leaves. That's pretty much the extent of his reign of terror and nefarious deeds until he canes a young boy in the streets and kills his fiancé's father.

FINAL WORD If you hated the previous year's rendition, you'll hate this one even more since it's more than double the length.

DR. JEKYLL AND MR. HYDE

(PARAMOUNT)
Release Date: March 28, 1920
Alternate Titles: *The Strange Case of Dr. Jekyll and Mr. Hyde*
(Czechoslovakia) *The Secret of Dr. Jekyll* (Finland) *Dr. Jekyll and the Devil* (Japan) *The Doctor and the Monster* (Mexico)

Directed by: John S. Robertson **Screenplay by:** Clara Beranger based upon the stage play by Thomas Russell Sullivan **Cast:** John Barrymore (Dr. Henry Jekyll/Mr. Edward Hyde) Brandon Hurst (Sir George Carewe) Martha Mansfield (Millicent Carewe) Charles Willis Lane (Dr. Richard Lanyon) Cecil Clovelly (Edward Enfield)

Academy Ratio, Black & White, 79 Minutes

SYNOPSIS Busy with medical work at a charity hospital for the poor, Dr. Jekyll accidentally stands up his fiancé, Millicent, and several colleagues at a restaurant. Arriving very late, Sir George, Jekyll's future father-in-law, chastises Jekyll that he's wasting away his youth at the charity hospital. Sir George takes Jekyll to a somewhat seedy dance hall, which awakens in Jekyll a desire to indulge in his baser natures. Jekyll devises a serum to transform into an alter ego, Mr. Hyde. Jekyll enjoys his nightlife as Hyde but eventually becomes repulsed by his deeds. Jekyll quits taking the serum, but Hyde emerges from him again with a vengeance. Sir George figures out that Hyde and Jekyll are one and the same and confronts Jekyll about it. Hyde kills Sir George soon after, devastating Millicent. As Jekyll's struggles with Hyde continue, Millicent goes to see Jekyll but is met by the monster. Millicent manages to get away, and Jekyll takes control of his body long enough to poison himself. Hyde dies and reverts back to Jekyll right in front of Dr. Lanyon, who tells Millicent that Hyde killed Jekyll, sparing her the ugly truth.

COMMENTARY This is one of the more highly regarded, early versions of *Dr. Jekyll and Mr. Hyde*, so much so that it completely overshadowed another adaptation made and released that same year. The high marks afforded to it are mostly due to lead actor

John Barrymore. This was also the first time that Jekyll was portrayed as young and handsome to better contrast with the grotesque Hyde. In a testament to Barrymore's acting abilities, there are no special effects used during the transformation scenes, just Barrymore contorting his face and body. In the seven-year interim between this and the last adaptation, cinema had matured considerably. Movies were still silent but were now longer and had more complex storylines as a result. The sets and costumes are also much more luxurious. (There's even a well-done flashback to explain the origin of a poison-carrying ring.)

The dialogue is well done, particularly a dinnertime conversation between Jekyll and some other scientists on the nature of dual identities and natures. One character says, "A man cannot destroy the savage in him by denying its impulses. The only way to get rid of a temptation is to yield to it." (A line that came not from the book, but from Oscar Wilde, by the way.) The line seems to have an unsettling effect on Jekyll and puts him on the path to creating Hyde and he says, "Wouldn't it be marvelous if the two natures in man could be separated—housed in different bodies!"

Hyde's design is good, definitely better than the ones that preceded it, with long spindly fingers, which is a nice touch. (In one of his more animated scenes, you can see Barrymore accidentally fling one off.) Mr. Hyde is less a cartoon caricature in this version and more of an actual character, seen engaging prostitutes in conversation rather than terrifying them. The most exciting scene comes when Jekyll confronts Sir George, telling him that it was he who encouraged him to fall into sin. Hyde then beats Sir George to death with his cane and appears to bite his throat at one point. In another terrifying, entertaining scene, Jekyll has a nightmare that a giant spectral spider attacks him in his sleep. (Barrymore also played the spider via suitmation, and as odd as it might sound, it's spectacularly creepy.)

The film was a success, and until the 1931 version, it was the reigning champion of the novel's many adaptations.

FINAL WORD Although it's still a chore for younger generations to watch, I can concede that it's still silent cinema at its finest.

NOSFERATU: A SYMPHONY OF HORROR

(PRANA FILM)

Release Date: March 4, 1922 (Germany)
Alternate Titles: *Nosferatu* (Latin America) *The Twelfth Hour: A Night of Horror* (Austria; recut version) *Vampire Nosferatu* (Japan)

Directed by: F. W. Murnau **Screenplay by:** Henrik Galeen **Music by:** Hans Erdmann **Cast:** Max Schreck (Count Orlok) Gustav von Wangenheim (Thomas Hutter) Greta Schröder (Ellen Hutter) Alexander Granach (Knock) Georg H. Schnell (Shipowner Harding) Ruth Landshoff (Ruth) John Gottowt (Professor Bulwer) Gustav Botz (Professor Sievers)

Academy Ratio, Black & White, 94 Minutes

SYNOPSIS In Wisborg, Germany, in the year 1838, real estate broker Thomas Hutter is given the unusual task from his boss, Herr Knock, to travel to Transylvania to collect a Count Orlok so that he may buy a property in Wisborg. Hutter finds Orlok to be a strange, rat-like man who craves his blood and who is infatuated with a portrait of Hutter's wife, Ellen. Eventually, Orlok puts the bite on Hutter and sets off for Wisborg on his own via sailing ship. On the journey, the crew fall victim to not only the vampire but also plague-ridden rats. The ship arrives in Wisborg with the entire crew dead, and the rats spread the plague from the ship to the town. Herr Knock, who has since gone insane, is blamed for the strange goings-on, as the town is unaware of the presence of Count Orlok. Eventually, Hutter, who escaped the castle, makes his way home in a weakened state. He warns Ellen that Orlok is a vampire. When Ellen reads that the only way to kill the vampire is to lure him into the sunlight via a pure maiden, she decides to sacrifice herself for the town. Orlok comes to her bedroom to feed on her, and forgets about the impending sunrise, which swiftly turns him into vapor after Ellen's death.

COMMENTARY The production history behind *Nosferatu: A Symphony of Horror*, which nearly became a lost film, is a fascinating one. Though Prana Studio founder Albin Grau claimed

15

he was inspired to produce the film due to a wartime experience where he encountered a man purported to know a real vampire, the true inspiration for the film was simply Bram Stoker's *Dracula*. Grau and his partner in the studio, Enrico Dieckmann, instructed screenwriter Henrik Galeen to simply adapt Stoker's novel for a German audience, relocating it to Germany and renaming the characters.

First off, Knock is the crazy Renfield equivalent, envisioned here as an old man. Though we're not sure what the connection is between Knock and Orlok, he seems to know there's something fishy about the Count, as he tells Hutter that he might have to give a little blood on his journey. Hutter is obviously the Jonathan Harker stand-in, and fulfills the exact same function, traveling to Transylvania, etc. Count Orlok is wildly different from the mustachioed Dracula envisioned by Stoker, who is pale, bald, and rat-like. And, nor does Orlok regain any semblance of youth or humanity as he feeds. For that matter, none of Orlok's victims rise again as vampires, they simply die. Hutter's wife, Ellen, is the Mina stand-in, who stays with the equivalents of Arthur and Lucy Holmwood while her husband is away. The film's version of Van Helsing, Professor Bulwer, is introduced to the audience via a lecture where he shows his students a Venus flytrap (the footage of which was probably sensational for a 1922 audience). However, considering he really doesn't do anything to confront the vampire, it may not be appropriate to even compare him to Van Helsing. In a move that was ahead of its time, it is Ellen who is the unabashed hero of the film rather than one of the men. None of the male characters aid her in vanquishing the vampire at all, and she gives her life to save her town and her husband from evil.

Another significant way in which this film differs from future *Dracula* adaptations is that very little of it takes place at Hutter/Harker's hometown. Most of it takes place in Transylvania and on the sailing ship, which makes for this version's most interesting visuals. In the hull, Orlok rises rigidly from his coffin in a manner that would be imitated from there on out. His crates of Transylvanian earth are also filled with rats that bring the plague. The idea of the plague carrying rats was this version's most unique twist on the mythos, and it's a shame that more Dracula adaptations in the future didn't carry this over as well. Unlike the Bela Lugosi and Christopher Lee Draculas of the future, Count Orlok, though terrifying, really has no dignity. Not only is he physically repulsive, and in no way attractive to his victims, he also carries his own coffin off of the ship! Lee or Lugosi's versions wouldn't be caught (un)dead doing such a thing, and if anything, one of their lackeys would be shown doing the grunt work.

The film was well-received upon its release, but trouble arose when Prana Film had to declare bankruptcy. (The studio, founded in 1921, had intended to produce multiple horror films, but ultimately only managed this one.) Making matters worse, the Stoker Estate became aware of the film and its obvious parallels to *Dracula*. They sued the producers, and the courts decreed that all prints of the film be destroyed. Fortunately, one survived, and through this print the legend and legacy of Nosferatu survived. Today, the expressionist horror film is highly regarded by horror fans, critics, and serious scholars alike.

FINAL WORD Of all the silent-era horror films, this one is regarded by many as the greatest thanks to its captivating imagery, particularly Orlok's shadow creeping along the wall, and his long, spindly fingers in shadow form reaching for Ellen.

PHANTOM OF THE OPERA

(UNIVERSAL)
Release Date: November 15, 1925 (original release)
February 16, 1930 (sound reissue)

Directed by: Rupert Julian **Screenplay by:** Walter Anthony, Elliott J. Clawson, Bernard McConville, Frank M. McCormack, Tom Reed, Raymond L. Schrock, Jasper Spearing & Richard Wallace **Makeup by:** Lon Chaney **Music by:** Gustav Hinrichs **Cast:** Lon Chaney (the Phantom) Mary Philbin (Christine Daaé) Norman Kerry (Vicomte Raoul de Chagny) Arthur Edmund Carewe (Ledoux) Gibson Gowland (Simon Buquet) John St. Polis (Comte Philippe de Chagny) Snitz Edwards (Florine Papillon) Virginia Pearson (Carlotta)

Academy Ratio, Black & White, 107 Minutes (original version)
93 Minutes (sound reissue)

SYNOPSIS The new season at the Paris Opera House has just debuted with a production of *Faust*. Mysterious events plague the opera with rumors of a ghostly phantom pulling the strings behind the scenes. For instance, an understudy named Christine has just replaced the lead performer of *Faust*, who departed under mysterious circumstances. Christine is also being tutored by an unseen figure, in fact the Phantom, who drags her to his underground lair. Shocked by his disfigured appearance, Christine begs him to let her go. The Phantom agrees so long as she returns, but instead Christine makes plans to escape with her fiancé, Raoul. The Phantom learns of this plot, and kidnaps Christine after a performance. Raoul and a French detective, Ledoux, go to rescue Christine. The Phantom absconds with her in a carriage, which Christine jumps out of. An angry mob chases the Phantom to the pier, where he is apparently killed, while Raul consoles Christine.

COMMENTARY Though *Nosferatu* is beloved as the greatest silent-era horror film, this one might be better—or, if not better, certainly more epic. With its grand architecture and numerous extras filling the screen, *Phantom of the Opera* is undeniably

18

sprawling in scale for a silent film. It was, of course, based on the classic work by Gaston Leroux, who Universal studio head Carl Laemmle met in Paris. Reportedly, upon receiving Leroux's novel as a gift, Laemmle read it in one night and immediately secured the screen rights and eyed Lon Chaney for the title role right away.

Filming did not get off to a smooth start, with Chaney and director Rupert Julian at odds. Actually, it wasn't just Chaney, but reportedly much of the crew who disliked Julian. Communications eventually broke down between the two to the point that they quit speaking, and Chaney essentially directed himself as the Phantom, which certainly wasn't bad. Just as Bela Lugosi is Dracula, and Boris Karloff is the Frankenstein monster, Lon Chaney is the definitive Phantom. The reveal of his disfigured face is one of the most iconic scenes in cinema history. (The Phantom's line is worth repeating: "Feast your eyes — glut your soul, on my accursed ugliness!") Reportedly, some audience goers fainted at the Phantom's unveiling! It's tough to say whether or not there was a missed opportunity to make Chaney's Phantom more sympathetic like in the book. In the book, Christine grants the Phantom a kiss at the ending, which causes him to "die of love". Although considered for a while, there is no such ending here. In what turned out to be a prototype of Universal finales to come, instead, an angry mob rushes the monster to dispatch him. Specifically, the Phantom absconds with Christine in a runaway carriage. (This chase sequence was reminiscent of some of the later Hammer Draculas, notably *Dracula has Risen from the Grave.*)

As stated before, there is no sympathy for the disfigured Phantom at his time of death. Because, throughout the film, the Phantom is quite the movie villain—almost a precedent for the overblown, charming villains of the Bond films. For instance, he traps Raoul and Ledoux in a torture chamber similar to something Bond would need to escape. Around the same time, when an alarm alerts him to the fact that an intruder is in the catacombs, he tells Christine, "It seems we have callers." The Phantom sets out into the sewers, takes a snorkel and stealthily glides under the water. Creeping under the water unseen, he comes upon the intruder, Raoul's brother, and flips over his boat dragging him to his death. This was a notable first in cinema for unseen horrors beneath the waters that would continue with *Creature from the Black Lagoon* and *Jaws.*

This release also featured two scenes in color, most notably the Bal Masque de l'Opera. "Beneath your dancing feet are the tombs of tortured men—thus does the Red Death rebuke your merriment!" the Phantom decrees as he exits the main hall back to the catacombs. He carries a scepter with a snake coiled around it topped by a skull. The colorized footage continues into the next scene, colorized a dark blue, on the rooftop. Christine and Raoul talk and the Phantom, perched like a gargoyle amidst some statues listens in. Notably, he is still wearing the great red robe, but minus his mask. The robe billows in the wind, making for some of the most dramatic imagery of the silent era.

Despite its classic status today, the film's preview showing in January of 1925 was not well received. One reviewer claimed, "There's too much spook melodrama. Put in some gags to relieve the tension." And that Universal did, shooting additional scenes that reportedly turned the movie into a romantic comedy! This cut was literally booed offscreen, and so Universal went back to the drawing board. A few more additional scenes were shot, a new cut was made, and the final version was finally unleashed. While critical reception was mixed, audiences loved it, and it made a good profit. In fact, only a few years later upon the advent of talking pictures, Universal immediately set about to do a partial remake of *Phantom of the Opera* with sound. Their only problem: Chaney not only refused to loop in dialogue but would not even allow a voice actor to voice the Phantom for him! However, Universal still wanted to do the film so badly that they went on with production, shooting new scenes. The actors who played Christine and Raoul, Mary Philbin and Norman Kerry, returned for the reshoots (now nearly five years later). Ultimately, about half of the picture was reshot, and to fill in the blanks in the case of actors no longer available for the minor parts, Edward Martindel, George B. Williams, Phillips Smalley, Ray Holderness, and Edward Davis were added in. As to scenes with the Phantom, they simply played out as they did in the original version with the dialogue written on screen. Universal wasn't bashful about this, though, and advertised the fact that everyone but Chaney spoke.

This version of the *Phantom*, too, was a hit and grossed either a half million or a million dollars, depending on the source. Unfortunately, most of this version of the film was lost in a fire. And though the soundtrack survived, the reshot footage did not, leaving us with the original Phantom alone.

FINAL WORD A good competitor with *Nosferatu* as the seminal silent horror film and quite possibly still the best adaptation of *Phantom of the Opera* that there is.

The EDISON
KINETOGRAM

VOL. 2   MARCH 15, 1910   No. 4

SCENE FROM

FRANKENSTEIN

FILM No. 6604

EDISON FILMS RELEASED FROM
MARCH 16 TO 31 INCLUSIVE

DRACULA

(UNIVERSAL)
Release Date: February 12, 1931
Alternate Titles: *Dracula-The Ancient Vampire* (Finland) *Majin Dracula* (Japan) *Dracula the Vampire* (Netherlands)

Directed by: Tod Browning **Screenplay by:** Hamilton Deane & John L. Balderston, based upon the play adapted from Bram Stoker's Dracula by Garrett Fort **Makeup by:** Jack P. Pierce **Music Supervisor:** Heinz Roemheld **Cast:** Bela Lugosi (Dracula) Helen Chandler (Mina Seward) David Manners (John Harker) Dwight Frye (Renfield) Edward Van Sloan (Van Helsing) Herbert Bunston (Dr. Seward) Frances Dade (Lucy Weston)

Academy Ratio, Black & White, 75 Minutes

SYNOPSIS A man named Renfield has just traveled to Castle Dracula in Transylvania on real estate business to broker a deal for Count Dracula to purchase the Carfax Abby estate in England. Renfield gets more than he bargained for when the vampiric Dracula drives him mad and makes him his slave as they travel to England. Upon arrival, Renfield is institutionalized and Dracula becomes enamored with the beautiful Mina Seward. It's then up to Mina's fiancé, John Harker, and vampire hunter Van Helsing to destroy Dracula before he can make Mina one of the undead. In the end, Dracula kidnaps Mina and takes her to Carfax Abby. However, it is close to sunrise, so the Count must return to his coffin. Van Helsing tracks him there and stakes him, while John rescues Mina who is freed from the vampire curse.

COMMENTARY Ever since the founding of Universal Pictures back in 1912, studio head Carl Laemmle had been pining to do an adaptation of Bram Stoker's *Dracula*. The project was considered off and on until the late 1920s. Early iterations would have been a bit more faithful to the book, not to mention costly. Two things had a major impact on the burgeoning film adaptation. First was the stock market crash of October 1929. Next was the death of Lon Chaney, the original choice for Dracula. As a way of saving on budget and streamlining Bram Stoker's epic story, Universal chose to adapt a stage play of the book that was seeing success in Britain. The title role in the play was performed by Bela Lugosi, who would be carried over into Universal's film.

Though a few other actors had played the Count prior to this, Lugosi's version of the character, notably the thick Hungarian accent and dark look, would thoroughly imbed itself the public consciousness as the definitive version of the role for many years. In fact, to this day, some consider it the definitive portrayal, even when compared to Christopher Lee's version that would emerge in the late 1950s. While Lugosi's Dracula wasn't quite as suave as Lee's, something interesting about Lugosi's Dracula was that he at least occasionally changed wardrobe. He more or less disguises himself as a very creepy coach driver to meet Renfield early in the movie, and later he looks dapper in a suit and coat sans his famous cape. Lee's Dracula was rarely, if ever, seen out of his cape. Also, Lugosi's Count frequently changed himself into a bat or a wolf throughout the film, even if the transformations took place off-screen.

Behind Bela Lugosi, the other standout performance in the film is Dwight Frye's Renfield. His dialogue is wonderfully quotable, and his spiel about the rats (often touted in the trailers) is very memorable. Of course, in the novel, it was Jonathan Harker that went to Castle Dracula. But, for the sake of condensing the novel, Renfield made for a wise replacement. Likewise, Mina Murray has become the daughter of Dr. Seward, thus making her Mina Seward, another good way to narrow down the characters. And whereas the book had three young male leads in the form of Harker, Arthur Holmwood, and Quincey Morris, the movie only has Harker.

The first twenty minutes of the film have a rather epic feel to them, mostly due to a few outdoor locations and the sprawling Castle Dracula set. Once the story reaches London, the film becomes a bit more claustrophobic mostly bouncing back and forth between the Seward home and the Sanitarium in the last half of the film. As such, it's heavily dialogue-driven. Though Edward Van Sloan's Van Helsing doesn't hold a candle to Peter Cushing's later interpretation, his interactions and verbal sparring matches with Dracula make for some of the best scenes in the whole film. Van Helsing doesn't waste any time in outing the vampire either and exposes him the moment he notices that he casts no reflection in a small mirror.

If there's one thing that's disappointing about *Dracula*, it's the ending. Of course, we are talking about a film made nearly 100

26

years ago now, but the ending of *Dracula* really isn't exciting at all—especially if compared to the ending of *Frankenstein* made less than a year later. While in that film the monster burns up in a windmill, Dracula's death is a simple affair. As Dracula absconds with Mina into the catacombs of Carfax Abby, Van Helsing and Harker follow close behind. Dracula foolishly seems to think that once he's in his coffin, he'll be safe. But, once Van Helsing gains ingress, he walks over to the coffin, pries off the lid, and stakes Dracula, who doesn't even wake up to put up a fight. And that is how the film ends.

When released in February of 1931, the film was unlike anything audiences had seen before. Word of mouth spread quickly, and within only two days, it had managed to sell 50,000 tickets. By the time it had finished its run, it had become Universal's highest grosser for the entire year.

FINAL WORD Though it might be a bit boring when compared to later versions like *Horror of Dracula* (1958), the film is still enjoyable to watch for its great performances and deserves respect as the father of the Universal horror genre.

DRACULA
(SPANISH VERSION)

(UNIVERSAL)
Release Date: April 24, 1931

Directed by: George Melford **Screenplay by:** Baltasar Fernández Cué based upon the play adapted from Bram Stoker's Dracula by Garrett Fort **Music by:** Heinz Roemheld **Cast:** Carlos Villarías (Conde Drácula) Lupita Tovar (Eva Seward) Barry Norton (Juan Harker) Pablo Alvarez Rubio (Renfield) Eduardo Arozamena (Van Helsing) José Soriano Viosca (Doctor Seward) Carmen Guerrero (Lucía Weston)

Academy Ratio, Black & White, 104 Minutes

SYNOPSIS When Renfield travels to Castle Dracula in Transylvania on real estate business, he gets more than he bargained for. Renfield is brokering a deal for Count Dracula to purchase the Carfax Abby estate in England. The vampiric Dracula drives Renfield mad and makes him his slave as they travel to England. Upon arrival, Renfield is institutionalized and Dracula becomes enamored with the beautiful Eva Seward. It's then up to Eva's fiancé, Juan Harker, and vampire hunter Van Helsing to destroy Dracula before he can make Eva one of the undead.

COMMENTARY Back in the 1930s, Universal had a practice of shooting pictures back-to-back. One would be in English, and the other would be in Spanish for countries in Latin America. This was notably done with *Dracula*. After the English language version finished shooting for the day, in the evenings, the Spanish crew would come to film using the same sets and props with Spanish-speaking actors. And, as much of a classic that *Dracula* would go on to become, many fans and critics consider its Spanish counterpart to be better. One reason why this version was superior likely stemmed from the fact that the Spanish crew sometimes got to watch the dailies from the English version. They would look at the scenes, then sometimes restage them to look better for their version. Carlos Villarias was also encouraged to imitate Bela Lugosi, whose performance he got to see via the dailies. Scenes of

Dracula enticing Mina to come to him in the yard are particularly well staged. Some differences between the two versions are quite minor. For instance, rather than a paperclip as in the English version, Renfield cuts his finger on a knife at dinner instead, which works better. One more notable difference between the two is that when the brides all line up to attack Renfield, Dracula doesn't stop them as he did in the English version. There's an additional character in the form of the maid, who shares a memorable scene with Renfield. When she faints at the sight of the madman, he begins to crawl towards her unconscious form. Just when we think he's going to attack her, it turns out he was really just after a fly!

The Spanish *Dracula* is longer not only because it has a few extra scenes, but because many of the scenes present in both versions are longer in the Spanish version. The main reason that this version has additional scenes wasn't because anything was added to it; it was because some scenes went unshot on the English version. As it was, the director, Tod Browning, literally ripped out pages from the shooting script when he didn't like them! Another reason the Spanish *Dracula* had extra scenes was that executives requested the removal of a few scenes from *Dracula* that they felt were too scary, which they apparently didn't worry about in the Spanish version.

The ending of the Spanish *Dracula* is a major improvement over the English version. For starters, it has an extra scene in it that either went unfilmed or got deleted from the English cut. The scene shows a spooky graveyard set. A woman's scream is heard. Van Helsing and Harker walk out of the fog, revealing they've just staked Lucy. Considering a set was built for the scene it stands to reason it was shot for the English version too and removed. Also, the ending is more suspenseful: as Dracula leans in for the kill on Eva, suddenly the sun begins to rise, and he races back to his coffin. Overall it has an element of excitement lacking from the other version. For a time, this version was a lost film until a print was found and restored in the 1970s. By the 1980s, it began reaping praise from viewers who regarded it as superior to the English language version. Today it always accompanies *Dracula* on its home video releases.

FINAL WORD Though I would 100% argue the direction and production values are better in the Spanish version, I still feel the performances of Bela Lugosi and Dwight Frye are better in the English version.

FRANKENSTEIN

(UNIVERSAL)
Release Date: November 21, 1931
Alternate Titles: *Frankenstein, the Man Who Created a Monster*
(France) *Dr. Frankenstein* (Hungary) *Frankenstein: The Man Who
Created Man* (Sweden)

Directed by: James Whale **Screenplay by:** Francis Edward Far-
agoh, Garrett Fort & John L. Balderston, based upon the novel by
Mary Shelley **Makeup by:** Jack P. Pierce **Music Supervisor:**
Bernhard Kaun **Cast:** Colin Clive (Henry Frankenstein) Mae
Clarke (Elizabeth Lavenza) John Boles (Victor Moritz) Boris Karloff
(the Monster) Edward Van Sloan (Dr. Waldman) Frederick Kerr
(Baron Frankenstein) Dwight Frye (Fritz) Lionel Belmore (the
Burgomaster)

Academy Ratio, Black & White, 71 Minutes

SYNOPSIS Henry Frankenstein, the son of a wealthy baron, has
just dropped out of medical school to perform a controversial
experiment. With his hunchback assistant, Fritz, Henry sews
together various corpses to create a brand new body. When Henry
sends Fritz to steal a brain preserved in a college classroom, Fritz
drops it, and so grabs an abnormal brain instead. On the night of
the experiment, Henry is shocked to see his fiancé Elizabeth, his
friend Victor, and also his old professor, Dr. Waldman, show up at
his laboratory. The group watches in amazement as Henry's
experiment is a success. The dead body is brought back to life by
lightning. Dr. Waldman helps Henry study the monster, which
becomes violent when Fritz teases it with fire. The monster kills
Fritz, and Waldman argues the monster should be put down.
Henry agrees to let Waldman do so on the day of his wedding to
Elizabeth. The monster kills Dr. Waldman and goes on a rampage.
Henry and his father lead a group of villagers in pursuit of the
monster. The monster finds Henry first and drags him into a
windmill, which the villagers set on fire. Henry is thrown from the
windmill by the monster but lives, while the monster appears to
perish in the flames.

COMMENTARY With *Dracula* having proven to be a big success, Universal was keen to find more horror thrillers to star Bela Lugosi. It was French director Robert Florey who suggested that Universal adapt *Frankenstein.* Though Florey envisioned Lugosi as the doctor, Universal head Carl Laemmle Jr. insisted he play the monster instead, and so roughly 20 minutes of test footage was shot with Lugosi in the famous Jack P. Pierce makeup. Ultimately, Lugosi passed on the role due to there being no lines for the monster, and when he exited, so did Florey. The duo was replaced by director James Whale and actor Boris Karloff.

Whereas *Dracula* ended with a special message from actor Edward Van Sloan, this film begins with a message from Sloan, giving audience members one last chance to back out before the show begins. Sloan is one of two returning cast members from *Dracula,* the other being Dwight Frye. In *Dracula,* Frye gave a standout performance as Renfield. Here he plays the hunchbacked servant, Fritz (not Ygor, that character would come later). Though he doesn't surpass Renfield, a pretty tall order, he does walk away with one of the film's most memorable characters. Fritz might just be the true villain of the film, as it is his misdeeds that lead to Frankenstein's creation becoming a monster. It is also Fritz who grabs an abnormal brain (after damaging a normal one). This is only his first mistake with the monster. Fritz compounds the already bad situation by teasing the creature with fire. This, it could be argued, just as much as the brain, is what made the monster cruel.

Colin Clive gives an excellent performance as Henry Frankenstein. In fact, it's uncanny how well he portrays the character, which was described in the first script well before he was cast as having the look of an intelligent man with a fanatical streak. And that he certainly does, as evidenced by his oft-imitated "It's alive!" line in the lab. Boris Karloff is still easily the standout performance, and not just because of Jack P. Pierce's excellent makeup (which has gone on to become the definitive look of the monster). Karloff's best scenes occur when he generates sympathy. This, it seems, is a key ingredient for a monster. There was nothing sympathetic about Dracula, but the poor monster, on the other hand, is a different story. The best example of this is his scene with the little girl, Maria. It's clear that the monster is elated to have found someone who's not frightened by him. In the famous scene, he has some fun with the young girl, tossing lilies into the water to watch them float. As we all know, the monster gets to having too much fun and tosses Maria into the water, though it's fairly clear he's not aware of what he's doing. If anything, he seems upset by what he's done when the girl dies.

The film does an excellent job of building the tension towards the ending. Scenes of the villagers dancing and celebrating, unaware of the monster in their midst, brings to mind *Jaws* when the beaches are packed on the 4th of July. The film's ending would serve as the blueprint for many Universal monster films to follow, as the villagers all grab their torches and pitchforks and go out to find the monster. The flaming windmill also serves as a great locale for the climax, which was originally a bit bleaker. You see, Henry was supposed to die, but a test screening convinced Universal of two things: 1. Perhaps a happy ending would be better suited. 2. Maybe they needed Henry Frankenstein to survive for a possible sequel.

Originally, after the monster throws Henry from the windmill, he would die; that simple. The newly filmed scenes of the villagers finding Henry's body, which confirm he is still alive, stick out like a sore thumb and interrupt the natural flow of the scene. Even worse is the tacked-on ending of Baron Frankenstein looking in on his son in bed while he talks to the maids. The film would've ended better with the credits rolling over the burning windmill, Henry Frankenstein's fate unknown. Another thing that this revised ending bungled was the love triangle between Elizabeth, Victor, and Henry. Victor existed mostly to give Elizabeth a happy alternative after Henry had died, and one of the early scripts ended with she and Victor in a church together mourning Henry's death with his father.

Frankenstein was a massive hit, with critics lauding it and audiences flocking to it. By 1953, after counting the re-releases, the film had managed to gross $12 million, which was quite a sum for the time.

FINAL WORD Though *Dracula* may have begun Universal's classic horror cycle, it was *Frankenstein* that truly cemented it. More so than *Dracula*, this one is full of iconic scenes that would be repeated in not only future Universal horror films but horror films for the rest of all time.

DR. JEKYLL AND MR. HYDE

(PARAMOUNT)
Release Date: December 31, 1931
Alternate Titles:
The Phantom of London (Austria/ Czechoslovakia)
The Doctor and the Monster (Brazil) *Doktor Jekyll* (Greece)

Directed by: Rouben Mamoulian **Screenplay by:** Samuel Hoffenstein and Percy Heath based upon the novel by Robert Louis Stevenson **Makeup by:** Wally Westmore **Cast:** Fredric March (Dr. Henry Jekyll/Mr. Edward Hyde) Miriam Hopkins (Ivy Pierson) Rose Hobart (Muriel Carew) Holmes Herbert (Dr. John Lanyon) Halliwell Hobbes (Brigadier-General Danvers Carew) Edgar Norton (Poole) Tempe Pigott (Mrs. Hawkins)

Academy Ratio, Black & White, 98 Minutes

SYNOPSIS Dr. Jekyll shocks the scientific community with his announcement that he believes man has two distinct natures that he can separate via chemical reaction. This doesn't bode well with the father of his fiancé, General Carew, who wishes for Jekyll to wait before marrying his daughter, Muriel. One night while walking home, Jekyll attends to a prostitute, Ivy, whose been beaten in the streets. The beautiful Ivy becomes enamored with Jekyll, who does his best to repress his desires for her. Jekyll turns his energies to creating the formula he proposed earlier and is successful, unleashing an ape-like version of himself called Hyde. Mr. Hyde wastes no time in courting Ivy, who, although disgusted by Hyde, becomes ensnared in his web when he begins paying her rent. Jekyll keeps up his dual life as Hyde while Muriel and her father are out of the country. Once they return, Jekyll vows to never turn into Hyde again. This coincides with a visit from Ivy, who beseeches Jekyll to free her from Hyde. Jekyll vows that Hyde will never harm her again. However, Hyde emerges from Jekyll without the serum and goes to kill Ivy. Disgusted by what he's done, Jekyll breaks his engagement with Muriel, leaving them both devastated. When he leaves, Jekyll turns into Hyde unexpectedly, who reenters the home. Muriel naturally rejects

Hyde's advances, and the enraged monster kills Muriel's father and flees the house. Hyde is traced back to Jekyll's lab where he is shot and killed by the police.

COMMENTARY It's unknown if the current success of *Dracula* and *Frankenstein* ushered this film into production or not, but either way, the success of the aforementioned two movies certainly didn't hurt this film. As it was, it had been over ten years since the last major adaptation of the tale. In fact, initially John Barrymore was courted to return to the role he had played so well in the 1920 version, but he was under contract with MGM. As this film was being produced by Paramount, that made Barrymore unavailable and Fredric March was cast instead, which was likely for the best. As would turn out, this adaptation of the book would become the seminal version much in the same way that Universal's adaptations of *Dracula* and *Frankenstein* were.

The film was produced before the Production Code, and as such got away with more horror and sexual content than would be afforded films only a few years later. Of all the different designs and makeup used for Mr. Hyde over the years, this adaptation did it best. The secret to the transformation sequence, not revealed for many years, was that the makeup was applied in contrasting colors. Colored filters that corresponded to the different colors were used, which, when exposed, gradually made the different colors visible, so to speak, on the black and white film. The image of Hyde as a sort of ape-man, with his sharp teeth, would more or less define the look of Mr. Hyde for years to come. (It was also adopted for Universal's only real turn at the character during their classic cycle in *Abbott and Costello Meet Dr. Jekyll and Mr. Hyde*.)

The film personalizes Jekyll in an interesting way right off the bat. The first images we see are a P.O.V. shot from Jekyll's perspective as he plays the organ and humorously interacts with his butler, Poole. We keep this P.O.V. for quite a while and only see Jekyll once he looks at himself in the mirror. As with Jekyll, we are introduced to Hyde via a P.O.V. shot in the same mirror. As odd as this sounds, in his first few scenes, there's something endearing about the ape-like Hyde. Perhaps this was meant to illustrate how at first evil things can seem friendly and attractive before turning to horror. And to horror Hyde turns upon going to the club where Ivy works, where he goes from an amusing ape-man to an abusive, unredeemable monster.

Apart from its great production values and performances, it should also be noted that the film is much more lively than its contemporaries. I am speaking, of course, of *Dracula* and *Frankenstein*. Though that's not saying much in regards to *Dracula*, I would argue that this film is still more exciting than *Frankenstein* at times. Hyde's acrobatic escape from the apartment complex in particular is a highlight for its time, as is the final duel between the monster and the police.

The film grossed $1.3 million, an impressive amount right on par with Universal's *Frankenstein* and *Dracula*. Not only that, but the film was also well received by critics and it garnered an Academy Award win for Best Actor in a Leading Role for Fredric March (technically he tied with Wallace Beery for *The Champ*).

FINAL WORD Easily the definitive version of *Dr. Jekyll and Mr. Hyde* to this day.

THE MUMMY

(UNIVERSAL)
Release Date: December 22, 1932
Alternate Titles: *The 3,000 Year Old Man* (Hungary)
Imhotep (working title)

Directed by: Karl Freund **Screenplay by:** John L. Balderston based off of a story by Nina Wilcox Putnam **Makeup by:** Jack P. Pierce **Music by:** James Dietrich **Cast:** Boris Karloff (Imhotep/Ardeth Bey) Zita Johann (Helen Grosvenor/Princess Anck-su-namun) David Manners (Frank Whemple) Arthur Byron (Sir Joseph Whemple) Edward Van Sloan (Dr. Muller) Bramwell Fletcher (Ralph Norton) Noble Johnson (the Nubian) Kathryn Byron (Frau Muller) Leonard Mudie (Professor Pearson) James Crane (Pharaoh Amenophis)

Academy Ratio, Black & White, 73 Minutes

SYNOPSIS In 1922, archeologist Sir Jospeh Whemple opens the forbidden tomb of Imhotep, a priest cursed to come back to life if the tomb is disturbed. Ten years later, Whemple's son, Frank, meets a mysterious man named Ardeth Bey, who leads him to the lost tomb of Anck-su-namun. What Frank doesn't know is that Ardeth Bey is really the revived Imhotep, and he only wanted him to find the tomb so that he could resurrect Anck-su-namun. Around the same time both Frank and Imhotep meet a woman named Helen who greatly resembles the long dead Anck-su-namun. When Imhotep attempts a ceremony to make Helen immortal, he is thwarted by Frank.

COMMENTARY After the double hit of *Dracula* and *Frankenstein*, Universal was quickly establishing itself in the horror genre. Looking for a new property to adapt, they turned to Nina Wilcox Putnam's *Cagliostro, King of the Dead*. The story was based on the real Italian mystic who founded the Egyptian branch of the Masons. The first treatment was heavy on sci-fi rather than horror and had a death ray and an all-seeing TV. Those two inventions carried over into the first screenplay, along with a great deal of Egyptian mysticism. Eventually, it was decided to move the story from America to Egypt and to substitute the Italian Cagliostro for the full-on Egyptian figure of Imhotep.

Even though it was the first in the Mummy series, 1932's *The Mummy* is sort of the odd man out of the franchise. In a series famous for its iconography of shuffling mummies wrapped in bandages, *The Mummy* features only one such scene. Even though the movie's most iconic scene is over within the first ten minutes, that doesn't mean the rest of the film is bad; it's just different when compared to Universal's sequels and Hammer's films. The 1932 *Mummy* is in many ways a retelling of *Dracula* in Egypt. This should come as no surprise since it was written by some of the same writers who had made the Dracula stage play: John L. Balderston and Nina Wilcox Putnam. There are similar characters and dialogue when one compares the two films. While it's obvious that Imhotep is the Dracula stand-in and Helen is the equivalent of Mina, it could be argued that Dr. Muller is meant to be Van Helsing. It is he who possesses the arcane knowledge needed to defeat the mummy, and just as Van Helsing gives out a crucifix necklace for protection, Muller hands out an Egyptian trinket in a similar way. Driving this parallel home is the fact that Edward Van Sloan played both Van Helsing and Muller. To a lesser extent, one could perhaps argue that Ralph Norton, the character who opens the forbidden chest, is a bit like Renfield, though he's out of the picture pretty quick.

All that said, *The Mummy* betters *Dracula* in many ways. It doesn't have the claustrophobic interior setting and at least has a few good exterior sequences with plenty of extras. It also has some wonderful sets, chief among them the Egyptian Museum. Imhotep is also a more sympathetic figure than Lugosi's Dracula when it comes to his relationship with Helen. Even though Imhotep doesn't have the iconic look of Kharis throughout the picture (again, he's only bandaged in his first scene), Karloff's Imhotep is a spooky character all his own. While he may not have the classic Mummy look, he does have powers that Kharis doesn't. For instance, he can open a window to the past within a mystic pool and he can use the same pool to spy on his enemies. One also has to wonder if George Lucas took inspiration from *The Mummy*, as one scene essentially has Imhotep "Force choke" the hero from a long distance. Imhotep's disintegration scene also likely inspired the ending of Hammer's *Horror of Dracula* and probably the ending of *Raiders of the Lost Ark* to some degree as well.

Like *Dracula* and *Frankenstein* before it, *The Mummy* was a hit when released during Christmas of 1932. Though they might have considered it a "one-off" hit at the time, little did Universal realize that they had birthed a rather enduring creation. Not only would *The Mummy* spawn five sequels, a meeting with Abbott and Costello, and a Hammer remake, but also a wildly successful reimagining in the more action-adventure oriented 1999 *Mummy,* which would itself produce sequels and yet another reimagining in 2017.

FINAL WORD If you grew up on the adventures of Kharis, then this first Mummy movie might be something of a letdown for you. But, if you can accept that it's something entirely different, then you should be able to enjoy it.

THE INVISIBLE MAN

(UNIVERSAL)
Release Date: November 13, 1933
Alternate Titles: *H.G. Wells' The Invisible Man*
(Australian TV title)

Directed by: James Whale **Screenplay by:** R. C. Sherriff based upon the novel by H.G. Wells **Special Effects by:** John P. Fulton & Jack P. Pierce (makeup) **Music by:** Heinz Roemheld **Cast:** Claude Rains (Dr. Jack Griffin/the Invisible Man) William Harrigan (Dr. Arthur Kemp) Gloria Stuart (Flora Cranley) Henry Travers (Dr. Cranley) Una O'Connor (Jenny Hall) Forrester Harvey (Herbert Hall) Dudley Digges (Chief Detective) E. E. Clive (Constable Jaffers)

Academy Ratio, Black & White, 71 Minutes

SYNOPSIS On a dark and snowy night in Sussex, a mysterious man clad in bandages arrives at the Lion's Head Inn demanding a room. This man turns out to be a chemist by the name of Dr. Jack Griffin, whose experiments turned him invisible. The experiments also made him mad. After several outbursts, he's evicted from the inn but refuses to leave. The police are brought in and Griffin takes off his clothes revealing his invisibility. He escapes and begins a reign of terror. Griffin goes to stay with an old colleague, Dr. Kemp, who he forces to aid and abet him in his effort to take over the world. Kemp alerts the police as well as Griffin's old mentor, Dr. Cranley, and Griffin's fiancé, Flora Cranley. The Cranley's come to Kemp's home where Griffin is delighted to see Flora again. When the police arrive, he escapes and vows revenge on Kemp. Griffin goes on a deadly killing spree, even derailing a train. He captures Kemp and sends him careening off a cliff in his automobile. Griffin takes refuge in a barn one snowy night, where he is found by the owner, who alerts the police. The police arrive outside the barn and shoot Griffin, whose footprints appear in the snow when he attempts to flee. A few hours later, Griffin dies in a hospital with Flora at his side as he becomes visible again.

COMMENTARY Even though it had a classic book as its source material, that of course being H.G. Wells' 1897 novel, *The Invisible Man* went through a true myriad of storylines. Rather than adapting Wells' novel outright, James Whale first wrote a completely originally treatment not using any of the character names or major events from Wells' story and it ended with the title character stabbing the female lead to death! The main character, called Farralane, also achieved invisibility with help from the devil, giving the story a supernatural edge not present in the original. For a time, Whale was off the project, which begat a revolving door of other writers and concepts. Ultimately the screenplay was tailored after Wells' novel in the end. Due to Wells disliking Universal's *Island of Lost Souls* (a 1932 adaptation of *Island of Dr. Moreau*), he had since gained final approval on the film adaptation of *Invisible Man* from Universal. As such, the final result was closer to the novel. Luckily, James Whale even became available again, and another classic was born.

As stated before, the film is basically faithful to the novel, with a few deviations. For instance, though the character names are the same, the setting has been moved up from 1897 to the present day of 1933. Notably, Griffon has no fiancé in the book but is given one in the movie. Also, Dr. Kemp survives in the novel but is killed in the film. This is a bit surprising, as Kemp is the de facto heroic male lead (although perhaps sympathetic male lead might be more appropriate as he's not particularly heroic).

Really the film belongs solely to its villain: the Invisible Man. Originally intended for Boris Karloff, Claud Rains makes an indelible impression in the role. In fact, it wouldn't be an understatement to say that this film belongs to Rains and Rains alone. The only actor who dominates the screen besides him is Una O'Connor, who is delightful as usual as the landlady. (Reportedly Whale could barely stop himself from laughing while watching her perform. She was also one of Wells' favorite aspects of the film, though he didn't care for changes to his source material in general.) While Rains does have an iconic look with his bandage-swaddled face, it's his voice that does the heavy lifting for the film. It's really a testimony to Rains as an actor to carry the film mostly through his voice. It's also impressive that his face isn't seen until the last moments of the movie. Most actors are too vain to accept a role where their faces can never be seen (and though Rains wasn't thrilled by this fact initially, he eventually accepted it). Though Rains would never return to play the Invisible Man a second time as Lugosi and Karloff did with their respective monsters, Rains remains the definitive Invisible Man. And Rains, like Karloff did in *The Mummy*, would return to play a second great Universal monster in 1943 as *The Phantom of the Opera*.

For the era in which it was released, *The Invisible Man* was quite a novelty. The ingenious visual effects were carried out by John P. Fulton, John J. Mescall and Frank D. Williams. To make Claud Rains disappear when he disrobes, they had wrapped the actor in black velvet and shot him against a black background. These shots were then superimposed into the new backgrounds giving him the impression of being invisible. (Rather than wires, this was also how objects were manipulated in mid-air.) While the first few acts keep the Invisible Man's chaos fairly low-key, towards the end of the picture he's causing car crashes, explosions, derailed trains, and bank robberies. It was pandemonium on a grand that delighted audiences.

Filmed throughout the summer of 1933, *Invisible Man* was a huge hit when released that November (apparently more popular than *The Mummy* as it was described as Universal's most successful horror film since *Frankenstein*). "The story makes such superb cinematic material that one wonders that Hollywood did not film it sooner. Now that it has been done, it is a remarkable achievement," raved Mordaunt Hall of the *New York Times*, which also named it one of their "Ten Best Films of 1933". Today the film is still highly regarded, being nominated for spots on various best of lists, notably those created by the American Film Institute.

FINAL WORD Though it spawned many lesser sequels that never ever quite lived up to the original, the original is a true classic ranking up there with *Dracula* and *Frankenstein* and arguably beats *The Mummy*. The film is also regarded by many as the best adaptation of an H.G. Wells novel ever.

BRIDE OF FRANKENSTEIN

(UNIVERSAL)
Release Date: April 20, 1935
Alternate Titles: *Frankenstein's Return* (Austria)

Directed by: James Whale **Screenplay by:** William Hurlbut & John L. Balderston, based upon characters created by Mary Shelley **Makeup by:** Jack P. Pierce **Music by:** Franz Waxman **Cast:** Colin Clive (Henry Frankenstein) Ernest Thesiger (Doctor Pretorius) Boris Karloff (the Monster) Valerie Hobson (Elizabeth Frankenstein) Elsa Lanchester (Mary Shelley/the Monster's Bride) Gavin Gordon (Lord Byron) Douglas Walton (Percy Bysshe Shelley) Una O'Connor (Minnie) E. E. Clive (the Burgomaster)

Academy Ratio, Black & White, 75 Minutes

SYNOPSIS In the aftermath of the great fire at the windmill, it is revealed that not only did Henry Frankenstein survive, but so did his monster. That very night, Henry's old mentor Dr. Pretorius comes to see Henry upon hearing word of his experiment. Pretorius invites Henry to join forces with him to create a mate for his monster, and he reluctantly agrees. Meanwhile, the poor monster is captured by the villagers but manages to escape. He finds comfort and friendship in the form of a blind man, who teaches him to speak. The friendship is short-lived when visitors recognize the monster and attack him. The monster has a chance meeting with Pretorius, who takes the misguided monster under his wing and uses him to kidnap Elizabeth when Henry backs out of their agreement. Henry and Pretorius create a mate for the monster as planned, but upon her birth, she rejects the monster. Enraged, the monster pulls the self-destruct lever on the laboratory, burying himself, his bride, and Pretorius. However, before he does so, he orders Henry and Elizabeth to leave so that they may live. "We belong dead," the monster says and then seals their fate.

COMMENTARY James Whale's 1935 production of *Bride of Frankenstein* is that rare sequel that outshines the original. In fact, many critics consider it to be the best Universal horror film ever made. However, it almost didn't turn out that way, and some proposed ideas for the sequel were downright campy. The ludicrous ideas that were pitched involved everything from circus animals to death rays! Eventually those aspects were done away with to create a draft called *The Return of Frankenstein*, which is fundamentally similar to the finished film except for one crucial detail: it didn't include the character of Dr. Pretorius.

Bride did what any good sequel should by exposing a new layer to returning characters. The monster is undeniably the heart and soul of the film, its emotional core all around. Though he's still naturally enraged when he emerges from the windmill, in his next scene he's peaceable and out to make friends. Of course, he's already got a bad reputation and a frightening look, so everyone screams and shoots at him. It's when he meets the blind man that the film really hits it home. The scenes are touching to the core, not something one would expect when compared to the monster of the first film. It also makes us wonder if we should forgive the monster for his past deeds. After all, the blind man makes it clear that all the monster was missing was a loving father figure, which Henry never provided in the first film. (One could also argue that the monster was like an over-powered newborn baby in the first film, not entirely accountable for its actions).

And, with the monster no longer the villain, a new character had to fit that bill. Enter Dr. Pretorius, who absolutely steals the show, whereas the human characters are concerned. Younger viewers might draw comparisons between Ernest Thesiger's performance and Ian McDarmid's acting in the Star Wars saga as Palpatine/Darth Sidious. Some of Pretorius's lines are full of a dark vigor and are quotable in the same way that the Emperor's lines from *Return of the Jedi* are.

On the other end of the spectrum, Henry is rather pathetic in this outing. For instance, Elizabeth has to speak for him when Pretorius comes to see him for a second time (though, at the same time, it does make Elizabeth's character more interesting and proactive than it was in the previous film). In a way, Henry is like a recovering drug addict, tempted back into the fold by his "dealer," in this case Pretorius. To his credit, Henry at least denies his addiction eventually and refuses to aid Pretorius. It is at this point that one of the great lines of the film, and there are many, are spoken. Pretorius calls in the monster to see Henry, who is naturally flabbergasted to hear it speak. To this astounding revelation, Pretorius says, "Yes, there have been developments since he came to me." This again helps to hit home the danger of absentee parents. In the lack of good influences, the monster has fallen under the sway of Pretorius.

Though the entire film is fantastic, it's still the final scenes in the laboratory that top it all off as Henry and Pretorius bring the Bride to life. As many great sequels would do in the future, *Bride of Frankenstein* puts a twist on a signature line from the original. As opposed to shouting, "It's alive!" again, this time around, Henry says, "She's alive, alive!" This may have been the first example of a sequel cleverly mimicking a line from the original, which many films would do in the future ("They're here," and "They're back," in the Poltergeist films, for instance). The titular Bride is great fun to watch, and one is certainly left wanting more time with her character. However, sometimes that is the secret of great art, to leave the audience wishing for more. Her attitude is a double-whammy for the poor monster. Not only does she reject him as a suitor, but she is also given the love of the father (Henry) that rejected him. To the monster's credit, he doesn't kill his father but lets him escape. He even has enough sense to know, somehow, that Pretorius belongs dead.

Overall, there aren't very many films from the 1930s that can hold the attention of later generations, but *Bride of Frankenstein* can for several reasons. For starters, it's not a talky picture full of superfluous exposition. It's brisk, and every scene counts. In fact, the "talky" scenes are equally as entertaining as the monster scenes. This is why the film holds up so well: its amazing characters. The film is also full of good humor, something the first film lacked, in the form of Minnie, Henry's maid. Though she almost overstays her welcome in a few scenes, she's somewhat irresistible, so it's no surprise that the editors didn't shorten her screentime. The other funny moments belong to Pretorius's miniature creations that he entraps within bottles like other men would insects.

The film was another hit when released in 1935, and again the critics were mostly positive, though the film has grown in esteem today.

FINAL WORD Not just one of the greatest classic horror films of all time, it's also one of the greatest films of all time. Easily, this is the best of Universal's Classic Monster series.

MARK OF THE VAMPIRE

(MGM)
Release Date: April 26, 1935
Alternate Titles: *Vampires of Prague* (Italy)
Demon of the Old Castle (Japan)

Directed by: Tod Browning **Screenplay by:** Guy Endore & Bernard Schubert **Special Effects by:** Tom Tutwiler **Music by:** Domenico Savino (stock tracks) **Cast:** Lionel Barrymore (Professor Zelen) Elizabeth Allan (Irena Borotyn) Bela Lugosi (Count Mora) Lionel Atwill (Inspector Neumann) Jean Hersholt (Baron Otto von Zinden) Henry Wadsworth (Fedor Vincente) Carroll Borland (Luna)

Academy Ratio, Black & White, 60 Minutes

SYNOPSIS An investigation into the unsolved murder of the wealthy Sir Karell Borotyn, drained of blood, makes locals think vampires are to blame. However, Inspector Neumann has his eyes set upon Fedor Vincente, the fiancé of Sir Karell's daughter Irena, as the suspect. Although a mysterious pair of ghoulish vampires appear to be haunting the neighboring house, owned and inhabited by Baron Otto von Zinden, it turns out that Zinden himself killed Sir Karell. The vampires were, in fact, stage actors hired by Neumann and his associate, Professor Zelen, a hypnotist. Zelen hypnotizes Zinden into believing it is the night of the murder. In the old house, a look-alike actor portrays Sir Karell, who Zinden attempts to poison. Zinden is caught red-handed, and the ruse is explained to all.

COMMENTARY This film is unique as a remake of one of the most famous lost films of all time: *London After Midnight* (1927). If you've ever seen stills of Lon Chaney looking macabre in a beaver hat, that's the movie. It featured Chaney in dual roles as an inspector and a faux vampire (the inspector in disguise). *Mark of the Vampire* follows *London After Midnight's* plot but changes the locales, the character names, and a few story details. Notably, the writers of *London After Midnight* weren't credited on this film. However, one

45

of the writers of that film was Tod Browning, who directed the original and the remake.

If you've seen TCM's 45 minute reconstruction of *London After Midnight*, the parallels between the two productions are obvious. What they have in common is a vampire couple moving into the home of an unsolved murder. Notably, both films had a scene where the rich neighbor's servants spot the vampires while passing by in a horse and carriage. There are many other similar scenes throughout, but there's also a major difference. Here, Irena is in on the ruse to catch Zinden, whereas she was not in *London After Midnight*. And the biggest difference of all, Lugosi's character is not the inspector in disguise. Here he is a totally separate character, specifically an actor hired to play a vampire.

Although he rarely ever speaks, Lugosi's scenes as Count Mora are the next best thing to actually getting to see him play Dracula again. Almost more noteworthy is the female vampire, Luna, who gets an astounding shot gliding through the air when her gown takes on the appearance of a bat. It's comparable to a similar scene in the 1979 *Dracula* which was also amazing. However, it also creates something of a plot hole. Remember, these aren't real vampires and it's doubtful the hired actors could put on such convincing wireworks in an old house! A good deal of the movie is played for laughs, and the ending scene is great fun. In it, Mora speaks for the first time, raving about what a good job he did portraying a vampire until he's more or less told to shut up and help load up the props. The vampire scenes are so well done it's a bit of a shame they all had to be a sham.

FINAL WORD An odd little film, the main reason horror fans will want to watch it is out of curiosity for *London After Midnight*, or they may want to watch it as a quasi-*Dracula* sequel for Lugosi (though *Return of the Vampire* might fit that bill a little better).

WEREWOLF OF LONDON

(UNIVERSAL)
Release Date: June 3, 1935
Alternate Titles: *Dr. Yogami from London* (Denmark)
The Monster of London (France) *Werewolf* (Hungary)
The Unholy Hour (Canada) *The Secret of Tibet* (Italy)

Directed by: Stuart Walker **Screenplay by:** John Colton, Harvey Gates, Edmund Pearson, James Mulhauser, Aben Kandel & Robert Harris (story) **Special Effects by:** John P. Fulton & Jack P. Pierce (makeup) **Music by:** Karl Hajos **Cast:** Henry Hull (Dr. Wilfred Glendon) Warner Oland (Dr. Yogami) Valerie Hobson (Lisa Glendon) Lester Matthews (Paul Ames) Lawrence Grant (Sir Thomas Forsythe) Spring Byington (Miss Ettie Coombes) Clark Williams (Hugh Renwick) J. M. Kerrigan (Hawkins) Charlotte Granville (Lady Forsythe)

Academy Ratio, Black & White, 75 Minutes

SYNOPSIS Dr. Wilfred Glendon is on a mission in Tibet to find the rare flower, the Mariphasa lupino lumino, which blooms only in the moonlight. While harvesting a sample of the plant, he is attacked by a wolf-like creature. Although he fights it off, it bites his arm. When Glendon returns to London, he meets the enigmatic Dr. Yotani, who is also obsessed with Glendon's lupino lumino sample. The reason why soon becomes apparent. The rare plant is the only cure for lycanthropy, and Dr. Yotani is the very werewolf who attacked Glendon in Tibet. Yotani warns Glendon that he too will become a werewolf, and specifically, Glendon will seek out to kill what he loves most: his wife Lisa. While out with a childhood sweetheart, Paul Ames, Lisa is indeed attacked by Glendon in wolf-form, who Paul recognizes. Unfortunately for Glendon, Yotani has stolen the last bloom of the lupino lumino and used it on himself. Glendon turns into a wolf and kills Yotani. When he goes after Lisa again, he is shot and killed by the police. In his last moment, he expresses his love for Lisa and then dies.

COMMENTARY Having adapted Stoker's *Dracula,* Shelley's *Frankenstein,* and Wells's *Invisible Man,* one would have thought that Universal would have acquired Guy Endore's 1933 novel *Werewolf of Paris* next. Instead, Universal concocted *The Werewolf of London,* perhaps as a way of being frugal and not having to buy screen rights to the book. Whatever the case, the movie was the first major Hollywood production to center on a werewolf (previous werewolf subjects had been short films only).

Strangely enough, the film is often criticized somewhat harshly by Universal horror fans, mostly citing Stuart Walker's direction and Henry Hull's performance. In this author's opinion, Walker did a fine job, and his use of shadows throughout the film was particularly impressive. The opening scenes set in Tibet (by way of the famous Vasquez Rocks in California) are quite spooky as Glendon and his partner are seized by unseen forces on their trek up the mountain. In addition to horror, the film also sports some sci-fi elements in the form of the massive carnivorous plants and Glendon's closed-circuit TV system in his laboratory.

This film is naturally overshadowed by the better-known and loved *The Wolf Man* (1941) in that the transformation scenes were not as elaborate as those done six years later. For instance, the first transition doesn't show Glendon's face change in a continuous shot. Instead, we watch Glendon walk through the yard, and each time a pillar or some other object obscures him from our view, he's transformed further into a wolf each time. Later he does have a full facial transformation in front of the camera, but it isn't quite as elaborate or as seamless as *The Wolf Man's.*

Though many consider this film's makeup to be inferior, there are a few points to consider. First of all, supposedly Jack Pierce's initial design was similar to the Wolf Man's. Actor Henry Hull argued that this makeup made the character unrecognizable, and according to the script, the characters needed to be able to recognize the werewolf as Dr. Glendon. Second, the Werewolf of London is a bit more sinister looking than Lon Chaney Jr.'s Wolf Man, which in later films, like *Abbott and Costello Meet Frankenstein,* even took on a heroic edge. Glendon's werewolf is nothing but sinister. It's also more intelligent. Whereas Larry Talbott's werewolf was all animal, Glendon's werewolf was intelligent and capable of deception. Case in point, he masks himself in a cap and cloak to hide his appearance while he's out on the prowl for female victims. This is much more horrifying than the Talbott werewolf. The ending is also somewhat more touching than *The Wolf Man's.* In his last moments, but still in the guise of the wolf, Glendon speaks to his wife lovingly one last time. The final line, spoken by the policeman who shot the werewolf, is also touching as he states that in his report he will say, "I shot him by accident when he was trying to protect his wife."

Though many lament the fact that Boris Karloff and Bela Lugosi didn't play the roles of Glendon and Dr. Yogami as originally planned, it's hard to imagine anyone other than Henry Hull as Glendon (though it might've been nice to see Lugosi as Yotani). The love triangle in the film is similar to the one in *Frankenstein* (an eccentric scientist neglects his fiancé, who clearly has an attraction to another man) only done better. In *Frankenstein* the triangle between Henry, Elizabeth, and Victor was undeveloped. In this film, we know Glendon is doomed the minute he's been bitten. In that sense, the story shares similarities with romantic dramas that concerned terminally ill husbands pondering their wife's future and well-being after their death. Though Glendon was naturally resentful of Paul while he was alive, one has to wonder if during his death that he's somewhat comforted by the fact that Lisa has a good man to look after her. And, unlike *Frankenstein*, which was denied a somber ending in favor of a badly tacked-on happy ending, *Werewolf of London* is afforded the tragic ending that it deserved. (An additional ending scene, focusing on the hilarious two old crones from the inn, was scripted but wisely excised.)

FINAL WORD Understandably overshadowed by the more popular Wolf Man films of the 1940s, *Werewolf of London* is still a landmark Universal horror.

DRACULA'S DAUGHTER

(UNIVERSAL)
Release Date: May 11, 1936
Alternate Titles: *Woman Dracula* (Japan)
Human Vampire (Portugal)

Directed by: Lambert Hillyer **Screenplay by:** Garrett Fort based upon characters created by Bram Stoker **Special Effects by:** John P. Fulton & Jack P. Pierce (makeup) **Music by:** Heinz Roemheld **Cast:** Gloria Holden (Countess Marya Zaleska) Otto Kruger (Dr. Jeffrey Garth) Marguerite Churchill (Janet Blake) Irving Pichel (Sandor) Halliwell Hobbes (Hawkins) Billy Bevan (Albert) Nan Grey (Lili) Hedda Hopper (Lady Esme Hammond) Claud Allister (Sir Aubrey) Gilbert Emery (Sir Basil Humphrey) Edward Van Sloan (Professor Von Helsing)

Academy Ratio, Black & White, 71 Minutes

SYNOPSIS Shortly after Van Helsing stakes Dracula through the heart, he is arrested for murder by the police. Van Helsing sends for a colleague, Dr. Jeffrey Garth, with a background in psychology and hypnosis to help prove his innocence. At the same time that Dracula's body is stolen, a woman named Countess Marya Zaleska arrives. Secretly Dracula's daughter, she hopes that the death of her father will release her from her vampiric urges. When that proves not to be the case, she recruits Garth to see if he can help her overcome her evil desires. Eventually, she succumbs to her vampire ways and kidnaps Garth's assistant, Janet, to lure him to Castle Dracula in Transylvania. Garth goes there to rescue Janet, and at the last moment, Marya is shot by her jealous servant, Sandor, who is then himself shot by the police. Janet revives, Dracula's daughter dies as a freed Van Helsing examines the body, and all is well.

COMMENTARY The development of this sequel to *Dracula* was rather complicated. You see, back in the 1930s, the Bram Stoker novel was not in the public domain (that wouldn't occur until the early 1960s). As such, Universal needed the Stoker Estate's permission to make a sequel. Furthermore, it was rather touchy to write a sequel since Stoker had never written one himself. The only source material available was a deleted chapter from Stoker's novel, published two years after Stoker's death as a short story called "Dracula's Guest." After the success of *Dracula* in 1931, MGM producer David O. Selznick craftily purchased the rights, presumably so that either he could cash in on *Dracula's* success or resell the rights to Universal for more money when they decided to produce the inevitable sequel. Whatever Selznick's intentions, the latter occurred, with Universal purchasing the rights to do their sequel, which, other than featuring a female vampire, had nothing in common with *Dracula's Guest*.

Though he was scripted to appear in early story drafts, all we see of Bela Lugosi's Dracula in the final film is a plastic dummy stand-in for his dead body in the first scene, picking up right where *Dracula* left off. Because it was shot five years later, the sets naturally don't match perfectly, and Van Helsing actor Edward Van Sloan has aged just a tad (and the character's name is now Von Helsing with an 'o'). Those aren't the only continuity flaws plaguing the sequel, either. While the last film never stated what year it took place, the ship on which Dracula and Renfield sailed to England looked to be quite old. In this film, there are automobiles and airplanes. Another strange thing to ponder is, why aren't John Harker, Dr. Seward, and Mina there to testify on Von Helsing's behalf after he's arrested? As it is, Van Helsing is the only returning character from the first film. (This is coincidentally similar to Hammer's first *Dracula* sequel, which featured Van Helsing but not the Count in 1960's *Brides of Dracula*.)

As is to be expected, there are numerous callbacks to the first film. In one, Gloria Holden does the famous "I don't drink...wine," line, only she doesn't pause quite long enough to give it the proper effect. In another scene, when Dr. Garth visits Marya's home, he mentions how she's the only woman he's ever met who doesn't have a single mirror. The Countess replies with a joke about how Garth's friend Von Helsing might think that she was a vampire. As a character overall, the Countess is actually a much more rounded character than Dracula. In her case, she despises her vampirism and wishes to be rid of it. In a very interesting scene, she even does a sort of exorcism at her father's funeral barge (one of the film's most atmospheric scenes) and holds a cross (though she can't bear to look at it). As the film progresses, she sadly loses a bit of her appeal when she gives in to her temptations and becomes nothing but a villain who needs to be vanquished by the time she kidnaps the heroine. Had the film kept emphasizing her tragic nature, as was done years later in *The Wolf Man*, the story might've been more interesting.

Whereas the first film began in Transylvania and ended in London, this film is just the opposite. It begins in London and ends at Castle Dracula, similar in a way to the novel. Therefore, if one watches *Dracula* and *Dracula's Daughter* back to back, it's a rather interesting experience. This film's ending is a huge improvement over its predecessors, which wasn't exciting in the least. Here there's at least some suspense in terms of rescuing Janet, and the Countess's death is a bit more shocking than her father's. In this case, her treacherous servant shoots her through the heart with a crossbow.

It's something of a marvel that *Dracula's Daughter* turned out as well as it did. The film was rushed into production, because if it failed to meet a proper start date, film rights to *Dracula's Guest* would revert back to Selznick. As such, the final script still wasn't finished until three weeks after filming had begun in late February. And even though it's highly regarded today, whether or not the film was a financial success is hard to determine. All most sources will say is that it didn't equal the grosses of *Dracula*, and it certainly didn't replicate the success of *Bride of Frankenstein*. Some will also point to the fact that Universal didn't return to the monster/horror genre again for another three years, but that was more so because censors were getting incredibly hard to please when it came to these films. In fact, horror films were banned in Britain altogether around this time. On top of that, the Laemmle family had recently lost control of Universal Studios, which ended up putting the classic monsters on ice for the next three years.

FINAL WORD If you're the sort of fan who prefers monster-mash movies like *Frankenstein Meets the Wolf Man* to Universal's earlier monster movies, this one will probably be a little boring for you. But, if you enjoy the more subdued, dialogue-driven entries, *Dracula's Daughter* is enjoyable as the last of Universal's first wave of monster movies.

53

MAX GLUCKSMANN
PRESENTA LA MAS SENSACIONAL TRAGEDIA DE GRAND GUIGNOL QUE HA FILMADO UNIVERSAL PICTURES
"DRACULA"
TOTALMENTE HABLADA EN ESPAÑOL
Creación de
CARLOS VILLARIAS
LUPITA TOVAR
BARRY NORTON
PABLO ALVAREZ RUBIO
JOSE SORIANO VIOSCA
EL FILM TERRORIFICO, CON ESCENAS FANTASTICAS, DONDE SE COMBINA LA MAGIA Y LO SOBRENATURAL

PARAMOUNT presents
Dr. JEKYLL
AND
Mr. HYDE
A ROUBEN MAMOULIAN PRODUCTION
FREDRIC MARCH
MIRIAM HOPKINS
ROSE HOBART
a Paramount Picture

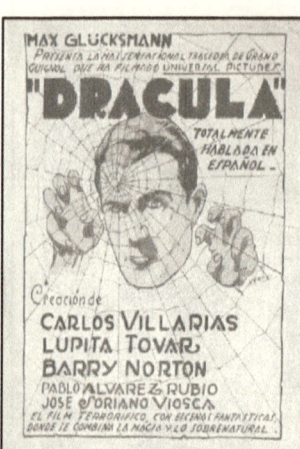

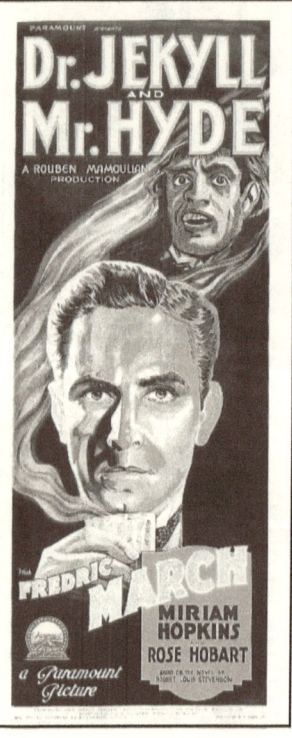

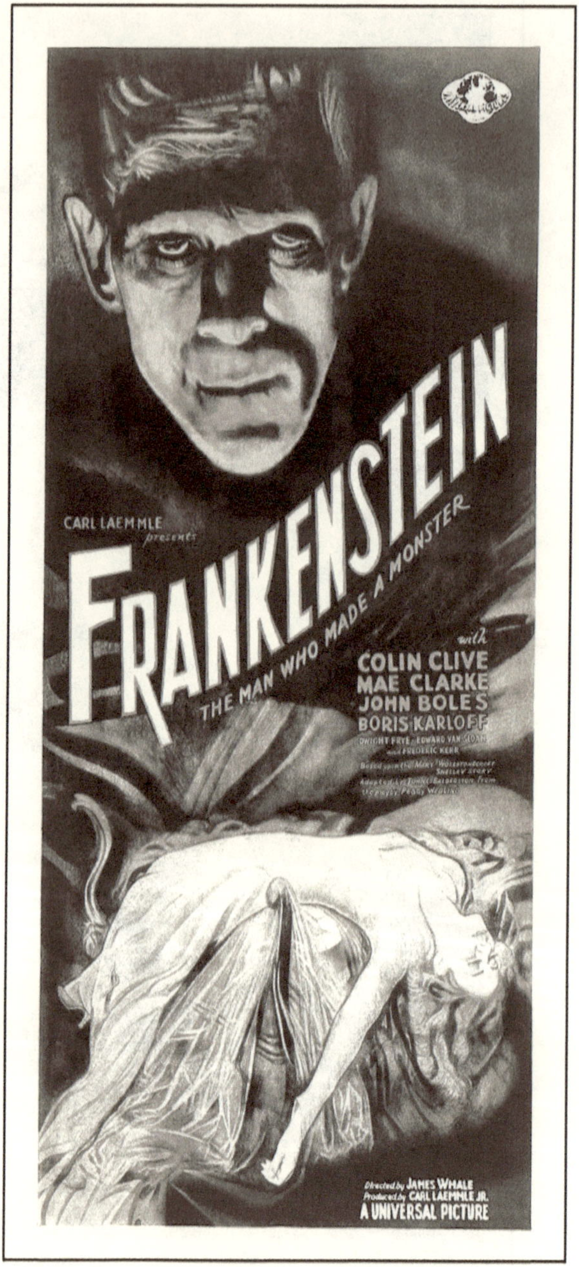
CARL LAEMMLE presents
FRANKENSTEIN
THE MAN WHO MADE A MONSTER
with
COLIN CLIVE
MAE CLARKE
JOHN BOLES
BORIS KARLOFF
Directed by JAMES WHALE
Produced by CARL LAEMMLE JR.
A UNIVERSAL PICTURE

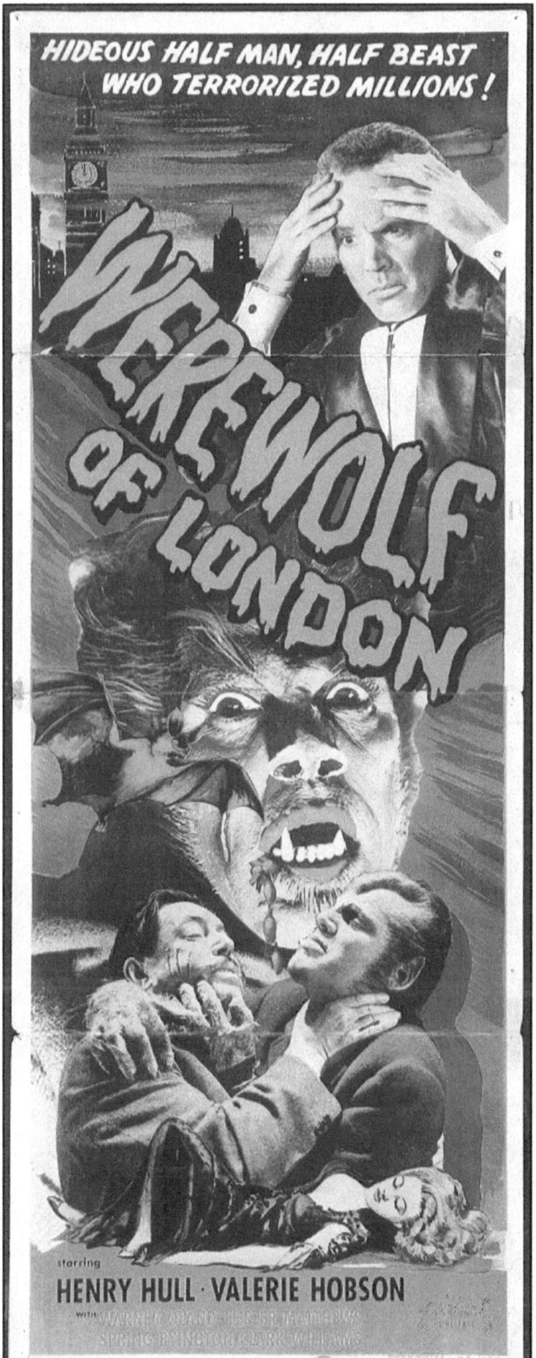
HIDEOUS HALF MAN, HALF BEAST
WHO TERRORIZED MILLIONS!
WEREWOLF OF LONDON
starring
HENRY HULL · VALERIE HOBSON

STRANGER THAN "DRACULA" ...MORE FANTASTIC THAN "FRANKENSTEIN" ...MORE MYSTERIOUS THAN "THE INVISIBLE MAN"
KARLOFF THE UNCANNY
IN
"The MUMMY"
WITH
ZITA JOHANN · DAVID MANNERS
EDWARD VAN SLOAN · ARTHUR BYRON

CARL LAEMMLE presents
H.G.WELLS'
FANTASTIC SENSATION
THE INVISIBLE MAN
with
GLORIA STUART - CLAUDE RAINS
Wm. HARRIGAN - DUDLEY DIGGES - UNA O'CONNOR
HENRY TRAVERS - FORRESTER HARVEY
A UNIVERSAL PICTURE

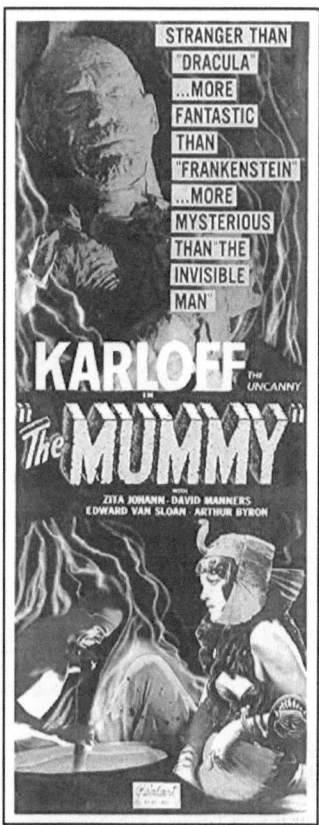

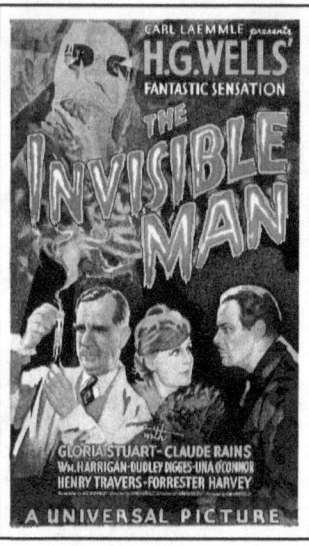

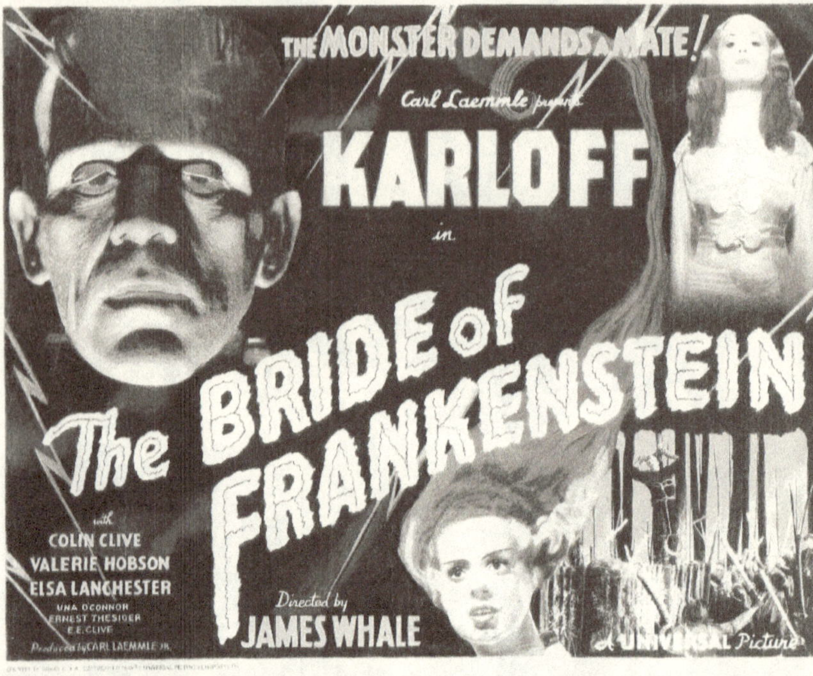
THE MONSTER DEMANDS A MATE!
Carl Laemmle presents
KARLOFF
in
The BRIDE of FRANKENSTEIN
with
COLIN CLIVE
VALERIE HOBSON
ELSA LANCHESTER
UNA O'CONNOR
ERNEST THESIGER
E.E. CLIVE
Produced by CARL LAEMMLE JR.
Directed by
JAMES WHALE
A UNIVERSAL Picture

She gives you that
WEIRD FEELING
DRACULA'S DAUGHTER
with
OTTO KRUGER · GLORIA HOLDEN
MARGUERITE CHURCHILL
EDWARD VAN SLOAN IRVING PICHEL
NAN GRAY
Realart

LIONEL BARRYMORE
IN
MARK OF THE VAMPIRE
with ELIZABETH ALLAN BELA LUGOSI
LIONEL ATWILL
JEAN HERSHOLT
TOD BROWNING'S
PRODUCTION
A
METRO
GOLDWYN
MAYER
PICTURE

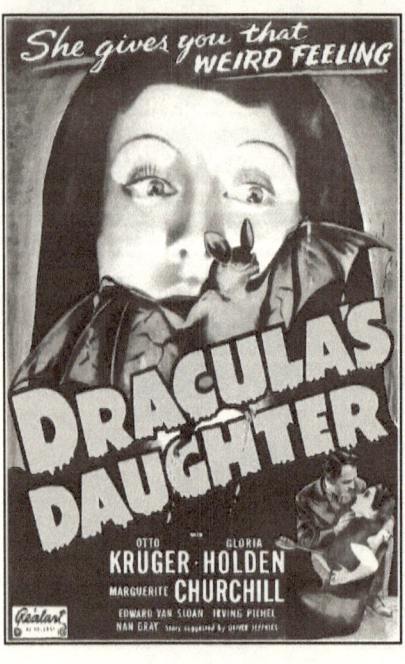

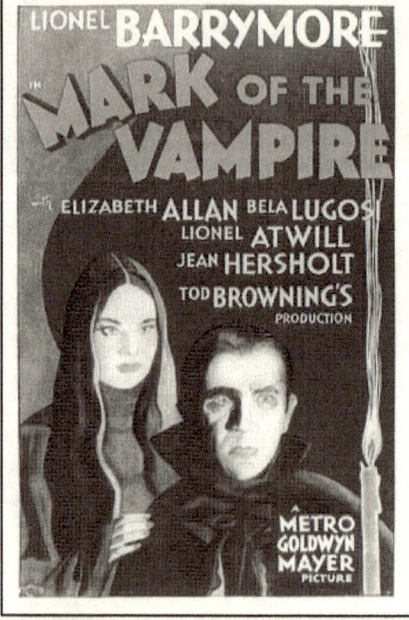

SON OF FRANKENSTEIN

(UNIVERSAL)
Release Date: January 13, 1939
Alternate Titles: *Frankenstein's Revival* (Japan)
The Shadow of Frankenstein (Spain)

Directed by: Rowland V. Lee **Screenplay by:** Willis Cooper & Rowland V. Lee (uncredited) based upon characters created by Marry Shelley **Special Effects by:** John P. Fulton & Jack P. Pierce (makeup) **Music by:** Frank Skinner **Cast:** Basil Rathbone (Baron Wolf von Frankenstein) Boris Karloff (the Monster) Bela Lugosi (Ygor) Lionel Atwill (Inspector Krogh) Josephine Hutchinson (Elsa von Frankenstein) Donnie Dunagan (Peter von Frankenstein) Emma Dunn (Amelia) Edgar Norton (Benson)

Academy Ratio, Black & White, 99 Minutes

SYNOPSIS Upon his father's death, Wolf Frankenstein returns to the town of Frankenstein with his wife, Elsa, and young son, Peter. The villagers are none too happy upon his arrival and begrudgingly hand over his father's property as designated in the will. However, Wolf does at least manage to strike up a friendship with Inspector Krogh. Things start to go awry when Wolf meets his father's old assistant, the hunchback Ygor, who was hanged years ago but didn't die. Ygor shows Wolf his father's creation. Unbeknownst to the villagers, the monster wasn't destroyed and is simply in a weakened state. It is Ygor's hope that Wolf can restore the monster to its full power. Wolf can't help himself and revives the monster, which Ygor then uses to get revenge on the men who hung him. With dead bodies piling up, this strains the friendship between Wolf and Krogh, who thinks a monster may be afoot. Eventually the truth comes out that Wolf has revived the monster. Wolf shoots Ygor dead and knocks the monster into a sulfur pit. Wolf and his family then leave the town of Frankenstein on good terms, bequeathing the castle to the town to do with as they please.

COMMENTARY By 1939, it had been three years since Universal had released a classic monster movie and four years since their last Frankenstein film. The reason was a silly ban on horror films that lasted only two years, and once the ban was lifted, Universal got right back at it with *Son of Frankenstein*. (The ban lifting wasn't the only reason for production, there had also recently been a wildly successful reissue of *Dracula* and *Frankenstein* on a triple bill with *Son of Kong*.) The first draft of the Frankenstein sequel by Willis Cooper was fundamentally similar to the finished film with Wolf Frankenstein coming to claim his inheritance. The main difference is that it didn't include Ygor, one of the favorite characters in the Frankenstein franchise!

On the note of Ygor, the cast/characters is a huge reason why this film is as well-loved as it is. Whereas many times "Son of" characters are pale imitations of their progenitors, Basil Rathbone's performance as Wolf is possibly just as iconic as Colin Clive's. While it's certainly over the top, it suits the film perfectly. When speaking to his servant, Benson, Wolf even manages to get in an excellent reference to the iconic line of the first film. Upon finding out that the monster has revived, Wolf says, "Benson, it's alive! Alive, alive!" Bela Lugosi is gruesomely delightful as the grotesque, hunchbacked, broken-necked Ygor, and many critics and fans alike consider the role to outshine even *Dracula*. One of Ygor's best scenes is a humorous one, where he intentionally coughs on one of the town constables and then apologizes. "Bone gets stuck in my throat," he explains. As is usual, there's a bit of retconning going on in the sequel. As the audience, we are led to believe that Ygor is the same hunchback from the first film, named Fritz. Not only was Fritz killed by the monster in that film, the monster hated Fritz above everyone else because he tortured him. That Fritz/Ygor could go on to befriend the monster he once tormented seems unlikely. Further compounding the confusion is the fact that Ygor was a blacksmith, which Fritz wasn't, but Ygor does talk numerous times about grave robbing. (Back then audiences had little sense of continuity without the aid of television broadcasts or home video. Therefore screenwriters didn't worry too much about what was to them a trivial matter.)

The most interesting relationship in the film is easily that between Wolf and Inspector Krogh, whose friendship is always on shaky ground. Krogh's story of having his arm ripped out as a child is easily one of the film's best scenes. Add to this his regret that it kept him from fulfilling his lifelong dream of becoming a soldier and the character easily emerges as the most sympathetic and likable of the whole film. In a touching scene, when Peter asks Krogh how he lost his arm, Wolf answers for him and tells Peter that Krogh is a soldier who lost his arm in the war. This moment bonds the two characters together, making their heated arguments later in the film more interesting than they would have been without it. The most famous scene between the duo, of course, is the infamous game of darts that they play towards the end. Really, it's a testament to Lionel Atwill that his character was spoofed years later in *Young Frankenstein*, which mostly only referenced the original and *Bride*, but not any of the post-*Son* sequels.

Unfortunately, the characterization of the monster regresses back to the mute brute of the first film, even though he spoke wonderfully in *Bride*. But then again, what would the monster and Wolf have had to talk about? Perhaps it was better this way. Karloff still gets some great moments of characterization, though. The reflection scene in *Bride* is referenced and expanded upon here when the monster stares at himself in the mirror. One could argue in *Bride* that he wasn't 100% sure that the reflection he saw was his own. But here, when he sees himself and Wolf reflected in the same mirror, he realizes the ugly truth. His moments mourning the loss of Ygor are also well done and push him over the edge so that he can wreak the mandatory amount of mayhem throughout the climax. And it's a great ending, too, with Wolf swinging from a chain like Douglas Fairbanks Jr. and knocking the monster into a sulfur pit.

If there's one flaw to be found with the ending, it's that it has a certain stop and go problem in terms of pacing, though this was apparently because they weren't sure of just how to get to the ending since the script was still being rewritten during filming! The project finished shooting on January 5, 1939, only two days before its preview date of January 7th! When released, it was reported that the film broke records and was the highest-grossing Universal horror film yet. In fact, it was so successful that it helped to get the studio back into the black. The film effectively ushered in a new era of Universal horror, and yet, ironically, in many ways it was the last great Universal horror film on par with earlier efforts like *Bride*. The pictures that followed were certainly fun, but they were basically "kid stuff" and though profitable, critics were not kind to them.

FINAL WORD Though it's not superior to *Bride*, *Son* just might still be better than the original *Frankenstein*, but it's a tough call. In either case, it's predominantly considered to be both the end of an era and the beginning of a new one.

THE INVISIBLE MAN RETURNS

(UNIVERSAL)
Release Date: January 12, 1940
Alternate Titles: *The Return of the Invisible Man*
(alternate title) *Invisible Man's Counterattack* (Japan)

Directed by: Joe May **Screenplay by:** Curt Siodmak, Lester Cole & Joe May (story) **Special Effects by:** John P. Fulton **Music by:** Hans J. Salter & Frank Skinner **Cast:** Vincent Price (Sir Geoffrey Radcliffe) Nan Grey (Helen Manson) Sir Cedric Hardwicke (Richard Cobb) John Sutton (Dr. Frank Griffin) Cecil Kellaway (Insp. Sampson) Alan Napier (Willie Spears) Forrester Harvey (Ben Jenkins), Harry Stubbs (Constable Tukesberry)

Academy Ratio, Black & White, 81 Minutes

SYNOPSIS Sir Geoffrey Radcliffe has been framed for the murder of his brother and sits on death row. However, he just happens to be friends with Dr. Frank Griffin, brother of the late Jack Griffin (the Invisible Man). On a visit, Griffin injects Radcliffe with the invisibility serum, allowing him to escape. On the run, the invisible Radcliffe reunites with his fiancé Helen Manson. It's now a race against time for Radcliffe to prove who the real killer is and for Griffin to devise a cure for the serum before the new Invisible Man goes mad just like the old one did. Ultimately, Radcliff clears his name by proving that his brother was murdered by Richard Cobb, though Radcliffe is shot by police while confronting Cobb. The wounded Radcliffe is given a blood transfusion, which ends up curing both his impending descent into madness and his invisibility.

COMMENTARY It's interesting to note that when *Son of Frankenstein* set the box office afire in 1939, the first monster franchise Universal eyed for a reprise wasn't Dracula or the Mummy, but the Invisible Man. *The Invisible Man Returns* was announced in March of 1939 with either Boris Karloff or Bela Lugosi eyed to anchor the picture. (Doesn't necessarily mean they were to play the title character, they might have been eyed for the villain, Cobb.) Joe May was announced to direct, and though he ultimately did, Universal replaced him with *Son of Frankenstein* director Rowland V. Lee for a time. To script the story W.P. Lipscomb (*Les Miserables*; 1935) was hired then replaced by Michael Hogan, though in the end, it would be the ever-reliable Curt Siodmak who wrote the movie. Actually, this was Siodmak's first Universal Horror work and was the suggestion of director Joe May when he came back on the project. Siodmak would go on to write many of Universal's seminal horror films of the Forties.

The script by Siodmak is typical of most sequels of the era in that it inevitably retreads many beats and plot points from the original while at the same time giving them a twist. The most repetitive aspect from the original has the new Invisible Man going to stay at a lonely inn right away. As in the original, one of the innkeepers walks in on Radcliffe while he's in a state of undress/invisibility. On that note, though it's a similar scene, John P. Fulton shows off new and improved effects. When Radcliffe removes the glasses from his bandaged head, we can see through the eye holes into the back of the bandage-wrapped skull! (It's very impressive for the year 1940.) Doing what any good sequel should do, Fulton finds new and exciting ways to play with the Invisible Man. Notably we get shots of the Invisible Man in rain and smoke, giving his body a discernable outline. One of the best scenes has the police scouring a house for Radcliffe by filling it with smoke. As they are all wearing protective gas masks, Radcliffe knocks one of them out and steals their uniform, allowing him to escape the house as one of their own. While that scene was unique, the ending is repetitive of the first film in that the Invisible Man gets shot by the police. In the last moments, he lays dying in a hospital bed while his fiancé looks on... only here the formula gets flipped. Radcliffe doesn't die. The blood transfusions he receives not only cure his madness, but also his invisibility.

While Claud Rains' Invisible Man was a villain through and through, Radcliffe, played by Vincent Price, is a sympathetic character. How could he not be? Rotting in a prison cell for a crime he didn't commit, invisibility is a last resort for him rather than a desire to meddle with nature. As such, though he's committed acts of violence in his invisible form, Radcliffe at least had a good reason. Many of Radcliffe's scenes are presented in a fairly mischievous light as well. As for Prices' iconic voice, his first scenes as Radcliffe downplay his powerful voice. It's only after he begins his descent into madness that the rich voice we all recognize becomes more prevalent, which is rather interesting. He also doesn't do anything horrible enough to bring him past the point of no return, thus allowing his survival in the end. This ending was also telling for future sequels, which would make their invisible characters heroes rather than villains. And on the note of sequels, the reason that so many followed (four more to be exact) was that this film, though not a hit on the level of *Son of Frankenstein*, still managed to gross four times its production budget. It was even nominated for an Academy Award for Best Special Effects. With a track record like that, it's no wonder that so many sequels followed.

FINAL WORD Easily the best of the Invisible Man sequels, the films that followed would mostly revolve around novelties to get by. This sequel would be remade (unofficially) twice, first as *Abbott and Costello Meet the Invisible Man* (1951) and then as the Mexican produced *The New Invisible Man* (1958).

THE MUMMY'S HAND

(UNIVERSAL)
Release Date: September 20, 1940
Alternate Titles: *Resurrection of the Mummy* (Japan)

Directed by: Christy Cabanne **Screenplay by:** Griffin Jay & Maxwell Shane **Makeup by:** Jack P. Pierce **Music by:** Frank Sinner & Hans J. Salter **Cast:** Dick Foran (Steve Banning) Peggy Moran (Marta Solvani) Wallace Ford (Babe Jenson) Eduardo Ciannelli (High Priest) George Zucco (Prof. Andoheb) Cecil Kellaway (Tim Sullivan, the Great Solvani) Charles Trowbridge (Dr. Petrie) Tom Tyler (Kharis)

Academy Ratio, Black & White, 67 Minutes

SYNOPSIS On their last dime in Egypt, two down on their luck explorers, Steve Banning and Babe Jenson, stumble upon an ancient vase that might lead the way to the lost tomb of Ananka. Though an expert in the field, Professor Andoheb, denounces it as a fake, Steve and Babe press on anyways. The duo secures funding for the expedition from a magician named the Great Solvani, though his daughter Marta is none too pleased about this. During the course of the expedition, the ancient tomb is found and Steve and Marta begin to fall in love. In secret, a High Priest of Karnak (really Professor Andoheb) uses Tanna leaves to resurrect Kharis, the mummified guardian of Ananka. Kharis begins killing off members of the expedition one by one and eventually kidnaps Marta. Andoheb wants to make Marta immortal like Kharis, so they can live forever, but Steve and Babe stop the ceremony, killing Andoheb and lighting Kharis on fire.

COMMENTARY With both *The Son of Frankenstein* and *The Invisible Man Returns* proving to be big hits at the box office, rather than turning to Dracula, Universal next chose to revive the Mummy. Unlike *Dracula* and *Frankenstein*, *The Mummy* never received a sequel during Universal's first horror cycle of the 1930s. Nor did the studio have as much faith in a Mummy sequel's potential as it was budgeted at a modest $80,000 (compare that to *Son of Frankenstein's* budget of over $400,000). In fact, to save money, even *Son of Frankenstein's* classic score was reused, and the Egyptian temple sets were leftovers from James Whale's *Green Hell* (1940).

More so than 1932's *The Mummy*, it was this film that set the formula for the entire franchise. It's all here: the Tanna leaves that need brewing to awaken Kharis, the High Priest of Karnak, the girl that the Mummy thinks looks like Ananka, and stock-footage flashbacks to past Mummy movies to pad out the run time. *The Mummy's Hand* is probably what general movie-going audiences *think* that 1932's *The Mummy* is (if they haven't seen *The Mummy*, of course). As it is, a bandage-clad zombie shuffling through a camp in the Egyptian desert and killing off the expedition's numbers one by one is what most audiences associate with Universal's Mummy franchise. (In fact, *Hand* is the only entry of the series where this happens, as the next three sequels were set in America). It's also worth noting that this film's expedition scenes finding the tomb were the real inspiration behind the 1999 *Mummy's* first act when the characters discover the tomb of Imhotep. (In a touch of irony, the 1999 *Mummy* was accused of ripping off Indiana Jones, but it's said that *The Mummy's Hand* also helped to influence the Indiana Jones films itself. So, in fact, 1999's *Mummy* was just coming full circle in a way.)

However, nothing as grand as Indiana Jones or the Mummy films of the 2000s occurs in *Hand*, which is painfully evident at the film's end. You'd think that once the Mummy was defeated that the tomb would begin to quake and collapse—or something—and the heroes would make a hasty exit, but nothing like that occurs. As Kharis lies flat on the ground to lick up the Tanna fluid, he gets lit on fire. That's it. He doesn't even get back up to chase the heroes out of the tomb. That nitpick aside, *Hand* is still regarded as the best Mummy sequel of the original cycle, which is somewhat remarkable considering that Kharis doesn't revive and go into action until the last 25 minutes of the movie. Why the film works so well is that it actually has likable, interesting characters to fill out the run time before the killing starts. This is undoubtedly one of the most important aspects of any horror picture: sympathetic characters for the audience to fret about when the monster gets loose. On the other end of the spectrum, George Zucco's Professor Andoheb makes for a thoroughly interesting and unlikable villain. That the priest of this ancient cult is a highly respected academic is a great touch as opposed to him being some kind of uneducated, unrefined zealot.

Most importantly of all, this film also introduced the central character of the sequels, that being the mummy of Kharis. Whereas the first *Mummy* featured only one very memorable scene of the mummified Imhotep coming to life, this film keeps the Mummy wrapped up for the entire picture. Though he would later be played almost exclusively by Lon Chaney Jr., in his debut outing Kharis is portrayed by stuntman and B-Western star Tom Tyler. Tyler's version of Kharis established the character's rather limited parameters, those being the mostly immobile right arm, the shuffling walk, and the weakness for pretty girls. One thing his Kharis had that was not only unique but quite impressive when compared to Chaney's iteration was his black, soulless eyes. To accomplish this, Tyler's eyes in close-ups as Kharis were painted black frame by frame and the results are spectacular. They were probably also quite time-consuming, hence them being a one-off trait.

Though box office information on this film is hard to find, it must've been successful, for it was eventually followed by three sequels plus a meeting with Abbott and Costello.

FINAL WORD If you didn't like the 1932 *Mummy*, this is probably the film you're looking for as it has all the tropes you'd expect from a Universal Mummy film.

THE INVISIBLE WOMAN

(UNIVERSAL)
Release Date: December 12, 1940

Directed by: A. Edward Sutherland **Screenplay by:** Kurt Siodmak & Joe May **Special Effects by:** John P. Fulton & John Hall **Music by:** Charles Previn **Cast:** Virginia Bruce (Kitty Carroll) John Barrymore (Prof. Gibbs) John Howard (Dick Russell) Charlie Ruggles (George) Oscar Homolka (Blackie Cole) Edward Brophy (Bill) Donald MacBride (Foghorn) Charles Lane (Growley) Thurston Hall (John Hudson) Margaret Hamilton (Mrs. Jackson) Mary Gordon (Mrs. Bates) Anne Nagel (Jean) Maria Montez (Marie) Shemp Howard (Hammerhead/Frankie) Kathryn Adams (Peggy) Kitty O'Neil (Mrs. Patton) Eddie Conrad (Hernandez)

Academy Ratio, Black & White, 72 Minutes

SYNOPSIS Dick Russell is a wealthy young playboy at the end of his financial rope, with most of his money getting drained by his father's old inventor friend, Professor Gibbs. However, Gibbs swears to Russell that he's on the verge of creating a formula that can make him a millionaire again. Specifically, it's an invisibility formula. The kooky professor puts a want ad in the paper for a test patient and receives an unlikely reply in the form of fashion model Kitty Carroll, who thinks it would be fun to turn invisible and terrorize her overbearing boss. The experiment goes off without a hitch, except for Kitty takes off in her new invisible form to cause mischief at the modeling agency. Therefore, when Russell shows up, he thinks the professor has lost his mind. Eventually, Gibbs gets Kitty and Russell in the same room together and proves that his experiment worked. Another problem arises when mob men, who wish to become invisible, steal Gibb's invisibility machine. They also kidnap Gibbs and the now visible Kitty and take them down to a hideout in Mexico. Kitty, who can activate the invisibility serum in her blood via alcohol, turns the tables on the mob men by drinking some liquor. In her invisible form, she incapacitates all of the mobsters by the time that Russell arrives to rescue her. She and Russell are married and later have a baby.

66

COMMENTARY Encouraged by *The Invisible Man Returns* good grosses, Universal produced another sequel by the end of the year. Rather than repeating the formula, writers Curt Siodmak and the previous film's director Joe May turned it on its head. Instead of being somber and serious, the new film would be satiric. And, in place of another man turning invisible, a woman would become so. And though horror fans and H.G. Wells (who did get paid for the concept) may not have been pleased with the resultant film, *The Invisible Woman* is a good film. It isn't a great film, but for what it is, it's very well rounded. The pacing is good, the dialogue is punchy, and it ends with a great little tag scene.

As to the production history, comedy writers Frederic I. Rinaldo and Robert Leeshe were brought in to further punch up the script in terms of humor and dialogue. The title role was originally cast with Margaret Sullavan, an esteemed actress who ultimately considered the picture to be beneath her. Though she was already under contract for the film, when she received an offer to appear in *So Ends Our Night* (1941) under director John Cromwell, she literally didn't show up for the production of *Invisible Woman!* In Sullavan's place, Universal then cast Virginia Bruce. And Bruce does a swell job as the title character and is aided along by the other members of the cast, all of whom work well with the comedic material given to them.

Notably, the titular Invisible Woman goes against type in that she is the lone hero of the ending; the male lead really doesn't help her. In fact, she pretends to be in distress for his benefit once all the bad guys are defeated! There's also a unique little love story between the two in that Russell doesn't know what Kitty looks like but still falls in love with her by the picture's end. No attempt is really made to equate Kitty to her male predecessors. Or, in other words, there is no scene of her swaddled in bandages. The closest she comes to that is wearing a big, brimmed hat with a veil over her face. Other unique looks for the character included her waltzing around in a dress on the runway, giving the viewers the impression that either a headless woman or a ghost had come before them. In another scene that was probably quite risqué and sexy for the time, Kitty puts some panty hose on her shapely legs to taunt Russell, who chides her that she's probably ugly! However, this is early on in the relationship and takes place during a humorous scene where both have consumed copious amounts of alcohol. By the film's tag scene, the duo has been married. This, in turn, allows for a great little ending where, as they admire their newborn son, he turns invisible! And thusly, *Invisible Woman* ends on a nice little comedic button.

Grossing about $200,000 less than the previous film, it wasn't as big of a hit. *Invisible Woman* also had a slightly larger budget at $300,000, meaning that its final gross only doubled its budget, whereas *Returns* had quadrupled its budget in terms of gross returns. This might be why the series went back to playing it straight in the next entry.

FINAL WORD Even if it's not a traditional horror movie, *Invisible Woman* is a fine film in its own right. And, if you're a fan of movies like *Hold That Ghost* and *Abbott and Costello Meets Frankenstein*, then you should like this one as well.

DR. JEKYLL AND MR. HYDE

(MGM)
Release Date: August 12, 1941
Alternate Titles: *Man and Beast* (Argentina)

Directed by: Victor Fleming **Screenplay by:** John Lee Mahin, Percy Heath & Samuel Hoffensteinby based on the book by Robert Louis Stevenson **Makeup by:** Jack Dawn **Music by:** Franz Waxman **Cast:** Spencer Tracy (Dr. Henry Jekyll/Mr. Edward Hyde) Ingrid Bergman (Ivy Pearson) Lana Turner (Bea Emery) Donald Crisp (Sir Charles Emery) Ian Hunter (John Lanyon) Barton MacLane (Sam Higgins) C. Aubrey Smith (Bishop Manners) Peter Godfrey (Poole)

Academy Ratio, Black & White, 112 Minutes

SYNOPSIS One day at church, the kindly Dr. Jekyll is shocked by a once peaceful man's outburst. Jekyll determines that a traumatic event brought out the dark side of the man's personality. Jekyll endeavors to prove that man has two natures which can be separated, which does not sit well with his father-in-law to be, Sir Charles. One night, Jekyll has a chance meeting with a dancer, Ivy, who needs medical attention. Despite a mutual attraction, Jekyll makes no advances on Ivy and leaves her apartment. When Sir Charles delays the wedding and takes Jekyll's fiancé, Bea, abroad, it's too much for Jekyll. He takes his experimental serum and turns into Mr. Hyde. It doesn't take long for Hyde to ensnare Ivy in his web and an abusive relationship begins between the two. Hyde reverts back to Jekyll when news comes that Bea and her father are returning. Sir Charles agrees to let the two wed sooner rather than later and Jekyll is overcome with joy. He sends money to make amends with Ivy and prepares to wed Bea, only Hyde remerges and kills Ivy. A guilt-ridden Jekyll goes to break it off with Bea, but turns into Hyde again after he's done so. The police chase Hyde down to Jekyll's lab where he is shot and killed.

COMMENTARY Remembering the great success of the Paramount adaptation in 1931, plus no doubt aware of Universal's continuing success with horror films, MGM decided to remake *Dr. Jekyll and Mr. Hyde* yet again. To do so, they first bought up the rights to the popular Paramount version and the John Barrymore adaptation from 1920 for a whopping $1,250,000. Nothing wrong with that except for afterward MGM went about destroying every print of the classic 1931 version (though thankfully a print was discovered and restored in later years). Perhaps for that reason, more than anything else, this version isn't highly regarded.

The film's pedigree is certainly impressive even if the final results were not. Its director was none other than Victor Fleming, who had helmed *Gone with the Wind* and co-directed *The Wizard of Oz*. Spencer Tracy was one of the great actors of his time, but most everyone agrees that he was miscast in this film. To his credit, though, Tracy had different ideas for the story during pre-production, which might have worked better to set itself apart from its predecessors. Tracy wanted to take a more realistic approach, where the tale would be more of an allegory than a literal manifestation of evil. Tracy envisioned Jekyll taking drugs and drinking heavily in a poor neighborhood where he was virtually unknown. There he would take on the moniker of Mr. Hyde and commit his atrocious deeds. In other words, there was no magic formula. Still, MGM wanted a straight remake of the 1931 version, and that's what they did.

The film is by no means a shot-by-shot remake, which makes for interesting viewing for Jekyll-Hyde completists. The production values are also a notch above the 1931 version when it comes to the more elaborate sets and matte paintings. Where this remake falls flat for most fans is Hyde's appearance, kept secret in the marketing they say to shock audiences when it finally debuted. However, the more likely answer is that the design was hidden so that it wouldn't underwhelm potential ticket buyers. As it stands, Tracey's Hyde is basically just Tracey with longer hair and some extra lines to age his face a bit. This version does have one major improvement on the original, though. In the 1931 ending, after a dejected Jekyll leaves his fiancé, we see Jekyll transform into Hyde outside and return to torment the girl. This film has a wonderful shock element by comparison. After Jekyll leaves Bea, she collapses on her porch steps, sobbing. Jekyll pauses upon hearing this in the distance and turns back around to go to her. However, as the camera pans up Jekyll's legs as he approaches Bea, it's revealed that he's turned into Hyde. If you've seen the 1931 version, you know this, of course, but if not, it's a wonderful moment of shock and horror.

Although it eventually grossed $2 million worldwide, the film was still a critical failure and isn't well-loved today. Likewise, Tracy described it as one of his least favorite films and even called his own performance as "awful".

FINAL WORD If not for its superior predecessor and the fact that MGM attempted to erase it from existence, this adaptation might be more highly regarded.

THE WOLF MAN

(UNIVERSAL)
Release Date: December 12, 1941
Alternate Titles: *The Werewolf* (Latin America)

Directed by: George Waggner **Screenplay by:** Curt Siodmak
Special Effects by: John P. Fulton & Jack P. Pierce (makeup)
Music by: Charles Previn, Hans J. Salter & Frank Skinner **Cast:**
Claude Rains (Sir John Talbot) Lon Chaney, Jr. (Larry Talbot/the
Wolf Man) Warren William (Dr. Lloyd) Ralph Bellamy (Capt. Paul
Montford) Patric Knowles (Frank Andrews) Bela Lugosi (Bela)
Maria Ouspenskaya (Maleva) Evelyn Ankers (Gwen Conliffe) Fay
Helm (Jenny Williams) Leyland Hodgson (Kendall) Forrester
Harvey (Victor Twiddle) J.M. Kerrigan (Charles Conliffe)

Academy Ratio, Black & White, 70 Minutes

SYNOPSIS After the death of his older brother, Lawrence "Larry"
Talbot returns to his ancestral home in Wales, England. Looking
through his father's telescope, he spies a beautiful girl, Gwen, in
the village and goes to see her where she works at an antique shop.
He buys a silver wolf's head cane and manages to persuade her to
go to the gypsy carnival that night. While there, a wolf attacks
Gwen's friend, and Larry kills it with his silver cane. However, the
beast also bit him, and later Larry begins to transform into a
werewolf. The curse is explained to him by Maleva, a gypsy woman
who also happens to be the mother of the werewolf that Talbot
killed. She takes pity on Larry, but there is no way to help him.
While Maleva believes Larry, his father and everyone else think
that he is going insane with his werewolf talk. As the Wolf Man,
Talbot kills several people drawing the attention of the locals. On
the night that a great hunt to catch the wolf is going on, Larry's
father ties him to a chair to prove to him that it's all in his head.
Instead, Larry transforms and goes on the prowl. In the woods, he
goes after Gwen (there looking for Larry) but she is saved by Larry's
father, who beats the werewolf to death with the same silver cane
Larry used to kill the other werewolf earlier. Gwen, Larry's father,
and the other onlookers are shocked to see the Wolf Man revert
back to the now dead Larry.

COMMENTARY The story of *The Wolf Man*, Universal's fifth big famous monster after Dracula, Frankenstein, the Invisible Man, and the Mummy, began exactly ten years before it saw release. In late December of 1931, Universal purchased rights to a screenplay from French director Robert Florey entitled *The Wolf Man*. However, the story bears no similarities to the 1941 film that would eventually carry that name. Florey's story concerned a young boy whose mother was killed by wolves. When he's carried away by a she-wolf, he suckles her teat, and years later the wolf's milk enables him to become a werewolf. (It's actually a great deal more like *Curse of the Werewolf* [1960] and *Legend of the Werewolf* [1974].) Boris Karloff had been the original choice for the role in the 1930s, and years later, when the film geared up for production, Bela Lugosi lobbied for the part. Ultimately, he was passed over in favor of the son of another famous Universal horror star: Lon Chaney Jr. His father had portrayed *The Phantom of the Opera* in 1925, and Chaney Jr. had recently impressed as Acoba, leader of the Rock Tribe in Hal Roache's *One Million B.C.* (1940).

The new version of *The Wolf Man* had been given to George Waggner, whose stock was rising at Universal after proving himself to be a dependable director. Waggner then hired writer Curt Siodmak to do the script. Siodmak never even bothered to read Robert Florey's old screenplay. Universal liked the title and that was all Siodmak needed. He was also told who the cast would comprise of, what the budget was, and that the picture was to begin shooting in ten weeks. And with that information in mind, he wrote the script.

Like *Dracula, Frankenstein,* and *The Mummy* before it, *The Wolf Man's* excellent story features the tragic love triangle common to many Universal horrors. For instance, in *Dracula* and *The Mummy*, the titular characters/monsters are involved in a love triangle with the leading lady and the hero. (In *Frankenstein*, this is true to a lesser extent in that Victor Moritz provides competition for the affections of Elizabeth.) But whereas Dracula and Imhotep are evil, Larry Talbot is not. He just has an evil affliction which he received, ironically enough, while performing a good deed. As such, this easily makes this one the best of Universal's monster love triangles. Naturally, it is most similar to *Werewolf of London*, only better done. The film's ending is similar in a way to *Werewolf of London*, where an inspector says he will claim that the main character was trying to defend his wife. Here, an inspector character says to Larry's bereaved father, "The wolf must've attacked and Larry came to the rescue. I'm sorry, Sir John."

Another factor that made this film more popular than Universal's previous werewolf film was the makeup, which was more elaborate. (Actually, the makeup used in *The Wolf Man* was a discarded design from *Werewolf of London*.) The transformation scenes in the film have since gone on to become legendary amongst horror fans. Just as much as Jack Pierce's makeup, the sets are also a huge asset to *The Wolf Man*. The forest set and gypsy camp in particular make for the most memorable ones. The scene where the gypsies all pack up to leave upon hearing that a werewolf is loose in camp in particular has a chilling atmosphere. But it also makes one sit back and ask, "Why didn't they feel the same way about Bela's werewolf?" Did he have his lycanthropy under control? And for that matter, why was Bela's version a mere wolf while Larry is a half-wolf half-man? (Tom Weaver speculates that the scene was shot based on an older version of the script where *The Wolf Man* was meant to simply turn into a wolf.)

Though Universal feared audiences would be in no mood for horror after the recent bombing of Pearl Harbor, the film was a huge hit, especially in comparison to Universal's earlier *Werewolf of London*. The film's release was even credited for inspiring RKO's slew of horror films from Val Lewton. It also cemented Lon Chaney Jr. as Universal's top new horror star, securing him future roles as not only the Mummy, Frankenstein's monster, but even Dracula himself! Though it provided the birth of the Wolf Man, for many this film was still the end of an era as Universal's last great horror film.

FINAL WORD Many fans consider this to be the best werewolf movie of all time. Whether you agree with that statement or not, it certainly set the tone for werewolf films to follow.

THE GHOST OF FRANKENSTEIN

(UNIVERSAL)
Release Date: March 13, 1942
Alternate Titles: *Frankenstein Returns* (Austria)

Directed by: Erle C. Kenton **Screenplay by:** Scott Darling & Eric Taylor (story) **Special Effects by:** John P. Fulton & Jack P. Pierce (makeup) **Music by:** Hans J. Salter **Cast:** Cedric Hardwicke (Dr. Ludwig Frankenstein) Lon Chaney Jr. (the Monster) Bela Lugosi (Ygor) Lionel Atwill (Dr. Theodore Bohmer) Evelyn Ankers (Elsa Frankenstein) Ralph Bellamy (Erik Ernst) Barton Yarborough (Dr. Kettering) Janet Ann Gallow (Cloestine)

Academy Ratio, Black & White, 67 Minutes

SYNOPSIS When angry villagers blow up the ruins of Castle Frankenstein, they unknowingly revive the monster. Ygor, who also survived the attack, leads the monster to the village of Vasaria, where Ludwig Frankenstein, Wolf's brother, lives. Ygor convinces Ludwig to operate on the monster to fix him, or so he thinks. Really Ludwig plans to destroy the monster until a visit from his father's ghost prompts him to fix the monster by giving it a new brain. Ludwig decides to use the brain of his dead colleague, Dr. Kettering, killed by the monster, to fulfill his father's dream. However, Ygor makes a deal with Ludwig's double-crossing companion, Dr. Bohmer, to transplant his brain into the monster instead. Dr. Bohmer agrees, removes Ygor's brain, and switches it with Dr. Kettering so that Ygor is transplanted into the monster. Ludwig is horrified when he discovers what he's done. The villagers are also aware of his experiment and storm his estate. In the violence, Ludwig, Bohmer, and Ygor/the monster all perish in a fire that consumes the house.

COMMENTARY *Son of Frankenstein's* success made another sequel a no-brainer. Though initially it was intended for Basil Rathbone to return as Wolf Frankenstein, ultimately only Bela Lugosi was brought back as Ygor along with Lionel Atwill (but as a completely new character). In place of Wolf, Frankenstein's heretofore unknown other son Ludwig is introduced. Though he's ably played by a fine actor in the form of Cedric Hardwicke (*The Ten Commandments*), his character can't hold a candle to the wonderful Wolf Frankenstein as played by Rathbone. Neither is Atwill's new character, Dr. Bohmer, on par with Inspector Krogh from *Son*. Lugosi is great again as Ygor at least, even if it seems incredulous he could have survived the three bullets fired into his stomach in the last film.

Of course, the biggest absence from *Son* was that of Boris Karloff himself. During the end of *Son's* production, Karloff had claimed that would be his last major appearance as the monster, which it was. And, even if Universal could have lured him back, he was currently contracted to theater, and Universal didn't want to wait on him. And so, *The Wolf Man's* Lon Chaney Jr. was chosen as his successor during filming of the aforementioned film. Overall Chaney looks good in the Jack Pierce makeup, but it's easy to differentiate him from Karloff. Mainly, it's the fact that his face is much puffier (this was compounded by Chaney having an allergic reaction to the makeup). Chaney offers a different, simpler characterization of the monster that would carry over into the next few sequels. It's not a bad effort at all, it's just that Karloff was so much better in terms of his expressions. However, this dull characterization was partly due to time constraints. Case in point, there was supposed to be a scene of the monster reacting in joy to seeing his friend, the little girl Cloestine, when she enters the courtroom. It was decided the happy facial expressions would necessitate redoing the makeup later that day, and so it was decided to keep the monster expressionless in the scene.

This one begins the way that most Universal horrors end: with angry villagers converging on the castle and blowing it up. It's certainly an exciting way to start off the movie, not to mention an easy way to free the monster from the hardened sulfur pit he is trapped in. As the monster emerges, chalky white, he indeed looks like a ghost himself. There's a lot of great visuals in the first ten minutes, especially Ygor and the monster watching the castle explode from a distance. After this, they walk through a classic cemetery that represents Universal Horror to a tee. Next up is a lightning storm amidst a forest of dead trees wherein lightning directly strikes the monster's neck bolts in another excellent shot. Visually speaking, these scenes easily make for the highlight of the film. After that it's up to the story to carry the movie. It does a decent enough job but isn't anywhere near as absorbing as *Bride* or *Son*. If anything, it's just a rehash of the last film (fixing the monster but with a twist: giving the monster a new brain). The idea from this comes via an appearance of the ghost of Henry Frankenstein, thus making the film's title literal. In the scene, Henry berates Ludwig for contemplating dismantling the monster piece by piece. Instead, he suggests gifting the monster with a proper brain, something he wasn't able to do himself. Ludwig decides to transplant the brain of his dead colleague, Dr. Kettering, into the very monster that killed him. However, due to the treachery of Atwill's Dr. Bohmer, he secretly removes Ygor's brain and switches it with Kettering's. As such, the film ends with Ygor essentially possessing his old friend's body (more or less proving Ygor only hung around the poor monster to take advantage of his strength).

The ending is good enough, except for that it's just a repeat of the opening. Villagers storm Ludwig's home crying for the monster's blood and the house burns down. End of movie. Though the script had called for the monster to appear to literally disintegrate during the fire, Universal was smart enough not to do that and simply had a flaming beam fall on top of him. The film naturally wasn't as well reviewed as *Son*, but was still profitable enough to guarantee more sequels. However, this would be the last standalone Frankenstein movie from Universal. From here on out, all of the monster's appearances would be in conjunction with other Universal monsters.

FINAL WORD Though it's an enjoyable enough monster movie, that's really all it is. As the last standalone Frankenstein movie before the monster mash era began with *Frankenstein Meets the Wolf Man, Ghost of Frankenstein* goes out with more of a whimper than a bang.

INVISIBLE AGENT

(UNIVERSAL)
Release Date: July 31, 1942
Alternate Titles: *Invisible Agent Against Gestapo*
(Brazil/Denmark/France) *Transparent Spy* (Japan)

Directed by: Edwin L. Marin **Screenplay by:** Curt Siodmak
Special Effects by: John P. Fulton **Music by:** Hans J. Salter **Cast:**
Ilona Massey (Maria Sorenson/Maria Goodrich) Jon Hall (Frank
Raymond/Frank Griffin) Peter Lorre (Baron Ikito) Sir Cedric
Hardwicke (Conrad Stauffer) J. Edward Bromberg (Karl Heiser)
Albert Basserman (Arnold Schmidt) John Litel (John Gardiner)
Holmes Herbert (Sir Alfred Spencer) Keye Luke (Surgeon

Academy Ratio, Black & White, 79 Minutes

SYNOPSIS Frank Raymond appears to be a simple print shop
owner in Manhattan until he receives a surprise visit from Hitler's
S.S. The men, led by Baron Ikito and Major Stauffer, know
Raymond's real last name: Griffin. Frank is actually the grandson
of the famous Invisible Man, Dr. Jack Griffin, and the S.S. wants
his formula. Frank manages to escape from the S.S. men and goes
to the U.S. Army, where he eventually offers his services. Frank,
in his invisible form, is airdropped into Germany where he
rendezvous with a beautiful female spy, Maria Sorenson, who
Frank thinks might be playing both sides. Through Maria, Frank
is to obtain a secret list of Japanese spies hiding in America.
However, Frank and Maria are eventually both captured by
Stauffer and Ikito. The duo manages to escape with the secret list
and commandeer a German plane which they escape in. Maria
pilots the plane while Frank drops bombs onto the German planes
on the airfield below. After this, Frank passes out, apparently
wounded in the escape. When they get into British airspace, their
plane is shot down, leaving it up to Maria to parachute out and
save Frank's life, which she does. When Frank wakes up, he finds
that the lovely Maria was always on the side of the good guys and
the two begin a romance.

COMMENTARY Like the last Invisible sequel, a gimmick or twist on the formula is used again. The twist utilized here is rather ingenious, even if it does deviate from the original's origins in horror, but then again, so do did the last picture. And, even though this one has a very straightforward action concept in the form of an Invisible Secret Agent, tonally the picture still plays towards comedy like *Invisible Woman*. The film started out with a slightly different title, *Invisible Spy*, under a different producing team, Frank Lloyd and Jack Skirball, who had produced Alfred Hitchcock's *Saboteur*. It's unknown how—or even if—their idea differed from the final film, but Skirball dropped out and was replaced by George Waggner.

Like the last film, our invisible protagonist is nothing but heroic. And, whereas the last film didn't reference the preceding two in any way, this one has a continuity thread in the form of introducing another member of the Griffin family: Jack Griffin's grandson. How did Frank perfect his grandfather's formula and not descend into madness? We never find out, but it really doesn't matter as this is a light, fluffy popcorn flick. As a WWII-era thriller, one will notice many similarities to more modern films. The opening German interrogation scene is a bit like something from *Raiders of the Lost Ark*. Peter Lore's villain, Baron Ikito, could have even been an inspiration for Ronald Lacey's character, Toht, in *Raiders*. Another scene that brings to mind current-day films is Frank's first transformation into the titular character. The transformation occurs when he parachutes out of an airplane being shot at over German airspace, which might bring to mind a similar scene in *Captain America: The First Avenger* (2010) for some.

Visually speaking, there is no callback to the iconic Invisible Man-look from the first two films. Frank never takes on the appearance of his two male predecessors. Instead, he uses greasepaint to make his face visible when he wants to (this was an idea from an aborted Invisible Man script by Richard Schayer from 1932). I'd like to say that the invisibility gimmick is put to good use in a spy film, but Frank really isn't a good spy. He brazenly interferes with a dinner between Maria and an important Nazi contact, ruining her operation in the process. The movie even regurgitates the drinking scene from *Invisible Woman*, though it's less humorous here. That all this was to service the film's comedic aspect is fine except for it does undermine the hero in the process. Griffin can't even be mindful to watch the door when he's rifling through Stauffer's office and gets caught! All that said, Griffin is capable when it comes to getting out of his sticky situations, which is fun to watch. The climax is also fairly grand and exciting, recalling *Raiders* again when the hero and heroine cause chaos at a German airfield before escaping.

Despite the fact that *Invisible Woman's* grosses were less than the previous sequel's, Universal still treated this production with prestige. Some attribute this to the fact that H.G. Wells was very popular at this time, and it's possible his contract wouldn't allow Universal to make a B Picture with his properties. In any case, Universal's faith in the project paid off. It ended up becoming the most successful of all their *Invisible Man* sequels, grossing a little over $1 million.

FINAL WORD If you're a fan of more modern films like *Raiders of the Lost Ark* and *Captain America: The First Avenger*, this WWII actioner might prove entertaining enough for you, but it is not a horror film in any way, shape, or form.

THE MUMMY'S TOMB

(UNIVERSAL)
Release Date: October 23, 1942
Alternate Titles: *Mummy's Graveyard* (Japan)

Directed by: Harold Young **Screenplay by:** Griffin Jay, Henry Sucher & Neil P. Varnick (story) **Special Effects by:** Tim Baar & Jack P. Pierce (makeup) **Music by:** H.J. Salter **Cast:** Lon Chaney Jr. (Kharis) Dick Foran (Professor Stephen Banning) John Hubbard (Dr. John Banning) Elyse Knox (Isobel Evans) Wallace Ford (Babe Hanson) Turhan Bey (Mehemet Bey) George Zucco (Andoheb) Mary Gordon (Jane Banning) Cliff Clark (Sheriff) Virginia Brissac (Ella Evans) Paul E. Burns (Jim) Frank Reiclier (Professor Norman)

Academy Ratio, Black & White, 60 Minutes

SYNOPSIS Thirty years after opening the tomb of Ananka and taking her body back to America, the priests of Karnak decide to take revenge on the tomb's desecrators: Stephen Banning and Babe Hanson. Banning is now the father of an adult son, Dr. John Banning, in New England. Stephen is the first person that the mummy, Kharis, kills upon arriving in America. When Babe comes for the funeral, his death follows. However, rather than setting Kharis after John, the High Priest sends Kharis on a mission to bring him John's beautiful fiancé, Isobel. The High Priest plans on forsaking his vows and making himself and Isobel immortal with the Tanna leaves. When John and the townspeople show up to rescue Isobel, Kharis whisks her away while the priest goes to deal with the angry mob. He is killed and Kharis makes it back to the Banning house. In the end, John rescues Isobel, and the house is set on fire with Kharis inside.

COMMENTARY Universal apparently thought enough of *The Mummy's Hand* to produce a direct sequel to that film as opposed to whipping up a new Mummy and new victims for it to stalk. Oddly, the film takes place 30 years after *Hand*. And to that end, Universal didn't even recast the roles of Steve Banning and Babe with older performers, but simply applied makeup to the returning actors which doesn't look half bad. This new story, in a way, undoes the happy ending of *Hand,* as Babe and Steve both die at the hands of the Mummy. (Maybe that's why they set it thirty years later, so the duo could have happy lives before their demises?) Steve and Babe aren't the only ones who are back. Just like Ygor from *Son of Frankenstein* into *Ghost of Frankenstein,* the fatal bullet shot into Andoheb in *Hand* turned out to not be so fatal as Andoheb lived... just long enough to pass the torch to a new high priest, Mehemet Bey, before he seems to die of old age! Like Renfield and Dracula, Bey and Kharis head west via steamer ship. In America, the duo take up residence in an old cemetery which makes for an excellent setting and scenes of Kharis stalking the American countryside are very well done. Whereas the last film was already half over by the time the Mummy showed up, here Kharis gets into action pretty quick. But, then again, he has to, as the movie is only one hour long, and ten minutes' worth of the run time is devoted to flashbacks to the previous film.

This film's ending is at least a little more exciting than the last picture's, albeit a bit silly. Despite taking place in modern day America, like the Frankenstein films, the villagers... er, townsfolk, all grab their torches and go on the warpath to face the monster. (Some of this sequence is comprised of footage of the peasants from the Frankenstein films.) They head first for the cemetery, giving Kharis one last chance to walk among the tombstones to escape with the damsel in distress. Rather incredulously, Kharis climbs a terrace while still holding Isobel as though he were King Kong! The house erupts into flame due to the townsfolk tossing torches at the Mummy and the picture ends. But not until after another happy coda like the previous film, in this case showing that John and Isobel do get married. (This was attributed to WWII era audiences needing a happy ending, typically a film like this would roll the credits once the monster is defeated.)

Lon Chaney Jr. had just re-upped his contract with Universal that year and so was cast as Kharis. But whereas in the old days the Laemmles would have taken great care to groom Chaney into stardom like they did Boris Karloff, with Chaney, all that mattered for the new studio heads was that they found more monster makeup to put Chaney in. And that they did, suiting him up as the Mummy, a role Chaney thoroughly disliked. This was no surprise, as a great deal of makeup was needed. However, instead of the cotton-based makeup used on the previous two mummies, this time Jack Pierce simply put a high quality rubber mask on Chaney (it still took eight hours to wrap him in bandages though!).

As usual, critics were dismissive of the film, which isn't terribly surprising all things considered. *The Mummy's Tomb* (which really would have been a more appropriate title for the last film set in Egypt) was double-billed with *Night Monster*. *Tomb*, though a rather weak entry in the series, was profitable enough to guarantee a few more sequels before the jig was up.

FINAL WORD Not as good as the film that preceded it or the one that would follow, *The Mummy's Tomb* is still a decent flick if you're in need of a quick mummy fix.

FRANKENSTEIN MEETS THE WOLF MAN

(UNIVERSAL)
Release Date: March 5, 1943
Alternate Titles: *Wolf Man Meets Frankenstein* (working title)
Frankenstein vs. Werewolf (France) *Frankenstein and Werewolves*
(Japan)

Directed by: Roy William Neill **Screenplay by:** Curt Siodmak
Special Effects by: John P. Fulton and Jack P. Pierce (makeup)
Music by: Hans J. Salter **Cast:** Lon Chaney Jr. (Larry Talbot), Bela
Lugosi (the Frankenstein monster), Ilona Massey (Baroness Elsa
Frankentein), Patric Knowles (Dr. Frank Mannering), Maria
Ouspenskaya (Maleva)

Academy Ratio, Black & White, 74 Minutes

SYNOPSIS When thieves disturb the tomb of Larry Talbot, the
Wolf Man emerges and lives again. A distraught Talbot, desperate
to end his eternal suffering, seeks the help of Maleva, the old gypsy
woman. Maleva takes Talbot to the village of Vasaria where they
hope to find a certain Dr. Frankenstein who may be able to end
Talbot's misery. Talbot suffers a transformation into the Wolf Man
and runs for the hills. After his transformation ends, he wakes up
in the ruins of the old Frankenstein castle, where he finds the
monster. The monster helps Talbot to find Frankenstein's old
journal, and Talbot even befriends the pitiful creature. In the
village, Talbot is able to find Elsa Frankenstein, who with Dr.
Frank Mannering eventually agrees to help Talbot. Unfortunately,
Mannering's mad scientist side gets the best of him, and he
decides to revive the monster to its full power. On the night he is
set to operate on Talbot and the monster, Talbot transforms at the
same time that the monster becomes strong from the experiment.
The monster and the Wolf Man fight, while Elsa and Mannering
escape at the last minute when the castle is flooded.

COMMENTARY Had it not been for a joke cracked by *Wolf Man*
writer Curt Siodmak over lunch at the Universal commissary, this
film would have never happened. In fact, had Siodmak not made

84

his joke, Universal's inevitable sequels to *The Ghost of Frankenstein* and *The Wolf Man* would have likely been standalone adventures. But that's not what happened. Wanting to make Yvonne De Carlo and Mary MacDonald laugh, Siodmak joked to George Waggner that, "George, why don't we make a picture *Frankenstein Wolfs the Meat Man*—I mean *Frankenstein Meets the Wolfman.*" To Siodmak's shock, Waggner ordered him to make his joke a reality and actually write the script!

Initially, Lon Chaney Jr. was to play both the monster and Larry Talbot/the Wolf Man! If Universal had planned to have Bela Lugosi at least read the monster's lines for continuity's sake is unknown. (Remember, as established at the ending of *Ghost of Frankenstein*, Ygor's brain was in the monster's body.) Either way, on October 14, 1942, *Variety* reported that "Lon Chaney Jr. plays a double header as both Monsters in THE WOLF MAN MEETS FRANKENSTEIN which goes to bat at Universal this week..." Instead, Universal cast Lugosi not just as the monster's voice but as the monster himself. It was a strange turn of events, as Lugosi had passed on playing the monster years ago in the original, but now in need of work, took on the arduous task of sitting in the makeup chair. Ultimately, the role would prove too much for Lugosi, and much of the part would end up being played by stuntmen.

The film itself is quite fun, and to his credit, Siodmak actually does come up with a good excuse for the two monsters to cross paths. Larry Talbot would revive from the grave. Discouraged, he would seek out Dr. Frankenstein in an effort to end his life and, therefore, his curse. In his travels, he meets Ygor in the Frankenstein monster. Ygor wants just the opposite, to find Dr. Frankenstein so that he might live. And if that doesn't sound right to you in remembering the film, you're right. You see, though the final edit of *Frankenstein Meets the Wolfman* ignored the fact that Ygor's brain was now in the monster's body, the shooting script did not. Was it removed during shooting you ask? No, actually not. Bela Lugosi actually spoke as the monster during filming and had a decent amount of dialogue. Furthermore, the monster is blind, and this is why he stumbles around with his hands in front of him. In the finished film, this is no longer the case, he's just a dumb brute, and that characterization would ironically stick throughout the rest of the series. Had Lugosi known that his dialogue would be cut in post-production, he may have never taken the role (but, then again, he also took the role because he really needed the money, so maybe not). It was decided to remove his dialogue because test audiences laughed at it, which is odd considering that *Ghost of Frankenstein* ended with Lugosi speaking as the monster after Ygor's brain had been transplanted.

And just how much did the deletion of Lugosi's lines affect the film? Quite a bit, it could be argued. The final battle in the context of the script and in the film is entirely different due to the removal of the subplot regarding Ygor planning to one day rule the world. This actually made the monster the villain and Larry/the Wolf Man the hero in a way. Or, in other words, the Wolf Man was the monster you were supposed to root for in the climax. After all, if he lost, the monster might take over the world! But, with this subplot deleted, the film's ending is shaded with a bit of tragedy. It seems that the "innocent, dumb monster" is fighting his "friend" the Wolf Man. In a strange way, both versions have their merits, different though they may be.

FINAL WORD This film presents an interesting turning point in Universal's horror franchise that not only established that their monsters inhabited the same world, but also encouraged the studio to do more team-up pictures in the future in addition to standalone entries. One could argue that it not only paved the way for similar shared "monsterverses" on the part of Toho studios in Japan, but even the Marvel Cinematic Universe of today.

PHANTOM OF THE OPERA

(UNIVERSAL)
Release Date: August 12, 1943

Directed by: Arthur Lubin **Screenplay by:** Samuel Hoffenstein, Eric Taylor & John Jacoby (story) based upon the book by Gaston Leroux **Special Effects by:** John P. Fulton & Jack P. Pierce (makeup) **Music by:** Edward Ward **Cast:** Claude Rains (Erique Claudin/the Phantom) Nelson Eddy (Anatole Garron) Susanna Foster (Christine DuBois) Edgar Barrier (Raoul Dubert) Jane Farrar (Biancarolli) J. Edward Bromberg (Amiot) Fritz Feld (Lecours) Frank Puglia (Villeneuve)

Academy Ratio, Technicolor, 92 Minutes

SYNOPSIS At the same time that Erique Claudin is let go from the Paris Opera's orchestra, he also comes to believe that his concerto has been stolen by a powerful publisher. In his rage, Claudin attacks the publisher and has etching acid thrown in his face in the process. Now disfigured and wanted for murder, Claudin hides in the catacombs of the Paris Opera. As the "Phantom of the Opera," he instigates a string of accidents to get a young performer named Christine thrust into the limelight. Christine then becomes integral into an investigation into the mysterious goings-on at the opera, which are led by a suitor named Raoul. Also vying for Christine's affections is Anatole, a baritone. When Christine is kidnapped and taken underground by the Phantom, Raoul and Anatole team up to rescue her. A gunshot in the catacombs causes them to collapse, burying the Phantom as Christine, Raoul, and Anatole escape. Later, Christine chooses neither man and decides to pursue her career in the opera to the fullest.

COMMENTARY Of all Universal's "Classic Monsters," the Phantom is sometimes the odd monster out, which is ironic considering that he was actually the company's first monster. Still, there are several reasons for the Phantom not being promoted as often as Frankenstein, Dracula, and the Mummy. First of all, the groundbreaking 1925 Phantom adaptation from Universal slipped into public domain, making it less lucrative for Universal in terms of home video sales. But, perhaps the most significant difference between the Phantom and Universal's other monsters was that his film was the only one to be done in Technicolor rather than black and white. (Even the first Phantom had a few color sequences in it.)

Universal had been mulling over a Phantom remake since 1935. Even then Universal was thinking of a less gruesome, more romantic version of the Phantom. This version was set to be played by either Boris Karloff or Feodor Chaliapin (a famous Russian opera singer). In this case, the Phantom apparently would not be physically disfigured. Instead, due to psychological trauma suffered in World War I, he only thinks that he is disfigured and, as such, hides his face. Of course, 1935 was around the time that Universal briefly gave up on horror films, and so this version was shelved. After the monsters became popular at the box office again, Universal went back to their Phantom remake, this time planning to reimagine the Phantom and Christine as estranged father and daughter, to be played by Charles Laughton and Deanna Durbin. That idea was floated in 1941, and by the time production began, the father-daughter idea had been done away with (mostly) and Claude Rains of *The Invisible Man* had been cast as the Phantom, with Susanna Foster as Christine.

The character structure of this film is a bit different than either that of the book or the 1925 movie. Like the previous adaptation, the character of the Persian is done away with. While in that version, the Persian had been replaced by an inspector, here it is romantic lead Raoul who has become the inspector. A rival love interest in the form of Anatole Garron (played by matinee idol Nelson Eddy) is added into the story. But, as both men compete for Christine, one might wonder just where this leaves the Phantom? Earlier had been mentioned the father-daughter idea, and in terms of the characters' respective ages, Erique could very well be Christine's father. The film tip-toes around whether his affections for the much younger woman are romantic or paternal. Because of this, some say as earlier version of the script had this Phantom as Christine's long-lost father.

Anyhow, this version of the Phantom is a completely different character than Lon Chaney's horrific villain. While Chaney's version really garnered no sympathy, the same cannot be said for Erique. This is due in large part to the fact that we actually get the Phantom's backstory in the film's first act. If I were to compare this movie and its lead character to something relatable to modern audiences I would choose 2019's *Joker*. Both films are similar in that both present "nice guys"—a little quirky, yes, but nice—who are driven mad due to unfortunate circumstances. In Erique's case he is losing the sensation in his fingers, which makes his performance in the orchestra suffer. He's let go from the Opera, and as it turns out, he was funneling most of his income into expensive opera lessons for Christine (anonymously, of course). Therefore, his beloved Christine will no longer receive the tutelage she needs. The final straw from Erique is when his concerto, submitted to a famous publisher, appears to have been stolen by that same publisher. Enraged, Erique attacks the man and has acid thrown in his face, causing the disfigurement. (In the book, the Phantom was born that way, so this provided another significant deviation.) However, Erique's disfigurement as the Phantom is only shown once. As it is, this version of the Phantom is iconic for his look while wearing his mask, while Chaney's version, by contrast, is iconic for the way he looks without it. (Most audiences barely recall Chaney's Phantom's mask and only recall his unmasked form.)

Another reason this film is a bit disjointed from Universal's other monster movies of the era is that it's more of a romantic melodrama with a few horror elements in it. Yes, the Phantom still kills plenty of people despite his more sympathetic portrayal, but he just isn't as scary as Chaney's Phantom, though he wasn't meant to be. Then, of course, there are the grand operas and huge sets which differentiate the *Phantom* from the smaller budgeted *Frankenstein, Dracula,* and *Invisible Man* sequels of the same era. The film also has quite a few comedic scenes, mainly those that focus on the romantic rivalry between Anatole and Raoul. The story ends with neither one winning Christine's affections, who more or less leaves them both to ascend as an opera star. As both men had recently asked her to dinner, they humorously agree to go to dinner together without her and that's how the picture ends! In this author's opinion, the film should have ended after the catacombs beneath the opera collapsed. There's an excellent lingering shot of the dead Phantom's mask and violin amongst the rubble the film could have ended upon, but instead, it leaves us with the rather unnecessary coda involving Christine and her two suitors.

Phantom was a huge hit for Universal when released in 1943. Not only that, it was actually their biggest hit yet among their "Classic Monster" films and even won two Academy Awards for Cinematography and Art Direction.

FINAL WORD Whether or not you consider this version of the Phantom to be superior to the 1925 original or not probably depends on whether you prefer horror to melodrama. In that case, Chaney's Phantom wins hands down. But, if you like musicals and melodrama over horror (unlikely though that may be as you are reading a book on horror), then the 1943 *Phantom* might be more so your cup of tea.

SON OF DRACULA

(UNIVERSAL)
Release Date: November 5, 1943
Alternate Titles: *Night Devil* (Japan)

Directed by: Robert Siodmak **Screenplay by:** Eric Taylor & Curt Siodmak (story) **Special Effects by:** John P. Fulton & Jack P. Pierce (makeup) **Music by:** Hans J. Salter **Cast:** Lon Chaney, Jr. (Count Alucard/Dracula) Louise Allbritton (Kay Caldwell) Robert Paige (Frank Stanley) Frank Craven (Dr. Harry Brewster) J. Edward Bromberg (Professor Lazlo) Patrick Moriarity (Sheriff Dawes) Evelyn Ankers (Claire Caldwell) Adeline De Walt Reynolds (Madame Queen Zimba)

Academy Ratio, Black & White, 80 Minutes

SYNOPSIS Despite being engaged to Frank Craven, Kay Caldwell has just invited the Hungarian Count Alucard to her family plantation in New Orleans in hopes of marrying him. The Count, really a descendant of Dracula, arrives and immediately kills Kay's wealthy father and then marries Kay to Frank's shock. Frank shoots Alucard, but the bullets pass through him and kill Kay instead. Frank is eventually committed on the basis that he is insane. Later, a vampirized Kay sneaks into Frank's jail cell in the form of a bat. In bat form, she feeds on Frank, then transforms back into a human. She tells Frank that she invited the vampire Alucard here so that she could be immortal with Frank. She tells Frank where the Count sleeps and instructs him to kill the Count. After that, Frank will be like her. Frank does escape the jail and kill Alucard, but once that's done, he also goes and kills the vampiric Kay.

COMMENTARY Before Kharis journeyed to the bayou in *The Mummy's Curse*, Dracula, or rather his "son," did in 1943. Though the film is called *Son of Dracula*, the title character's lineage really isn't addressed aside from one throwaway line. Due to this fact, some fans speculate that this film was initially to star Bela Lugosi as Dracula again. Author Robert Guffey even speculates the title was likely *The Bride of Dracula*, as a great deal of the film's focus is on the character of Kay. (In fact, Kay is defeated after Dracula, another way in which she is the central villain in a sense.) It is assumed that Lugosi was to simply reprise the role of Dracula, and according to the writer of the first treatment, Curt Siodmak, he wrote it with Lugosi in mind. Curt was later removed from the project by the director (also his brother), Robert Siodmak (Curt attributed this to sibling rivalry!). As to why Lugosi didn't return, it is thought that it was because Lugosi had such difficulty playing the Frankenstein monster in *Frankenstein Meets the Wolf Man* (never mind the strain of the makeup on the 60-year-old actor!). Ultimately, Lugosi's return to the role in *Abbott and Costello Meet Frankenstein* would prove that he most certainly was not too old to play the Count again. As it was, this was Lugosi's second missed opportunity to reprise the role, the first being when his rather epic scenes were cut from *Dracula's Daughter*.

With Lugosi out, Lon Chaney Jr. was then cast in the role, which may or may not have been retrofitted to become the Count's heretofore unknown son. To further differentiate the characters, Chaney's version went under the alias of Count Alucard (Dracula spelled backward). Of all the monsters Lon Chaney Jr. ever played (the Wolf Man, Frankenstein's monster, Kharis) his Count Alucard is easily the weakest of the bunch. As it is, Chaney Jr. just doesn't have the Dracula look. Though he's certainly tall, he's also rather broad, while Dracula is usually thought of as tall and thin. Ultimately, John Carradine would have made for a better replacement.

However, there's still some pretty neat stuff in *Son of Dracula*. Alucard's coffin rising out of the swamp, then the vampire exiting it as a white mist is a striking visual (even if the idea of the Count's coffin submerged underwater seems silly). The animation effects used for Chaney Jr. to transition from bat back to human are also well done for their time. The bayou and plantation offer an atmospheric setting as well, and ultimately, it would have suited Lugosi ill. Imagining his Dracula cavorting around a Southern swamp and trying to marry a rich heiress somehow doesn't fit him as opposed to Chaney's Count Alucard.

The ending is certainly more exciting than either that of *Dracula* or *Dracula's Daughter*, in which both vampires are staked through the heart. Here, like in *Horror of Dracula*, it is sunlight that does the vampire in. It all starts with our hero Frank lighting Alucard's casket on fire right before dawn. The two wrestle around a bit before the struggle takes itself outside and once the sunlight hits Alucard, it's all over. As it was, it would be the first time that

Dracula would decompose onscreen in a Universal film. The disintegration of Alucard was to be seen in full, but the censors considered this too much. Therefore, Alucard falls into a pool of water obscuring his body with only his hand visible. It is the hand that we see turn into a skeleton, notably wearing the famous Dracula ring.

Box office information is hard to find for this film. But, whether it was a hit or not, Chaney never returned to the role, and nor did Universal ever produce another solo Dracula movie (though that could have been attributed to the success of *Frankenstein Meets the Wolf Man* more than anything else).

FINAL WORD Though it has its fans, and it's also more lively than the previous two Dracula films, *Son of Dracula* more or less cemented Universal's Dracula branch as the weakest link of their horror series when compared to Frankenstein, the Wolf Man, and the Mummy.

THE INVISIBLE MAN'S REVENGE

(UNIVERSAL)
Release Date: June 9, 1944

Directed by: Ford Beebe **Screenplay by:** Bertram Millhauser **Special Effects by:** John P. Fulton **Music by:** Hans J. Salter **Cast:** Jon Hall (Robert Griffin) Leon Errol (Herbert Higgins) John Carradine (Dr. Peter Drury) Alan Curtis (Mark Foster) Evelyn Ankers (Julie Herrick) Gale Sondergaard (Lady Irene Herrick) Lester Matthews (Sir Jasper Herrick) Halliwell Hobbes (Cleghorn) Leyland Hodgson (Sir Frederick Travers) Ian Wolfe (Jim Feeney)

Academy Ratio, Black & White, 77 Minutes

SYNOPSIS After years of being locked up in a Capetown asylum, Robert Griffin returns to England to avenge himself on the people he believes left him for dead. Years ago, Griffin had discovered a diamond field in Africa with Sir Jasper Herrick and his wife Maria. Griffin became injured in the jungle and the duo left him behind, or so he says. The couple calls the police on Griffin, making him a fugitive. Griffin finds his way into the home of Dr. Drury, looking for a test subject for his invisibility experiments (so far he has performed them only on animals). Griffin is all too happy to oblige, and upon becoming invisible, runs away from the lab to do away with the Herricks. Eventually, when Griffin wishes to regain his visibility, he witnesses Drury turn his invisible dog to visibility via blood transfusion. Griffin then murders Drury and uses his blood to become visible again. He makes his way back into the Herrick household to woo their daughter, Julie. However, Griffin begins to become invisible again and so knocks out Julie's beau, Mark Foster, and begins to drain him of his blood. At the last moment, Drury's faithful dog tracks down Griffin and mauls him to death in an act of retribution. Mark is saved in the nick of time before he can be drained of all blood.

COMMENTARY With *Invisible Agent* having been the most successful Invisible Man film since the original, Universal naturally cranked out another sequel. Unlike the previous two

94

entries, which featured gimmicky storylines to tweak the formula, Universal returned the series to its roots in horror. Though played by the same actor in the previous film, John Hall, this Invisible Man is an outright villain with no redeeming qualities. Nor does he appear to have any ties to past entries despite having the surname of Griffin (no mention is made of Dr. Jack Griffin from the original). The surname seems to be nothing more than a nod to the novel, and it is a new scientist character who transforms Robert Griffin into an Invisible Man. (It's possible this film began as a direct sequel to the original as sources say Claud Rains was approached to star, but he turned Universal down.)

The film's story is a little hard to follow at first as it tells us about the characters' pasts rather than showing us. There is a somewhat hackneyed backstory where Griffin and two accomplices found a diamond mine in the jungle. Griffin appeared to suffer an accident and got left behind, and was then later committed to an asylum which he escaped from. (Again, all of this is unseen in the film and thrown at us in the form of expositional dialogue.) We're also not entirely sure if Griffin's accomplices on the jungle expedition, Sir Jasper Herrick and his wife Irene, are innocent victims of the crazed Griffin or if the Invisible Man's revenge of the title upon them is justified.

Mediocre writing aside, the film does offer up a few novelties and new tricks for the franchise. Griffin dips his arm in an aquarium at one point, an interesting effects shot. He throws water on his face to make himself semi-visible to Jasper and Irene, which looks rather creepy. This Invisible Man murders people for their blood, which can render him visible again via transfusion. When the transfusion begins to wear off, we see Griffin turn a pale white before beginning to disappear. Otherwise, it's mostly tricks we had seen before, and Griffin also dons the classic bandaged look of the character not seen since *The Invisible Man Returns*. (This seems to have been done mostly for tradition's sake, as it really didn't seem to fit the parameters of Griffin's character in this story.) The film also features an invisible dog of note. Even though the franchise had played with invisible animals before, the dog serves as a minor character and even ends up being the hero of the picture when it kills the villainous Griffin. (The dog being the hero of the film isn't an understatement, as the picture lacks a solid sympathetic male or female lead. All of the main characters are mostly unlikable.)

Despite not having a gimmick to make the film stand out from its predecessors, it was still profitable for Universal. The studio even secured the rights from H.G. Wells for two more Invisible Man pictures. Ultimately, they wouldn't utilize those rights until nearly six years later on *Abbott and Costello Meet the Invisible Man* (1951). (Universal also initially inserted the Invisible Man into the script for *House of Frankenstein* but later removed him, along with the Mummy.) So, as it stands, this was Universal's last traditional Invisible Man entry in their line of classic horror films.

FINAL WORD If you disliked the light tones of the previous two films, then you might prefer the more serious, horror-oriented *Invisible Man's Revenge.*

THE MUMMY'S GHOST

(UNIVERSAL)
Release Date: July 7, 1944
Alternate Titles: *The Specter of the Mummy* (Argentina) *The Mummy's Shadow* (Brazil) *The Princess and the Mummy* (Mexico) *The Phantom Mummy* (Portugal)

Directed by: Reginald Le Borg **Screenplay by:** Griffin Jay, Henry Sucher & Brenda Weisberg **Makeup by:** Jack P. Pierce **Music by:** Frank Skinner **Cast:** Lon Chaney Jr. (Kharis) Ramsay Ames (Amina Mansori/Ananka) Robert Lowery (Tom Hervey) John Carradine (Yousef Bey) Barton MacLane (Inspector Walgreen) George Zucco (Andoheb) Frank Reicher (Professor Norman)

Academy Ratio, Black & White, 62 Minutes

SYNOPSIS Several years after Kahris seemed to perish in a fire in the Banning home, Yousef Bey, a High Priest of Arkham, comes to America looking for the Mummy, who didn't actually burn to ashes in the fire. What's more, a girl named Amina is really Ananka reincarnated. As Kharis and Yousef Bey continue their reign of terror in search of Ananka's body, they too learn the truth about the girl. One night, Kharis abducts Amina, who reverts back to the ancient form of Ananka. The Mummy and his bride sink into an abysmal swamp as Amina's fiancé Tom watches in horror.

COMMENTARY It was another year and another Mummy movie at Universal. Aside from a little retconning going on (the Priests of Karnak are now the Priests of Arkam and the Hill of the Seven Jackals is now the Hill of Arkam), *The Mummy's Ghost* has good continuity ties to *The Mummy's Tomb* and again takes place in Mapleton... mostly. The film begins in Egypt, with John Carradine's character waltzing into the High Priest's tomb as though he were James Bond receiving his assignment from M. In this case, the assignment is to go to America and find Kharis. (George Zucco is back again—Andoheb still isn't dead!) Speaking of Egypt, since the film can't have the Mummy loose in familiar Egypt, it does the next best thing and sets him loose in the Egyptian wing of a museum in America. In one of the more interesting scenes there, he reaches down to caress the dead mummy of Ananka. Only when he touches it, it shrivels up and deflates. At the same time, Amina wakes from a nightmare, making it clear to the audience that Amina is now Ananka. Just in case we don't get it, Carradine also vocalizes this plot point, which enrages Kharis, who begins destroying the museum.

On that note, this is probably the best that Chaney's Mummy ever looked, and he also gets a great deal of screen time compared to the previous two Mummy movies. Not only that, it doesn't take long to get to him either, as he pops up only ten minutes in. That said, he doesn't get any interesting type of resurrection scene. He simply comes shuffling out of the woods into frame with some bombastic music to herald him. The same plot formula is used once again where Kharis is betrayed by the High Priest, who is beginning to fall for Ananka himself. This is the first entry where Kharis actually gets to deliver the death blow to the priest, though, as he knocks him out a window.

As for Amina/Ananka, she presents what is probably the best female lead of Universal's Mummy movies. As the film progresses, a white *Bride of Frankenstein*-like streak grows across Amina's hair, and I have to wonder if it was intentional. (Say, do you think they considered *Bride of the Mummy* as a title?). This film resurrects the old reincarnation plot from the first film, but while that one ended happily with the heroine saved from danger, this one doesn't. In *Mummy's Ghost*, Amina/Ananka turns into a female mummy/quasi-monster herself in the last reel. As Kharis carries her in her arms, she turns into an old woman. Kharis and Ananka sink into a swamp leaving a heartbroken Tom behind. (This was apparently not in the original script, for director Le Borg claims that it was his idea to end the picture somberly.)

The Mummy's Ghost is one of the more highly-regarded Mummy sequels, second only to *Hand*. Though poorly reviewed by critics, it was profitable for Universal. It would be followed by one more Mummy movie, but after that, it would be the end of the road for Kharis until it was his turn to tangle with Abbott and Costello.

FINAL WORD Better than both its predecessor and the film that would follow it, *The Mummy's Ghost* is easily the best of Kharis's adventures in America.

BASIL
RATHBONE
BORIS
KARLOFF
BELA
LUGOSI in
THE NEW UNIVERSAL PRESENTS
SON OF FRANKENSTEIN
with
Lionel ATWILL
JOSEPHINE
HUTCHINSON
DONNIE DUNAGAN
Emma Dunn - Edgar Norton

THE MUMMY'S HAND
DICK FORAN
PEGGY MORAN
WALLACE FORD
Cecil KELLAWAY
Eduardo CIANNELLI
George ZUCCO
Tom TYLER

THEY HEAR HIM! THEY FEEL HIM!
But They Can't Stop Him!
H.G. WELLS'
The INVISIBLE MAN RETURNS
SIR CEDRIC HARDWICKE
VINCENT PRICE NAN GREY
SUTTON Cecil KELLAWAY

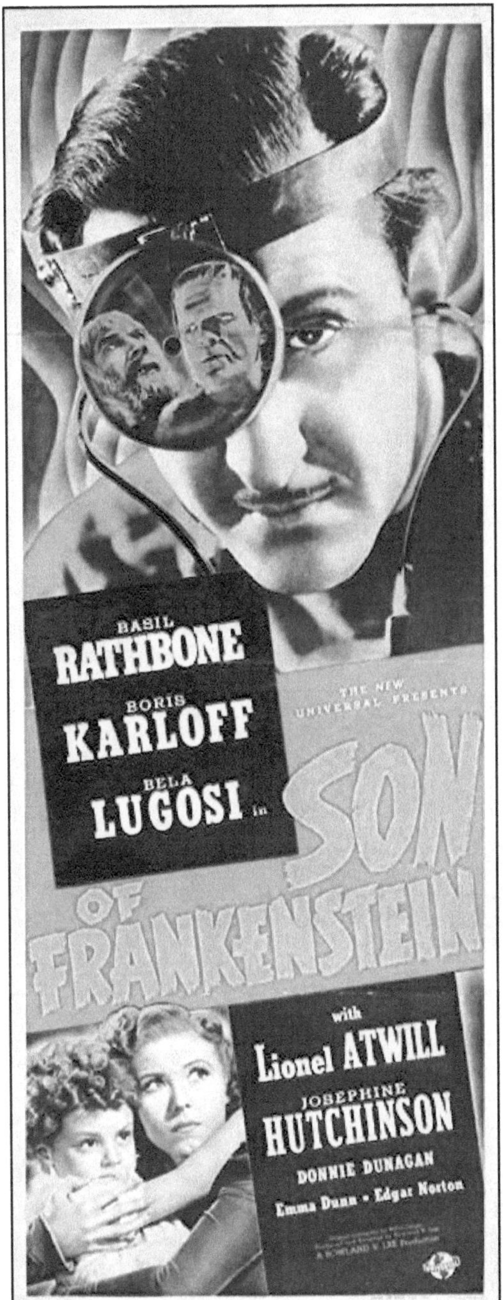

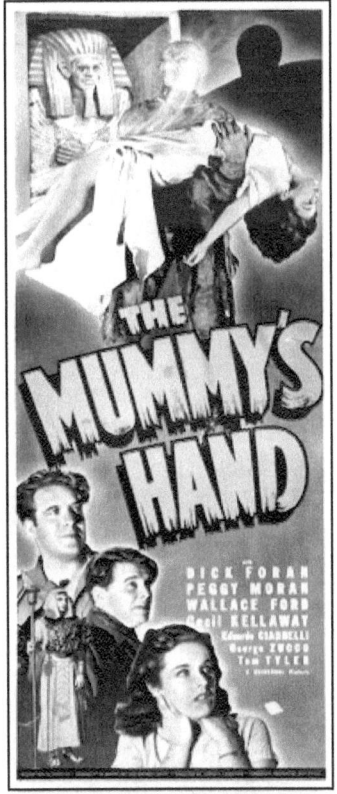

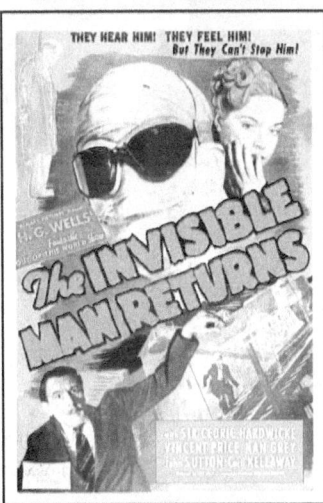

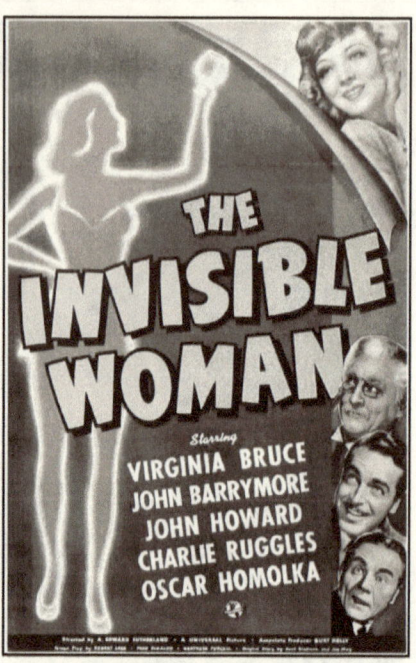

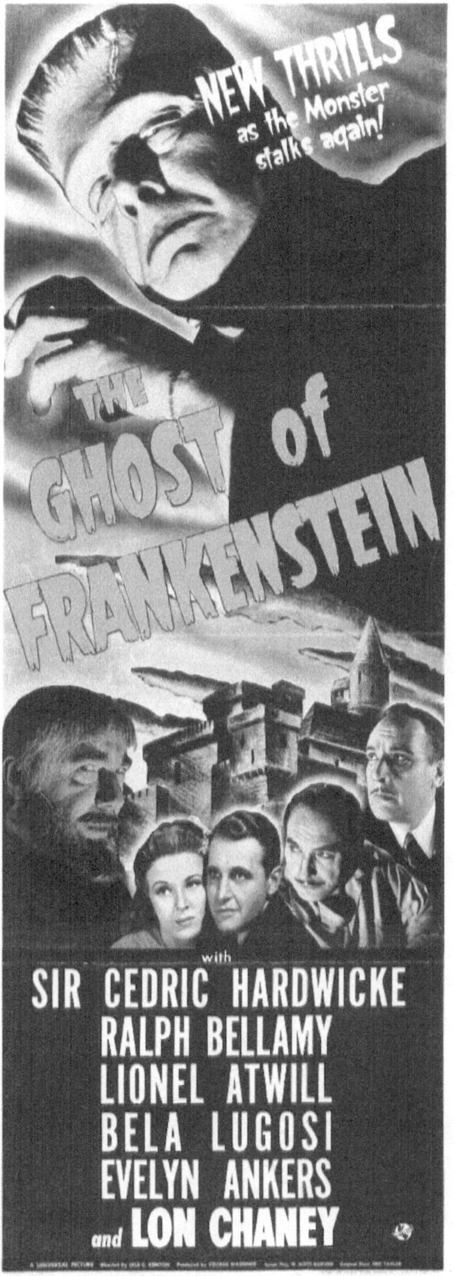
NEW THRILLS
as the Monster
stalks again!
THE
GHOST of
FRANKENSTEIN
with
SIR CEDRIC HARDWICKE
RALPH BELLAMY
LIONEL ATWILL
BELA LUGOSI
EVELYN ANKERS
and LON CHANEY

FRANKENSTEIN
meets THE WOLF MAN

THE SCREEN'S CLASSIC OF TERROR!
PHANTOM
OF THE
OPERA
IN TECHNICOLOR
NELSON EDDY
SUSANNA FOSTER
CLAUDE RAINS
EDGAR BARRIER
LEO CARRILLO JANE FARRAR
J. EDWARD BROMBERG
FRITZ FELD HUME CRONYN
A CAST OF THOUSANDS

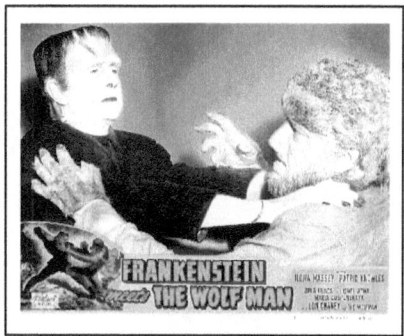

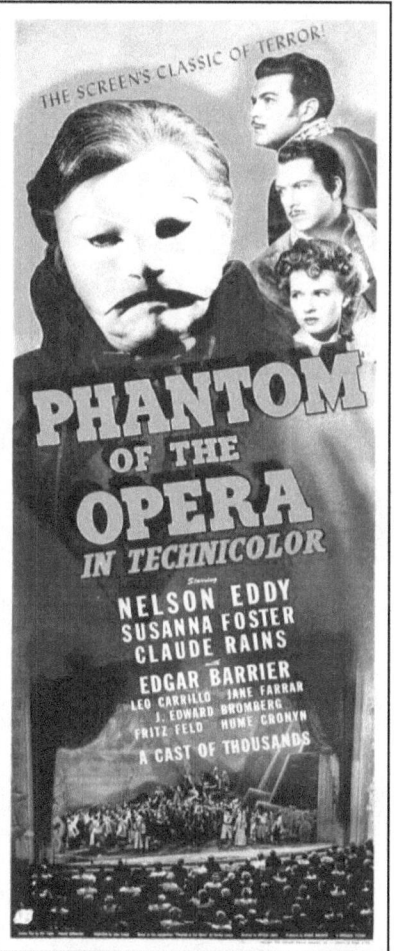

A HORROR FILM SUITABLE ONLY FOR ADULTS
SON of DRACULA
with
LOUISE ALLBRITTON
ROBERT PAIGE
EVELYN ANKERS
FRANK CRAVEN
J. EDWARD BROMBERG
SAMUEL S. HINDS
LON CHANEY
as Count Dracula
A UNIVERSAL PICTURE

NO CHAINS CAN HOLD IT! NO TOMB CAN SEAL IT!
ALL NEW TERROR!
The MUMMY'S GHOST
Starring
LON CHANEY
as KHARIS, THE MUMMY
with
JOHN CARRADINE
RAMSAY AMES
BARTON MacLANE
GEORGE ZUCCO
ROBERT LOWERY

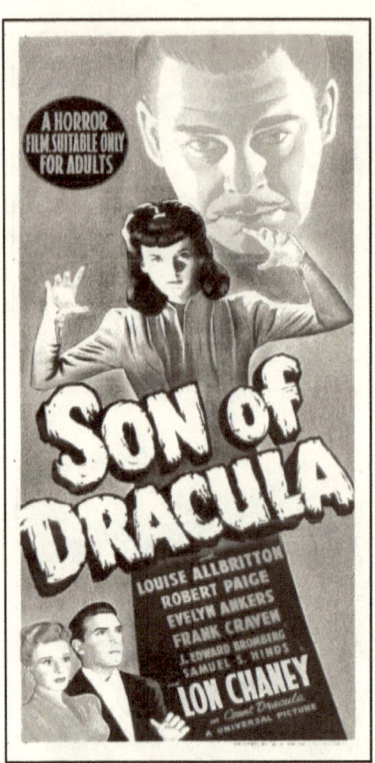

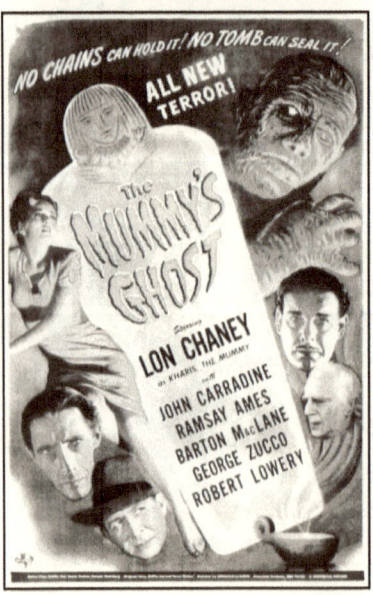

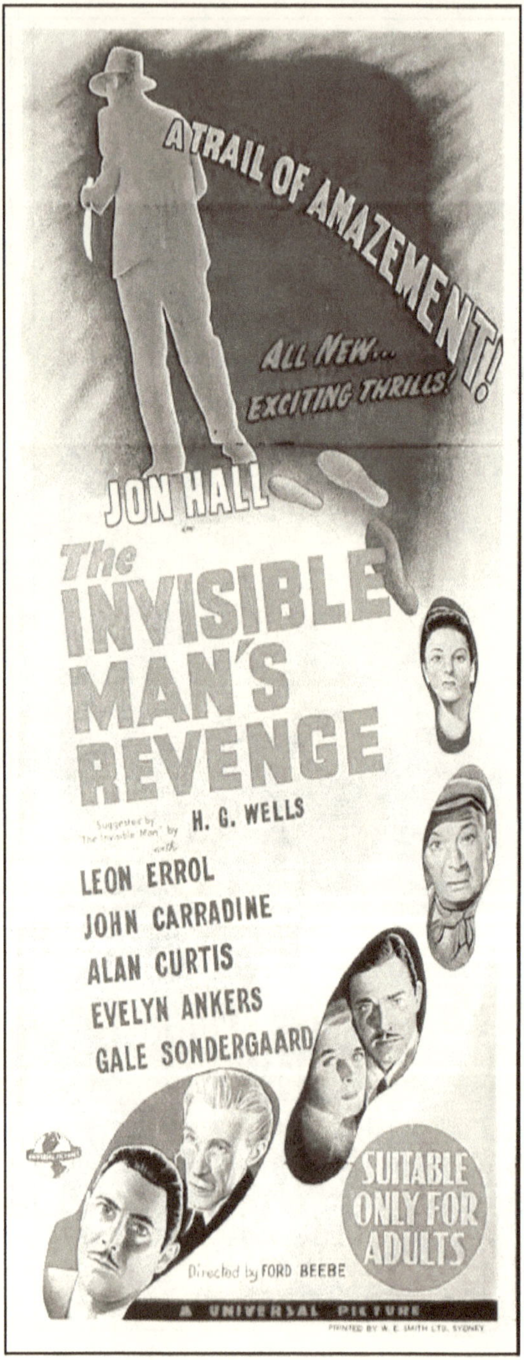
A TRAIL OF AMAZEMENT!
ALL NEW... EXCITING THRILLS!
JON HALL
in
The INVISIBLE MAN'S REVENGE
Suggested by "The Invisible Man" by H. G. WELLS
with
LEON ERROL
JOHN CARRADINE
ALAN CURTIS
EVELYN ANKERS
GALE SONDERGAARD
SUITABLE ONLY FOR ADULTS
Directed by FORD BEEBE
A UNIVERSAL PICTURE
PRINTED BY W. E. SMITH LTD. SYDNEY

HOUSE OF FRANKENSTEIN

(UNIVERSAL)
Release Date: December 15, 1944
Alternate Titles: *The Gypsy and the Monsters* (Spain, alternate title) *Doom of Dracula/Destiny/The Devil's Brood* (working titles)

Directed by: Erle C. Kenton **Screenplay by:** Edward T. Lowe & Curt Siodmak (story) **Special Effects by:** John P. Fulton & Jack P. Pierce **Music by:** Hans J. Salter & Paul Dessau **Cast:** Boris Karloff (Dr. Gustav Niemann) Lon Chaney Jr. (Larry Talbot/the Wolf Man) J. Carrol Naish (Daniel) Elena Verdugo (Ilonka) Glenn Strange (Frankenstein's Monster) John Carradine (Count Dracula) Anne Gwynne (Rita Hussman) Peter Coe (Karl Hussman) Lionel Atwill (Inspector Arnz) Sig Ruman (Bürgermeister Hussman) George Zucco (Professor Lampini) Philip Van Zandt (Müller) Michael Mark (Strauss) Frank Reicher (Ullman)

Academy Ratio, Black & White, 71 Minutes

SYNOPSIS Dr. Gustav Niemann is an inmate at an asylum for the criminally insane for trying to imitate the experiments of Dr. Frankenstein in Visaria. A freak accident frees he and a hunchbacked accomplice named Daniel. The duo commandeers Professor Lampini's traveling horror exhibit, which includes the skeleton of Dracula. Niemann resurrects Dracula by removing the stake from his heart and then uses him to kill the Burgermeister who helped sentence him years ago. Dracula kills the Burgermeister and is then killed himself while Niemann and Daniel escape. Coming into Visaria, they pick up a gypsy girl named Ilonka. Next they find the Frankenstein monster and the Wolf Man frozen in ice. They thaw them out and use Larry Talbot to lead them to Dr. Frankenstein's notes on the promise that Neimann will cure Larry of lycanthropy. Ultimately, Neimann fails to come through on his promise, being too caught up in getting revenge on two Visarian officials, Strauss and Ullman. Talbot transforms into the Wolf Man, alerting the villagers to strange happenings at the castle. In the end, Ilonka, who has fallen in love with Larry, shoots him with a silver bullet. Neimann revives the monster, who breaks free of his restraints, first killing Daniel and then carrying Neimann outside. The villagers chase the monster into a swamp with torches, and there he sinks into the muck with Niemann.

COMMENTARY With *Frankenstein Meets the Wolf Man* proving to be a hit, Universal decided that their next movie would feature all of their monsters: Dracula, the Mummy, the Ape Woman, the Mad Ghoul, and the Invisible Man!!! Another reason for this celebration was due to the fact that Boris Karloff had just finished his run on the theater circuit for *Arsenic and Old Lace* and signed a multi-picture deal with Universal. The idea was that Karloff would be the ringleader of this carnival of horrors, which, ultimately, only Dracula joined in the end. It was simply too difficult to juggle that many monsters in one story, and the finished product shows this to some degree.

In some ways you get two movies in one within *House of Frankenstein*. The first thirty minutes, in terms of monsters, belong to Dracula, while the final forty go to the Wolf Man and Frankenstein's monster. Though it makes the film a bit disjointed, it surprisingly works just fine. John Carradine does quite well in the role of Dracula and managed to carve out his own unique niche in the Universal pantheon with his portrayal. He doesn't try to imitate Bela Lugosi's Hungarian accent and portrays the Count as more of an English aristocrat. His brief scenes manage to be exciting, with him transforming into a bat (via shadow) and killing the Burgomeister. His signet ring also gets a new power, with the people who peer into it being able to see into the Netherworld from which Dracula came. The chase between the police, Dracula's stolen carriage, and Niemann's caravan of wagons is quite exciting. Towards the end of the chase, Niemann suggests that they ditch Dracula's coffin and so Daniel climbs to the top of the caravan and hops from one wagon to the next until he reaches the casket. For an old Universal chiller, the stunt work is impressive. The chase ends with Dracula crawling to his discarded casket and succumbing to the sunlight. It's basically just a reprise of the ending of *Son of Dracula*, with only his hand shown decomposing into a skeleton. (The film might've been more interesting if Dracula had managed to survive this encounter somehow, and then pop back up at the climax to take revenge on Niemann.)

After the Dracula portion (where Niemann and Daniel notably fade into the background), the real story begins in earnest when Daniel rescues a gypsy girl named Ilonka in the village of

Frankenstein. It is Ilonka who provides the film with a much needed sympathetic character and moral center (the characters of Rita and Tony in the Dracula segment were, after all, just guest stars). The one-sided love story between Ilonka and Daniel, which was inspired by the Hunchback of Notre Dame, is complicated upon the resurrection of Larry Talbot. Ilonka immediately falls for the more handsome, brooding Talbot, and the friendship she previously had with Daniel all but evaporates. Though Daniel doesn't deserve a full dose of the audience's sympathy—don't forget, he is a cold-blooded murderer—he does pull at the heart strings a bit. (One could argue that Daniel is being manipulated by the more clever Niemann, after all, and that the murders aren't entirely his fault). The villainous doctor is not only duping Daniel into thinking that he'll be getting a new body, but Larry Talbot as well.

Talbot does very well in this outing and continues to be an interesting character despite the fact that it's still the same storyline from the last film. Aiding this along is his tender love story with Ilonka. Actually, it's remarkable that the love story comes across as well as it does considering that it has only a little under thirty minutes to make its mark. Ilonka's killing of the Wolf Man, which costs her own life, is an excellent scene with a great deal of emotional impact. It could be argued that it even tops the death scene in *The Wolf Man.*

Though the Wolf Man had only two relatively brief scenes in the film, the Frankenstein monster doesn't actually become active until the last five minutes of the movie! Thankfully, Universal didn't try to reprise the ending of the last movie by having him fight the Wolf Man again, and the monster essentially just goes on a mission to kill Daniel, who tormented him earlier. Though his time is brief, actor Glenn Strange is actually an improvement upon Lugosi and Chaney, and resembles Karloff in the makeup more so than the other two did. Not only that, since he was already there, Karloff helped to coach Strange on how to play the monster. The final scenes have the monster carrying Niemann in a protective manner, which was done deliberately as a way of showing respect to Karloff who originated the role. (In an early script, Niemann and the monster had more animosity in the final moments which was done away with.) The final scenes of Strange and Karloff sinking in quicksand have a nice touch of irony to them and could have closed out the Universal horror cycle on a highpoint. But, the movie was a hit, which naturally meant another sequel...

FINAL WORD Though it may not be as "good" or highly regarded as earlier entries in Universal's horror pantheon, *House of Frankenstein* may well be the most fun of the whole bunch for monster kids.

THE MUMMY'S CURSE

(UNIVERSAL)
Release Date: December 22, 1944
Alternate Titles: *The Mummy's Plague* (Brazil)

Directed by: Leslie Goodwins **Screenplay by:** Bernard Schubert based upon an original story by Leon Abrams & Dwight V. Babcock **Special Effects by:** Joe McGee & Jack P. Pierce **Music by:** William Lava & Paul Sawtell **Cast:** Lon Chaney Jr. (Kharis) Dennis Moore (Dr. James Halsey) Kay Harding (Betty Walsh) Virginia Christine (Princess Ananka) Addison Richards (Pat Walsh) Peter Coe (Dr. Ilzor Zandaab) Martin Kosleck (Ragheb) Kurt Katch (Cajun Joe) Ann Codee (Tante Berthe) Holmes Herbert (Dr. Cooper)

Academy Ratio, Black & White, 60 Minutes

SYNOPSIS Dr. James Halsey arrives in "Bayou country" in hopes of draining a swamp and finding the mummies of Kharis and Princess Ananka. Though skeptical, the landowner Pat Walsh allows it, while his niece Betty develops feelings for Halsey. Unbeknownst to Halsey, his colleague, Dr. Ilzor Zandaab, is the new High Priest of Karnak. Working with a man named Raghed, Zandaab resurrects Kharis, who sets out to find Ananka, who has also surfaced from the swamp. Ananka is taken in by Halsey and Betty, but eventually Kharis captures her. Ragheb captures Betty and takes her to a monastery hideout. Halsey arrives to save her, and when Ragheb kills Zandaab, Kharis retaliates by killing him. In the process, the monastery collapses, burying Kharis and Ananka.

COMMENTARY This last entry of the classic Mummy movies plays more havoc with the series continuity than usual. While Kharis and Ananka did indeed sink into a river at the end of the previous film, they did so in New England. This story explicitly takes place in a swamp in the "Bayou country" (though the state is never identified). Ananka was a mummified old woman when she sank into the swamp, and here she's young again. Furthermore, *Curse* also takes place 25 years after the previous film, which itself took place over thirty years after *The Mummy's Hand*, stated to take place in 1940. As such, if one does the math all the way from *Hand* to *Curse*, that means this film takes place around the year 1997!

Those small gripes aside, there's a lot to like about *The Mummy's Curse*. The swampy setting is a perfect backdrop for Kharis to stalk his victims, and one could argue that Hammer's utilization of a similar setting for their 1959 remake probably came from this film. Though the romantic leads only meet cookie-cutter standards at best, some interesting things are done with Kharis and the High Priest, Zandaab. As it is, Zandaab is one of the more sympathetic high priests of the bunch when compared to his predecessors. In fact, in early scripts, he even agrees to let Betty live when she finds out what they are up to! In both the film and the script, Ragheb emerges as the real villain when he kills Zandaab. In an interesting turn for the series, Kharis gets to play the hero for once when he turns his anger on Ragheb and kills him (also saving Betty and Halsey in the process). Had the film been shot as originally written, Kharis would have also been given a rather human moment when he reacts to the killing of Zandaab with some grief.

The film's ending makes it clear that this wasn't intended as the final outing for Kharis. As it stands, it presents one of the weakest means of "death" for Kharis yet as a building simply falls on him. Compared to past endings in the series, that was small potatoes. Halsey even states that they will dig up Kharis and put he and Ananka in a museum. Clearly, Universal was leaving the door open for a sequel that never happened. And yet, *Curse* does offer a satisfying conclusion for the saga of Kharis and Ananka buried together forever. (In the original script's version, which was much better, Ananka had a line where she essentially told Kharis she wanted to be laid to rest with him for good that sadly went unfilmed. Had it been shot, it could have afforded the series some nice closure.)

The Mummy's Curse was released on a double bill with *House of Frankenstein*, which incidentally Kharis was also supposed to appear in at one point but didn't. Though Universal would produce a few more classic monster movies before throwing in the towel on the genre, this turned out to be the Mummy's last go until *Abbott and Costello Meet the Mummy*.

FINAL WORD Disliked by some, this certainly isn't the worst that the Mummy series had to offer, and had it been filmed as originally written it might have emerged as one of the better sequels.

HOUSE OF DRACULA

(UNIVERSAL)
Release Date: December 7, 1945
Alternate Titles: *The Wolf Man's Cure* (Yugoslavia)

Directed by: Erle C. Kenton **Screenplay by:** Edward T. Lowe
Special Effects by: John P. Fulton & Jack P. Pierce **Music by:**
William Lava **Cast:** Lon Chaney Jr. (Larry Talbot/the Wolf Man)
Onslow Stevens (Dr. Franz Edelmann) John Carradine (Count
Dracula) Martha O'Driscoll (Milizia Morelle) Jane Adams (Nina)
Lionel Atwill (Inspector Holtz) Ludwig Stössel (Ziegfried) Glenn
Strange (Frankenstein's monster)

Academy Ratio, Black & White, 67 Minutes

SYNOPSIS Count Dracula comes to the castle of Dr. Franz
Edelmann under the auspices of seeking a cure for his vampirism.
Dr. Edelmann agrees, and soon after Larry Talbot, the Wolf Man,
also shows up seeking a cure. When Edelmann tells Talbot he is
not able to cure him before the next full moon, Talbot jumps off a
cliff into the sea. Edelmann goes down looking for him and gets
more than he bargained for when he finds the dormant
Frankenstein monster in a seaside tunnel as well. Meanwhile, it
turns out that Dracula isn't there seeking a cure, he's just out to
seduce Edelmann's assistant, Milizia. Furthermore, Dracula gives
Edelmann a transfusion of his own blood, which slowly drives him
mad. When Dracula makes his final move on Milizia, he is chased
back to his coffin by Edelmann, who exposes the Count to sunlight
turning him to ash. Edelmann still cures Talbot of lycanthropy at
least, but then begins a descent into madness that ends in him
reviving the Frankenstein monster and destroying his lab. Talbot
and Milizia, now in love, happily manage to escape after Edelmann
and the monster perish.

COMMENTARY This film began life as *The Wolf Man vs. Dracula*
and it shows, as the Frankenstein monster seems to be a mere
afterthought in the story. However, that's okay as the movie is
titled *House of Dracula*. Curt Siodmak used to joke about how the

109

Universal writers tried to paint each other into corners by killing off the monsters in definitive ways so that "the next guy" would have a great deal of difficulty resurrecting them. Well, the game was apparently up, because Dracula shows up with no explanation whatsoever in this film. Neither is Larry Talbot's off-screen resurrection ever addressed or explained. The only time the last film is referenced is when the Frankenstein monster is found, entirely by coincidence mind you, in a tunnel under the castle. Dr. Edelmann then explains that the monster must have drifted down from the mud pits, and even points out the skeletal remains of Dr. Niemann.

Seeming like more of a guest star in the last picture, here Dracula is front and center. Again Dracula uses his Baron Latos alias, and this may have been Universal's way of differentiating Carradine's Dracula from Lugosi's, the same way that Lon Chaney Jr.'s Dracula was called Count Alucard. His best scene is probably the one of him and Milizia at the piano, where the latter plays a beautiful melody (Moonlight Sonata) that she says reminds her of the netherworld from which Dracula came. Overall, the scene is similar to the one in the previous film of the girl seeing the Netherworld in Dracula's signet ring. Monster-wise, Dracula is arguably the star of the show and gets some decent special effects scenes transforming into a bat (though you can see the wires). He expires well before the film ends, though, but at least we get to see a full body decomposition shot this time rather than just his hand as was the case with his previous two appearances. The Wolf Man gets two great scenes that present the monster in new localities. In his first appearance, he transforms within a jail cell. The next time we see him, he's lurking in an ocean cave. Of all the monsters, it is again the Frankenstein monster who gets shortchanged and doesn't awaken until the last moments of the movie as was the case in *House of Frankenstein*.

Though it's less episodic than the previous film in terms of its pacing, *House of Dracula* also goes off the rails a bit towards the end, as though it's unsure of what to do with itself other than tie up loose ends. Dr. Edelmann, though advertised as a "mad scientist," really becomes more of a second-rate Mr. Hyde due to Dracula's blood transfusion, and scenes of him attacking innocent victims are rather silly. There is at least one good scene at the end of Talbot being bathed in the moonlight for the first time in years without turning into a wolf. As Talbot does this, Dr. Edelmann suddenly rushes to his lab—probably realizing that movie literally only has three minutes left in its run time—to revive the

Frankenstein monster. In these three minutes a lot happens: the monster revives, Edelmann strangles Nina, Talbot shoots Edelmann, and Talbot fights the monster. This aspect is at least rather interesting from a continuity standpoint. The last time the monster saw Talbot (in human form), he was a friend, but the monster attacks him right away (presumably for shooting Edelmann). It's also exciting to see Talbot have to face off against the monster in human form rather than his wolf form and win the fight at that. (This is similar to *Wolf Man vs. Dracula* script where Talbot triumphed over the Count in human form as well.)

Overall, though it's a rehash of the last entry in many ways, *House of Dracula* still presents some interesting twists on the mythos. That the hunchback is a beautiful girl for once is an excellent deviation, and Nina makes for the film's most sympathetic and likable character. (The way in which her affliction is revealed by the director, who at first hides it behind miscellaneous lab equipment, is also fantastic.) The aspect of Dracula and the Wolf Man both coming to a doctor seeking a cure for their afflictions is interesting (albeit both at the same time is a bit contrived). While Dracula's intentions aren't pure, Talbot's are. He's even cured of his werewolf curse, which perhaps implies that Universal felt this might be the last film in the series. (However, this might've just been because it was the last film in Chaney's contract, not to mention that he was difficult to work with.) And even though the monsters would return only a few years later in *Abbott and Costello Meet Frankenstein*, in many ways *House of Dracula* was the last hurrah for the Universal monsters in terms of straight horror pictures.

FINAL WORD Even if it manages to squeeze a few fresh twists out of the established characters, at the end of the day this is still something of a tired rehash and easily inferior to the preceding film.

SHEWOLF
OF LONDON

(UNIVERSAL)
Release Date: May 17, 1946
Alternate Titles: *The Curse of the Allenbys* (U.K.) *The Wolf Woman* (Portugal)

Directed by: Jean Yarbrough **Screenplay by:** George Bricker **Music by:** William Lava (uncredited) **Cast:** June Lockhart (Phyllis Allenby) Don Porter (Barry Lanfield) Sara Haden (Martha Winthrop) Jan Wiley (Carol Winthrop) Lloyd Corrigan (Det. Latham) Dennis Hoey (Inspector Pierce) Martin Kosleck (Dwight Severn) Eily Malyon (Hannah)

Academy Ratio, Black & White, 61 Minutes

SYNOPSIS Beautiful young heiress Phyllis Allenby is set to be married to Barry Lanfield. Phyllis resides at the Allenby Mansion with her aunt Martha and cousin Carol. Before the wedding can occur, a strange series of attacks by a "Wolf Woman" occur in the park nearby the mansion. Phyllis becomes convinced that she is the Wolf Woman due to an old legend pertaining to the curse of the Allenby family. Though her Aunt Martha tries to convince Phyllis that she is crazy for believing this, an investigation by Barry later proves that Aunt Martha is herself the killer! Martha is not, however, a werewolf, and simply perpetrated the werewolf idea in the hopes of getting Phyllis committed to an insane asylum so that she wouldn't have to share the estate with her.

COMMENTARY *She Wolf of London* really doesn't deserve to be in this book apart for two reasons. Its title implies it's a sequel/spin-off/female version of *Werewolf of London*, and Universal saw fit to put *She Wolf of London* in their Classic Monsters Complete 30 Film Collection Blu-Ray set. (Maybe they did it to round out the set to an even number, but it still doesn't belong and should have been placed in their single volume Universal Horror Collection releases with movies like *Captive Wild Woman*.) As it is, *She Wolf of London* is more of an "old dark house" psychological thriller than it is a monster movie because it doesn't have an actual monster. *She*

112

Wolf of London simply dupes its main character, and the audience along with her, into thinking that she's a werewolf. Naturally, this is an unforgivable sin for monster kids.

It would be nice to think that maybe this did start out as a real monster movie, and budget cuts necessitated the removal of said monster, but this apparently isn't the case. A female twist on the werewolf legend would have certainly been interesting, but this was apparently never the intent and it was always just a psychological thriller with a misleading title. There are plenty of nice red herrings to make us think Phyllis is a werewolf, too. For instance, in one scene she mysteriously gets singled out and cornered by a dog (again, if she's not a werewolf, why does this happen?). Phyllis also mentions having dreams about being a wolf. The "monster" that we do get—another red herring—is a cloaked woman. Considering that the title character in *Werewolf of London* disguised himself with a coat and a cloak, why wouldn't the She Wolf of London follow suit? Later, when this cloaked figure attacks a man, it even utters a dog-like growl. (Aunt Martha is really going all out!) And, ironically, while in *Werewolf of London* police were skeptical of a werewolf on the loose when that really was the case, here an investigator believes wholeheartedly that a werewolf is to blame when it isn't. Making the film even worse is the fact that its plot was a retread of many similar films, like *Devil Bat's Daughter* (also 1946). Adding insult to injury, *She Wolf* would more or less be remade with a monster this time as *Daughter of Dr. Jekyll* (1957).

Audiences weren't happy at being duped into thinking this was a sequel to *Werewolf of London*, and *The New York Times* Thomas M. Pryor rightly described the film as coming "from Universal's bottom-drawer." Universal didn't care though, their horror cycle was at an end and the title had managed to lure a few patrons into theaters, and that was all that mattered.

FINAL WORD Unless monster-less Universal chillers like this are your bag, not even werewolf completists need waste their time on this film.

ABBOTT AND COSTELLO MEET FRANKENSTEIN

(UNIVERSAL)
Release Date: June 15, 1948
Alternate Titles: *The Brain of Frankenstein* (working title) *Abbott and Costello Grappling with Ghosts* (Brazil) *Two Simpletons against Frankenstein* (France) *Abbott and Costello Meet the Monsters* (Greece) *Frankenstein's Brain* (Italy) *Abbott and Costello vs. the Ghosts* (Mexico) *Abbott and Costello and the Monsters* (Portugal)

Directed by: Charles Barton **Screenplay by:** Robert Lees, Frederic I. Rinaldo & John Grant **Special Effects by:** Jerome Ash, David S. Horsley, Fred Knoth & Bud Westmore (makeup) **Music by:** Frank Skinner **Cast:** Bud Abbott (Chick Young) Lou Costello (Wilbur Grey) Lon Chaney Jr. (Larry Talbot/the Wolf Man) Bela Lugosi (Count Dracula) Glenn Strange (Frankenstein's monster) Lenore Aubert (Dr. Sandra Mornay) Jane Randolph (Joan Raymond) Frank Ferguson (Mr. McDougal) Charles Bradstreet (Professor Stevens)

Academy Ratio, Black & White, 83 Minutes

SYNOPSIS Chick Young and Wilbur Grey are two delivery men charged with unpacking two very important crates at the McDougal House of Horrors. Though Chick thinks it's all a bunch of hooey, Wilbur knows that the two crates contain the real Count Dracula and Frankenstein's monster. When Wilbur watches them walk away, no one believes him, including McDougal, who thinks the duo is responsible for his lost property. Soon after an insurance investigator named Joan Raymond feigns romantic interest in Wilbur to learn more about the case. She and Wilbur plan to go to a masquerade ball together; only Wilbur already has a date: Dr. Sandra Mornay. Unbeknownst to all involved, Dr. Mornay is working with Dracula and is only interested in Wilbur so that she can transplant his brain into the monster. At the ball, Chick and Wilbur are also joined by Mornay's associate, Professor Stevens, who takes an interest in Joan, and Larry Talbot, on the trail of Dracula and the monster. Dracula ends up kidnapping Wilbur and Joan both and taking them back to the island before

114

the night is over. Chick, Larry, and Professor Stevens go to rescue Joan and Wilbur just seconds before the macabre operation can take place. Larry transforms into the Wolf Man and takes out Dracula, while the monster breaks free and kills Dr. Mornay. Wilbur and Chick escape from the monster via boat while Professor Stevens and Joan light the pier on fire, causing the monster to perish.

COMMENTARY Back in 1943, a full five years before this film came out, comedy duo Bud Abbott and Lou Costello pondered doing a Broadway show in which they interacted with Universal's monsters. In 1948, after the duo made the hit horror-comedy *Hold That Ghost*, it was decided to finally team Abbott and Costello with the monsters. (The initial idea was for all the monsters to appear, including the Mummy.) Ironically, Abbott hated the initial script, called *The Brain of Frankenstein* even though he had wanted to work with the monster (so to speak). Little did he know that the eventually titled *Abbott and Costello Meet Frankenstein* would go on to become the team's seminal film and biggest box office hit.

It's debatable whether or not this picture is truly an in-continuity sequel to *House of Dracula* or not. On the one hand, it continues the rivalry established between Larry Talbot and Count Dracula in that film, but we don't know how the vampire has been resurrected or why Larry is once again a werewolf (he was cured in *House of Dracula*). But it's probably all for the best, it really didn't matter why the monsters were back, and the little details would've bogged down the story's excellent pacing. Perhaps part of the reason why the film works so well is that the basic story could still be a solid Universal monster movie without the comedy. The basic premise is really pretty cool from a straightforward perspective: Larry Talbot is out to stop Count Dracula from resurrecting the Frankenstein monster while at the same time trying to keep his own lycanthropy in check. One thing monster kids probably really wanted to see in *House of Dracula* was for the Wolf Man to fight Dracula, which didn't happen. Here, the end battle between the Wolf Man and Dracula is quite the crowd pleaser and ends on a high note with both monsters tumbling into the ocean. The locale, a castle on a tropical island, makes for an interesting fusion of Gothic horror and adventure that would've worked in another "House of sequel". (*House of the Wolf Man* this time perhaps?)

Another impressive aspect of the film is that after 17 years Bela Lugosi finally returns to the role that made him famous. Actually, it was probably his portrayal of the character in this film that truly cemented him in the role of Dracula forever, as it was easily the more popular and widely seen of the two. Besides, it doesn't get much cooler than Dracula driving his victims away in a speedboat on their way to his island castle! Glenn Strange is billed before many other members of the cast for once, too. Furthermore, he gets much more to do here than he did in either of the two *House* movies as well, in which he didn't really do anything until the last reel. Here he shares a few scenes up and walking before the end monster mash, which truly is a monster mash. Furthermore, the fact that Universal chose to call this movie *Meet Frankenstein* as opposed to "Meet Dracula" or "Meet the Wolf Man" proved that they still considered him to be their most marketable monster. And, for the first time since *Bride of Frankenstein,* the monster even speaks! (Technically Ygor spoke as the monster's new brain in *Ghost of Frankenstein.*) As for the Wolf Man, his transformations scenes are some of the most seamless of the whole series. Though it's all fun and games for a while with the Wolf Man, eventually somebody does get hurt. That person, ironically enough, is Mr. McDougal. (Food for thought: will McDougal later become a werewolf himself?) However, due to the film's comical nature, the Wolf Man never kills anyone (plus, if he did, according to the censors the Wolf Man himself would need to die at the film's end).

Costello gets several great scenes with each of the monsters, but all the best occur between him and the Wolf Man. You see, Costello's character is positively terrified of Dracula and the Frankenstein monster, neither of which is likely to hurt him (because they want his brain in that case). The irony lies in the fact that Wilbur is blissfully unaware of the Wolf Man, the most dangerous monster of them all, in most of their scenes together. In the first, the werewolf silently stalks Wilbur in Talbot's hotel room so quietly that he's unaware a monster is behind him. Their second encounter at a costume ball is even better. As Chick had earlier worn a werewolf mask, Wilbur assumes that Chick is the Wolf Man. Thus ensues bits of Wilbur kicking and slapping the Wolf Man when he thinks Chick is just messing around. The duo's chase with the monster in the halls of the castle is not only hilarious, it's also great fun in terms of comedic action. The film is topped off by an excellent end gag. The fact that Vincent Price voices the Invisible Man makes it even better (Price starred in *The Invisible Man Returns*).

The film went on to become a huge success that guaranteed future pairings with other monsters, was Universal's second highest grossing movie that year and also their second cheapest to produce! Historically speaking the film has landed on several distinguished Top 100 comedy lists, including AFI's 100 Years...100 Laughs.

FINAL WORD Not only is it a great comedy for the ages, it's also probably one of the best ways to introduce Universal's monsters to kids with short attention spans.

INVISIBLE MAN APPEARS

(DAIEI)
Release Date: September 25, 1949

Directed by: Nobuo Adachi **Screenplay by:** Nobuo Adachi, Akimitsu Takagi (story) & H. G. Wells (novel) **Special Effects by:** Eiji Tsuburaya **Music by:** Goro Nishi **Cast:** Kanji Koshiba (Shunji Kurokawa/Invisible Man) Daijiro Natsukawa (Kyosuke Segi) Chizuru Kitagawa (Machiko Nakazato) Ryunosuke Tsukigata (Dr. Kenzo Nakazato) Takiko Mizunoe (Ryuko Mizuki) Teruko Omi (Kimiko Chosokabe) Kichijiro Ueda (Otoharu Sugimoto) Shosaku Sugiyama (Ichiro Kawabe) Mitsusaburo Ramon (Matsubara)

Academy Aspect, Black & White, 82 Minutes

SYNOPSIS Dr. Nakazato has recently developed a serum for invisibility, but hides this fact from his two protégés: Dr. Kurokawa and Dr. Segi. Instead, he creates a competition between the two to see who can create the invisibility formula first. The prize will be his daughter Machiko's hand in marriage. A group of jewel thieves, led by Ichiro Kawabe, kidnap Dr. Nakazato, fully aware of his invisibility serum. The same thieves trick Kurokawa into taking the professor's invisibility serum under what he thinks are the professor's wishes. Kurokawa gladly obliges thinking this will win him Machiko's hand in marriage. The jewelers then reveal to Kurokawa that before they will give him the cure to restore his visibility, he must steal a famous necklace belonging to his sister called the Tears of Amour. Kurokawa reluctantly agrees as the invisibility serum begins to affect his mind. Kurokawa's sister, Ryuko, works with a police inspector to protect the necklace from the invisible man, unaware it is her own brother. Kurokawa goes to visit Segi, revealing to him what has happened and how he has been deceived. Machiko walks into the room, unaware of Kurokawa's presence, and declares her love for Segi. This enrages Kurokawa who runs away, now more determined than ever to steal the necklace. Ryuko disguises herself as the invisible man and infiltrates the jewelers' hideout to free Dr. Nakazato. It is there that Kurokawa learns there is no cure for his condition. Kurokawa engages in a gun battle where he kills Kawabe, and then is gunned down himself by the police.

COMMENTARY Recognized as Japan's oldest surviving special effects picture, Daiei's *Invisible Man Appears* is overlooked for many reasons. Of course, the biggest reason it remains relatively unknown is the fact that it came out before *Godzilla* (1954) which put Japanese effects films "on the map" so to speak. In fact, *Invisible Man Appears* special effects director was none other than Eiji Tsuburaya, famous for creating Godzilla. Sadly, more people are aware of Tsuburaya's later Invisible Man film for Toho released shortly after *Godzilla* than they are this one.

Right away the film's opening sets itself up as a smarter thriller than its successors, Toho's *Invisible Avenger* (1954) and Daiei's later effort *Invisible Man vs. the Human Fly* (1957). Firstly, the film begins with these words: "There is no good or evil in science but it can be used for good or evil purposes." The first scene then introduces the main characters in a scientific discussion about the color black in the color spectrum (and how it could be used to render an object invisible) that is far ahead of the two future films which don't spend much, if any, time discussing how their titular Invisible characters were rendered such.

This film is of merit for being Eiji Tsuburaya's first major fantastical film as director of special effects. Tsuburaya's first trick is making a guinea pig turn transparent. Interestingly, the hair briefly turns black, then back to white, before becoming a ghostly image that fades away, implying an imaginative chemical reaction going on within the animal. There's also an invisible pet cat that runs around, though we don't see its transformation. The scene is played for shock as much as it is humor, as Machiko is unaware that her father has turned the cat invisible (let alone invented an invisibility formula) as it walks through the house, tipping over vases and causing some minor mayhem.

As for the film's invisible man, his design is directly inspired by the original Universal Studios Invisible Man with iconic bandages, sunglasses, hat, and trench coat look. The famous unveiling scene in this film happens 25 minutes in when Kurokawa walks into the jewelry store and requests to speak to the manager in private. When he makes his demands to the manager known, he tells him that he is an invisible man and first takes off his glasses, revealing the absence of eyes. Next, he unravels the bandages around his head which is an excellent effect on par with the Universal films.

He then strips off all his clothes until only his gloved hands remain.

At the same time, later unveiling scenes also become somewhat gimmicky. At one point, the Invisible Man (naked and completely invisible) accosts an old drunk for his clothes, which he steals. However, all this does is draw attention to himself as he now has the appearance of a headless man in a trench coat! A cop spots him, causes a ruckus, and soon the Invisible Man has discarded the clothes he has only just stolen from the bum as he runs off into the night.

Though some may be tempted to classify this as a Japanese imitation [read: rip-off] of the Universal Studios' Invisible Man films, it too is a quasi-adaptation of the H.G. Wells story which, like the Universal film, transports the action into the present day. The Japanese version does specifically lift one plot aspect unique to the Universal film wherein the invisibility formula causes the user to become psychotic. Conversely in the H.G. Wells novel, the Invisible Man is psychotic before becoming invisible.

FINAL WORD Overall, *Invisible Man Appears* isn't a terribly entertaining film, but horror fans will find it worth a watch for its historical significance. And for a film of its time, it is a quality production all around.

ABBOTT AND COSTELLO MEET THE INVISIBLE MAN

(UNIVERSAL)
Release Date: March 19, 1951
Alternate Titles: *In Sherlock Holmes' Footsteps* (Austria)
Two Boobies and the Invisible Man (Belgium)

Directed by: Charles Lamont **Screenplay by:** Robert Lees, Frederic I. Rinaldo & John Grant **Special Effects by:** David S. Horsley **Music by:** Joseph Gershenson (director of stock tracks) **Cast:** Bud Abbott (Bud Alexander) Lou Costello (Lou Francis) Arthur Franz (Tommy Nelson/the Invisible Man) Nancy Guild (Helen Gray) Adele Jergens (Boots Marsden) Sheldon Leonard (Morgan) William Frawley (Detective Roberts) Gavin Muir (Dr. Philip Gray) John Daheim (Rocky Hanlon)

Academy Ratio, Black & White, 82 Minutes

SYNOPSIS Tommy Nelson, a prize boxer, is accused of killing his manager, when in fact the mob did it. On the run, Tommy first acquires the services of two novice detectives, Bud and Lou, and then goes to see a scientist, Dr. Gray. The man injects Tommy with an invisibility serum, which allows him to evade the police and also try to catch the real killers. When Bud and Lou investigate Tommy's old gym, Tommy throws real punches while Lou shadowboxes, thus making Lou the hot new fighter in town. A new fight is set up between Lou and Tommy's old nemesis, Rocky Hanlon. However, the same mob men who tried to throw Tommy's last fight pay Bud and Lou to lose in the fifth round. Tommy won't have it, however, and still sees to it that Lou wins the fight. In the locker room after the fight, the mob men accost Bud and Lou, who fight them off with Tommy. Though the mob men are arrested, Tommy is injured in the fight, necessitating a blood transfusion. Lou is the donor, who restores Tommy's visibility. But, when a bit of Tommy's blood backs up into Lou's veins, Lou briefly becomes invisible himself.

COMMENTARY To some viewers, the end of *Abbott and Costello Meet Frankenstein* had promised a sequel featuring the Invisible Man. In reality, it was just a fun twist ending for the film, but when

121

it ended up being a massive hit, Universal did indeed produce *Abbott and Costello Meet the Invisible Man.* (However, it's not an in-continuity sequel, as all the characters are brand new.) What is surprising is that it took Universal three years to produce the follow-up (although, there was a related picture in the form of 1949's *Abbott and Costello Meet the Killer, Boris Karloff*). Furthermore, more than a few sources ascertain that this began life as a straight Invisible Man sequel which the comedy duo was inserted into. This theory doesn't really hold water though. While Universal had paid H.G. Wells for the rights to more Invisible Man movies, after 1945's *House of Dracula* Universal had quit making their usual monster movies. *The Invisible Man's Revenge* had been released in 1944, and yet Universal didn't move on their sequel option (though they did ponder throwing the character into *House of Frankenstein.*) It seems that the idea that Bud and Lou were added in to the story later is a mis-amalgamation of the facts. As it is, *Meets the Invisible Man* is really a remake of *Invisible Man Returns*. The storylines are the same in that a wrongly accused man takes the invisibility serum to hide from the police and catch the real killers. More than that, bits of dialogue from the film and even a few effects shots are repurposed. The only twist on the story is that the wrongly accused man is a boxer. So, perhaps when sources claim Bud and Lou were added in later, what is more likely is that Bud and Lou were added into the story structure of *Returns* to create *Meets Invisible Man.*

Regardless of the film's origins, one thing is for certain: it works. Though it doesn't have the classic status of *Meets Frankenstein*, in many ways, *Meet the Invisible* Man is possibly better. After all, Bud and Lou interacting with an invisible man is a comedy gold mine, and mine the concept they do. Initially, the laughs come from Lou claiming to have caught Tommy/the Invisible Man, except every time the police inspector is fetched, Tommy has disappeared. (The police inspector, by the way, is another great comedy presence in the form of William Frawley of *I Love Lucy* and *My Three Sons.*) Another fantastic bit has Bud, Lou, and Tommy going to the latter's gym, where the Invisible Tommy makes Lou look like a world class boxer (whose punches are so fast that no one can see them). Though every routine is a winner, the best bit occurs when Bud, Lou, and Tommy go to a fancy bar and restaurant. By this point, all the important elements are at play. Lou is currently touted as a highly respected fighter called "Lou the Looper" on a date with a beautiful woman, while a depressed Tommy is on a drunken bender, leaving Bud to babysit him. In this regard, Bud, who is usually relegated to being the straight man, gets to engage in some wonderful comedy of his own for a change. In this case, the drunk Tommy is becoming boisterous, so whenever the waiter arrives at him and Bud's table, Bud has to begin acting drunk himself to drown out the invisible Tommy's ranting. More hilarity ensues when Bud and Lou decide to take on some wise guys at the bar, having become accustomed to Tommy bailing them out, only he doesn't.

The end match has a lot of story elements riding on the outcome. For one, Lou has to have Tommy backing him up or he'll get massacred by the other boxer. He has also recently been paid by the mob to throw the fight in the fifth round. This conflicts with Tommy's need to beat Rocky and help clear his name. In essence, there are two opposing conflicts. And though the boxing match can't top the earlier scenes in the bar, it's still spectacular. Like many of the Invisible Man films before it, it ends with Tommy being shot and requiring a blood transfusion. The blood transfusion, coming from Lou, restores Tommy's visibility, but also briefly makes Lou invisible. The gags from Lou's newfound invisibility service the final moments well and allow the film to end on another memorable button.

FINAL WORD Though it can't top the classic monster content of *Meets Frankenstein*, from a purely comedic standpoint this sequel is actually superior in some ways.

THE SON OF DR. JEKYLL

(COLUMBIA PICTURES)
Release Date: October 31, 1951
Alternate Titles: *The Monster of London* (Austria) *Cursed Inheritance* (Brazil) *The Will of the Physician and the Monster* (Portugal)

Directed by: Seymour Friedman **Screenplay by:** Mortimer Braus, Jack Pollexfen & Edward Huebsch **Makeup by:** Clay Campbell **Music by:** Paul Sawtell **Cast:** Louis Hayward (Edward Jekyll/Dr. Henry Jekyll and Mr. Hyde) Jody Lawrance (Lynn Utterson) Alexander Knox (Dr. Curtis Lanyon) Lester Matthews (Sir John Utterson) Gavin Muir (Richard Daniels) Paul Cavanagh (Insp. Stoddard) Rhys Williams (Michaels)

Spherical, Black & White, 78 Minutes

SYNOPSIS In the year 1860, the madman Mr. Hyde is killed, thus leaving Dr. Henry Jekyll's wife a widow and his infant son an orphan. The boy is adopted by Jekyll's old friend John Utterson and his wife. Thirty years later, Edward Jekyll is unaware of his true parentage until he inherits his father's old mansion. He moves there but is not kindly received by his neighbors due to his father's legacy. In an effort to clear his family name, he resumes his father's experiments. His first experiment is successful, but when he attempts to duplicate the experiment in front of a crowd, it fails. Edward's life spins out of control as a series of attacks and murders follow, all blamed on him. An old friend of Jekyll, Dr. Lanyon, takes Edward under his care. However, it eventually becomes apparent that Lanyon is the one framing Edward for the crimes. Since his association with Jekyll nearly ruined his career, Lanyon is out to usurp the Jekyll estate from Edward. Lanyon and Edward get in a fight in the old Jekyll mansion, which burns down amidst the chaos. Lanyon is killed, and Edward's name is cleared.

COMMENTARY This film's opening couldn't help but remind me of the better-known *Hands of the Ripper* from Hammer in 1971. That film opens with Jack the Ripper murdering his wife and being chased down the streets of London by angry townsfolk. This film begins excitingly with Hyde being pursued through London by an angry, torch-wielding mob. A text slate informs us that Hyde has just killed his wife, so we don't see that part, but the similarities between it and *Hands of the Ripper* are there just the same. Despite not showing the murder, this one is still more exciting than *Ripper's* opening scene, as it shows Hyde running across rooftops and even jumping down onto the roof of a carriage. Hyde is tracked back to Jekyll's residence, which is promptly set on fire. Hyde, who we finally get to see, then darts about the flaming house. (Already this film's beginning is ten times more exciting than the Jekyll and Hyde adaptations of the past!) In a fantastic death scene, Hyde falls from the flaming rooftop onto the ground below, where onlookers watch him revert to Jekyll.

After that exciting opening, does the rest of the film live up to it? While it doesn't necessarily keep up that exciting momentum, the story itself is engaging enough... for a while at least. The new Mr. Hyde doesn't pop up until forty minutes later, and just as a single hairy hand at that. (A good effect comparable to *The Wolf Man*.) As in the famous 1931 adaptation, makeup artist Clay Campbell used colored filters to illustrate the illusion of change. Campbell applied red-colored makeup to actor Louis Hayward's hand first and then passed a two-color filter in front of the camera. The makeup looked normal on the hand under the first filter but turned dark as the second lens passed in front of the camera.

As it turns out, the single hairy hand is Hyde Jr.'s only appearance! We're also not exactly sure if Edward didn't hallucinate the whole thing. As the film progresses, Edward is framed for being a Hyde-like murderer when he is not. The story then goes into Scooby-Doo territory when it is revealed that Lanyon was behind the new Hyde murders all along. Unfortunately, the plot gets so muddied that it becomes unclear if there ever was a real Mr. Hyde to begin with, and that includes the monstrous figure from the opening scene! If nothing else, the film at least has an exciting ending that mirrors the opener where Edward and Lanyon fight it out in a burning building. There's also some nice symmetry in that history repeats itself with Lanyon plunging to his death from the roof of the burning mansion.

FINAL WORD The exciting opening and ending aren't enough to make up for this film's confusing plot and lack of a real Mr. Hyde. For Jekyll completists only.

DRACULA
IN ISTANBUL

(AND FILMS)
Release Date: March 4, 1953

Directed by: Mehmet Muhtar **Screenplay by:** Turgut Demirag, Umit Deniz, Mehmet Muhtar & Ali Riza Seyfi (novel) based upon the book by Bram Stoker **Music by:** Turgut Demirag & Karlo Kapoçelli **Cast:** Atif Kaptan (Dracula) Annie Ball (Güzin) Bülent Oran (Azmi) Cahit Irgat (Turan) Ayfer Feray (Sadan) Kemal Emin Bara (Dr.Nuri) Münir Ceyhan (Dr.Akif)

Academy Ratio, Black & White, 102 Minutes

SYNOPSIS Azmi, a lawyer, travels to Romania to meet his client, Count Dracula, to discuss a real estate transaction. Over the course of his stay, Azmi learns that Dracula is a vampire. When the Count attacks Azmi, he is saved by the Count's hunchback servant due to an act of kindness on Azmi's part earlier. Azmi escapes, though the servant is killed. In Istanbul several months later, Azmi's wife Güzin, a dancer, goes to see her ill friend, Sadan. The young woman is mysteriously withering away, and it turns out it's because Dracula has arrived and is feeding on her. Sadan dies and rises again as a vampire around the same time that Azmi finally returns from Romania. Azmi teams with Dr. Nuri, an expert on vampires, to put Sadan at peace. While they go to stake Sadan, Dracula attacks Güzin. He forces her to do a solo dance for him at her nightclub. Azmi thankfully comes along and chases him away, all the way to a cemetery where the Count has hidden his coffin. Azmi opens it and destroys the sleeping Dracula with a stake through the heart. He returns home and he and Güzin resume their old life.

COMMENTARY This Turkish adaptation of *Dracula*, though not well-known, is significant for a number of reasons. First off, it's the first talking picture to give Dracula fangs. It is also possibly the first adaptation to depict Dracula's crawl down the castle wall before 1970's *Scars of Dracula*. The Count also has a very significant line where he states that "The locals believe that I, like my ancestor Voyvodo Drakula, am ruthless." This is fascinating, for even though Bram Stoker based Dracula on Vlad the Impaler, that the fictional Dracula was a descendant of Vlad was never stated in any film or story before this one. Later, this would become an important part of the mythos thanks to *Bram Stoker's Dracula* (both the 1974 version by Dan Curtis and the 1994 version by Francis Ford Coppola).

This iteration follows the Bram Stoker novel more closely than the 1931 *Dracula*, though it's not technically based on the Stoker novel. Instead, it was based upon on a 1928 novel *Kazıklı Voyvoda* (*Impaler Voivode*) by Ali Riza Seyfi. Still, it was more or less a translation of Stoker's novel with certain variations. As you could see from the synopsis, the character types of Harker, Mina, Lucy and Van Helsing are all there but have had their names changed to Azmi, Güzin, Sadan, and Dr. Nuri, respectively. The Count himself is more or less the same, though, and is portrayed capably by Atif Kaptan.

The best portion of the film takes place within Castle Dracula. And, as with any film, it has good traits and bad traits. Sometimes, compared to the Lugosi version, this Dracula is rather pathetic. Like Lugosi, he picks up Harker in his carriage, but unlike Lugosi is completely undisguised when he does so. This would be fine except for Dracula later tries to pretend as though that wasn't him who picked up Azmi! As for the good, there's a scene where Azmi attacks Dracula in his coffin only to have him open his eyes and scare him away. Best of all, after Azmi runs away, Dracula levitates the lid of his casket back on. Like Lugosi, this Dracula too can turn into a giant bat which doesn't look too bad for the time. (This version says that Dracula transforms with the help of his cloak. This is a nice touch, explaining why Dracula doesn't need to be naked between transitions as the clothes are enchanted.) This version of Dracula also has a hunchbacked servant who seems to be modeled after Lugosi's Ygor from *Son of Frankenstein*. Via jump cuts, Dracula has the ability to suddenly "pop up" in front of the characters for a good scare here and there, too. The castle portion of the movie ends with Azmi shooting Dracula in his casket and then running away (which is silly considering that Azmi had earlier read a book all about how to kill vampires!).

Whereas the first act was faithful to past movies and books, once we hit Istanbul it's an entirely different story. And though we didn't know the exact year of the first act, in the second we learn it is the current year of 1953. With the modern setting and characters, one feels they have suddenly switched channels to a soap opera. An unnecessarily long amount of time lapses before the normal story resumes, and Dracula begins feeding on Sadan. Like Lucy, Sadan eventually becomes one of the undead. However, Sadan's staking scene is positively pathetic, and might as well have been left unseen it's so lackluster. During the end portion, in a very un-Dracula move, the Count walks up behind a janitor, taps him on the shoulder, and then punches him out when he turns around! Dracula then makes Güzin dance for him, and psychically plays the piano keys while she does. After this, Azmi chases Dracula, defrocked of his cape, through the streets. In an ending only slightly better than the 1931 version, Azmi tracks Dracula to a cemetery. As in the 1931 version, no fight occurs between the two, he stakes Dracula, and the threat is over. The movie then ends with a humorous epilogue of Azmi and Güzin returning to their home where Azmi tells her that he never wants to have to smell garlic again.

FINAL WORD Though it has a fairly promising first act at Castle Dracula, it begins to lose interest once this film reaches Istanbul.

ABBOTT AND COSTELLO
MEET DR. JEKYLL AND MR. HYDE

(UNIVERSAL)
Release Date: August 12, 1953
Alternate Titles: *Abbott and Costello Against the Man and the Monster* (Latin America) *Two Boobies Against Dr. Jekyll and Mr. Hyde* (France) *Terrible Detective* (Greece) *Gianni and Pinotto Against Dr. Jekyll* (Italy)

Directed by: Charles Lamont **Screenplay by:** Lee Loeb & John Grant based on a story by Sid Fields & Grant Garett **Special Effects by:** David S. Horsley & Jack Kevan (makeup) **Music by:** Joseph Gershenson **Cast:** Bud Abbott (Slim) Lou Costello (Tubby) Boris Karloff (Dr. Henry Jekyll) Craig Stevens (Bruce Adams) Helen Westcott (Vicky Edwards) Eddie Parker (Mr. Hyde) Reginald Denny (the inspector) John Dierkes (Batley)

Academy Ratio, Black & White, 76 Minutes

SYNOPSIS When a Women's Suffrage Rally in Hyde Park turns into an all-out brawl, two American policemen working for the London Police Force step in to deescalate it but only make it worse. The two men, Slim and Tubby, are jailed along with one of the suffragettes, Vicky, and a reporter, Bruce, who begins to fall for Vicky. All but Tubby and Slim are bailed out by Vicky's guardian, Dr. Henry Jekyll, who immediately becomes jealous of the blossoming romance between Vicky and Bruce. Unbeknownst to all, Jekyll is the cause of a string of recent murders as his alter ego, Mr. Hyde. Jekyll sets his sights on killing Bruce but is thwarted accidentally by the bumbling duo of Tubby and Slim. Though Jekyll intends to turn Bruce into a monster, Tubby gets the injection by accident at the same time that Jekyll turns into Hyde. As such, Bruce, Slim, and the London Police force end up chasing down two Mr. Hydes. The real Mr. Hyde falls to his death from a window, while Slim catches Tubby thinking him to be a monster. When he turns him into the police, Tubby reverts back to normal.

COMMENTARY This third entry in the "Abbott and Costello Meet the Monsters" series produced for Universal ironically saw them doing battle with a monster that Universal never produced: Mr. Hyde. As it was, Universal had never tackled the subject before, probably due to the fact that the story was adapted by Paramount in 1931 and MGM in the 1940s. As such, this was Universal's only classic take on the Jekyll and Hyde story. And their version of Mr. Hyde would have been right at home with Chaney's Wolf Man and other classic makeup jobs. Their design is quasi similar to the one seen in the 1931 film, but more ape-like in general. Their version of Hyde is not played by Boris Karloff, but by stuntman Eddie Parker, though Karloff is certainly great as Jekyll. His interpretation is a more villainous one, as he has no guilt or remorse in terms of Hyde's misdeeds.

In terms of comedy, many fans and critics consider this one inferior to the duo's run-ins with Frankenstein and the Invisible Man. This is true to an extent, as the film emphasized violent getting-bashed-over-the-head physical comedy over the pair's great dialogue exchanges. The reason for this was supposedly because the duo was doing that on television, either on *The Abbott and Costello Show* or the *Colgate Comedy Hour*. However, the film is still pretty funny even in the absence of their great dialogue driven skits. It does get off to something of a rough start though, padded out by a few song and dance numbers. Plus, for a while, Tubby and Slim disappear for so long that they feel like guest stars in their own movie, as more emphasis is given to the two romantic leads and Karloff's Dr. Jekyll. However, once the title act are integrated into the story properly, the movie moves along quite well.

The best remembered bit for many occurs when Tubby takes a potion in Jekyll's lab. Rather than turning into an ape, he turns into a giant mouse. Slim is so dismissive of his friend that he barely looks at him and so doesn't notice the transformation when the duo walks into a bar. The other patrons, the bartender, and even a mouse all react in horror while the duo are blissfully unaware still. When the barflies run out, Tubby says, "Hey Slim, those guys must be seeing things?" Slim says, "Pay no attention to them, they're drunk!" There's also a lengthy reprisal of the wax museum from *Meets Frankenstein*, and actually makes better use of the wax museum this time around. In *Meets Frankenstein* most of the comedy was generated by Dracula and the monster as opposed to the museum itself. Here there's more interaction with the exhibits themselves. For instance, the guillotine gag is

130

repeated, but this time a stray cat crawls into the severed head causing it to creep across the floor to Tubby's horror. Dracula and the Frankenstein monster also get cameos as exhibits in the museum, and an electrical shock caused by Tubby somehow makes the monster's dummy walk!

The ending is pure monster mayhem, with both Tubby and Jekyll loose in Hyde form (due to an accident where Tubby gets injected with Hyde serum in the butt). Though not as fun or clever as the climax of *Meets Frankenstein*, there's still plenty of great visual gags, such as Hyde hiding out in a baby carriage and also jumping onto the middle seat of a three-person bicycle. The real Hyde meets his demise by falling out a window, wrapping up that portion of the story, leaving us to wonder what's going to happen to Tubby's version of Hyde. Slim has captured his friend, thinking him to be the real Hyde, and proudly takes him to the police department. What happens next isn't downright hilarious, but it makes for a perfect end note similar to the Invisible Man's cameo at the end of *Meet Frankenstein*. Here, when Tubby reverts back to his normal form, Slim gets scolded and isn't in for the big reward he thought he was. However, when he was hauled into the station, Tubby bit everyone who handled him (except Slim). Therefore, all the policemen turn into Hyde copies (like werewolves) and chase Tubby and Slim from the station.

Even though this film was released at a time when theaters were oversaturated with Abbott and Costello flicks, it still managed to be a huge hit, and reportedly audiences laughed all the way through. However, this oversaturation would eventually lead to the duo's downfall at the box office, and their penultimate film would be *Abbott and Costello Meet the Mummy* (1955).

FINAL WORD Though considered the weakest of the "Meet the Monsters" series it's still undeniably funny and one of Abbott and Costello's best.

CREATURE FROM THE BLACK LAGOON

(UNIVERSAL)

Release Date: February 12, 1954

Alternate Titles: *Monster of the Black Lagoon* (Austria) *Monster of the Swamp* (Belgium) *Horror of the Amazon* (Germany) *Terror of the Black Lagoon* (Greece)

Directed by: Jack Arnold **Screenplay by:** Harry Essex, Arthur Ross, & Maurice Zimm (story) **Creature Design by:** Milicent Patrick, Bud Westmore, Jack Kevan & Chris Mueller Jr. **Music by:** Henry Mancini, Hans J. Salter & Herman Stein **Cast:** Richard Carlson (Dr. David Reed) Julie Adams (Kay Lawrence) Richard Denning (Dr. Mark Williams) Antonio Moreno (Dr. Carl Maia) Nestor Paiva (Captain Lucas) Whit Bissell (Dr. Edwin Thompson) Bernie Gozier (Zee) Henry Escalante (Chico)

Academy Ratio, Black & White, 79 Minutes

SYNOPSIS During a dig in the Amazon, Dr. Carl Maia discovers skeletal remains of a Devonian creature that has characteristics of land and water-dwelling animals combined. Maia goes off to fetch his former student, ichthyologist Dr. David Reed, to aid him in an expedition to find more fossils in the Amazon. Funding the excursion is Dr. Mark Williams, and he joins the expedition with Reed and Maia. Complicating the matter is that Reed is currently courting Williams' ex-girlfriend, Kay Lawrence. The expedition sets sail on the boat *Rita* on the Amazon River. Eventually they find themselves in a haunted locale called the Black Lagoon by the locals. The expedition sights a living version of the fossil found by Maia and does their best to capture the creature, dubbed the Gillman. Their efforts only enrage the Gillman, who traps their boat in the river when it tries to escape. Mark and David don scuba gear to dislodge the tree blocking their way out and Mark is killed by the Gillman in the process. David manages to use a drug on the monster to keep him at bay while he moves the tree. As the boat sails down the river, the Gillman climbs on board and abducts Kay. David and the crew follow the Gillman to his hidden cave, where they rescue Kay and the creature is riddled with bullets.

COMMENTARY In terms of Universal's classic monster roster, the Gillman is something of an odd fit. As opposed to Gothic horror, the Gillman fits more into the mutant genre that was popular in the 1950s. Nor is the Gillman based on classic literature like *Frankenstein* and *Dracula*, nor is it even based upon a well-known legend like vampirism or lycanthropy. That said, the Gillman is based on a real-life cryptid, or mystery animal, said to haunt South America. (Though not as popular as Bigfoot, reports of fish people do surface in cryptozoology more often than you'd think.)

During the shooting of *Citizen Kane*, writer William Alland was at dinner at Orson Welles's home when he heard a very interesting story. It came from a cinematographer named Gabriel Figueroa who told the guests how in the Amazon River lived a half-man half-fish monster that would venture from the depths once a year to abduct a maiden. Then, for a year, the village would be safe. Alland was intrigued by the concept and pitched it to Universal International. They liked it, and so Alland got Maurice Zimm to write the first treatment. Zimm's story was interesting in that it depicted the Gillman as totally sympathetic, and the monster only killed in self-defense. But, as other writers came on board, the Gillman evolved into a vicious killer. (Though there are those who argue that the Creature was just defending its turf...)

The film gets off to a semi-epic start, depicting God creating the Earth. (The film tries to have it both ways by first depicting creation, while the rest of the film hinges upon evolution with the Gilman hinted as a sort of missing link.) Right after this prologue, we get an exciting shot of diggers in the Amazon jungle running to the site of a startling new discovery, which turns out to be the skeletal hand of a prehistoric monster. Shortly after, a still living version of the clawed hand reaches from out of the water to tease the audience. That's another thing this film does well is tease the audience about the Creature's appearance, not giving him a full reveal until an underwater shot later. The monster also benefits from an amazing design that has gone on to become quite iconic.

Initially, the Gillman was designed in a sleek way reminiscent of the Oscar statue. A headpiece was built with this design but all the Universal executives agreed that it looked awful in test footage. And so it was back to the drawing board for the monster's design. As it turned out, the monster's final design was done by Disney animator Milicent Patrick. Unfortunately, her role in creating the Creature was downplayed and more credit was given to make-up artist Bud Westmore. (Back in the 1950s, they didn't want anyone to know that a girl had designed the monster, oh the horror!)

In addition to the Creature's excellent design, the other standout of the production is the thrilling underwater cinematography. Two scenes in particular stand out in this regard. The first is Kay's swim in the Black Lagoon. While her beautiful form graces the surface, the Gillman swims below her in a mirror formation. In some ways the scene might have been inspired by a similar swim from *Tarzan and his Mate* (1934). Likewise, shots of Kay's legs kicking in the water undeniably influenced similar P.O.V. shots in *Jaws*. Director Jack Arnold said in interviews that for him, much of the film was based upon the strange sensation of something tickling at your feet in the water. Arnold said, "You know the feeling when you are swimming and something brushes your legs down there - it scares the hell out of you if you don't know what it is. It's the fear of the unknown. I decided to exploit this fear as much as possible."

Arnold also said that he wanted to instill a sense of dread throughout the picture. This is exemplified especially well in the scene where the bed-ridden, bandaged doctor watches the Creature slip onboard unnoticed by the rest of the crew. The score for the film helps in building the suspense immensely. In fact, it's spectacular throughout, from the creepy, mysterious opening to the more unnerving theme that plays whenever the monster is on the loose. The film was also noteworthy for being released in 3-D and proved to be a huge hit.

FINAL WORD If not the seminal monster movie of the fifties, its undoubtedly one of the seminal monster movies of the era.

INVISIBLE AVENGER

(TOHO)
Release Date: December 29, 1954
Japanese Title: *Invisible Man*

Directed by: Motoyoshi Oda **Screenplay by:** Shigeaki Hidaka & Kei Beppu (story) **Special Effects by:** Eiji Tsuburaya **Music by:** Kyosuke Kami **Cast:** Seizaburo Kawazu (Takamitsu Nanjo/Invisible Man) Miki Sanjo (Michiyo) Yoshio Tsuchiya (Komatsu) Keiko Kondo (Mariko) Minoru Takada (Yajima) Kenjiro Uemura (Ken) Kamatari Fujiwara (Mariko's grandfather) Haruo Nakajima (Invisible Man hit by car)

Academy Ratio, Black & White, 70 Minutes

SYNOPSIS An accident on a busy Tokyo street reveals the existence of an invisible man when he is hit by a car. A suicide note explains that the man was part of a top-secret program during the war that turned him and several other men invisible. Now that he is dead, the note says only one other survivor of the group remains. Hysteria takes over Japan for fear of the invisible men when this is revealed by the press. A gangster takes advantage of the situation by having a faux gang led by an invisible man (in fact just a normal man wearing bandages). The real invisible man, Nanjo, now works as a clown in order to hide his appearance. When the gangsters murder the grandfather of a young girl that he has befriended, Nanjo goes on the offensive to take down the gangsters. Nanjo chases down the gangster boss to a Tokyo oil refinery where both men fall to their deaths.

COMMENTARY With their production of *Godzilla* poised to be a hit, Toho wanted another effects picture ready in time to be the "New Year's Blockbuster" at the end of December. Someone pitched an invisible man film, which Eiji Tsuburaya already had experience with thanks to being the Special Effects Director for Daiei's *Invisible Man Appears* (1949). In that film, Tsuburaya recreated scenes from the classic Universal Studios' *Invisible Man* (1933) with the titular character revealing himself, so to speak, by unraveling bandages from his face.

In this film, Tsuburaya one-ups both himself and Universal by having his invisible man, Nanjo, unveil his true form by rubbing off his clown makeup. To create this effect, Tsuburaya had actor Seizaburo Kawazu actually rub a black makeup on his face while against a black background, thus making himself disappear on screen. Speaking of the clown angle, it's actually ingenious as it allowed Kawazu's face to be visible for most of the film. Though Universal's Invisible Man clad in bandages is more iconic in terms of visual appeal, Toho's version of the Invisible Man notably manages to connect with the audience through his facial expressions (visible due to the white face clown makeup). Also, this Invisible Man is nothing but heroic, and never takes a dark turn like many of the titular characters in other "Invisible Man" films. Nanjo's relationship with a young girl is particularly touching in this regard, as he does his best not only to avenge her dead grandfather but also to buy her a much coveted music box. Said music box plays into the film's final scenes, where it is revealed that Nanjo had it on his person as he dies.

Speaking of the climax, it is one of the film's weaker aspects, as it mostly consists of the gangster villains shadow-boxing the invisible Nanjo at an oil refinery. This author wonders if something more ambitious was planned for the finale and restrictions of either time or budget came into play. Otherwise, *Invisible Avenger* is a pretty solid Toho effects film from director Motoyoshi Oda. Actually, considering Oda would go on to direct *Godzilla Raids Again*—also co-written by *Invisible Avenger* writer Shigeaki Hidaka—Toho's Invisible Man movie actually makes for an interesting companion piece with the 1955 Godzilla sequel.

FINAL WORD Though often forgotten in the grand scheme of Toho's Transforming Human Series that "launched" with *The H-Man* in 1958, this film was actually the first. Toho's *Invisible Avenger* is also a unique and worthy addition to the pantheon of Invisible Man films produced worldwide.

REVENGE OF THE CREATURE

(UNIVERSAL)
Release Date: May 13, 1955
Alternate Titles: *Return of the Monster* (Argentina) *The Monster's Revenge* (Belgium) *Half-Fishman's Counterattack* (Japan) *The Creature from the Black Lagoon Returns* (Romania) *Revenge of The Creature from the Black Lagoon* (Serbia) *Monster Man's Revenge* (Spain) *The Monster Takes Revenge* (Sweden) *Return of the Creature/ Return of the Creature from the Black Lagoon* (working title)

Directed by: Jack Arnold **Screenplay by:** Martin Berkeley & William Alland (story) **Creature Design by:** Milicent Patrick, Bud Westmore, Jack Kevan & Chris Mueller Jr. **Music by:** William Lava & Harvey Stein **Cast:** John Agar (Professor Clete Ferguson) Lori Nelson (Helen Dobson) John Bromfield (Joe Hayes) Nestor Paiva (Lucas) Grandon Rhodes (Jackson Foster) Dave Willock (Lou Gibson) Robert Williams (George Johnson)

Academy Ratio, Black & White, 82 Minutes

SYNOPSIS An expedition led by Joe Hayes into the Amazon manages to finally capture the Creature from the Black Lagoon. The Gillman is brought to a large aquarium in Florida and put on display. He is studied by animal psychologist Professor Clete Ferguson and Helen Dobson, an ichthyologist. As the duo study the Gillman, both the Creature and Clete being to fall in love with Helen. Eventually the Gillman escapes the aquarium, killing Joe in the process. The Creature then begins stalking Helen from afar and abducts her from a pier-side club one night when she is with Clete. The police and Clete track the monster down to a Florida lagoon where Helen is able to escape the Creature's clutches and get ashore. After this, the police riddle the monster with bullets and he sinks into the depths.

COMMENTARY Smelling a hit, Universal was careful with just how they did in the Creature in his debut film. (They had finally learned their lessons after blowing up Frankenstein or burning up the Mummy only to bring them back virtually unscathed for sequels.) If you'll recall, at the end of the first film, the Creature sinks into the depths in a wounded state—small potatoes for any Universal monster. As such, starting off the story was a simple affair. As it is, the first part of the film serves as a brief but pleasant reprise of the first, with efforts to capture the Gillman in the Amazon. Just as the supporting characters of Maleva and Ygor often returned for sequels in the Wolf Man and Frankenstein films, here the boat captain from the last movie, Lucas, returns serving as a nice continuity thread. After the Creature's capture, we're in all new territory as the monster is put on display at an aquarium. In this sense, the story does exactly what a good sequel should in changing up the formula and the setting, as unleashing the Gillman in civilization is an excellent idea. That said, the story formula is still a little repetitive. For instance, there's another love triangle and the film's climax revolves around saving the girl from the Creature after it's killed the other male suitor.

The aquarium setting was well utilized in the film, particularly where the monster gets loose and terrorizes the patrons. As a testament to this concept's popularity, it popped up in more than one proposed *Creature* remake in the 1980s that never went before cameras. It also inspired the storyline of *Jaws 3-D*, taking place at Sea World in Florida. (In fact, Universal was set to remake the *Creature* until someone suggested *Jaws 3-D* in its place!) The film has an excellent three-act structure and sense of pacing. The opening takes place in the Amazon and focuses on capturing the Creature. Act II is all about the Creature in captivity and developing the three leads (one of which dies at the end of Act II). Act III then treats us to the Gillman loose in civilization. A particularly shocking scene, for 1955 at least, has the Creature pick up a poor teenager and throw him sideways into a palm tree. The teen's companion is found dead with blood on his neck later, which is also much edgier than the Universal horror of the previous decades.

Like the first film, this one too was shot in 3-D (it was the only sequel to be shot in 3-D up to this time, too). Not surprisingly it was an even bigger hit than the first film, which naturally ensured Creature #3. The only question was, where does the Gillman go from here?

FINAL WORD Many fans consider the first *Creature* film to be superior, but this sequel just might be better depending on your tastes.

ABBOTT AND COSTELLO MEET THE MUMMY

(UNIVERSAL)
Release Date: June 23, 1955
Alternate Titles: *Abbott and Costello in the Mummy* (Australian
TV title) *Abbott and Costello as Mummy Robbers* (Austria) *Two
Simpletons among the Pharaohs* (Belgium) *Hunting Mummies in
Egypt* (Brazil) *Abbott and Costello in Egypt* (Finland) *Adventures
in Egypt* (Greece) *The Mystery of the Pyramid* (Italy)

Directed by: Charles Lamont **Screenplay by:** John Grant **Special
Effects by:** Clifford Stine & Bud Westmore (makeup) **Music by:**
Joseph Gershenson (supervisor) **Cast:** Bud Abbott (himself) Lou
Costello (himself) Marie Windsor (Madame Rontru) Michael Ansara
(Charlie) Dan Seymour (Josef) Richard Deacon (Semu) Kurt Katch
(Dr. Gustav Zoomer) Richard Karlan (Hetsut) Mel Welles (Iben)
George Khoury (Habid) Eddie Parker (Klaris, the Mummy)

Academy Ratio, Black & White, 79 Minutes

SYNOPSIS Bud and Lou are two down-on-their-luck Americans
stranded in Cairo. When they overhear Dr. Zoomer stating that he
needs two men to transport the mummy, Klaris, to America, they
go to his home to inquire about the job. However, members of a
cult devoted to Klaris have already been there and killed Zoomer.
As such, Bud and Lou then get the murder pinned on them. To
make matters worse, the duo also picked up a sacred medallion
from Zoomer's home, which is desired not only by the Klaris cult,
but also a group of criminals led by Madame Rontru. Lou
accidentally eats the medallion, which leads to the secret treasure
of Princes Ara, and is captured by Rontru. Eventually the leader
of the Klaris cult, Semu, comes along posing as an archeologist
and agrees to lead Rontru and the boys to the temple where the
treasure is housed. Things come to a head at the temple where
Klaris revives and mixes it up with the criminals and cultists alike.
Some dynamite meant to excavate the treasure accidentally
explodes killing Klaris. In the end, Bud and Lou convince everyone
to honor Klaris's memory by turning the temple into a Klaris
themed club.

COMMENTARY After having met Frankenstein's monster, Dracula, the Wolf Man, the Invisible Man (twice), Mr. Hyde, and even the Gillman (albeit on TV rather than a film), there was only one Universal monster left for Abbott and Costello to meet: the Mummy. (Although they could've met the Phantom of the Opera too...)

Ironically, this spoof of Universal's Mummy sequels appears to have a higher budget than every single one of Universal's straight Mummy movies with bigger sets, more extras, and exterior locations that look much more Egyptian than those found in *The Mummy's Hand*. And yet, that said, the Mummy makeup is the series worst. Rather than being swaddled in bandages, it's apparent that the actor is wearing a literal suit. As for the face, it's rather comical, which is okay since this *is* a comedy. Furthermore, it's unknown if this was an error in continuity or an in-joke of some sort, but Kharis has become Klaris, and Ananka is now Princess Ara. (However, had they tried to play into the series continuity, this entry would have had to have been set in America and Egypt suited this film much better.)

Whereas you could've removed the comedy duo from *Meet Frankenstein* and still had a pretty solid monster movie, the same can't be said for *Meet the Mummy*. Perhaps that's one reason it can't hold a candle to *Meet Frankenstein*, even if it is a solid Abbott and Costello effort and is certainly better than *Meets Dr. Jekyll and Mr. Hyde*. The duo has some great bits that would've been excellent in any of their films, but still have a unique touch for the Mummy franchise. In one, they are in possession of a cursed amulet that neither wants to hold, so they keep planting it on the other in secret. Eventually, it ends up in Lou's hamburger and he eats it (this skit was a hybrid of both the "Slipping the Mickey routine" from *The Naughty Nineties* and had also played out in an episode of *The Colgate Comedy Hour*). Soon after, they are captured by the villains who X-ray Lou's stomach to find a multitude of other miscellaneous items like marbles and paperclips. (Bud quips that he lost a tie clip two years ago and to see if it's in there, too.) One of the duo's classic plays on words occurs when they're digging a hole in the Egyptian desert. When choosing between a shovel and a pic, Bud picks a pic, leading to a classic "Who's on first?" misunderstanding.

The film ends with some true Mummy madness within an ancient tomb, which kicks off with Lou finding a secret passageway that contains a giant iguana of all things. Later, one of the villains dresses up as Klaris to replace the real Mummy, who they bash over the head when he wakes up. Bud then gets the same idea and dresses up as the Mummy as well, so that during the picture's end, three mummies are running around. The movie ends with Bud and Lou keeping Klaris's legacy alive by opening up the Kafe Klaris (similar in a way to the club "Imhotep's" in *Mummy: Tomb of the Emperor Dragon*).

As it turned out, this was the penultimate Abbott and Costello film, and also their last picture under contract at Universal. They only did one more film together for a different studio called *Dance With Me, Henry* before ending their partnership in 1956.

FINAL WORD Though it may not be as good as *Meets Frankenstein* or *Meets the Invisible Man*, *Meets the Mummy* is still a solid effort that should please fans of either Abbott and Costello or the Mummy franchise.

THE CREATURE WALKS AMONG US

(UNIVERSAL)
Release Date: April 26, 1956
Alternate Titles: *The Avenging Monster* (Argentina) *The Monster is Among Us* (Belgium/Germany) *Monster Hunt* (Brazil) *Terror Over the World* (Italy)

Directed by: John Sherwood **Screenplay by:** Arthur A. Ross **Special Effects by:** Clifford Stine **Music by:** Irving Gertz, Heinz Roemheld & Henry Mancini **Cast:** Jeff Morrow (Dr. William Barton) Rex Reason (Dr. Thomas Morgan) Leigh Snowden (Marcia Barton) Gregg Palmer (Jed Grant) Maurice Manson (Dr. Borg) Ricou Browning (Gill-man/water scenes) Don Megowan (Gill-man/land scenes)

Academy Ratio, Black & White, 78 Minutes

SYNOPSIS Dr. William Barton is on a mission to capture the Gillman and unlock the creature's secrets in hopes of advancing man's own development. To help capture the Creature, loose in the Florida Everglades, he hires Dr. Thomas Morgan and Jed Grant. Along with Barton's adventurous wife, Marcia, they set out on a yacht and manage to capture the Creature, but it is badly burned in the process. Emergency surgery is performed on the Gillman which makes him an air breather, and the Creature recovers on the yacht as it sails to California. At Barton's ranch there, the Creature is placed in a livestock pen for study. Tensions mount at the ranch as Marcia becomes attracted to Morgan, while Grant often makes advances on her. One night Barton catches Grant and kills him. He throws his body in the pen with the Creature, hoping to pin the murder on the Gillman. The Creature becomes angry and breaks out of his pen, chasing down Barton until he's killed. He then leaves Marcia and Morgan alone and wanders off towards the ocean, his fate uncertain as he walks towards the waves.

COMMENTARY When Universal asked for the inevitable third Creature movie, Creature creator William Alland was at a loss for storylines. Resurrecting the monster was no problem, as *Revenge*

142

of the Creature had ended similarly to the first film, with a wounded Gillman sinking into the depths, destined to rise again. The problem was, what to do with the Creature now? Alland turned to Arthur Ross, who had helped to develop the first film. Ross's storyline doesn't mirror the first two films in any way. Both of those films had followed the same formula, more or less, just in different locations. The common core of both entries had a love triangle between a girl, and two suitors, who must also compete with the Creature for the girl's affections. Both films ended with the Creature kidnapping the girl after killing one of the suitors, leaving the remaining romantic male lead to rescue her. The third Gillman film has none of this, not even the Beauty and the Beast aspect at the center of the last two outings. (One could argue that the Creature in captivity aspect is similar to *Revenge*, though.)

Ross took inspiration for his new treatment from the news, where a scientist had made bold claims about performing surgery on an ape to induce the evolutionary process on it (more or less). Ross then wondered what would happen if someone tried that on the Gillman, and converted him into an air-breather. (This no doubt thrilled Universal's money men, as this would lessen the amount of underwater photography.) While the surgery storyline served as the film's "gimmick," the core of the story harkened back to a very early treatment for the first film. It was called *Black Lagoon*, where the Creature was a sympathetic figure that kills only twice (both instances are in self-defense). That treatment also had the female lead engaged to the story's villain-scientist, and she eventually falls in love with another character and leaves her fiancé to be with the other man.

This story has the female lead as the wife of a villainous scientist, who over the course of the story falls for another scientist. The Gillman starts off the story violent, but after his surgery, is presented only in a sympathetic light. For instance, he never harms any of the livestock in the pen with him, and saves the lesser animals from a marauding mountain lion. At the film's end, the Creature only breaks loose upon witnessing a murder committed by Dr. Barton. He then goes on a delightful rampage, tearing through a ranch house in his efforts to kill Barton, which he does. The film ends on a thought-provoking shot of the escaped Creature standing on the beach, looking into the ocean. Will he die in the depths? We don't know, but that gloomy fate seems likely for the Gillman.

Indeed, this is a very different Gillman film. It wasn't uncommon for violent yet beloved movie monsters to go through transformations and become heroes. King Kong's first sequel, *Son of Kong*, immediately recognized this, as did every King Kong movie thereafter where the big ape was always sympathetic. Even the Wolf Man plays hero, albeit accidentally, at the end of *Abbott and Costello Meet Frankenstein*. Speaking of Frankenstein, the big, bulked-up Creature has essentially been turned into the Frankenstein monster. (To prep audiences for his new physique, the first thing they see is a drawing of the Creature who appears much bigger than he did in previous entries. However, when he appears a bit later, he's just as lean as he's always been!) The climax is also similar to many Frankenstein films, with the monster chasing down the mad scientist across a large estate.

The film did not do well with test audiences. One reviewer remarked that it was the best comedy in years not to feature Abbott and Costello, while another commented they would have felt less gypped if it had at least been in color. Though this test screening didn't bode well, the film wasn't a disaster, but it wasn't a big hit either. Though the first two Creatures had grossed over a million dollars, *The Creature Walks Among Us* did not. This, more than the Creature's new status quo as a land-lubber probably cancelled future sequels. (Had Universal wanted to, they could have just claimed that the Creature regrew his gills in the water, or perhaps just discovered another member of the same species.) As it stands, this is sadly the last official Creature film, even though there have been talks of a remake for years.

FINAL WORD Many Gillman fans don't love this film, primarily due to the lack of underwater antics. (The first underwater sequence is a showstopper, and is possibly superior or at least on par with the previous two film's underwater scenes, though.) That all said, the film deserves points for trying something different with the Creature. It also serves as a somber end to the Gillman saga.

146

SHEER, STARK TERROR GRIPS YOU IN UNDERWATER... 3-D
CREATURE FROM THE BLACK LAGOON
RICHARD CARLSON · JULIE ADAMS

ALL NEW THRILLS! SHOCK! SUSPENSE!
REVENGE OF THE CREATURE
JOHN AGAR · LORI NELSON · JOHN BROMFIELD

RICHARD CARLSON · JULIA ADAMS
RICHARD DENNING · ANTONIO MORENO
L'ETRANGE CREATURE DU LAC NOIR

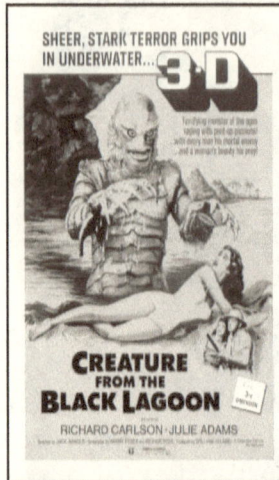

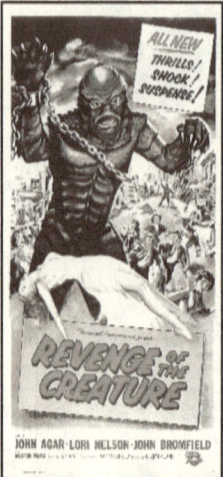

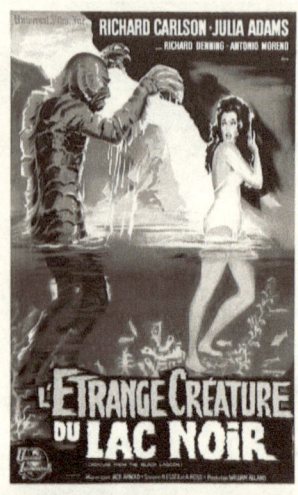

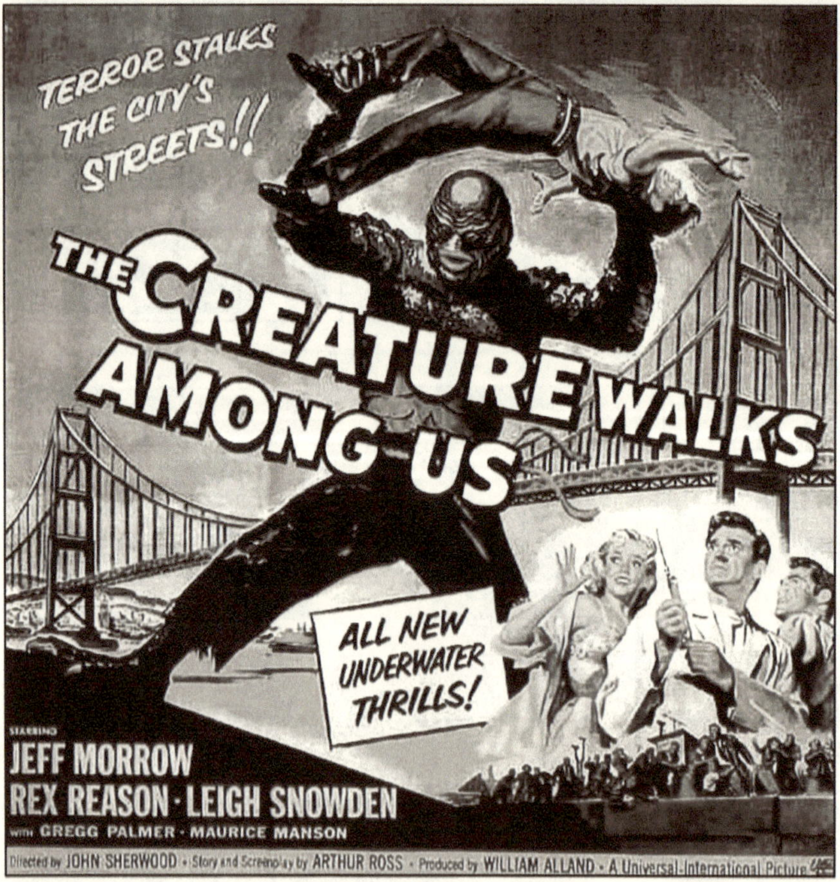
TERROR STALKS THE CITY'S STREETS!!
THE CREATURE WALKS AMONG US
ALL NEW UNDERWATER THRILLS!
STARRING
JEFF MORROW
REX REASON · LEIGH SNOWDEN
WITH GREGG PALMER · MAURICE MANSON
Directed by JOHN SHERWOOD · Story and Screenplay by ARTHUR ROSS · Produced by WILLIAM ALLAND · A Universal-International Picture

CURSE OF FRANKENSTEIN

(HAMMER)
Release Date: May 20, 1957 (U.K.) June 25, 1957 (U.S.)
Alternate Titles: *Mask of Frankenstein* (Germany)
Frankenstein's Counterattack (Japan) *Frankenstein* (Netherlands)

Directed by: Terence Fisher **Screenplay by:** Jimmy Sangster based upon the book by Mary Shelley **Special Effects by:** Les Bowie & Philip Leakey **Music by:** James Bernard **Cast:** Peter Cushing (Baron Victor Frankenstein) Robert Urquhart (Dr. Paul Krempe) Hazel Court (Elizabeth) Christopher Lee (the creature) Valerie Gaunt (Justine) Paul Hardtmuth (Professor Bernstein) Alex Gallier (the priest) Melvyn Hayes (young Victor)

Spherical, Eastmancolor, 83 Minutes

SYNOPSIS After the death of his parents, young Baron Victor Frankenstein sends for a tutor who arrives in the form of Paul Krempe. Within only a few years, Victor outpaces his tutor and the duo begin to experiment with reviving the dead. Victor creates a new body from corpses and even murders a brilliant scientist to utilize his brain. This becomes too much for Paul, and during a fight between he and Victor the brain is damaged. Victor presses on anyways and gives life to his monstrous creation. It escapes the lab, but Victor and Paul are able to track it down. Paul shoots and kills the monster to Victor's disappointment. Paul leaves but returns to the Baron's estate after being invited to the Baron's wedding, where Victor will wed his cousin Elizabeth (who Paul is also fond of). After the wedding, Paul learns that Victor has resurrected the monster. It gets loose again, terrorizing Paul, Victor, and Elizabeth until it falls into a vat of acid and dies. Victor is sentenced to be executed via guillotine for his crimes.

COMMENTARY By the late 1950s, it seemed that audiences were no longer interested in the classic monsters of yore, which were being supplanted by space monsters and mutants. Then along came Hammer Films with their gory color version of Frankenstein, and the classic monsters returned to the big screen once more.

149

(That said, they were still popular on television, which probably aided in this film's success somewhat.) However, Hammer's first foray into Frankenstein started out very differently in its inception. In 1956, Max J. Rosenberg and Milton Subotsky reached out to Elliot Hyman of Associated Artists about a remake of the Frankenstein story. Hyman suggested the pair contact Hammer because of their recent sci-fi hit *The Quartermass Experiment.* The duo brought their script to James Carreras, the head of Hammer, who decided to take on the production. Initially, it was to be filmed in black and white and bears only a passing resemblance to the finished *Curse of Frankenstein.* This version was entitled *Frankenstein and the Monster,* and like the title, was perfunctory at best. While it does chronicle the exploits of a younger Baron Frankenstein than the one portrayed in Universal's 1931 film, its main similarity to *Curse* is that it begins and ends in a jail cell where the Baron recounts his story.

Once Hammer announced the project, Universal was quick to step in and advise Hammer not to copy anything unique to their version, namely the beloved Jack Pierce makeup applied to Boris Karloff. This gave Hammer an excuse to do something they had wanted to do anyway: throw Rosenberg and Subotsky's script out the window. According to Anthony Hinds, the duo's script was just a watered-down version of the Universal film anyways. Carreras paid the men, and then handed off the story to Jimmy Sangster. Carreras not only instructed Sangster to deviate from the Universal film as much as possible; he also told Sangster to keep it cheap. Above all else this meant no villagers with torches and pitchforks (as a way to avoid paying the extras). The other way to keep it cheap was to set it in only a few locations, which meant less sets to build and less time to shoot. Carreras also gave Sangster some interesting character direction in that he told him to make Baron Frankenstein "a shit." And that he did.

"I was more interested in Baron Frankenstein than the monster," Sangster said in his autobiography *Do You Want It Good, Or Tuesday?* and it shows. As it is, Sangster's Baron Frankenstein is more of a monster than his own creation. Over the course of the film the sociopathic Baron murders his maid (carrying his unborn child) and also an elderly professor in order to get a good brain to transplant into his creation. Furthermore, in keeping with not emulating the Universal film too much, there is no "It's alive!" scene. The monster is actually brought to life by accident when Victor and Paul are out of the lab, thus creating an entirely different type of reveal when the men walk back into the lab to find

150

the creature alive. When it rips off its face bandages, it reveals a creature much more grotesque than Karloff's Frankenstein monster. It then goes on a rampage as in the 1931 film, only in place of the monster meeting the little girl Maria by the side of a lake, the creature has a run in with a blind man and his grandson. The blind man was probably an allusion to the blind man from the book and *Bride of Frankenstein*. However, unlike the blind man in the book and *Bride*, this man and the monster do not make friends. Victor and Paul arrive on the scene, and in a shocking visual for the time, the latter shoots the monster in the head. It was one of only several gory visuals to burn itself into the minds of the audience, including severed hands and disembodied eyes and brains. The film even ends with the monster falling into a vat of acid.

Of course, what really makes this film work in addition to the color photography and added gore are the performances, chief among them Peter Cushing and Christopher Lee. Of the two, Cushing shines the brightest as the Baron, though Lee would eventually outpace Cushing when he became renowned for playing Count Dracula. However, while Lee's Dracula teeters between being held in equal or higher esteem to Bela Lugosi's Dracula among fans, Cushing's Baron Frankenstein easily trumps Colin Clive's version of the character, memorable though it may be. (It doesn't help that Clive only got to play the character twice while Cushing reprised the role five more times.)

Curse of Frankenstein was shot over five weeks on a budget of only £65,000. Upon release, critics hated it and audiences loved it. It was unlike anything they had ever seen before. Due to word of mouth, the film made more money on its second week of release rather than its first! In fact, the film grossed more than 70 times its production cost.

FINAL WORD This film's significance as Hammer's first true horror-hit withstanding, it's still an excellent horror film and possibly Hammer's best Frankenstein flick.

I WAS A TEENAGE WEREWOLF

(AIP)

Release Date: July 19, 1957 (U.S.)
Alternate Titles: *The Teenage Monster* (Argentina) *The Claws of the Werewolf* (Belgium) *Spirit Transplant Human* (Japan)
Death has Black Claws (West Germany)
Blood of the Werewolf (working title)

Directed by: Gene Fowler Jr. **Screenplay by:** Herman Cohen & Aben Kandel **Makeup by:** Phillip Scheer **Music by:** Paul Dunlap **Cast:** Michael Landon (Tony Rivers/the Teenage Werewolf) Yvonne Lime (Arlene Logan) Whit Bissell (Dr. Alfred Brandon) Malcolm Atterbury (Charles Rivers) Barney Phillips (Detective Sgt. Donovan) Robert Griffin (Police Chief Baker) Vladimir Sokoloff (Pepe, the janitor)

Academy Ratio, Black and White, 76 Minutes

SYNOPSIS Tony Rivers is a hot-headed teenager who frequently gets into fights at school. A local detective takes an interest in Tony and encourages him to go see a special psychiatrist. Tony initially turns down the offer, but after attacking a friend at a party he relents. Unfortunately, the doctor plans only on using Tony as a guinea pig, to see how far back he can get him to regress into a primal state of mind. Using his experimental drugs on Tony, the youth later transforms into a werewolf and kills one of his friends. Tony next transforms in the school gymnasium where several students are able to recognize him. Tony becomes the focus of a large manhunt. Eventually the police track him back to the doctor's lab where, in his werewolf form, he kills the doctor. The police arrive soon after and shoot the werewolf to death, thus killing poor Tony.

COMMENTARY After *The Wolf Man*, but before *Teen Wolf*, there was *I Was a Teenage Werewolf*. And despite that silly title, it was something of a landmark film. Though there had been horror movies involving teenagers before to some extent, this was the first film to make the central teenaged character an actual monster.

The movie was produced by American International Pictures, and studio head Samuel Z. Arkoff recalled getting some flak for making a monster out of a teenager. The teenaged werewolf really does look like it could be the Wolf Man's teenaged son. The big hair is pompadour-like, and, of course, the letterman jacket helps, too.

Though it's easy to dismiss this movie as corny or campy, it at least is able to emotionally invest the audience in the main character, which is more than a lot of films of this nature can say. Tony, played by Michael Landon, is a pretty big departure from the actor's future roles playing wholesome characters in shows like *Bonanza* and *Highway to Heaven*. Tony doesn't make a great first impression on the audience because we are introduced to him in the middle of a fight. It's not the fight that's the problem, it's that he fights dirty. He picks up a shovel and swings it at his opponent's head and then he throws dirt in his face, while the opponent keeps the fight fair. And yet, thanks to Landon's performance, Tony does manage to garner audience sympathy for the rest of the film, which is important when it comes to tragic werewolf characters.

If there's one major disappointment in this film it's the ending. A detective character and a policeman show up, pumps the titular character full of bullets, and he dies. Typically a werewolf film ends with the accursed character's loved ones surrounding them. This one would have benefited from having either Tony's father or girlfriend there to see him expire. The detective character at least has a preexisting relationship with Tony, but the duo hadn't really shared any scenes together since much earlier in the story.

The movie was shot in just one week on a $150,000 budget and remarkably went on to gross over $2 million when it was released on a double bill with *Invasion of the Saucer Men* (1957).

FINAL WORD Though it's not regarded as a "good" film by very many critics, not even horror fans, the movie deserves respect for starting the teenage horror genre.

THE DAUGHTER OF DR. JEKYLL

(FILM VENTURERS)
Release Date: July 28, 1957
Alternate Titles: *The Grave of the Dead of Dr. Jekyll* (Austria)
The Doctor's Daughter and the Monster (Brazil)

Directed by: Edgar G. Ulmer **Screenplay by:** Jack Pollexfen
Makeup by: Louis Phillipi **Music Supervisor:** Melvyn Lenard
Cast: Gloria Talbott (Janet Smith) John Agar (George Hastings)
Arthur Shields (Dr. Lomas) John Dierkes (Jacob) Molly McCard
(Maggie) Martha Wentworth (Mrs. Merchant)

Academy Ratio, Black & White, 71 Minutes

SYNOPSIS Upon her 21st birthday, Janet Smith inherits a large
estate in the English countryside. She also learns from her
guardian, Dr. Lomas, that she is actually the daughter of Dr.
Henry Jekyll, who in years past created a formula that turned him
into a werewolf. From that point forward, Janet begins having
dreams of attacking women in the forest. At the same time, the
women Jane dreams about turn up dead despite the fact that she
never left her room. Eventually it turns out that Dr. Lomas is the
werewolf, and is trying to convince Jane that she is the one doing
the killing. Jane's fiancé, George, along with the villagers, track
down Dr. Lomas in werewolf form and kill him.

COMMENTARY From the same man who wrote *Son of Dr. Jekyll*
came this 1957 "sequel". Actually, it's not really a sequel. It's not
even that close to a *Dr. Jekyll and Mr. Hyde* adaptation as it's
actually a werewolf movie. (The film was one of three werewolf
features that year, the other two being the better-known *I Was a
Teenage Werewolf* and *The Werewolf*.)

At first, *Daughter of Dr. Jekyll* seems like the same song and
dance from *Son of Dr. Jekyll*: A young person discovers they are
the secret child of Dr. Henry Jekyll and have inherited his estate
shortly before they are to be married. A guardian and former friend
of Dr. Jekyll then convinces the child that they are committing
murders as a monster when, in fact, they are the ones doing the
killing. But, where there was no monster in *Son*, here the guardian

154

turns out to be the real werewolf at least. (Still, you have to wait until the last ten minutes of the movie to even see him.) The werewolf's kill, stalking a woman alone in her home, is better than what we've seen earlier and seems like it came out of another movie. That said, Dr. Lomas still isn't much of a werewolf and is comparable to the *Werewolf of London* with even less makeup on if that tells you anything.

Like the last film, the narrative is again rather confusing. Was Dr. Jekyll ever really a werewolf? Or was it Lomas all along and he framed Jekyll for his deeds just as he tries to do to Jane? That's not clear. And, as stated earlier, this really isn't much of a Dr. Jekyll and Mr. Hyde adaptation. Dr. Jekyll might as well be Dr. Frankenstein in this version with his huge castle complete with servants. And even though Jekyll was said to be a werewolf, the villagers staked him through the heart like a vampire. So, in a sense, this movie is a pastiche of nearly every monster aside from the Mummy and the Invisible Man.

There is some sequel bait at the end. If you've seen the film, you know that it begins with a prologue depicting the death of Dr. Jekyll, where an unseen narrator states that Dr. Jekyll is dead. A werewolf then cackles, "Are you sure?" in a female voice. When the movie ends, the same thing happens only "Are you sure?" is asked in a man's voice. Then again, it may not have been sequel bait, and may have just been the typical horror film ending where it's hinted that the monster isn't really gone for good, which was true of plenty of one-off monster flicks.

The film started shooting in November of 1956 over the course of only a week's time (rather strange considering it wasn't released until more than seven months later). The film wasn't even shot on a studio set, but rather an actual Los Angeles residence (as such, modern traffic can occasionally be glimpsed outside of the Victorian home).

FINAL WORD More of a *She Wolf of London* than a *Dr. Jekyll and Mr. Hyde* movie; I wouldn't say this one is worth your time unless you're a sucker for any old black and white monster movie with the usual horror cliches.

INVISIBLE MAN VS. THE HUMAN FLY

(DAIEI)
Release Date: August 25, 1957
Alternate Titles: *Invisible Man and Fly Man* (Japan) *The Murdering Mite* (U.S.)

Directed by: Mitsuo Murayama **Screenplay by:** Hajime Takaiwa **Special Effects by:** Toru Matobu **Music by:** Tokujiro Okubo **Cast:** Ryuji Shinagawa (Dr. Tsukioka/Invisible Man), Yoshiro Kitahara (Chief Inspector Wakabayashi), Junko Kano (Akiko Hayakawa), Ichiro Izawa (Kokichi Kusunoki/Fly Man #2), Ikuko Mori (Mieko), Shizuo Chujo (Yamada/Fly Man #1), Jôji Tsurumi (Sugimoto), Shôzô Nanbu (Dr. Hayakawa), Yoshihiro Hamaguchi (Detective Hayama)

Academy Ratio, Black & White, 96 Minutes

SYNOPSIS On a flight to Tokyo, a man is found mysteriously murdered while in the bathroom—there is no sign of the culprit. Sitting next to the murdered man on the flight was Dr. Hayakawa. Chief Inspector Wakabayashi wonders if perhaps the killer was invisible and asks Dr. Hayakawa if this is possible. Dr. Hayakawa takes him to his secret lab to show him that he has an invisibility ray—though neither he nor his assistants, Dr. Tsukioka and Sugimoto—are the culprits. As more murders occur, Wakabayashi pieces together the clues and finds that all victims heard a mysterious buzzing before they were killed. Wakabayashi goes to visit the employer of one of the victims, Kusunoki, but finds him to be quite amiable. As it turns out, Kusunoki holds the strings of Yamada the Human Fly, whom he has given a formula that can make him shrink down to miniature size and fly! As the murders continue, Wakabayashi beseeches Tsukioka to use the invisibility ray on him to help solve the case. Tsukioka refuses, thinking it too dangerous, but when the Human Fly kills Dr. Hayakawa, he turns the invisible ray on himself. Tsukioka spies on Kusunoki and discovers he and the Human Fly are in cahoots. Soon afterward, Yamada is found dead and Tsukioka helps Wakabayashi arrest Kusunoki. However, Kusunoki takes the fly potion and flies away to escape. Kusunoki then bombs a bullet train as a testament to his power and demands that he be given the invisibility ray or he will set off another bomb. A trade is set between Wakabayashi and Kusunoki atop a building at midnight. Meanwhile, Akiko, Dr. Hayakawa's daughter and Tsukioka's fiancé, sets the invisibility ray on herself. Kusunoki arrives in a helicopter and despite Tsukioka and Wakabayashi's best efforts, absconds with the invisibility ray. To their surprise, it turns around and lands. An invisible Akiko was in the helicopter. Kusunoki tries to escape but is shot by Wakabayashi.

COMMENTARY This wackily-titled movie is just almost as fun as it sounds. Those expecting to see a classic, bandaged invisible man battling something that looks like the mutated man-bug from 1958's *The Fly* will be disappointed. Unfortunately, the titular "human fly" is not a mutated human-fly hybrid as in the 1958 film (which came out after this Daiei sci-fi caper). The human fly is merely a person who shrinks themselves down and can also fly (but no, they do not have wings). All the Invisible Man really needs to defeat his opponent is a newspaper. Not terribly exciting.

Yet, *Invisible Man vs. the Human Fly* is actually a very fun film, assuming you don't let the title give you grandiose expectations. It is more of a crime caper than a Universal-esque monster mashup. Within that crime caper are plenty of twists and turns to keep the viewer engaged. In that vein—as revealed in the synopsis—there are multiple Invisible Men and Human Flies, plus one Invisible Woman! This is yet another way in which Daiei's Invisible Man film makes itself unique compared to Toho and Universal's Invisible Man films—not to mention Daiei's own 1949 *Invisible Man Appears*, which featured a single, invisible fiend.

Overall, those that enjoy Japanese special effects movies should give this fun effort from Daiei a try, even if the film should have been titled "The Invisible Man vs. The Incredible Shrinking Man" instead. Though the film never did get a U.S. release, it was shopped around under the title of *The Murdering Mite*, which wisely would have subverted expectations had it been released there.

FINAL WORD If one can go into the film without too many preconceived notions as to what they are about to witness, this fun flick is worth tracking down.

I WAS A TEENAGE FRANKENSTEIN

(AIP)
Release Date: November 23, 1957 (U.S.)
Alternate Titles: *Frankenstein 1959* (Uruguay) *Teenage Frankenstein* (U.K.) *The Son of Frankenstein* (Mexico) *The Massacre of Frankenstein* (Italy) *Girls for Frankenstein* (Belgium)

Directed by: Herbert L. Strock **Screenplay by:** Herman Cohen (as Kenneth Langtry) **Makeup by:** Phillip Scheer **Music by:** Paul Dunlap **Cast:** Whit Bissell (Professor Frankenstein) Phyllis Coates (Margaret) Robert Burton (Dr. Karlton) Gary Conway (Frankenstein monster/Bob) George Lynn (Sergeant Burns) John Cliff (Sergeant McAfee) Marshall Bradford (Dr. Randolph)

Academy Ratio, Black and White, 74 Minutes

SYNOPSIS Professor Frankenstein, a descendant of the famous scientist, has come to America from England on a celebrated lecture tour. He has hopes of constructing a perfect being out of the dead bodies of teenagers. He picks the best bits out of a bad car crash where multiple teens were killed to create the monster, which has a perfect body but a mutilated face. As the monster learns from the doctor and becomes more sentient, Frankenstein acquires a new handsome face for the monster by having him murder a teenager named Bob. Frankenstein wants to disassemble his monster and ship him back to England. When the monster learns this he attacks Frankenstein and kills him and is electrocuted himself.

COMMENTARY With *I Was a Teenage Werewolf* proving to be a hit, that there would be a sequel was no surprise. The surprise was in how quickly it came about. According to Samuel Z. Arkoff, a major theater chain owner in Texas asked him if he thought AIP could create a similar double bill in time for the major Thanksgiving weekend. Arkoff said that they could, and it was off to the races for AIP. Production began in mid-September, and remarkably, the film was ready for release by November. The production brought back Whit Bissel again as the mad doctor, though this time he is a descendant of Frankenstein. This one's a bit more laughable than the last one, though. Case in point, Dr. Frankenstein is opining on how he'll use the bodies of teenagers, because they are youthful and healthy to make the body of a perfect being. As his very convenient luck would have it, a car wreck then occurs right in front of his office. A troubled bystander then more or less tells him how those darn teenagers were driving home recklessly from a party and crashed into each other. It sounds a bit like an after-school special combined with a horror film if anything.

The problem with this movie when compared to the last is that it doesn't have a central teen protagonist like in the previous entry. Our focus is almost entirely on the new Frankenstein. In a moment of out-of-place hilarity, Professor Frankenstein even takes his date to make out point where all the teenagers are! It has a few of the same elements of *Curse of Frankenstein*, such as a reluctant partner for Frankenstein and a snooping fiancé curious what he's up to in his lab. In fact, Frankenstein kills his fiancé by locking her in the room with the monster just like the Baron did to his maid in *Curse*. There's even some fairly gory bits, such as a severed head kept in a birdcage. The fact that the doctor disposes of his victims to a crocodile is a nice touch as well.

The teenage Frankenstein character is a bit hard to relate to because the face is essentially just a mask, devoid of expression even though the actor's voice at least has good emotion. The relationship between him and the Professor is that of overbearing overprotective parent and child. One of the creepier scenes has the Professor taking him out on the town—specifically to make out point—to pick out a face he likes. Or, in other words, to pick out a murder victim. After the doctor installs the new face comes the macabre idea that the doctor is then going to disassemble his monster and ship him in parts to England where he will be reassembled! But the monster gets loose and ends up throwing Frankenstein down into the alligator pit to be eaten. At the same time, the film transitions to color for the last few moments for added shock value. As for the monster, he simply gets electrocuted and that's it.

FINAL WORD If you liked the first one, this one's not as good, but it's still entertaining enough.

BLOOD OF DRACULA

(AIP)
Release Date: November 23, 1957 (U.S.)
Alternate Titles: *Blood of the Vampire* (Mexico) *I Was a Teenage Vampire* (working title) *Blood Is My Heritage* (U.K.)

Directed by: Herbert L. Strock **Screenplay by:** Aben Kandel (as Ralph Thornton) **Makeup by:** Phillip Scheer **Music by:** Paul Dunlap **Cast:** Sandra Harrison (Nancy Perkins) Louise Lewis (Miss Branding) Gail Ganley (Myra) Jerry Blaine (Tab) Heather Ames (Nola) Mary Adams (Mrs. Thorndyke) Edna Holland (Miss Rivers) Thomas B. Henry (Mr. Paul Perkins) Jeanne Dean (Mrs. Doris Perkins) Don Devlin (Eddie) Malcolm Atterbury (Lt. Dunlap) Michael Hall (Glenn)

Academy Ratio, Black and White, 69 Minutes

SYNOPSIS Six weeks after her mother has died, Nancy Perkins is dropped off at an all-girls boarding school by her father and new stepmother. There Miss Branding, the chemistry teacher, decides to use Nancy as her guinea pig in a dangerous experiment. She hypnotizes Nancy with a supernatural amulet from the Carpathian Mountains, which turns her into a vampire. Though Nancy is unaware of the murders she commits, the police begin to investigate the school. Eventually, Nancy's boyfriend, Glenn, comes to visit, and when she almost attacks him, she goes to confront Miss Branding. The two get into a struggle, with Nancy killing her teacher and then getting impaled on a wooden stake.

COMMENTARY Though it's often forgotten, *Blood of Dracula* is actually the female version of *I Was a Teenage Werewolf*. Why AIP didn't call it *I Was a Teenage Vampire* as originally planned is anyone's guess—perhaps they just wanted Dracula's name in the title?—but if they had, it might've been better remembered. More so than its double-bill feature, *Teenage Frankenstein*, *Blood of Dracula* is a remake of *Teenage Werewolf*. The similarities between the two are many. The main character again has social behavioral problems, though hers seem more justified than Michael Landon's

160

werewolf boy Tony. In this case, Nancy has lost her mother and her father has married the perennial wicked stepmother only six weeks later. When she's sent to an all-girls school, the other girls there aren't particularly nice to her. To make matters worse, the movie's "mad scientist," Nancy's chemistry teacher, decides she's the perfect subject for her experiment. There's even another horrible song and dance number, in this case, "Puppy Love," to mirror the song from *I Was a Teenage Werewolf.*

Some critics describe Nancy's monster as being part-werewolf and part-vampire, but I think the producers were going for a bat-girl. She has pointed ears like a bat, plus the fangs, nor does she grow extra hair on her face exactly; it's just that her eyebrows and widow's peak become more pronounced. Though this movie might just be the most laughable one of the bunch due to the makeup, at the same time, it's also the one with more emotional investment in the central character.

In many ways, it also improves upon the basic story outline copied from *Teenage Werewolf.* For instance, even though boyfriend Glenn doesn't show up until the last ten minutes, the relationship between him and Nancy still has more impact on the story's final moments than the relationship from *Teenage Werewolf.* Here there's some suspense as Nancy almost bites Glenn, whereas Arlene was never in any danger from Tony in *Teenage Werewolf.* Unfortunately, *Blood of Dracula's* ending is rushed instead of exciting. Nancy confronts Miss Branding in her vampire form, and in the struggle, some furniture is broken, creating a wooden stake that Nancy conveniently falls onto. One of her classmates, along with the headmistress and Glenn, walk in to find the duo dead, and the head mistress offers a quick condemnation of Branding's experiments to wrap the movie up.

This film and *I Was a Teenage Frankenstein* weren't the mega-hit that the previous film was, but they would still be followed by another quasi-sequel, *How to Make a Monster,* which featured the masks from *Werewolf* and *Frankenstein* both.

FINAL WORD Though the least well-known of the "I Was a Teenage Monster" trilogy, this one might be the best of the bunch.

RETURN OF DRACULA

(GRAMERCY PICTURES)
Release Date: April 1958
Alternate Titles: *The Fantastic Disappearing Man* (U.K.)
Curse of Dracula (U.S. TV title)

Directed by: Paul Landres **Screenplay by:** Pat Fielder **Makeup by:** Stanley Smith **Music by:** Gerald Fried **Cast:** Francis Lederer (Bellac Gordal/Count Dracula) Norma Eberhardt (Rachel Mayberry) Ray Stricklyn (Tim Hansen) John Wengraf (John Meierman) Virginia Vincent (Jennie Blake) Gage Clarke (Reverend Whitfield) Jimmy Baird (Mickey Mayberry) Greta Granstedt (Cora Mayberry)

Spherical, Black & White, 77 Minutes

SYNOPSIS Dracula is run out of Europe by a special task force and so he heads to America. On a train bound for California, he kills an artist by the name of Bellac Gordal. When Dracula finds Gordal's relatives waiting for him at the train station, and upon learning that the family matriarch hasn't seen Bellac in years, Dracula takes on his identity. The family, consisting of a mother, Cora Mayberry, her teenage daughter, Rachel, and young son, Mickey, are all too happy to take him back home. However, strange events soon plague the family. Rachel's sickly friend, Jenny, who is being treated at a local parish, mysteriously dies and then rises again as a vampire. This coincides with the arrival of the same Dracula task force in America from Europe, where they pick up the Count's trail. On Halloween night, Dracula puts Rachel under his spell and entices her to join him in an abandoned mine. Rachel is followed there by her boyfriend, Tim, and together the duo forces Dracula off a ledge with a crucifix. The Count falls into some old mining equipment and is pierced through the heart.

COMMENTARY This fun little horror flick might be better remembered today if not for one thing: after it was released in April of 1958, Hammer's *Horror of Dracula* came out in color only one month later. However, according to TCM's Ben Mankiewicz, this film was produced in anticipation of and with intent to beat *Horror* *of Dracula* to theaters. Anyhow, even if it is allegedly a cash grab at Hammer's better-known production, Gramercy Picture's *The Return of Dracula* is a fine film.

Being set in the then contemporary 1950s, it beat Hammer's *Dracula A.D. 1972* to the idea of putting the Count in the modern era by fourteen years. Though more than a few viewers have teased that this film is like *"Leave it to Beaver* meets *Dracula,"* it's by no means corny, and it arguably handles Dracula in a modern setting better than *A.D. 1972*. For instance, Dracula sometimes wears his overcoat on his shoulders, making it look like a cape, which is an interesting way of updating his look. Although, rather than comparing this film to *A.D. 1972*, it might be better described as a precursor of sorts to the vampire-next-door movie *Fright Night* (1985).

Despite the innovations, there are still plenty of callbacks to Bram Stoker, though. The bedridden Jenny character is the Lucy stand-in, for instance. (One has to wonder why they bothered to change her name?) Shots of Dracula entering Jenny's room as a supernatural mist are spectacular for the time and are comparable in atmosphere to the 1979 *Dracula*. The mist is probably this film's most effective visual concerning its vampires, as it also surrounds Dracula in his casket, and Jenny exits her chamber in the mortuary through the same type of mist. Later, in a first, Lucy—I mean Jenny—turns into a white wolf to attack a victim outside of a lonely train depot.

The film's version of Dracula never makes any animal transformations, though. (I have a sneaking hunch they wanted him to turn into a bat in the mine but ran out of money or time.) Nor is the climax terribly exciting compared to Hammer's *Horror of Dracula*. Its main claim to fame is that it has one brief, shocking color shot of Jenny being staked, and it's quite graphic for its time. However, Dracula is dispatched by simply tumbling over a precipice in the cave and impaling himself on some mining equipment, which is also quite bloody, though it is kept in black and white.

FINAL WORD If you enjoyed Dracula's romp through the 1970s courtesy of Hammer, then you might also enjoy this equally amusing, if not possibly superior, outing for the Count in the 1950s.

HORROR OF DRACULA

(HAMMER)
Release Date: May 8, 1958 (U.S.) May 22, 1958 (U.K.)
Alternate Titles: *Dracula* (U.K.) *Dracula's Nightmare* (France)
Vampire of the Night (Brazil) *Dracula, the Vampire of the
Carpathians* (Greece) *Dracula the Vampire* (Italy)
Vampire Dracula (Japan)

Directed by: Terence Fisher **Screenplay by:** Jimmy Sangster based off of the book by Bram Stoker **Special Effects by:** Les Bowie **Music by:** James Bernard **Cast:** Peter Cushing (Dr. Van Helsing) Christopher Lee (Count Dracula) Michael Gough (Arthur Holmwood) Melissa Stribling (Mina Holmwood) Carol Marsh (Lucy Holmwood) John Van Eyssen (Jonathan Harker) Valerie Gaunt (Vampire) Olga Dickie (Gerda) Janina Faye (Tania)

Academy Ratio, Technicolor, 82 Minutes

SYNOPSIS Jonathan Harker arrives at Castle Dracula posing as the Count's new librarian. In reality he is on a secret mission to kill the age-old vampire. Instead, Harker is himself vampirized, and Dracula sets out to find Harker's fiancé, Lucy Holmwood. On Dracula's trail is vampire hunter Van Helsing, Harker's mentor. Van Helsing arrives at the Holmwood home, where he meets Arthur and Mina Holmwood to give them the bad news that Jonathan is dead. While there he also attends to Lucy, growing weaker by the night for reasons unknown. When Van Helsing's advice isn't followed, Lucy dies and rises again as a vampire. Van Helsing takes Arthur with him to Lucy's tomb, where he witnesses her walk as one of the undead. Van Helsing stakes her, setting her soul free and the duo make it their mission to next find Dracula. Unfortunately for them, Dracula has begun seducing Mina, who has already hidden him in the cellar. Upon Van Helsing's discovery of this, Dracula flees with Mina, while Van Helsing and Arthur give chase. The chase ends at Castle Dracula, where Van Helsing dispatches the vampire king by exposing him to sunlight. Dracula turns to dust, and Mina is saved.

COMMENTARY Naturally, Hammer was thinking about remaking *Dracula* right after *Curse of Frankenstein's* record-breaking numbers at the box office. Actually, according to some sources, they were thinking about it before that, specifically in the latter half of 1956 as *Curse* was gearing up for production. However, unlike Mary Shelley's *Frankenstein*, Bram Stoker's *Dracula* would not be in the public domain until 1962 (constituting the 50th anniversary of Bram Stoker's death). As such, if Hammer wanted to make *Dracula*, they would have to negotiate with Universal. Horror fans should consider themselves lucky that Universal didn't try to remake *Dracula* themselves after *Curse's* success, and fortunately they played ball with Hammer, and eagerly at that as it turned out. The production was announced just a month after *Curse* was released to U.S. theaters in fact.

The budget was only slightly higher than it had been on *Curse* (£87,000 vs. £67,000) but the shooting schedule was about the same. It was a no-brainer to simply bring back the majority of the cast and crew that had made *Curse* a hit for Hammer. To that end, Terence Fisher returned to direct, Jack Asher did the cinematography, Bernard Robinson was again production designer, and James Bernard composed the score. Hammer also naturally wanted Peter Cushing and Christopher Lee to return, with the latter again playing the "monster". Lucky for Hammer, Lee was a looker underneath the makeup that transformed him into Frankenstein's monster. As such, his tall, dark good looks made him a shoe-in for the Count. All Lee needed in this case was fangs and contact lenses to turn his eyes bloodshot. However, even though Lee played the title character, Cushing still got top billing. As such, even though Van Helsing took a backseat to Harker in most adaptations, with Cushing in the role, Van Helsing became the focus in Hammer's version. In fact, Cushing more than anyone else popularized the character of Van Helsing. Before Cushing portrayed the character, no studio would have ever considered headlining a film with Van Helsing. (Case in point, Universal followed their popular Mummy movies of the early 2000s not with Dracula or Frankenstein remakes, but a movie called *Van Helsing* in 2004.)

Whereas Hammer's Frankenstein picture had been titled *Curse of Frankenstein*, as a remake this picture could simply be called *Dracula* (though it would be retitled *Horror of Dracula* in the U.S.). That said, the film doesn't stick to either the book or Universal's adaptations too closely. Most notably, there are no scenes set in London. The main reason that no portion of the film takes place

165

in England was because Hammer would have had to feature a boat scene, which was too costly, and so the action all stayed within riding distance of Dracula's castle (even if it was a long ride). Dracula wasn't given the ability to transform into a bat because that would also cost too much. The choice would stick, and though Dracula would command bats in *Scars of Dracula*, he would never turn into one in Hammer's films. Lastly, the character of Renfield was removed not for budgetary reasons, but simply because he didn't fit into Sangster's version of the story.

Fisher's direction works incredibly well with James Bernard's score (that was another plus this Dracula had over the 1930 version, which was unscored). The key scene for many was Dracula's arrival outside of Lucy's bedroom. The young girl seems excited for the Count's arrival, and Bernard's music in tandem with Fisher's direction heralds his entrance wonderfully. And in this version, when Dracula bites his victims, audiences actually got to seem them bleed. It wasn't just the added blood, color, and sex appeal that made this movie attractive to audiences, it was a heck of a lot more lively than the 1930 *Dracula*. Just compare the two endings. In the original, Dracula hides in his coffin and gets staked off-screen; there's no struggle or suspense whatsoever. Here Dracula nearly overpowers Van Helsing until the last second (reportedly people in the audience were screaming like mad at this point). Then Van Helsing performs a Douglas Fairbanks-like run across a large banquet table to bring down the curtains and expose Dracula to sunlight. And on that note, Cushing's famous dash across the table and pulling down of the curtains was his idea, as was Van Helsing making a makeshift crucifix out of two candlesticks (originally Van Helsing had a spare in his pocket).

Upon release in the spring of 1958, the film was an even bigger hit than *Curse*, even though critics still hated it. Christopher Lee even claims that the current Universal head told him that it saved the company from bankruptcy!

FINAL WORD For many, this is considered the best Hammer film ever made. While that's debatable, it certainly is their seminal film that cemented them as a studio to be reckoned with.

REVENGE OF FRANKENSTEIN

(HAMMER/COLUMBIA)
Release Date: June 1, 1958 (U.S.) August 27, 1958 (U.K.)
Alternate Titles: *Blood of Frankenstein* (working title)

Directed by: Terence Fisher **Screenplay by:** Jimmy Sangster (with additional dialogue by Hurford Janes) **Makeup by:** Philip Leakey **Music by:** Leonard Salzedo **Cast:** Peter Cushing (Dr. Victor Stein/Frankenstein) Francis Matthews (Dr. Hans Kleve) Eunice Gayson (Margaret) Oscar Quitak (Karl, the dwarf) Michael Gwynn (Karl in his new body) John Welsh (Bergman) Lionel Jeffries (Fritz)

Spherical, Technicolor, 90 Minutes

SYNOPSIS Before being taken to be executed, Baron Frankenstein makes a deal with his jailer, a hunchback named Karl. The Baron promises to give him a new body if he will help him fake his death, and so he does. Three years later, the Baron runs a successful practice in Carlsbrück as Dr. Stein. He also operates a hospital for the poor, though he really uses it to harvest body parts. Using the body parts of the homeless, he has constructed a near perfect new body for Karl to inhabit. The Baron is aided by a young admirer who recognized him from some years past, named Hans Kleve. Together the Baron and Hans transplant Karl's brain into a new body. However, an antsy Karl escapes the hospital when he becomes afraid of being exploited by the Baron. He gets into a fight which causes brain trauma. The body begins to reject the brain, and Karl becomes a malformed cannibal. Eventually he drops dead, but not before outing Dr. Stein as Baron Frankenstein. Back at his charity hospital, the Baron's patients turn on him and beat him until he is mortally wounded. The Baron is saved by Karl, who transplants the Baron's brain into a backup body, identical to his own, that he constructed some time ago.

COMMENTARY With *Curse of Frankenstein* proving to be a monumental hit for Hammer, it should come as no surprise that Hammer quickly produced a sequel. James Carreras managed to sell the film (based on a poster with the title of *Blood of Frankenstein*) to Columbia before any type of script had even been written. Carreras then asked Jimmy Sangster how fast he could write a script, as Carreras had already promised the distributer the film by a certain date! Sangster was then faced with something of a problem. Though we never saw the blade drop from the gallows in the last movie, that was where the Baron was headed. How would he get out of his predicament? At first, someone joked that they would simply sew the Baron's head back on. But then Sangster came up with the macabre, not to mention ingenious, idea of having the Baron escape by substituting him with the priest we saw in the last outing! As we eventually learn in the film, the Baron made a deal with his hunchbacked jailer, promising him a new body if he saved him from the guillotine.

The film has two great opening teasers in a way. The first is the Baron being marched off to the guillotine, as we the audience wonder just how he's going to escape. Before the critical moment, the camera focuses on the top of the guillotine only. We hear a sudden scuffle below, and then it drops. The next teaser has two grave robbers going out to dig up the Baron's grave (notably, one is played by Michael Ripper in his first of many bit parts for Hammer). The men dig up the grave and are shocked to find a headless priest in the casket. One of the men runs off, and the other stays behind. A moment later, Baron Frankenstein appears before him. The man has a heart attack and falls backward into the casket. (In my opinion, that might have been the more interesting pre-credits sequence, letting us wonder just how the Baron escaped, and then revealing that later when the Baron explains it all to Hans, his pupil.)

Unlike the next sequel, *Evil of Frankenstein*, which regurgitated the basic Frankenstein monster story, *Revenge of Frankenstein* does something wholly original: we see Frankenstein succeed at his experiments... at least for a while. And not only does he succeed in his work, he's also the most popular doctor in his new town under the alias of Dr. Stein. (Case in point is a humorous scene where a rich Countess tries to marry off her daughter to the doctor.) To top it off, Dr. Stein even runs a charity hospital for the poor. However, the die-hard Frankenstein fans will begin to put two and two together right away when they see that there's a high number of amputee patients in his ward. It's all rather horrific,

168

with the Baron telling various patients that this or that limb needs to be amputated when there's nothing wrong with it. As evidenced by the Baron's amputating a pickpocket's arm (they have sensitive fingers), he's literally picking and choosing the best body parts from the homeless population. The reason why he chooses the pickpocket's arm comes into play in a very clever way at the film's end.

As stated earlier, this film is also interesting for the reason that the Baron is successful in his experiment to create a perfect man, or at least perfect in the sense that it's not a malformed monster like the last one. The Baron's artificial brain in his laboratory is also quite interesting. The good doctor has rigged two tanks to some sort of electric brain he's made. One tank houses a pair of eyes, the other an arm. Through the electrical wires connected to both, they are able to move under their own power. It's all rather amusing as the eyes watch the Baron bring a flame close to the arm, which then begins trying to retract itself.

Creature-wise, the climax isn't terribly exciting. Karl, in his mangled cannibalistic form, breaks into an in-home concert at a wealthy countess's house. He doesn't attack anyone, just stumbles around and identifies Dr. Stein as Frankenstein before he drops dead. But, the twist ending that follows is one of Hammer's best. Now aware of his real identity, Frankenstein's patients at the "charity hospital" attack him and beat him until he becomes mortally wounded. It is then up to Hans to transport the Baron's brain into a backup body that he constructed for just such an occasion! This backup body looks just like the Baron and notably has the arm of the pickpocket, the sensitive fingers of which could be quite useful to a surgeon. The film ends with the Baron, now under the name of Dr. Franck, practicing in London.

Even though the film didn't feature a true monster, it still managed to be a sizeable hit upon release and pleased Hammer's production partner, Columbia.

FINAL WORD Easily the least "typical" Frankenstein movie in the Hammer pantheon alongside *Frankenstein Created Woman*, many Hammer critics consider this to be Jimmy Sangster's best script.

FRANKENSTEIN 1970

(AUBREY SCHENCK PRODUCTIONS)
Release Date: July 20, 1958 (U.S.)
Alternate Titles: *Castle of Frankenstein* (Latin America)
Frankenstein vs. the Invisible Man (France) *Frankenstein Takes
Revenge* (Sweden) *The Doctor Who Made a Monster* (Turkey)

Directed by: Howard W. Koch **Screenplay by:** Richard H. Landau,
George Worthing Yates, Charles A. Moses (story) & Aubrey
Schenck (story) **Makeup by:** Gordon Bau **Music by:** Paul Dunlap
Cast: Boris Karloff (Baron Victor von Frankenstein) Tom Duggan
(Mike Shaw) Jana Lund (Carolyn Hayes) Donald Barry (Douglas
Row) Charlotte Austin (Judy Stevens) Irwin Berke (Inspector Raab)
Rudolph Anders (Wilhelm Gottfried) Norbert Schiller (Schutter)
John Dennis (Morgan Haley) Mike Lane (Hans Himmler/The
Monster)

CinemaScope, Black & White, 83 Minutes

SYNOPSIS Due to disfigurement suffered at the hands of the Nazis
in WWII, plus the fact that he has no heirs, the grandson of the
original Baron Victor Frankenstein wishes to create a being in his
own likeness. To do so, the Baron needs a nuclear reactor. To fund
his secret experiment, the Baron allows a television film crew to
shoot a made-for-TV movie at his castle. In secret, the Baron
resurrects his grandfather's old monster to fulfill his experiment.
The unruly monster then begins killing off members of the TV
crew. In the end, a radiation leak kills the Baron and his monster.
Investigators unmask the creature to reveal that the Baron had
grafted the likeness of his own face before it was so badly scarred
onto the creature.

COMMENTARY Only a little over a year before this picture came
into being, Hammer was contemplating a black and white chiller
to star Boris Karloff as the Baron rather than the creature in what
was called *Frankenstein and the Monster*. This project was
bypassed in favor of *Curse of Frankenstein*, the success of which
ironically helped to inspire this black and white chiller starring
Boris Karloff as the Baron. The other influences behind the film

170

included *I Was a Teenage Frankenstein* (1957) and the success of Universal horror films released to television as part of the "Shock Theatre" package. The film was shot over the course of eight days on the set previously utilized in that same year's *Too Much, Too Soon*.

Based on the title, one might be forgiven for thinking this is something along the lines of *Dracula A.D. 1972*, which came out the year it was set. This film, however, takes place in 1958's conception of what 1970 might be like, which is really no different from 1958 aside from some futuristic technology, so it might as well have been called *Frankenstein 1960*. From the opening credits, set against a swampy background, you could be forgiven for mistaking this for a Universal film. Immediately following this the film gives the audience what it wants right away. With no explanation (but perhaps one really isn't needed), a shuffling monster chases a girl through foggy swampland. We never see its face, but it's certainly Frankenstein-like in its movements. It does differentiate itself a little by shuffling low to the ground like an ape and it has long fingernails. In what turns out to be a pretty suspenseful scene, it chases the poor woman into the swamp and then drowns her. But then something refreshing happens. A director yells cut, and it all turns out to be a movie within a movie. Though not original by today's standards, in the late 1950s this was probably one of the first horror movies to fake out the audience.

Since this movie hinges upon a real film crew shooting a movie in the "real" Castle Frankenstein, this plotline predates the better known *Halloween Resurrection* (2002), where a film crew spends a night in Michael Myer's old house. And like that film, *Frankenstein 1970* is a semi-spoof of the genre at times, while at other inopportune times, it takes itself seriously when it really shouldn't. The monster as it first appears is good enough for monster kids of the time, as it's a large, bandaged body topped off by a skeletal head. After the operation, it spends a good deal of the picture with its now oversized head wrapped in bandages. It's positively goofy looking as it resembles a man with a bucket on his head wrapped in bandages. It's a bit similar to *I Was a Teenage Frankenstein* except for that film at least did a better job! It does at least get a good scene where, as one of the filmmakers is doing a 360-camera shot alone beneath the castle, the monster suddenly comes into frame. The monster's face isn't revealed until after it's dead—due to a very unexciting ending where it's exposed to too much radiation. As it turns out, the monster's face is that of

171

Frankenstein's, who wanted the creature to continue his legacy since he was the last of the family line. Though it's a decent little twist, it's not enough to save the film from a lackluster finale. Warner Bros was supposed to distribute the film, but not surprisingly passed upon seeing it for the first time. Instead, Allied Artists purchased the rights for $250,000.

FINAL WORD If you're a fan of bad movies or are simply a Frankenstein completest, this film might be worth your time, but otherwise steer clear.

THE
NEW INVISIBLE MAN

(AZTECA FILMS)
Release Date: November 28, 1958 (Mexico)
Alternate Titles: *Invisible Man in Mexico* (U.K.)
The Case of the Invisible Man (Brazil)

Directed by: Alfredo B. Crevenna **Screenplay by:** Julio Alejandro,
Alfredo B. Crevenna & Alfredo Salazar (story) **Special Effects by:**
León Ortega, Jorge Benavides & Raúl Martínez Solares **Music by:**
Antonio Díaz Conde **Cast:** Arturo de Córdova (Carlos/Charles Hill)
Ana Luisa Peluffo (Beatriz Cifuentes/Beatrice Forsythe) Raúl
Meraz (Comandante Flores/Police Chief Charles Ford) Augusto
Benedico (Luis/Lewis Hall) Néstor de Barbosa (José Suárez/John
Hayes) Jorge Mondragón (Don Ramón Cifuentes/Mr. Forsyth)

Academy Ratio, Black & White, 96 Minutes

SYNOPSIS When Carlos walks in on a man being murdered in his
company office, the crime is pinned on him by his boss, Don
Ramon (who also happens to be the father of Carlos's fiancé,
Beatriz). Carlos's brother, Luis, is working on an invisibility
serum, and injects Carlos with it in prison, enabling him to escape.
Carlos then reunites with Beatriz and begins an investigation to
learn why he was framed. Snooping at the office, he witnesses
another murder committed by José Suárez (the unseen assailant
that murdered the first man). Eventually, Carlos learns that Jose
and Don Ramon are in cahoots, and Carlos forces Jose to write a
confession letter. Ultimately Jose and Don Ramon kill each other
in a struggle, and thus that problem has been solved. However,
the invisibility serum has slowly been driving Carlos insane, and
he develops an overinflated sense of justice, claiming to be a
messenger from God. Carlos feels it is his mission to rid the world
of all the horrid people that inhabit it. To do so, he plans to poison
the city water supply. Beatriz informs the police, who swarm the
area on high alert. Luis is killed in the crossfire when Carlos is
sighted holding a poisonous vile. Carlos, too, is shot,
apprehended, and taken to the hospital, where he regains his
visibility and his sanity.

COMMENTARY This Mexican version of *The Invisible Man* is half-remake of *The Invisible Man Returns* (1940) and half-adaptation of *The Murderer Invisible*, the novel which also helped to shape Universal's *The Invisible Man* (1933). Essentially, Acts I and II tell the story of *Returns*, while Act III turns into an adaptation of *Murderer Invisible*. *New Invisible Man* apes *Return* in the sense that it has the exact same story with a wrongly accused man using an invisibility formula to clear his name. Unlike *Returns*, where the backstory was told to us via exposition, *New Invisible Man* actually lets us see the crime committed and meet our main character before he turns invisible. (*Return* is almost confusing by comparison, as we hear all about Vincent Price's character and his alleged crime before we ever see him, invisible or otherwise.)

The most famous scene from *Returns*, where the Invisible Man evades the police in a gas-filled home, is recreated in this film as well. As in *Returns*, when the police gas the house to make Carlos visible, he hijacks one of their uniforms to escape with Beatriz. The scene offers one innovation over the original: before all this happens, the villain uses a whip to ensnare Carlos by the neck. Another interesting bit unique to this film takes place on a bus, where a young pickpocket tries to steal something from a woman's purse. Once he withdraws the item, his hand suddenly seizes, and the Invisible Man's hand forces him to return it. The thief then gets down on his knees and begs the Virgin Mother for forgiveness. Like *Invisible Agent* and Toho's *Invisible Avenger*, this film features a fairly impressive scene of the invisible man applying makeup to make himself visible. (Perhaps the producers were afraid that Universal's design with the bandages was trademarked as that look is never used in this film.)

As stated before, this story follows *Returns* up to the point that the real killers are dealt with at the end of Act II, after which Carlos goes from hero to villain. He even threatens to take over the world with his newfound power! After he hijacks a radio signal to inform the populace of this, people begin running in the streets as though Godzilla were on the loose! The ending, set at a water facility Carlos plans to poison, fails rather clumsy. While we know that Carlos lost his mind due to the serum, he's still become a much more unlikable character than Vincent Price's character in *Returns*. The film would have been better served in giving him a tragic death as a sympathetic figure. Instead, Carlos's brother Luis is shot and killed by accident. After Carlos is shot and apprehended by the police, the late Luis's cure works, making him visible. We end with Carlos being carted off to surgery with a loving

Beatriz at his side. But after all the trouble he's caused isn't he going to go to prison? Is it really a happy ending? Of that we are uncertain.

It's unknown how big of a success this film was in Mexico, but it did manage to secure an English language dub and make its way to the States in 1959. The character names were notably anglicized as well (see the cast listing in front matter). It's unknown if the U.S. version was simply dubbed or altered further, but the film has one of those stock music soundtracks in the U.S. version where the same music seemingly plays on a loop. Though you'd think the film would be more obscure, it can be found online easily and even on DVD.

FINAL WORD For Invisible Man completists only.

CURSE OF THE UNDEAD

(UNIVERSAL)
Release Date: May 1959 (U.S.)
Alternate Titles: *Diabolic Rage* (Brazil) *In the Clutches of the Vampire* (France) *Affairs of a Vampire* (working title)

Directed by: Edward Dein **Screenplay by:** Edward & Mildred Dein **Makeup by:** Bud Westmore **Music by:** Irving Gertz **Cast:** Eric Fleming (Preacher Dan) Michael Pate (Drake Robey) Kathleen Crowley (Dolores Carter) John Hoyt (Dr. Carter) Bruce Gordon (Buffer) Edward Binns (the Sheriff) Jimmy Murphy (Tim Carter) Helen Kleeb (Dora)

Academy Ratio, Black & White, 79 Minutes

SYNOPSIS At the same time that women in their town are suffering from a strange blood disease, the Carter family is in the middle of a feud over water rights with their neighbor, Buffer. When Doc Carter, the family patriarch, is killed mysteriously, his children, Dolores and Tim, think Buffer is to blame. Soon after, Tim is killed in a duel with Buffer, who claims that he didn't kill Doc. A black-clad gunman by the name of Drake Robey wanders into town and offers to kill Buffer for Dolores. This doesn't sit well with Dolores's beau, preacher Dan Young, who thinks there's something nefarious about Drake. He's right, and Drake turns out to be an undead vampire on the prowl. Eventually, Dan shoots Drake through the heart with a special bullet containing a tiny crucifix.

COMMENTARY Perhaps not surprisingly for some, this vampire western started out in the form of a joke. Husband and wife writer team Edward & Mildred Dein came up with the idea of a vampire in the Old West while sitting around their swimming pool. When the duo handed out their script to a friend as a joke, they took the concept seriously and got it picked up for production by Universal.

As the first vampire western, *Curse of the Undead* has a lot to live up to, which might determine just how well one likes the film. For example, a lot of people's expectations for this picture might have been fairly high if they loved Westerns and horror films. For those people, the film was probably a letdown. By contrast, the people who really enjoyed *Curse of the Undead* might have been those who stumbled across it on television and missed the opening title credits. If one were to miss the first few minutes of the movie, they might think that what they are witnessing is just a run-of-the-mill Western. (The film was shot on the same Universal Western town set as a million others and would blend right in with them.) The Western aspect of the plot is a typical one, with two competing landowners fighting over water rights. Then, imagine viewers' surprise when one of the main characters turns out to be a vampire! With their expectations shocked instead of subverted, I have a feeling those were the people who could have enjoyed *Curse of the Undead* the most. But, as it stands, those who go into the film expecting a bang-up "cowboys vs. vampires" movie might be disappointed.

Curse of the Undead does deserve a few points for deviating from common vampire mythology. Here, the writers chose to base their mythology on European folklore rather than past films. Drago, the vampire, can walk in the sunlight, and his bite doesn't turn the living (or the dead) into other vampires. Furthermore, Drago turned into a vampire as punishment for committing suicide after murdering his brother for putting the moves on his fiancé. (This flashback makes for one of the movie's better scenes.) And, as was typical with non-Hammer vampires of the time, Drago never shows his fangs.

The end duel is also interesting for two reasons. First, it's been established that Drago isn't quick on the draw at all. He's so overconfident in his immortality and immunity to normal bullets that he usually shoots after he's been shot to the shock of those astute enough to notice. As such, Drago isn't concerned when the hero wants to engage in a pistol duel with him at the film's end. What Drago doesn't know is that the hero has placed a cross on his bullet. And not just any cross, but one carved from a thorn found near the site of Christ's crucifixion. Sadly, this ending still isn't enough to make up for the rather boring earlier portion of the film. Despite there being no horror westerns to follow for many years, the film was quite profitable, thanks in part to its low budget but also due to its novel concept.

FINAL WORD For vampire and/or Western fans only.

THE MUMMY

(HAMMER)
Release Date: September 25, 1959 (U.K.)
December 16, 1959 (U.S.)
Alternate Titles: *The Curse of the Pharaohs* (France) *Revenge of the Mummy* (Finland) *Revenge of the Pharaohs* (Germany) *Mummy Ghost* (Japan) *Terror of the Mummy* (working title)

Directed by: Terence Fisher **Screenplay by:** Jimmy Sangster
Special Effects by: Les Bowie & Roy Ashton (makeup) **Music by:**
Franz Reizenstein **Cast:** Peter Cushing (John Banning)
Christopher Lee (Kharis/The Mummy) Yvonne Fumeaux (Isobel
Banning/Ananka) Felix Aylmer (Stephen Banning) Raymond
Huntley (Joseph Whemple) Eddie Byrne (Inspector Mulrooney)
George Pastell (Mehemet Bey)

Spherical, Eastmancolor, 86 Minutes

SYNOPSIS While on a dig in Egypt, father and son duo Stephen
and John Banning discover the lost tomb of Ananka. In the
process, Stephen, alone in the tomb, revives the mummy Kharis
and goes mad. John and his colleague Joseph Whemple finish up
the dig and have Ananka shipped to England. There, three years
later, a high priest of Karnak, Mehemet Bey, comes with the body
of Kharis to enact revenge on the expedition's leaders. Stephen, in
an asylum, is killed first, and then Whemple. John is saved from
Kharis by his wife Isobel, who looks exactly like Ananka. When she
asks Kharis to leave, he obeys. John suspects that an Egyptian
man—Mehemet Bey—who has moved in down the road is
connected and pays him a visit, which confirms John's suspicions.
Kharis returns to terrorize John, and Isobel again impersonates
Ananka to save her husband. Kharis picks up Isobel and carries
her away after killing Bey. John and the police chase the mummy
into the swamp, where he puts Isobel down at her request. When
Isobel is safe, the police all fire on Kharis, who sinks into the
swamp.

COMMENTARY After the success of *Horror of Dracula*, which was not produced as a straight remake of 1930's *Dracula*, Universal then turned around and wanted Hammer to remake their old classics. As such, Hammer would "remake" *The Mummy* (and later *Phantom of the Opera*). *The Mummy* was the one property that Hammer needed Universal's permission on more so than others, as the Mummy, specifically Kharis and Imhotep, were Universal creations based upon no classic literary sources. To bone up for the remake, Jimmy Sangster watched several of Universal's Mummy films (though in interviews, he claims it was only one!).

All that said, Hammer's version of *The Mummy* is by no means a remake of the film of the same name from 1932. Instead, it is an amalgamation of all of Universal's Mummy films. If what Sangster said about watching only one of the Mummy movies was true, then it was probably *The Mummy's Tomb*, which featured an elderly Steve Banning, his son John, and fiancé Isobel. Banning had originated as a young man (sans his son) in *The Mummy's Hand*, which took place entirely in Egypt. Hammer's *Mummy* opens in Egypt like *Hand*, with the elder Stephen Banning and his son John both present to uncover the tomb of Ananka. While Stephen is in the tomb, Hammer tips their hat for the first and only time to the 1932 *Mummy*. In the scene, Stephen reads from the Scroll of Life and awakens Kharis, who frightens Banning so badly that he goes insane, just like the famous scene from *The Mummy* with Bramwell Fletcher.

It was in *Tomb* that the Mummy came to America years later to kill the Bannings, but here the Mummy comes to England three years later to do so. As in *Tomb*, Stephen Banning is the first to die in a terrifying scene where Kharis corners him in a padded cell in an asylum. In the place of Babe (the comic relief character from *Hand* and *Tomb*) is Joseph Whemple, a character from the 1932 *Mummy*, who is the second to die. But, before this happens, in the long-running tradition of the Mummy films, John narrates a lengthy flashback detailing the history of Kharis and Ananka (though the footage is all new in this case, of course, unlike the old Universal sequels that repeated footage from *The Mummy* ad nauseam). As for the female lead of Isobel, in *Tomb* it was the High Priest of Karnak who had the hots for her, but in this film it's Kharis himself, as Isobel greatly resembles Ananka. So, in this way the film also acknowledges the major storyline from *The Mummy* and *The Mummy's Ghost*, though Isobel is never passed off as Ananka's reincarnation. The climax of *Ghost*, wherein Kharis carries Isobel into a swamp is recreated more excitingly here in

Hammer's version. In this case, Isobel is spared being dragged into the swamp's depths by Kharis, who is shot repeatedly by the police.

Having established a winning team in Peter Cushing as the monster slayer and Christopher Lee as the monster, the duo were reteamed again for this film. (His star having risen since *Horror of Dracula*, Lee is even credited alongside Cushing and female lead Yvonne Fumeaux in the opening titles.) Lee makes for one of the better mummies on film and possibly bests Lon Chaney's version. If you'll recall, Boris Karloff's "Mummy" Imhotep was always out of his bandages and Chaney Jr.'s Mummy was more of a shuffling caricature rather than a full-blown character. Lee's Mummy at least emotes a great deal of expression from his eyes, giving Kharis a pleading look when he sees Isobel for the first time. Lee's Mummy is also quite a bit quicker than Chaney's plodding Mummy. Lee's Kharis stands a good chance of actually catching his victims, rather than relying on their obliviousness to sneak up on them. The battle between John Banning and the Mummy is every bit as exciting as Van Helsing's fight with Dracula. In fact, it's quite possibly the most exciting fight Lee and Cushing ever shared, with Banning shooting the Mummy at close range with a rifle twice, blowing out dusty chunks of his torso in the process. Once again on the ball whereas choreography was concerned, it was Cushing's idea to stab the Mummy with a spear. (Cushing was keen enough to observe that the Mummy on the poster had a hole in it through which a searchlight shined. He knew that audiences would be disappointed by the false advertising and suggested that he impale the Mummy.)

With a higher £125,000 budget, *The Mummy* is noticeably more lavish than the preceding two pictures (*Curse of Frankenstein* and *Horror*). It was shot over the course of eight weeks at Bray Studios from late February into mid-April in 1959. Though critics were, as usual, relatively unkind to the film when released later that year, audiences flocked to it. Remarkably, *The Mummy* outperformed even *Horror of Dracula* at the box office! Clearly, Hammer was here to stay.

FINAL WORD Though Hammer's Mummy sequels were never as successful as their Dracula and Frankenstein follow-ups, this first entry is still among Hammer's best horror films. It also ended up rounding out a swell trilogy by director Terence Fisher, Cushing and Lee representing the big three of Frankenstein, Dracula, and the Mummy.

CURSE OF FRANKENSTEIN

HORROR OF DRACULA

FRANKENSTEIN SPILLS IT..! DRACULA DRINKS IT!

IN THE SCREEN'S GREATEST DOUBLE CREATURE FEATURE!

A DOUBLE DOSE OF FULL COLOR THRILLS!

STARRING PETER CUSHING • HAZEL COURT
ROBERT URQUHART AND CHRISTOPHER LEE
Screen Play by JIMMY SANGSTER
Directed by TERENCE FISHER
Executive Producer MICHAEL CARRERAS

starring PETER CUSHING • MICHAEL GOUGH
and MELISSA STRIBLING
with CHRISTOPHER LEE as DRACULA
Screenplay by JIMMY SANGSTER
From the novel by BRAM STOKER
Directed by TERENCE FISHER
Executive producer MICHAEL CARRERAS
Associate producer ANTHONY NELSON-KEYS
Produced by ANTHONY HINDS

PRODUCED BY HAMMER FILMS • RELEASED BY SEVEN ARTS PICTURES

R64/371

181

182

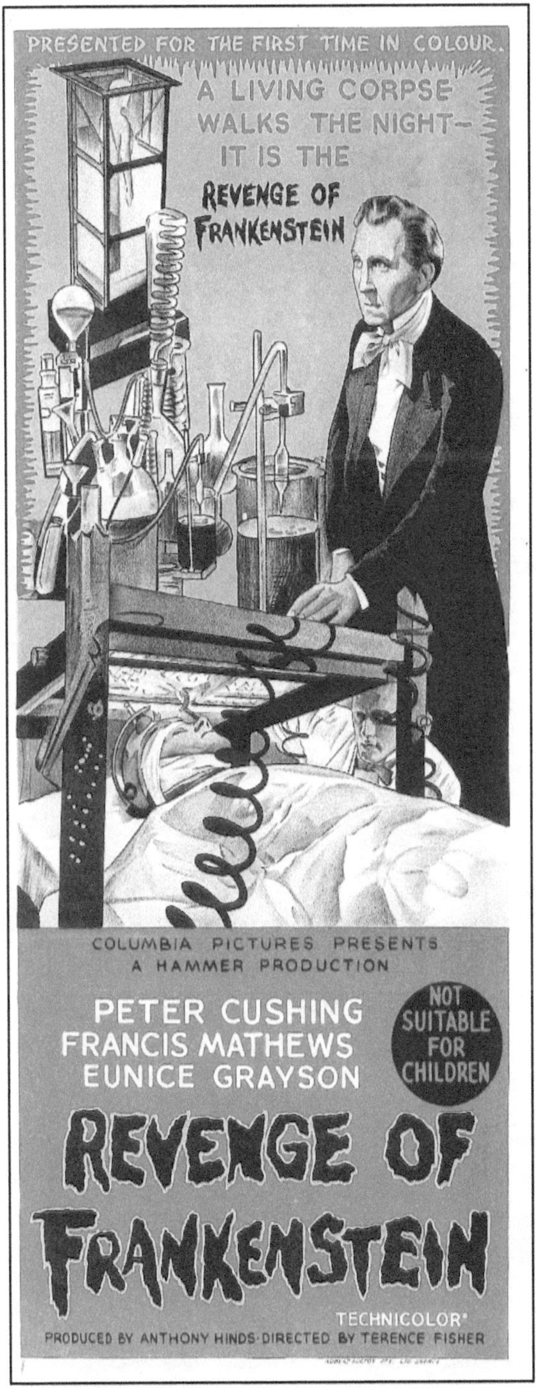
PRESENTED FOR THE FIRST TIME IN COLOUR.
A LIVING CORPSE WALKS THE NIGHT— IT IS THE
REVENGE OF FRANKENSTEIN
COLUMBIA PICTURES PRESENTS
A HAMMER PRODUCTION
PETER CUSHING
FRANCIS MATHEWS
EUNICE GRAYSON
NOT SUITABLE FOR CHILDREN
REVENGE OF FRANKENSTEIN
TECHNICOLOR®
PRODUCED BY ANTHONY HINDS · DIRECTED BY TERENCE FISHER

CURSE OF THE UNDEAD
ERIC FLEMING · KATHLEEN CROWLEY · MICHAEL PATE with JOHN HOYT · BRUCE GORDON

PEL MEX
presenta a
VIBRE USTED CON LA MAS EXTRAÑA Y VIOLENTA EMOCION...!
ARTURO DE CORDOVA
ANA LUISA PELUFFO en
EL HOMBRE QUE LOGRO SER INVISIBLE
ALFREDO B. CREVENNA

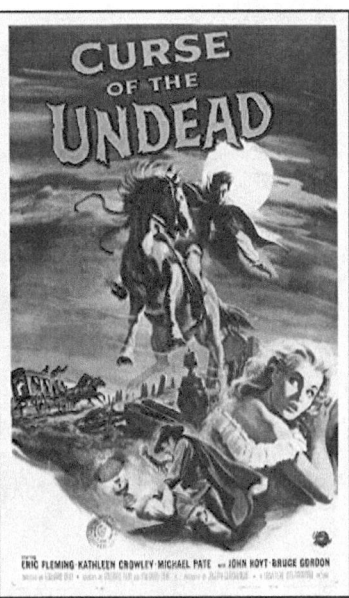

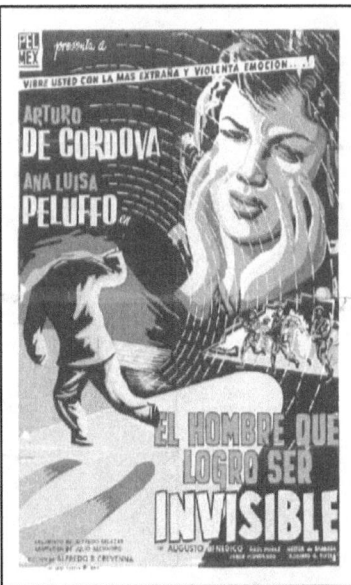

BRIDES OF DRACULA

(HAMMER)

Release Date: July 7, 1960 (U.K.) September 5, 1960 (U.S.)
Alternate Titles: *The Vampire Brides* (Brazil) *Exorcism of Dracula*
(Greece) *Dracula's Vampire Brides* (Japan)
Dracula - Bloodthirsty Vampire (Sweden)

Directed by: Terence Fisher **Screenplay by:** Jimmy Sangster,
Peter Bryan, Anthony Hinds (uncredited) & Edward Percy
(additional dialogue) **Special Effects by:** Sydney Pearson & Roy
Ashton (makeup) **Music by:** Malcolm Williamson **Cast:** Peter
Cushing (Professor Van Helsing) Yvonne Monlaur (Marianne)
David Peel (Baron Meinster) Martita Hunt (Baroness Meinster)
Freda Jackson (Greta) Miles Malleson (Doctor Tobler) Henry Oscar
(Herr Lang) Mona Washbourne (Frau Lang) Andrée Melly (Gina)

Spherical, Technicolor, 85 Minutes

SYNOPSIS On her way to teach at an all-girls finishing school,
Marianne becomes stranded in a small village not far from the
Chateau Meinster. Baroness Meinster arrives at the inn and
invites Marianne to stay the night at the Chateau. There Marianne
meets Baron Meinster, a prisoner of his cruel mother, or so he
claims. Feeling sorry for him, Marianne frees the Baron of his
chains and flees the castle. Marianne is found in the woods by
Professor Van Helsing, who agrees to take her to the school. At the
same time, mysterious killings occur in the village, which Van
Helsing recognizes as the work of a vampire. Eventually, he figures
out that it is Baron Meinster, who has vampirized his own mother,
who Van Helsing stakes and puts out of her misery. Meinster
proposes to Marianne, who is unaware of his true nature, and later
uses one of her vampirized colleagues from the school to bring her
to an old windmill. Van Helsing arrives to save Marianne and
vanquish the vampires, which he does by turning the sails of the
windmill into a gigantic cross which kills Meinster.

COMMENTARY Though this film was completed as a Dracula
spin-off starring Peter Cushing as Van Helsing, in its inception the
story featured Christopher Lee's Dracula returning without Van

Helsing. The original plot was similar to *Brides of Dracula* but was entitled *Disciple of Dracula* and featured a vampire hunter named Latour (a prototype of sorts to Professor Zimmer in *Kiss of the Vampire*). Latour rescues the Marianne character from Baron Meinster, but it is Dracula's ghost that does his disciple in! At the story's end, Latour summons the spirit of Dracula who appears and then sentences Meinster to death for violating the Code of the Undead. By the next draft, Dracula was gone, and Van Helsing had replaced Latour as a way to bring back Peter Cushing. Furthermore, this next draft ended with Van Helsing performing the occult ceremony from *Kiss of the Vampire* to destroy Meinster at the windmill. Cushing argued that Van Helsing would never use evil to defeat evil, and a new ending where good triumphs over evil—as opposed to evil triumphing over evil—was devised.

In this regard, Cushing and Christian director Terence Fisher were in perfect alignment. Fisher was happy to be off of the morally ambiguous *Two Faces of Dr. Jekyll* and back into black and white (morally speaking) territory with *Brides*. (Who knows, perhaps this film's extra emphasis on good vs. evil is thanks to the Jekyll film?) As it is, *Brides* is one of the more heavy good vs. evil films in the Hammer pantheon with many lines referencing the power of good over evil and God. And, whereas in some Hammer films the monster (the film's main draw) doesn't appear until halfway in, in this case it's our hero who doesn't arrive until around the halfway mark. In the absence of Dracula, Van Helsing himself was now the star attraction of the show, largely thanks to Cushing's star power. Usually the audience may be pining for the monster to show up, wondering what horrible deed it will perpetate next. But for many viewers in *Brides* it's the opposite, and we wonder what Van Helsing's got up his sleeve. Nowhere is this more evident than during the film's last minutes.

Though nearly every scene in *Brides* is wonderful, it's the ending portion that makes it a true classic—a term used a little too loosely on some films, but *Brides* deserves the distinction. As it was, topping the ending of *Horror of Dracula* was going to be a tall order. And as great as he was as Meinster, David Peel was no Christopher Lee. And yet, despite that, *Brides* just might top *Horror's* ending (depending on who you ask, of course). Allegedly, the scene to elicit the biggest scream in *Horror* was the one where Dracula almost bites Van Helsing. Imagine audiences' shock when, in this film, Meinster succeeds where Dracula failed. Viewers no doubt wondered if Van Helsing was going to be a goner after Meinster bites him, but being the ingenious character that he is, Van Helsing finds a way out. In a scene that will make anyone grimace, Van Helsing takes a branding iron to his neck to seal the wound, and then douses it with Holy Water, making him good as new again. And, for the *coup de grâce*, when Meinster is fleeing below the windmill, Van Helsing makes his famous jump onto the windmill sail, pulling it down to trap Meinster in its shadow. For some this may not be as exciting as watching Dracula burn to death in the sunlight, but you have to admit it is more clever and unique.

Despite all of its wonderful attributes, *Brides* is actually something of a divisive film among Hammer fans. Though a majority of fans consider it to be one of Hammer's best—and for some THE best—there are a few who consider it disjointed. The reason for this are lapses in logic that probably came about due to too many hasty script revisions. For instance, unlike Dracula, Meinster can turn into a bat. And, if Meinster can transform into a bat, why doesn't he do so to escape his chains in the castle? That is just one of a few lapses in logic that mars an otherwise near perfect film. (Fans who like to speculate and come up with their own backstories could suppose that perhaps it was some sort of enchanted anti-vampire chain that Meinster couldn't escape. But, even if that was the case, Greta could have undone if she really wanted to.) And, from a production standpoint, it was possible that Meinster transforms into a bat because bats had already been built for the original climax and Hammer didn't want them wasted? However, all that said, many other Hammer classics are guilty of similar conundrums.

The film was shot on a £120,000 budget in the early winter of 1960 (which therefore gives all the leafless trees a nice, dead look to match the fairytale setting). As the sequel to *Horror of Dracula*, it was perhaps more hotly anticipated than Hammer's first Frankenstein sequel. The film didn't disappoint at the box office and was reportedly even a bigger hit in America than it was in Britain.

FINAL WORD Whether you consider it the best Hammer film of all time or not, it's still certainly one of the best and quintessential Hammer.

187

THE TWO FACES OF DR. JEKYLL

(HAMMER)
Release Date: October 24, 1960 (U.K.) May 3, 1961 (U.S.)
Alternate Titles: *Stroke 12 in London* (Austria) *The Two-Face Monster* (Brazil) *House of Fright* (Canada) *The Dragon of London* (Greece) *The Monster of London* (Italy) *Jekyll's Inferno* (U.S.)

Directed by: Terence Fisher **Screenplay by:** Wolf Mankowitz **Makeup by:** Roy Ashton **Music by:** David Heneker, John Hollingsworth & Monty Norman **Cast:** Paul Massie (Dr. Henry Jekyll/Mr. Edward Hyde) Dawn Addams (Kitty Jekyll) Christopher Lee (Paul Allen) David Kossoff (Dr. Littauer) Francis de Wolff (the Inspector) Norma Marla (Maria)

MegaScope, Technicolor, 88 Minutes

SYNOPSIS Dr. Henry Jekyll has created a serum that allows him to unleash what he calls the "higher man." In Jekyll's case, it manifests as a younger, more suave version of himself that goes by the name of Mr. Hyde. While out at a London club, Hyde finds Jekyll's wife, Kitty, having an affair with Jekyll's friend, Paul Allen. Within a short span of time, Kitty turns down the advances of Jekyll and Hyde both, causing Hyde to become more and more depraved. Hyde arranges to have Allen killed, then rapes Kitty. Afterwards, Kitty commits suicide. A despondent Jekyll is unable to repress Hyde, who tries to frame Jekyll for murder and fake Jekyll's death. However, in the end, Jekyll manages to subdue Hyde once more, the transformation taking place in front of the police. Jekyll is then arrested for the crimes committed by he and Hyde.

COMMENTARY Though it wasn't a straight adaptation of Robert Louis Stevenson's novel, between 1959's *The Ugly Duckling* (a comedy) and 1971's gender-bending *Dr. Jekyll and Sister Hyde*, *Two Faces of Dr. Jekyll* was the closest that Hammer ever came to one. You can tell from the opening credits that this is going to be a very different type of Hammer horror flick. For starters, the music is a bit more upbeat (nor is it from James Bernard), and furthermore, the usual Hammer writers (Jimmy Sangster and Anthony Hinds) aren't listed at all. Written by Wolf Mankowitz, a writer outside of Hammer's usual stable, *Two Faces of Dr. Jekyll* presents more of a psychological thriller as opposed to a straight monster movie. This is evident fairly early on via two surprise twists.

When we are introduced to Dr. Jekyll, he is an older bearded man, married to the younger, attractive Kitty. Their first scene together has Kitty announcing an unwanted visitor in the form of Jekyll's friend, Paul Allen, who Kitty feels is taking advantage of Jekyll by always borrowing money from him. The big surprise comes when Kitty goes to see Paul and kisses him (the two are in the middle of an affair). The next big twist comes when Jekyll takes his serum. Instead of turning into a hairy, gnarled monster, he becomes a younger, better-looking, clean-shaven version of himself. Considering that Hammer had also made Dracula more attractive to women, it was an intriguing decision to do the same with Mr. Hyde. In a publicity release for Columbia, the film's distributor, Mankowitz said, "Evil is attractive to all men. Therefore it is not illogical that the face of evil should be attractive."

As it is, Jekyll, with his heavy beard and thick eyebrows, looks more like what audiences might expect Hyde to look like. Though undeniably interesting for the adult audience (which was what it was intended for), it no doubt disappointed "monster kids" who saw the film later. Though he's certainly diabolical, this version of Hyde doesn't even have superhuman strength. At one point he's even knocked out cold by a pimp. Nor does Hyde kill Paul himself, but locks him in a bathroom with a dangerous snake. Another interesting facet of this version of the tale is that each time he transforms into Hyde, when he reverts back to Jekyll, it has aged him similar to *The Picture of Dorian Gray.*

The film does well until the ending section when it begins to falter somewhat. For starters, two inspector characters suddenly come into the story, obviously there to push the picture along to its ending. (Had they appeared earlier or had a previous story function, they wouldn't seem shoehorned in.) From an action standpoint, the climax is pretty standard, with Hyde lighting Jekyll's lab on fire, a common staple of the old Universal films and Hammer alike. (This also gave way to the film's alternate release title in the U.S.: *Jekyll's Inferno.*) The very last scene, where Hyde reverts back to Jekyll in a police station is a tad underwhelming. Originally, rather than getting away with his scheme, Hyde was sentenced to the gallows. Right before he was to hang, in front of a crowd of onlookers, Jekyll would appear again to the crowd's shock. Jekyll would announce his triumph over his inner evil and then die. In this version, the film ends with Jekyll under arrest (in most versions of the story Jekyll always dies).

Another reason that the film didn't turn out as well as it could was that the script was ill-suited to Terence Fisher's more black and white depictions of good and evil. There aren't any sympathetic protagonists at all to be found in the picture, which was the screenwriter's intent. It might have been interesting to see how the film would've turned out with a different director, but as Fisher had proven himself on past horror remakes, Hammer wanted to stick with him. The film was a disappointment at the box office, in particular for Columbia. In fact, Columbia was so soured by the U.K. release, that in the U.S. they sold the film to American International for distribution. AIP retitled the film *Jekyll's Inferno*, and then later *House of Fright*. It wasn't a success there, either.

FINAL WORD Forgotten in the wake of Hammer's other, more unique take on the story in *Dr. Jekyll and Sister Hyde*, *Two Faces of Dr. Jekyll* will be of interest to Hammer historians and completists more so than typical horror fans.

CURSE OF THE WEREWOLF

(HAMMER)
Release Date: May 1, 1961 (U.K.) June 7, 1961 (U.S.)
Alternate Titles: *The Night of the Werewolf* (France; Brazil, reissue title) *Bloodsucking Wolfman* (Japan) *The Implacable Condemnation* (Italy) *The Curse of Siniestro* (West Germany)

Directed by: Terence Fisher **Screenplay by:** Anthony Hinds (as John Elder) based on the novel by Guy Endore **Special Effects by:** Roy Ashton (makeup) **Music by:** Benjamin Frankel **Cast:** Oliver Reed (Leon) Clifford Evans (Don Alfredo Carido) Yvonne Romain (jailer's daughter) Catherine Feller (Christina Fernando) Richard Wordsworth (Beggar) Anne Blake (Rosa Valiente) Warren Mitchell (Pepe Valiente) Anthony Dawson (Marquis Siniestro) Josephine Llewellyn (Marquesa Siniestro) George Woodbridge (Dominique) Justin Walters (Leon as a child) Hira Talfrev (Teresa)

Spherical, Technicolor, 93 Minutes

SYNOPSIS On the night of the Marquis's wedding celebration, a lonely beggar makes the mistake of crashing the event. Though initially the nobles delight in teasing the man, the Marquis has the beggar locked up for insulting him when he becomes drunk. Years pass, and a mute servant girl is locked in the cell with the beggar as punishment for denying the advances of the cruel Marquis. She is raped but manages to escape the castle. In a small village she is taken in by the kindly Don Alfredo and Teresa where she gives birth to a baby boy, Leon, and then dies. Alfredo and Teresa raise him as their son, but due to the traumatic circumstances of his conception, he becomes a werewolf. There is some hope for Leon when he grows up and falls in love with a girl named Christina, whose affections keeps the beast within at bay. However, Leon is eventually arrested for murders committed as a werewolf. He escapes jail, and his adoptive father must shoot and kill him with a silver bullet.

COMMENTARY This movie's genesis lies in an aborted co-production just as much as it does Guy Endore's 1933 novel, *The Werewolf of Paris*. The novel had been knocking around Hollywood since it was first published, though Universal passed it over (probably to avoid paying for the screen rights) to do their own original werewolf movie in the form of *Werewolf of London*. In 1961, Hammer obtained the rights to Endore's novel but relocated the story to Spain. They had planned to shoot the picture on the same sets as their Spanish-set *The Rape of Sabena*. The co-production was to be for Columbia, who disliked the idea of the Sabena picture as it was too far removed from Hammer's Gothic output. The Catholic League of Decency also objected to it, and so Hammer shelved that production and went on with the Werewolf film. With the £100,000 budget already stretched thin, Anthony Hinds decided to write the script himself rather than hire a screenwriter. And thus began the career of John Elder, Hinds's pen name, who would go on to script a bevy of Hammer horror films.

Among the similarities with the novel are mostly the main character's birth, which occurs on Christmas Day and is the result of a rape. Other than that, there's not much of *Werewolf of Paris* in the story. (This isn't surprising as the novel would be expensive to adapt as it's set against the backdrop of the Franco-Prussian War.) There are only two major werewolf scenes, and in the first you don't even see the full monster. The second transformation takes place within a jail cell shared with a terrified Michael Ripper. Though it really isn't terribly interesting when you stop to think about it—the werewolf just runs across various rooftops while the villagers chase him—the scene is still very well-staged. The final moments are much more exciting than those in any of Universal's werewolf films, though, which is something at least.

If anything, the film is widely remembered for being Oliver Reed's breakout role. Reed had recently impressed everyone at Hammer with his screen presence via a small role as a brawler in *Two Faces of Dr. Jekyll*. Actually, it was makeup man Roy Ashton who suggested Reed for the part. As it is, it takes a long time for Reed to come onscreen. The character of Leon isn't born until about thirty minutes in, and the adult Leon, played by Reed, doesn't make his appearance until the last forty minutes of the movie, less than half the runtime! And yet, despite this, Reed still dominates the movie as Leon. Though it's debatable whether his Leon character is more sympathetic than Lon Chaney Jr.'s Larry Talbot from *The Wolf Man*, Reed's character was younger and more relatable to the audience.

Curse of the Werewolf wasn't an outright flop as is sometimes claimed, it just didn't make a huge profit past recouping its production costs. Nor did it equal the heights of *Dracula* or *The Mummy*. As such, Hammer seemed to have no interest in any sequels or more werewolf movies, making this their lone foray into the genre.

FINAL WORD This film will always be remembered as Hammer's lone werewolf movie, but it's still much more than that and is one of the better werewolf movies in the entire genre.

THE PHANTOM OF THE OPERA

(HAMMER/UNIVERSAL)
Release Date: June 25, 1962 (U.K.) August 15, 1962 (U.S.)
Alternate Titles: *The Mystery of the Eerie Mask* (Germany)

Directed by: Terence Fisher **Screenplay by:** Anthony Hinds (as John Elder) based on the book by Gaston Leroux **Special Effects by:** Brian Johnson & Roy Ashton (makeup) **Music by:** Edwin Astley **Cast:** Herbert Lorn (Professor Petrie/The Phantom) Heather Sears (Christine Charles) Edward de Souza (Harry Hunter) Thorley Walters (Lattimer) Michael Gough (Lord Ambrose D'Arcy) Ian Wilson (Dwarf) Miles Malleson (Cabby) Harold Goodwin (Bill) Miriam Karlin (Charwoman) Martin Miller (Rossi) John Harvey (Sergeant Vickers) Renee Houston (Mrs. Tucker) Marne Maitland (Xavier)

Spherical, Eastmancolor, 85 Minutes

SYNOPSIS The London Opera is haunted by a string of mysterious murders during the run of an opera dedicated to Joan of Ark. Though it is said to be written by Lord Ambrose D'Arcy, it was actually composed by Professor Petrie, thought dead after a fire in a printing press. When a dead body turns up in the middle of a performance, the leading lady quits, necessitating that the play's producer, Harry Hunter, find a new starlet. He does so in the form of Christine Charles, who D'Arcy tries to seduce. When his efforts fail, he has her fired. Harry, romantically involved with Christine, quits, and begins an investigation that leads him to the truth of the play (that being that it was written by Petrie). Meanwhile, Christine is kidnapped by a dwarf and taken into the sewers, where she meets the mysterious Phantom, who turns out to be Petrie. It is his wish that Christine perform in his opera, and he gives her singing lessons. Harry eventually makes his way down to the sewer, where he is confronted by the murderous dwarf who committed the earlier killings. Harry overcomes the dwarf but doesn't kill him and enters the lair of the Phantom. He agrees to let him train Christine, and Harry overrides D'Arcy in getting Christine back into the lead of *Saint Joan*. The night of the

194

performance, the dwarf causes a chandelier to fall by accident. At the last moment, the Phantom pushes Christine out of the way and is killed.

COMMENTARY Of all Hammer's takes on properties once made popular by Universal, Hammer's version of the Phantom might be their weakest, though it's by no means bad. As a remake of the 1943 Universal *Phantom of the Opera* rather than a straight adaptation of the book, it naturally brings back many elements from the 1943 film. For instance, the Phantom in this version wasn't born deformed; he was scarred by etching acid during an incident at a printing press. And, like Claude Rains' sympathetic but still villainous Phantom, Hammer's version leans more towards the sympathetic as opposed to Lon Chaney's version. Actually, Hammer's version is nothing but sympathetic and claims no victims (to commit the murders, Hammer added in a dwarf character). And why exactly was Hammer's Phantom the kindest of the bunch?

This was done primarily because Cary Grant was supposed to play the Phantom, and if Grant was playing him, then he most certainly would not be a killer. By the time Grant left, it was too late to turn back and the story had to stay as it was. Though Christopher Lee would have been happy to play the Phantom (he said it would give him a chance to prove that he could sing) he was living in Switzerland at the time (for tax purposes). Therefore, Herbert Lom was cast instead. Lom was quite excited to play the part, and in his own words literally jumped at the chance, springing from his chair to call and accept right after he finished reading the story outline. Unlike Rains, who didn't want his face presented in the grotesque manner that Chaney's was, Lom apparently had no qualms. His Phantom not only has a blue-colored, scarred face, but hands to match. His mask is unique as well, as it has only one eye hole and no slit for the mouth at all. We only see the Phantom's face at the very end when he rips off his mask before saving Christine from a falling chandelier. (Why does he do this? That isn't exactly clear, but perhaps he can see better without it. That, and Hammer had yet to reveal his face and the audience would no doubt feel cheated if they didn't.)

If there's any major fault to be found in Hammer's take on the tale, it's that it's less grand than Universal's preceding adaptations. Those two films had the benefit of a huge soundstage (in fact, the same soundstage was used in both productions) to represent the Paris Opera House. Here, not only is the opera much smaller and less grand, it's not even in Paris! But, this was probably a wise move on Hammer's part, as they relocated to London, which would be easier for them to pull off. In fact, many of the stages and sets are recognizable from other Hammers (notably, the club is presumably the same one from *Two Faces of Dr. Jekyll*). As for one last detriment to Hammer's version, it lacked the novelty of their color remakes of *Dracula* and *The Mummy* since Universal had themselves already remade the Phantom in color. Still, the film had a larger than usual budget (a little over £170,000) for Hammer, and filming lasted around two months. Upon release, the film did better in America than it did in Britain, oddly enough.

FINAL WORD Though it may be the weakest of Hammer's "Classic Monsters" remakes, it's still a fine film in its own right.

KISS OF THE VAMPIRE

(UNIVERSAL)
Release Date: September 11, 1963 (U.S.)
January 26, 1964 (U.K.)
Alternate Titles: *The Mystery of the Castle* (Italy)
Kiss of Evil (U.S. TV title)

Directed by: Don Sharp **Screenplay by:** Anthony Hinds (as John Elder) **Special Effects by:** Les Bowie **Music by:** James Bernard **Cast:** Clifford Evans (Professor Zimmer) Edward de Souza (Gerald Harcourt) Jennifer Daniel (Marianne Harcourt) Noel Willman (Dr. Ravna) Barry Warren (Carl Ravna) Jacquie Wallis (Sabena Ravna) Noel Howlett (Father Xavier) Brian Oulton (Disciple) Peter Madden (Bruno) Isobel Black (Tanya) Vera Cook (Anna)

Spherical, Eastmancolor, 88 Minutes

SYNOPSIS When their motorcar breaks down on their honeymoon, Gerald and Marianne Harcourt find themselves stranded in a small village at the foot of a huge chateau. They take a room at the local inn and soon find themselves invited to the chateau by its owner, the enigmatic Dr. Ravna. Gerald and Marianne become quite taken with Ravna and his children, Carl and Sabena. Later they are invited to a costumed ball at the chateau, which turns out to be the gathering of a vampire sect, of which Ravna is the head. Gerald is drugged while Marianne is bitten by Ravna. The next day, as Gerald looks for Marianne, he is told that he came there alone, and that he has no wife! He is swiftly kicked out of the chateau, and when he returns to the inn, the innkeepers too allege that he had no wife. The only person who believes Gerald is Professor Zimmer, actually a vampire hunter out to avenge the death of his daughter. He helps Gerald to storm the chateau and rescue Marianne, who is under Ravna's spell. Zimmer then performs a ritual that summons a swarm of vampire bats from hell to destroy the vampires. With Ravna and his followers dead, his hold over Marianne disappears.

COMMENTARY In the early 1960s, Hammer still found itself unable to produce a sequel to *Horror of Dracula*, as Christopher

197

Lee was out of the country at the time. Nor could they do another Van Helsing spinoff since Peter Cushing was taking a sabbatical from Hammer. Though this film still began life as "Dracula III", it's unknown if Dracula was ever slated to appear. Furthermore, part of the intent of the film was to see if Hammer could come up with another star duo to mirror Lee and Cushing. As Clifford Evans had impressed in *Curse of the Werewolf*, it was decided to cast him as the vampire hunter, Professor Zimmer, and Noel Willman as the vampire, Dr. Ravna.

As it is, the new characters are fantastic. Zimmer presents a morally ambiguous vampire hunter compared to Van Helsing, one who is a borderline alcoholic and not above using the dark arts to combat evil. (Evans is so good in the part it's hard to even recognize him from *Curse of the Werewolf!*) Dr. Ravna is almost more Dracula than Dracula. Though the Count is often referred to as the King of the Vampires, this title seems more appropriate to Ravna, who has hordes of vampire subjects. Literally, this film features more vampires than any other Hammer film in the form of Ravna's sect of followers. On that note, the dance of the vampires in this film went on to become one of its best remembered scenes, and was notably spoofed in Roman Polanksi's *The Fearless Vampire Killers* in 1967.

While the dance of the undead is great, and original to *Kiss of the Vampire*, it should be noted that the best bits of what began as "Dracula III" came from a discarded draft of "Dracula II" (or *Brides of Dracula*). The early version of *Brides* would have begun with a man staking a recently buried woman through the heart with a shovel and would have ended with a swarm of bats destroying the vampires. This film used that opening to even better effect, with the man doing the staking turning out to be the vampire's bereaved father. Overall it makes for what just might be Hammer's best pre-credits scene ever. The ending of *Kiss*, where vampire bats swarm Ravna's chateau, came from the original ending of *Brides* where Van Helsing performed the ceremony that summoned the bats. However, Cushing correctly argued that Van Helsing wouldn't use evil to destroy evil and so it was dropped. In *Kiss*, the scene is pulled off surprisingly well, with a mix of animated bats and marionettes on wires swooping in to kill the vampires.

Kiss has a few other interesting callbacks to *Brides*. Like Van Helsing, bitten on the neck in *Brides*, Zimmer is bitten on the hand. Rather than using Holy Water and a branding iron, Zimmer douses his hand in alcohol and holds it over an open flame. There's also a scene where a vampire woman comes to check on the vampire that got staked in the pre-credit scene. Not realizing what has happened to her friend, she begins to dig through the grave, asking why she hasn't emerged yet. It's a bit like the vampire birth scene in *Brides*. The story structure, stranded travelers at the mercy of the vampires and a vampire hunter, is similar to *Brides* and is also an antecedent to *Dracula – Prince of Darkness*, where two couples are stranded as opposed to one. It could also be argued that Gerald and Mariane from this film are a bit more loveable than Charles and Diana in *Prince of Darkness*, so *Kiss* wins on that front.

Kiss of the Vampire was shot in the fall of 1962 but wasn't released until nearly a year later in the U.S. where it was another hit for Hammer. (The reason for the long delay was Universal's fear of the film's climax being compared to 1963's *The Birds*!) However, despite Hammer's hopes of establishing a new star duo in the form of Evans and Willman, they never resurrected Ravna or Zimmer. Soon, Cushing and Lee would both return to Hammer, and there was no need for replacement vampires and vampire hunters.

FINAL WORD It's tough to say which of Hammer's vampire films not featuring Lee or Cushing are its best, but this one is definitely a contender.

THE EVIL OF FRANKENSTEIN

(HAMMER/UNIVERSAL)
Release Date: May 8, 1964 (U.S.) May 31, 1964 (U.K.)
Alternate Titles: *Frankenstein's Punishment* (Argentina/Mexico)
Frankenstein's Monster (Brazil/Germany/Sweden) *The Mark of
Frankenstein* (Canada/France) *Frankenstein and the Human
Beast* (Denmark) *Frankenstein's Revenge* (Greece) *The Revolt of
Frankenstein* (Italy) *Wrath of Frankenstein* (Japan)
Frankenstein is Coming (Turkey)

Directed by: Freddie Francis **Screenplay by:** Anthony Hinds (as
John Elder) based on a story by Peter Bryan **Special Effects by:**
Les Bowie & Roy Ashton (makeup) **Music by:** Don Banks **Cast:**
Peter Cushing (Baron Frankenstein) Peter Woodthorpe (Zoltan)
Sandor Elès (Hans) Katy Wild (beggar girl) David Hutcheson
(Burgomaster) Duncan Lamont (Chief of Police) Kiwi Kingston (the
monster)

Spherical, Eastmancolor,
84 Minutes (theatrical)/96 Minutes (television)

SYNOPSIS Several years ago, Baron Frankenstein gave life to his
first creation on the outskirts of Karlstaad. The monster escaped
and became frozen in ice, while the Baron was run out of town.
Years later, the Baron has returned along with his assistant Hans.
With the help of a mute girl, Frankenstein finds his old creation
frozen in the ice. They thaw it out, take it back to the lab and revive
it. But, the monster is braindead. Using a hypnotist named Zoltan,
Frankenstein is able to revive his creation. However, Zoltan uses
his powers of hypnosis to use the monster to terrorize the villagers
for his own selfish ends. The villagers come to destroy the castle,
but before they can, the monster goes mad, killing Zoltan and
setting fire to the lab. Hans and the mute girl escape, but the
Baron does not and presumably perishes along with his creation
as the castle explodes.

COMMENTARY Hammer had announced Frankenstein #3 as far
back as June 5, 1958, before *Revenge of Frankenstein* even hit
theaters. However, a deal for a Frankenstein TV series with

Columbia/Screen Gems derailed plans for a third film. The pilot, which was a reimagining rather than a sequel, was shot in 1958. The network passed on the TV series, which would have been called *Tales of Frankenstein*. Then, after *Brides of Dracula* (1960), Peter Cushing took a brief sabbatical from Hammer, and it was uncertain if and when he would return. But, in mid-1963, he agreed to come back for a new Frankenstein to be produced as part of Hammer's deal with Universal. There was just one problem: there wasn't much time to write a script. Jimmy Sangster wasn't interested, and Anthony Hinds was busy rewriting *The Gorgon*. As such, Frankenstein #3 didn't get the attention it needed. To whip up a quick story, Hinds raided his old scripts for *Tales of Frankenstein* to make movie #3. One of them concerned a hypnotist controlling the monster, and it was fleshed out into a full screenplay. So if you've ever wondered why this entry's story was rather simplistic when compared to the previous two films, that's why.

One plus for Hammer on the production was that due to the involvement of Universal, they could finally utilize the famous Jack Pierce makeup. Or, at least, it should have been a plus. The makeup for the monster is atrocious, and many people compare it to a papier-mâché mask. The makeup is also applied so thick that it leaves little room for monster actor Kiwi Kingston to express himself. Aside from the monster design, there are many other callbacks to the Universal films. The pitchfork touting villagers scouring the woods for the monster is quite evocative of those films. The Baron's laboratory, described more in line with what we saw in *Curse of Frankenstein* in the script, was made to resemble the more elaborate labs from the Universal films at the insistence of director Freddie Francis (who replaced Terence Fisher). Even finding the monster in ice was a nod to both *Frankenstein Meets the Wolf Man* and *House of Frankenstein*. Speaking of that, in this film's story it's unclear if we're to assume that the Baron had two homes, and that perhaps after the events of *Curse* he went there and made another monster, or, if this film's flashback offers a retelling of *Curse*, where the monster didn't die in acid but escaped and became frozen in ice?

As Bruce G. Hallenbeck put it in *Little Shoppe of Horrors* #35, *Evil of Frankenstein* was more of what we would today call a reboot than a sequel. Whatever its intent was as to the flashback scene, it effectively retconned events from the first film. And yet, at the same time, it also carried over a major character, Hans, from *Revenge of Frankenstein*. (However, the fact that the doctor now inhabits a new body—great story potential there—isn't addressed.) Another way in which the film reboots the series is its portrayal of the Baron. While he was a sociopath in the first two films, here he is something of a sympathetic anti-hero, wronged by the villagers rather than the other way around (and, other than kill some sheep, what harm did his monster really do?). Of Cushing's six Frankenstein films, this is easily the one where he comes across as the most heroic and sympathetic. Some of his best moments occur when he craftily escapes his jail cell and then commandeers a horse and buggy to race back to his castle.

Structurally speaking, the film's last third is similar to a mummy movie in the sense that the monster is ordered to shuffle around and kill various villagers. Only in this case, rather than the desecrators of some Egyptian tomb, it is men who have wronged Zoltan who are slated to die. The film's ending is one of its better bits, and is clearly inspired by *Son of Frankenstein* (1939). As the monster begins wrecking the lab, the Baron shows up to try and subdue him. Like Basil Rathbone, Cushing's Baron even swings down into the lab by way of a chain hanging from the ceiling. This explosive ending tops off what was otherwise a lackluster entry in the series. And while the previous film let the Baron live, this one's ending was more dubious with his fate uncertain.

Lackluster story aside, the exterior locations shot at Black Park in the Autumn of 1963 are beautiful, as are most of the sets. (It is painfully evident that James Bernard didn't handle the score this time around though, as it's a bit repetitive and over dramatic throughout). When released in the late spring of 1964 the film was a disappointment in Britain (or so some sources say, *Hammer Complete* says that it was a hit in the U.K.). Whether it was a hit or not in its home country, the film was profitable in the U.S., where audiences were mostly lured in by the more Universal-esque monster.

FINAL WORD As far as Hammer Frankenstein movies go, this one will always be considered not only the weakest Cushing-led entry, but also the least Hammer-like in the way that it's really a throwback to the old Universal films by way of Hammer.

THE GORGON

(HAMMER/COLUMBIA)
Release Date: October 18, 1964 (U.K.)
February 17, 1965 (U.S.)
Alternate Titles: *The Castle of the Gorgon* (Argentina) *Gorgon Goddess of Terror* (Belgium) *The Killing Look* (Italy) *Witch Gorgon* (Japan) *Death Has Passed By* (Portugal) *Medusa* (Spain) *Petrified by Fear* (Sweden) *The Burning Eyes of Bartimore Castle* (Germany)

Directed by: Terence Fisher **Screenplay by:** John Gilling & Anthony Nelson Keys based upon a story by J. Llewellyn Divine **Special Effects by:** Sydney Pearson & Roy Ashton (makeup) **Music by:** James Bernard **Cast:** Peter Cushing (Dr. Namaroff) Christopher Lee (Professor Karl Meister) Barbara Shelley (Carla Hoffman) Richard Pasco (Paul Heitz) Patrick Troughton (Inspector Kanof) Michael Goodliffe (Professor Jules Heitz) Jack Watson (Ratoff) Joyce Hemson (Martha) Prudence Hyman (the Gorgon)

Spherical, Technicolor, 83 Minutes

SYNOPSIS In the early 1900s, the village of Vandorf is plagued by a strange series of deaths wherein the bodies are found turned to stone. The father of one of the victims comes to investigate and is himself turned to stone at the old Castle Borski. The man's other son, Paul, comes to town next to investigate. One night he is struck ill by the reflection of a snake-headed woman he sees in a pool of water. He recovers in a hospital under the care of Dr. Namaroff and his nurse Carla, who Paul falls in love with. However, not only is Dr. Namaroff also in love with Carla, he's the only one who knows that Carla is secretly the Gorgon, which even Carla herself doesn't know. Paul sends for his old professor, Karl Meister, to come to the village and help. Meister figures out that Carla is the Gorgon, but Paul refuses to believe it. At Castle Borski, Paul and Dr. Namaroff are both killed by the Gorgon's hideous face. Meister beheads her from behind, killing the monster.

COMMENTARY *The Gorgon* could probably be considered Hammer's seminal non-Frankenstein/Dracula/Mummy monster movie. It features Peter Cushing and Christopher Lee in star roles, it has that classic tension inducing Terence Fisher direction, and a standout score from James Bernard. The sets by Bernard Robinson (and the accompanied Technicolor photography by Michael Reed) are also absolutely gorgeous, and are decorated by an abundance of blowing autumn leaves for added affect. The only thing this film seems to be missing is a small role for Michael Ripper! That, and perhaps a better executed monster...

For the time period, Hammer's Gorgon looks well enough in this author's opinion. However, many people involved on the film haven't many nice things to say about the monster itself. Christopher Lee notably said that, "The only thing wrong with *The Gorgon* is the Gorgon!" That said, Lee did not blame Roy Ashton or Sydney Pearson for this, and argued that neither men were given enough time to create the Gorgon. As such, what we see is an otherwise good makeup job on the face, topped with a wig of obviously plastic snakes that have no semblance of realistic movement. Actually, Barbara Shelley wanted to play the part herself, and even suggested a wig with live snakes! Anthony Nelson Keys rejected this idea, but reportedly later told the actress that he should have listened to her. As to why Shelley didn't play the part in general, it was because Hammer wanted the monster to move with grace and so hired ballerina Prudence Hyman.

Initially, the Gorgon is only seen fleetingly in the beginning, either glimpsed in quick shots from a distance, or distorted in a reflection of some kind. The monster gets a proper close-up in the film's final reel, which Lee felt was something of an anti-climax. In some respects, it might have been interesting had the Gorgon not been revealed until the very end. Or, better yet, follow the model later employed in *Dracula–Prince of Darkness*, where tension builds and builds until it is finally released in the last act. Of course, children (and quite a few adults) would not have stood for the monster only appearing at the end, though.

As for other aspects, Barbara Shelley does great in her role as Carla, who essentially follows the pattern of the werewolf. At the full moon, Carla turns into the Gorgon, though she is blissfully unaware of this. And yet, she also knows that something is wrong with her, though she doesn't know what exactly. Cushing and Lee do well in their parts and are nothing like any of their signature roles of the past, not even Baron Frankenstein. We're really not sure how we should feel for Cushing's character, as he's not an outright villain. He is complicit in what's going on due to being in love with Carla. However, the hero of the picture, Paul, might have sunk to the same depths as the doctor. The ending is certainly downbeat, with Lee's character being the sole survivor.

The Gorgon was the result of Columbia's dissatisfaction with Hammer's recent non-gothic thrillers. Probably adding salt to the wound was the fact that Universal's release of *Evil of Frankenstein* had proved to be a hit in the U.S. With Columbia wanting a gothic monster film, rather than producing a vampire film for them, Hammer went a totally original route. Hammer held a story contest amongst the public, and the result was an idea based on the Greek legend of the Gorgon. Rather than the more famous Medusa, Megaera was the focal point (though technically she was a fury, not a Gorgon). The story was submitted by a fan from Canada, named J. Llewellyn Divine. The concept was turned into a script by John Gilling (then simply called *Supernatural*), which Anthony Hinds did his best to rewrite during production of *Evil of Frankenstein* (the sets of which would be repurposed for *The Gorgon*).

Luckily for Hammer and Columbia, *The Gorgon* brought in healthy returns at the box office, and even the critics were kind to it compared to their past reviews of Hammer horror.

FINAL WORD As it turned out, this was the final film to team Fisher, Cushing and Lee. Though there were probably better films that the trio could have parted ways on, *The Gorgon* is still classic Hammer, and is certainly a notch above similar films like *The Reptile*.

THE CURSE OF THE MUMMY'S TOMB

(HAMMER/COLUMBIA)
Release Date: October 18, 1964 (U.K.)
February 17, 1965 (U.S.)
Alternate Titles: *Tomb of the Mummy* (Greece) *Mystery of the Mummy* (Italy) *Mysterious Mummy* (Japan) *Curse of the Mummy* (Latin America) *Pharaoh's Revenge* (West Germany)

Directed by: Michael Carreras **Screenplay by:** Michael Carreras (as Henry Younger) with contributions by Alvin Rakoff (uncredited) **Special Effects by:** George Blackwell & Roy Ashton (Makeup) **Music by:** Carlo Martelli **Cast:** Terence Morgan (Adam Beauchamp) Ronald Howard (John Bray) Fred Clark (Alexander King) Jeanne Roland (Annette Dubois) George Pastell (Hashmi Bey) Jack Gwillim (Sir Giles Dalrymple) John Paul (Inspector Mackenzie) Dickie Owen (the Mummy)

TechniScope, Technicolor, 80 Minutes

SYNOPSIS Sir Giles Dalrymple and Professor Dubois have just unearthed the lost tomb of the Pharaoh Rah. Dubois is mysteriously killed before the mummy of Ra and other artifacts are shipped to London under the care of Alexander King, a showman. However, when King opens the sarcophagus as part of a live stage show, it is empty! As it turns out, Ra's immortal brother, Bey, posing as an aristocrat named Adam Beauchamp, has revived Rah with the Words of Life. Ra's mummy then kills King and Dalrymple. However, it cannot bring itself to kill Dalrymple's daughter, Annette, even when Bey commands him to do so. Instead, Rah kills Bey, and then commits suicide by collapsing a sewer tunnel onto himself.

COMMENTARY Though the Mummy was more famous than Megaera the Gorgon, the Mummy was decided upon to play second fiddle to the Greek monster as *The Gorgon's* support feature on the double bill for Columbia. *Curse of the Mummy's Tomb* was hastily shot at Elstree from February 24 to March 27, 1964. The film was unique in that it was a rare, widescreen production for Hammer

206

which does lend it a somewhat more epic feel, though the sets don't fill it out very well. (On that note, the best set in the film, rather than any of the Egyptian tombs, is the English study.)

There aren't any familiar Hammer faces in the film at all except for Michael Ripper in a small role. Specifically, this time Ripper plays an Arab which is both intentionally and unintentionally humorous at times. The character doesn't last long though and is killed early on. The male lead is terribly uninteresting, unfortunately, and is also a bit too old for the part. Far more interesting is the film's villain, Adam Beauchamp, who is himself an ancient Pharaoh who has survived for millennia (similar to Robert Quarry's character in *Dr. Phibes Rises Again*). As a wealthy, womanizing connoisseur, Beauchamp is a bit like an Egyptian Dracula in a way. You could even argue that you get two mummies for the price of one, except for this one doesn't wear bandages. Of course, this shocking revelation doesn't come about until the last fifteen minutes of the film. As such, *Curse of the Mummy's Tomb* makes for interesting repeat viewing when one watches Beauchamp with this information in mind. Notably, during the film's obligatory flashback sequence (which is well done), we never do see Bey, only Rah, as seeing Bey would have given away the surprise at the end.

One of the film's better characters is Alexander King, who seems to be patented after Carl Denham from *King Kong*. King even has a Kong-like unveiling for the Mummy. (This sequence seems a bit overlong and might have been done as a way of padding out the runtime). Before he dies, King also gets a nice scene where he gives a prostitute a few pounds to go and get a meal as a way of humanizing him before his demise. There's also a funny bit between King and Beauchamp. After the Mummy goes missing, Beauchamp asks King if there's anything he can do to help, and King makes a bitter joke that maybe he could wrap himself up in some dusty old bandages (unaware of the irony of his joke).

As for the Mummy that does wear bandages, played by stuntman Dickie Owen, it looks quite similar to the Lee Mummy in a few respects. The main differences are that the bandages are less detailed, and the Mummy seems to have a slight, blue/grey hue to it at times. There's also a very effective addition to this Mummy in that it has incredibly loud breathing that sounds like a subway vent. In fact, we hear this noise before we ever actually see the Mummy on the move, which is very effective. As for other visual differences between Owen's Mummy and Lee's, this one has no mouth and it's also missing a hand.

The movie has a fetish for lopping off hands. In fact, that's how the movie starts, with Professor Dubois (an uncredited Bernard Rebel) getting his hand lopped off in very gory fashion. In the flashback, we see Ra get his hand lopped off. Then, at the climax, Bey gets his hand cut off by a steel door. In addition to severed hands, this movie also has a few memorable skull crushings. In the first, the Mummy breaks into a study in a callback to the 1959 *Mummy*. The Mummy kills Sir Dalrymple by bludgeoning him on the head with a small statue that sits atop his desk. We don't see it of course, but the sound effect used is quite graphic. Later in the film, an Egyptian bows down to the Mummy in shame and asks him to kill him, which Ra does by crushing his head with his foot.

The Mummy gets several memorable scenes in the film. As mentioned earlier, his reveal is well done, with King hearing the loud breathing before he spots the Mummy standing atop a stairwell. Though the kill itself isn't that interesting—King just gets thrown down the stairwell—visually speaking it's quite haunting. The scene's parting shot has the Mummy standing atop the stairwell in the distance, shrouded by fog before it disappears. Another memorable scene has the heroes attempt to capture the Mummy by way of a giant net that it easily breaks free of. The ending isn't terribly exciting. In a way it's similar to the first film, except that rather than a swamp this Mummy perishes in a sewer (by its own hand no less).

If there's one problem with this film it's that it's a bit too talky and the Mummy doesn't revive until an hour in. Now, this was also true of the well-loved *Dracula – Prince of Darkness*, but in that case Terence Fisher had done an excellent job of carrying the first two acts via the tension alone. The same really can't be said for this entry. For this reason, *Curse* narrowly beats *The Mummy's Shroud* as the weakest of Hammer's four Mummy movies, but it's not a bad film by any means. However, audiences took to the film just fine, and it managed to be a decent hit at the box office in both Britain and the States.

FINAL WORD Though the parts are greater than the whole, the movie is easily worth sitting through to see them.

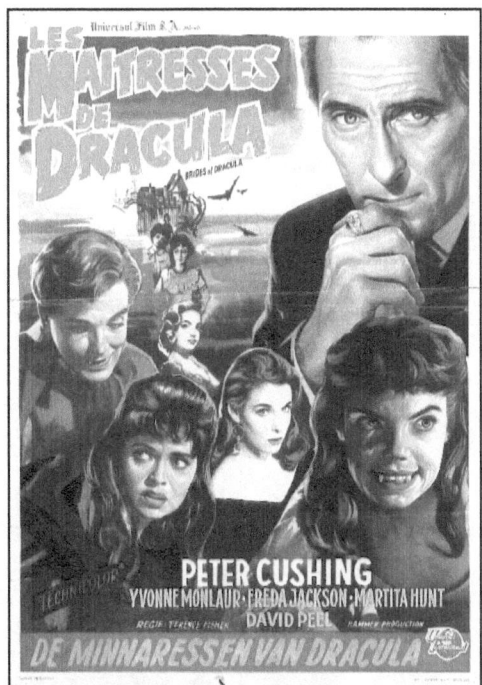

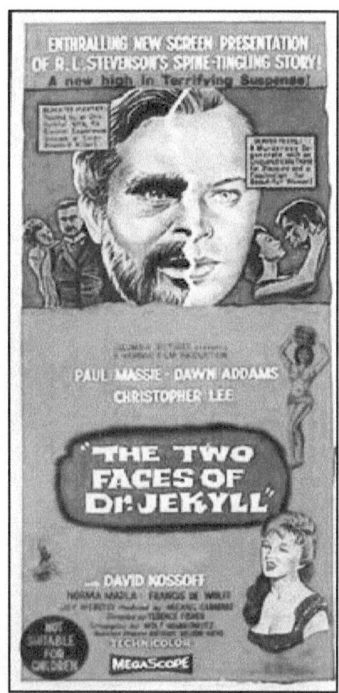

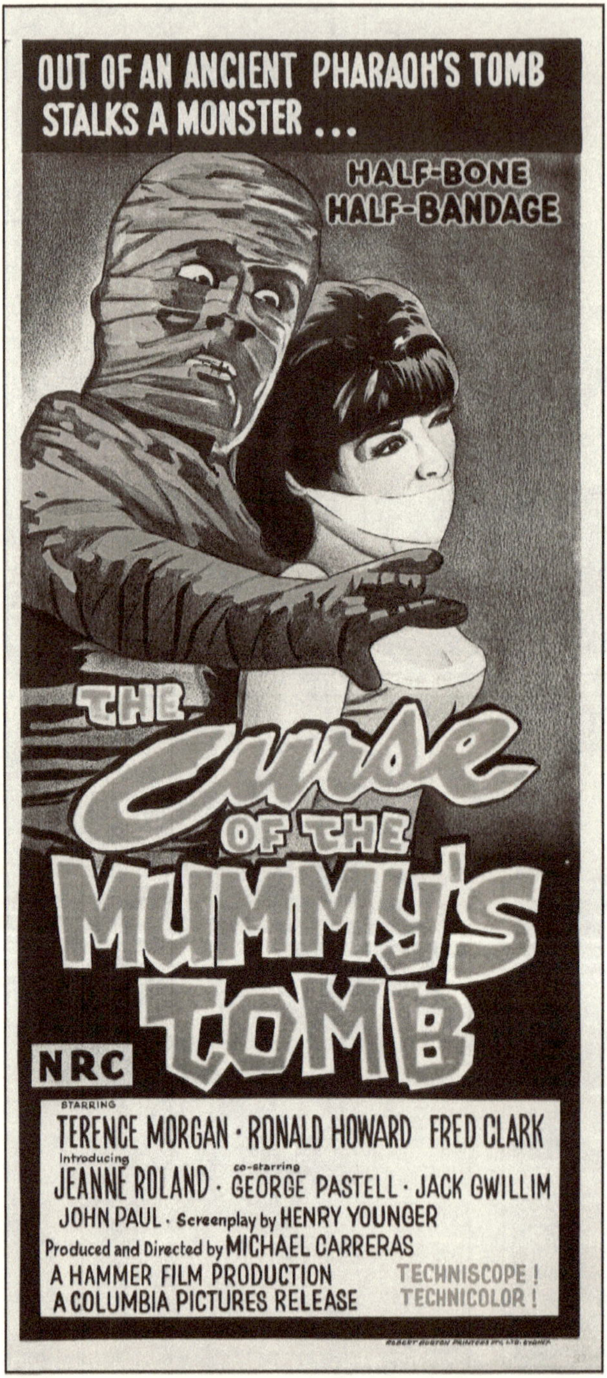
OUT OF AN ANCIENT PHARAOH'S TOMB
STALKS A MONSTER ...
HALF-BONE
HALF-BANDAGE
THE
Curse
OF THE
MUMMY'S
TOMB
NRC
STARRING
TERENCE MORGAN · RONALD HOWARD FRED CLARK
Introducing
JEANNE ROLAND · co-starring GEORGE PASTELL · JACK GWILLIM
JOHN PAUL · Screenplay by HENRY YOUNGER
Produced and Directed by MICHAEL CARRERAS
A HAMMER FILM PRODUCTION
A COLUMBIA PICTURES RELEASE
TECHNISCOPE!
TECHNICOLOR!

THE GORGON PETRIFIES THE SCREEN WITH HORROR!
THE
GORGON
SHE HAD A FACE ONLY A MUMMY COULD LOVE!
TECHNICOLOR
PETER CUSHING · CHRISTOPHER LEE RICHARD PASCO
MICHAEL GOODLIFFE · BARBARA SHELLEY
JOHN GILLING
ANTHONY NELSON KEYS · TERENCE FISHER
A HAMMER FILM PRODUCTION
A COLUMBIA PICTURES RELEASE

A COLORI
RIVOLTA
FRANKENSTEIN

The CURSE OF THE
WEREWOLF
COLOR
CLIFFORD EVANS · OLIVER REED · YVONNE ROMAIN · CATHERINE FELLER
JOHN ELDER · TERENCE FISHER · ANTHONY HINDS · MICHAEL CARRERAS

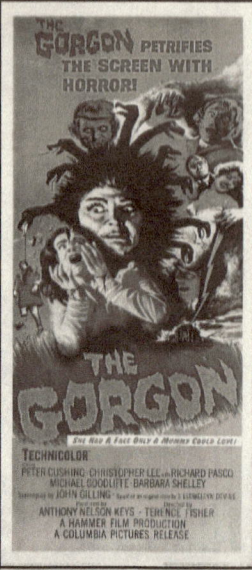

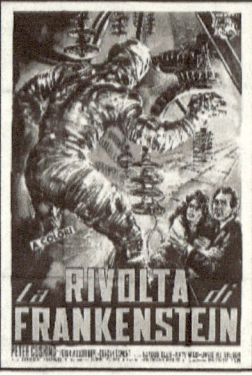

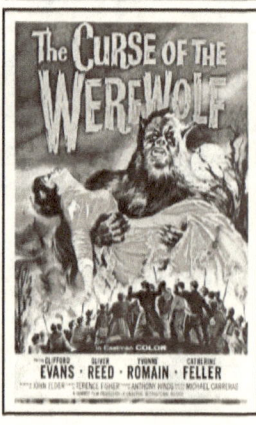

FRANKENSTEIN CONQUERS THE WORLD

(TOHO)
Release Date: August 08, 1965
Alternate Titles: *Frankenstein vs. Subterranean Monster
Baragon* (Japan) *Frankenstein Conquers the World* (U.S.)
Frankenstein: The Terror With an Ape Face (Germany)

Directed by: Ishiro Honda **Screenplay by:** Takeshi Kimura (as
"Kaoru Mabuchi") & Reuben Bercovitch **Special Effects by:** Eiji
Tsuburaya **Music by:** Akira Ifukube **Cast:** Nick Adams (Dr. Bowen)
Kumi Mizuno (Sueko) Tadao Takashima (Dr. Kawaji) Yoshio
Tsuchiya (Kawai) Koji Furuhata (Frankenstein) **Suit Performers:**
Haruo Nakajima (Baragon)

Tohoscope, Eastmancolor, 95 Minutes

SYNOPSIS During the waning days of WWII, the Frankenstein
monster's still-beating heart is captured by the Nazis in Germany
and taken to Hiroshima shortly before the bomb is dropped. Flash-
forward fifteen years later and American scientist Dr. Bowen runs
a radiation clinic with nurse Sueko and partner Kawaji. Reports
begin to surface of a strange teenage boy killing animals. They
discover the boy is perhaps the regenerated heart of the
Frankenstein monster. Growing at an astonishing rate, the boy
soon grows too large to be contained and escapes into the
wilderness. At the same time, an underground monster named
Baragon begins attacking villages and eating the inhabitants. The
military assumes Frankenstein is to blame and sets out to destroy
him. Bowen and Sueko don't want to believe the boy has turned
violent and search for him near Mt. Fuji but are attacked by
Baragon. Frankenstein shows up to save them and the two
monsters battle amidst a forest fire. After Baragon has been
defeated, a sudden tremor causes Frankenstein to sink into the
earth.

COMMENTARY The fact Toho, producer of the Godzilla series,
made a film about a giant Frankenstein is odd enough. Odder still
is that it's actually quite good. Unsurprisingly, the film began life
as "Frankenstein vs. Godzilla" written by Jerry Sohl (a future *Star*

211

Trek writer) in 1963 or 1964. The idea was brought to Toho executives, who were already keen on pitting their monster against yet another western icon in light of the success of *King Kong vs. Godzilla*'s. And, best of all, Frankenstein would not require expensive licensing rights like Kong. Supposedly, the final storyline (a Toho/United Productions of America co-production) was said to partly be the brainchild of Reuben Bercovitch, a UPA executive. However, much like the classic Frankenstein monster, the story was stitched together from so many "donors" that's hard to know what came from which writer or producer.

All that's known for sure is that Henry G. Saperstein of UPA had garnered the distribution rights to Toho's monster films in 1964, in a sense, becoming Godzilla's American agent. Because the films were playing so well in America, he pitched Toho the idea of utilizing American "stars" to make their releases more appealing internationally. Nick Adams, who appeared in such American classics as *Rebel Without a Cause, Mister Roberts,* and the TV series *The Rebel*, signed to play the lead in the film. Curiously, many sources indicate Adams was already cast in the movie by Toho before Saperstein officially became involved making Bercovitch's screenplay credit all the more mysterious. More likely, it was penned by Kaoru Mabuchi (the only writer credited it in the Japanese version), who seemed to simply adapt Sohl's "Frankenstein vs. Godzilla" treatment (which this author has read). Whatever the case, the screenplay and its monsters are quite entertaining.

Rather than a man in a suit, actor Koji Furuhata portrayed the Frankenstein monster via make-up effects with a slightly flattened head reminiscent of Universal's classic design. There are a few other tips of the hat to the Universal series, such as the distinctly Bavarian-style musical chords that open the Japanese version and credits that play over a laboratory set full of beakers and chemicals. Special effects master Eiji Tsuburaya even constructs a miniature German graveyard for one of the film's early scenes. At one point, Kawaji interviews an old German scientist who seems to reference the Universal films when he mentions how the monster had been killed many times before but always came back to life. The rest of the proceedings are distinctly Japanese and the highlight of the film is the monster Baragon, sporting a unique design amongst the pantheon of Toho kaiju. Because of the two monsters' smaller sizes, Tsuburaya was able to construct a bevy of larger scale miniature sets that convey a heightened sense of realism. The standout is a well-lit forest that becomes ablaze at dusk during the final battle between the monsters. This film is also famous for an elaborate alternate ending that appears in neither the Japanese or American versions. At UPA's behest, a scene was filmed where, after defeating Baragon, a giant octopus shows up— seemingly out of nowhere—to battle Frankenstein. The two beasts struggle about and then fall into a body of water. Although an exciting sequence, it throws the film for a loop and UPA wisely chose to go with the original Japanese ending. The "lost" sequence was edited into a special version of the film released on Japanese laserdisc in the 1990s and the octopus prop would be put to better use in the sequel, *The War of the Gargantuas*.

As for the film's American star, Nick Adams was much loved at Toho, frequently joking with his co-stars, all of whom admired him. He was also rumored to be having an affair with Kumi Mizuno. According to interviews with Mizuno, Adams once even proposed to her. Adams also headlined a Godzilla film, *Invasion of Astro-Monster* (better known as *Monster Zero*), during his time in Japan, which also starred Mizuno, and was able to squeeze one more picture in with her, the non-monster film, *The Killing Bottle*, released in 1967. Ishiro Honda remarked to David Milner that, "There should have been two or three more films produced with Mr. Adams whether they were monster movies or not." *Frankenstein vs. Baragon* managed to reach U.S. theaters in 1966 before the tragic death of Adams (some say it was a suicide though others claim it was murder) in 1968.

FINAL WORD Worth seeing based upon the concept alone. Whether it equals or surpasses one's expectations is all a matter of taste.

DRACULA,
PRINCE OF DARKNESS

(HAMMER)
Release Date: January 9, 1966 (U.K.) January 12, 1966 (U.S.)
Alternate Titles: *The Bloody Scream of Dracula* (Canada) *Blood for Dracula* (Germany)

Directed by: Terence Fisher **Screenplay by:** Jimmy Sangster (as John Sansom) based upon a story by Anthony Hinds (as John Elder) **Special Effects by:** Les Bowie & Roy Ashton (makeup) **Music by:** James Bernard **Cast:** Christopher Lee (Count Dracula) Andrew Keir (Father Shandor) Francis Matthews (Charles Kent) Suzan Farmer (Diana Kent) Barbara Shelley (Helen Kent) Charles Tingwell (Alan Kent) Philip Latham (Klove) Thorley Walters (Ludwig)

Techniscope, Technicolor, 90 Minutes

SYNOPSIS Two brothers, Charles and Alan Kent, are traveling through Karlsbad with their wives, Diana and Helen. At sundown they find themselves abandoned near the foot of Castle Dracula when their coach driver refuses to drive past the castle at night. Soon a driver-less carriage comes from out of nowhere. The weary travelers try to commandeer it, but the horses mysteriously take them straight to the castle. There they find an odd man named Klove, who offers them hospitality on the behalf of his dead master. That night, Klove kills Alan and uses his blood to resurrect Dracula. The count immediately vampirizes Helen, but Charles and Diana manage to escape. They find solace in a monastery run by Father Shandor. But, Dracula and Helen soon infiltrate the monastery's walls. Though Helen is caught and destroyed, Dracula escapes with Diana. Charles and Shandor pursue Dracula's hearse, driven by Klove, who Charles shoots and kills. Dracula's casket slips onto the frozen moat of his castle. As Charles attempts to stake him, the vampire king awakens and a struggle ensues. Diana and Shandor shoot a rifle at the ice, cracking it at strategic points so that Dracula is swallowed into the waters below while Charles escapes.

COMMENTARY This sequel was a long time coming, and supposedly Jimmy Sangster cooked up the basic outline all the way back in the late 1950s. It was alternately known as *Dracula, the Damned* and *Revenge of Dracula*, and supposedly had Dracula resurrected by a band of gypsies, but otherwise was similar to this film. Depending on what source you go by, either Christopher Lee wasn't interested in the role or Hammer wasn't interested in Lee returning to the role in a large capacity (as evidenced by his incredibly small role in the aborted *Disciple of Dracula*). Finally, Lee relented to return. Part of the reason Lee agreed to reprise Dracula was because he was also guaranteed the title role in *Rasputin, the Mad Monk* to be shot back to back on the same sets. Had that not sweetened the pot, it's unknown if Lee would've returned. (However, the actor has claimed that he didn't turn Hammer down for seven years, but rather they never asked him until then!)

That Hammer was finally making another Dracula with Lee was announced in 1963, as TV shows invited viewers to submit ideas for the film. That, by the way, was where Dracula's resurrection was devised when viewers suggested mixing blood in his ashes. The film is also somewhat notorious for the fact that Dracula has no dialogue in it. Conflicting sources state that Lee refused to read the dialogue, while Jimmy Sangster himself claimed that no dialogue was ever written! And then there's the fact that Van Helsing didn't return. Though Van Helsing had been inserted into *Brides of Dracula* where he originally wasn't, in this case the opposite was true. Van Helsing was in the first draft of the script, but when Peter Cushing became unavailable, Van Helsing was replaced by a new character, the gun-toting monk, Father Shandor. (Despite official materials to the contrary, his name is Shandor and not Sandor.) Played by Andrew Keir, Shandor is a welcome addition to the film and is one of the livelier characters. Despite Dracula and Shandor being the more dynamic figures in the film, most of the runtime is carried by the everyman characters represented by actors Francis Matthews and Suzan Farmer as a husband and wife stranded at Castle Dracula, where much of the film takes place.

It's actually a marvel that the film is as popular as it is in retrospect. The first fifty minutes of the film builds tension in the form of the travelers making their way to and spending the night in Castle Dracula. That's two-thirds of the film without much action and without the Count! And yet, this continual tension serves the story well, as the film's last forty minutes is mostly a non-stop rush of horror and action—a relief to the earlier tension. The monastery scenes are quite fun for many reasons. First, there's Thorley Walter's character of Ludwig, who Jimmy Sangster admitted was his version of Renfield (who there was no room for in *Horror of Dracula*). Barbara Shelley's scenes as the vampire version of Helen are also fantastic, made all the more effective by Shelley's earlier portrayal of the character as a shrewd Victorian woman. Helen's staking scene is pretty wild compared to the ones that came before it in *Horror* and *Brides*, too. And, though Lee spoke no dialogue, he did get to recreate a scene straight out of Stoker's book where Dracula tries to force Diana to drink his blood. The film's ending was also inspired by Stoker's novel even more so than *Horror* was in some respects. In the book, the heroes chase Dracula, who is being transported by gypsy servants in a hearse. When his casket slides out of the hearse, they stake him. Sangster's ending, where the heroes only attempt to stake Dracula on a precarious, frozen moat, is much more exciting than that. Though the first film could get away with dispatching Dracula in a rather typical way, audiences would have no doubt been disappointed had Dracula simply been disintegrated in the sunlight again. As such, this film's truly novel, exciting climax is probably one of the many reasons the movie is still so well-loved today.

Though shot back-to-back with *Rasputin: The Mad Monk*, this film was double-billed with Hammer's *Plague of the Zombies* so that audiences didn't get too much of a double-dose of the same sets and actors. The double bill was a huge hit for Hammer, which naturally pleased 20th Century Fox. As it turned out, Hammer would cap off 1966 with yet another huge moneymaker in the form of a subsequent 20th Century Fox co-production: *One Million Years B.C.* Coupled with *B.C.*, *Dracula – Prince of Darkness* set the company on a financial roll that would last all the way until the end of the 1960s.

FINAL WORD For many, this is the best of the Dracula sequels, with Hammer historian Marcus Hearn even calling it the quintessential Hammer.

PLAGUE OF THE ZOMBIES

(HAMMER)
Release Date: January 9, 1966 (U.K.) January 12, 1966 (U.S.)
Alternate Titles: *Invasion of the Living Dead* (Canada/France)
Rising from the Grave (Finland) *Big Night of Horror* (Greece/Italy)
Bloodsucking Zombie (Japan) *Curse of the Zombies* (Mexico)

Directed by: John Gilling **Screenplay by:** Peter Bryan **Special Effects by:** Les Bowie **Music by:** James Bernard **Cast:** Andre Morell (Sir James Forbes) John Carson (Clive Hamilton) Diane Clare (Sylvia Forbes) Brook Williams (Dr. Peter Tompson) Alex Davion (Harry Denver) Jacqueline Pearce (Alice Tompson) Michael Ripper (Sergeant Swift) Roy Royston (Vicar) Dennis Chinnery (Constable Christian) Marcus Hammond (Martinus)

Spherical, DeLuxe Color, 87 Minutes

SYNOPSIS When Sir James Forbes receives a mysterious letter from his old protégé, Dr. Peter Tompson, now the doctor of a rural Cornish village, Forbes's daughter Sylvia insists that they pay him a visit. They find Peter's wife, Alice, in a rather strange, almost trance-like state upon arrival. Soon after, Alice mysteriously dies. Around the same time, there are sightings on the village's outskirts of the recently deceased alive and walking. Via a joint investigation, Forbes and Tompson figure out that voodoo magic is reanimating the dead. The perpetrator of the evil deed is the wealthy Clive Hamilton, who is using the zombies to work in his mine. Alice becomes a zombie but is killed for good by Forbes. Sylvia soon falls under Hamilton's voodoo spell as well and marches to his mansion in a trance. Forbes and the widower Tompson save her in the mines, while the mine and the mansion both burn up in a fire.

COMMENTARY *Plague of the Zombies* began as a simple synopsis titled *The Zombie* by Peter Bryan all the way back in 1962. Anthony Hinds fleshed it out into a script which was announced in 1964 as *Horror of the Zombies*. (The promotional artwork copied Hammer's *Mummy* poster, with a searchlight shining through a hole in the zombie.) Then, in 1965, Anthony Nelson Keys had a rather inspired idea for Hammer to film not two, but four films all on the same sets. In the past they had indeed shot films back-to-back (like *Evil of Frankenstein* and *The Gorgon*), but four films was a tall order! The four films comprised of *Dracula – Prince of Darkness*, *Rasputin – The Mad Monk*, *Plague of the Zombies* and *The Reptile* to be shot in that order. *Plague* began shooting as soon as *Rasputin* finished filming in late July and the moat of Castle Dracula was converted into the zombie graveyard.

The productions weren't just similar in their set designs, in the case of *Reptile* and *Plague*, they also share similar scenes at times. For instance, both have scenes where the two male leads have to exhume a grave in secret to solve the mystery. They also feature actress Jacqueline Pearce in monster makeup of some sort, the titular Reptile in the next film and a zombie in this production. Both films also destroy their monsters via fire. For its part, *Plague* is a bit better than *The Reptile* and moves at a better pace.

Of the cast, Andre Morell is much better here as the blustery Forbes than he would be in *The Mummy's Shroud* the next year. John Carlson, later to endear himself to Hammer fans in *Taste the Blood of Dracula* and *Captain Kronos: Vampire Hunter*, does well enough as the villain, too. Michael Ripper has a supporting role as a police inspector as usual. Jaqueline Pearce is excellent here as Alice, and it's a shame she didn't get put to work in more Hammer films. Diane Clare is good as Sylvia, too, but one can't help but to feel that perhaps Jennifer Daniel would have been better suited to the part.

And, what of the marauding zombies? They aren't exactly hidden from the viewer (their makeup is very well done) but they're scarcely seen until the hour mark. In the film's best remembered scene, poor Alice rises as one of the undead and Forbes whacks her head off with a shovel. The sight causes her widowed husband to faint. When he awakens, in a spectacular green-tinted nightmare, a horde of zombies rise up from the graveyard. However, it's all a dream (not the decapitation, that happened, just not the mass zombie exodus from the ground). However, even though the scene is a cop-out, it's still fun, and the ending, where we see hordes of zombies hard at work in a mine, is excellently staged.

The climax is predictable Hammer. Much like one of their vampire films, Sylvia comes under a trance and slips from the supervision of the male lead to wander to her potential doom in the darkness. In this case, rather than Chateau Ravna or Castle

Dracula, she marches to the estate of Clive Hamilton. And like so many Hammer and Universal monsters before them, the monster and villains succumb to fire. However, the story serves up a twist: during a decently choreographed fight between Forbes and one of Hamilton's lackeys, a fire breaks out in the house. The fire spreads to the voodoo caskets of the zombies. When those catch fire, the zombies down in the mine start to spontaneously combust as well.

Because *Rasputin* and the *Dracula* sequel both resembled each other due to the same castle setting, it was decided to double-bill *Plague* with *Prince of Darkness*. It's always a bit tough to determine whether or not the supporting feature of a double bill was a hit, after all, most audiences were there to see Dracula. But, that said, *Plague* got some good reviews from critics and is fondly remembered by most Hammer fans.

FINAL WORD Though some might be tempted to watch this film back to back with *Dracula – Prince of Darkness*, they might enjoy watching it side by side with *The Reptile* instead to compare and contrast the sets.

THE REPTILE

(HAMMER)
Release Date: March 6, 1966 (U.K.) April 6, 1966 (U.S.)
Alternate Titles: *Death Comes Crawling* (Italy) *Threat of the Snake Woman* (Japan) *The Female Reptile* (Canada) *The Serpent* (Brazil) *Death Came from Borneo* (Greece)

Directed by: John Gilling **Screenplay by:** Anthony Hinds (as John Elder) **Music by:** Don Banks **Special Effects by:** Les Bowie & Roy Ashton (makeup) **Cast:** Noel Willman (Dr. Franklyn) Ray Barrett (Harry George Spalding) Jennifer Daniel (Valerie Spalding) Jacqueline Pearce (Anna Franklyn/the Reptile) Michael Ripper (Tom Bailey) Marne Maitland (Malay) John Laurie (Mad Peter) David Baron (Charles Edward Spalding) Charles Lloyd-Pack (Vicar)

Spherical, Color DeLuxe, 91 Minutes

SYNOPSIS After his brother dies a mysterious death in an English village, Harry Spalding and his wife, Valerie, inherit his cottage. When Harry teams with a local tavern owner, Tom Bailey, to investigate his brother's death, he learns that he wasn't the only one to die under the same, unusual circumstances. All the victims appeared to suffer the effects of extreme snake venom, and for some reason all the clues point to the home of Dr. Franklyn and his daughter Anna. As it turns out, Anna had been cursed to transform into a snake woman by an evil cult from Borneo, a member of which, Malay, lives with the Franklyns. Dr. Franklyn decides to finally end his poor daughter's suffering by killing her, but is stopped by Malay, who Franklyn forces into a sulfur pit. A fire erupts in the struggle, and Valerie arrives at the Franklyn home at the same time. Dr. Franklyn, now out of his mind, tries to force Valerie to stay in the burning home with him. She is rescued by Harry and Tom, while Franklyn is bitten by Anna. Father and daughter then perish together in the burning home.

COMMENTARY After wrapping *Plague of the Zombies*, director John Gilling and the crew gave themselves a well-deserved week off before jumping into movie #4 in the Hammer production cycle

220

that had started with *Dracula – Prince of Darkness* earlier that year. That film's castle moat had been reused as the castle in *Rasputin – The Mad Monk* and was then repurposed into a graveyard for *Plague of the Zombies*. *The Reptile* topped off the four-film cycle and again used the set as a graveyard.

Of all the Hammer Horrors ever produced, *The Reptile* might be the weakest, and it still isn't bad by a long shot. If anything, the film is most comparable to *The Gorgon*. Like that film, it utilizes a non-traditional monster that also happens to have reptilian traits. In *The Gorgon*, mysterious victims were found turned to stone. Here they are found with blackened, rotting skin, and grotesquely foam at the mouth due to the venom in their systems. Unlike *The Gorgon*, we do get better, longer shots of the titular monster. Anna's Reptile gets a superb jump scare, literally coming out of the shadows in her first reveal, and she's not kept hidden in the shadows for the climax. The reason for this is because the makeup is quite good. Roy Ashton used a mold made from a real snakeskin for the makeup. Perhaps appropriately, this was Ashton's swan song for Hammer (appropriate in the sense that he went out with a bang). The Reptile is much better done than Medusa, who had been marred by the stiff, plastic snakes protruding from her head. However, the Reptile lacks an exciting death when compared to Medusa, whose own demise wasn't anything spectacular when compared to Dracula's numerous defeats. There is no real confrontation with the creature, the heroes merely escape it and leave it to burn in the house.

In terms of the cast, the film also lacks *The Gorgon's* star power, which had Peter Cushing, Christopher Lee and Barbara Shelley. Here, our main familiar faces are Noel Willman and Jennifer Daniel from *Kiss of the Vampire*. The standout characters are easily the tragic Anna and her father Dr. Franklin. Like his role as Dr. Ravna a few years before, Willman positively commands audience attention when he speaks, and we aren't sure what to make of him. Anna, on the other hand, is quite endearing and sympathetic, and you can't help but feel sorry for her. This was also, notably, another Hammer film that awarded Michael Ripper a larger than usual role. While his character here doesn't leave as big of an impression as the one he would play in *The Mummy's Shroud*, he does get to play an assertive, heroic character for a change, which is interesting.

When released in the Spring of 1966, *Rasputin* and *The Reptile* proved to be the lesser of the pair of the four-film package and didn't perform nearly as well as *Dracula – Prince of Darkness* and *Plague of the Zombies* did.

FINAL WORD As stated previously, it may be one of Hammer's weakest films, but it's still a unique piece of Hammer Horror, and that's always worth something.

BILLY THE KID
VERSUS DRACULA

(CIRCLE PRODUCTIONS INC.)
Release Date: April 10, 1966

Directed by: William Beaudine **Screenplay by:** Carl K. Hittleman
Makeup by: Ted Coodley **Music by:** Raoul Kraushaar **Cast:** John
Carradine (James Underhill/Dracula) Chuck Courtney (Billy the
Kid) Melinda Casey (Betty Bentley) Virginia Christine (Eva Oster)
Walter Janovitz (Franz Oster) Olive Carey (Dr. Henrietta Hull) Roy
Barcroft (Sheriff Griffin)

Spherical, Pathécolor, 74 Minutes

SYNOPSIS Travelling through the Old West, a vampire going
under the name of James Underwood is one of four passengers
onboard a stagecoach. When one of the travelers shows him a
picture of her beautiful daughter, Betty Bentley, Underwood sets
his sights on her. The vampire manipulates a Native American
band into killing the passengers, and then shows up in town
posing as Betty's uncle. Unbeknownst to the vampire, Betty's
fiancé is none other than a reformed outlaw named Billy the Kid.
When Underwood takes Betty into the mines to make her one of
the undead, Billy comes to her rescue and stakes the vampire
through the heart.

COMMENTARY Though it's called *Billy the Kid versus Dracula*,
this picture could have just as easily been titled "Cowboy vs.
Vampire." As it is, the name Dracula is never spoken during the
film's entire runtime. For that matter, other than being a quick
draw, there's nothing that makes the male lead particularly like
the real-life Kid. Of course, one doesn't go into a movie called *Billy
the Kid versus Dracula* expecting historical accuracy, but the fact
is both characters' histories are grossly neglected.

Though never stated, it's presumable that this version of Billy
the Kid was based upon the myth that an impostor was killed on
the night of July 14, 1881, that later went on to become known as
Brushy Bill. This is likely, as this piece's sister film, *Jesse James
Meets Frankenstein's Daughter*, used a similar real-life myth

wherein Jesse James escaped his alleged 1882 death. No mention of the Kid's past exploits in New Mexico are ever brought up so it's presumed he's on the run, having fled the aforementioned state. Likewise, it's never said where James Underwood, the unnamed Dracula, came from. Or, in other words, how did Dracula get from Transylvania to the Old West?

John Carradine plays Dracula again for the first time in 20 years, and acknowledged that this was the worst film he ever appeared in. It wasn't that Carradine was too old to be playing Dracula, the problem was he was too old to be making googley eyes at his younger co-stars. Making it even more laughable is the fact that this film was released in the Christopher Lee era, where Dracula was indeed a suave lady-killer. Carradine's character is more devil than Dracula, as his mustache and pointed goatee gives him the look of a classic devil more so than the Count. (Whenever he says something evil, a red glow is projected onto his face.)

The Western aspects of the film, notably a raid on a stagecoach by Native Americans, is fairly polished (though it's possible this fine footage was lifted from another film). The sets and color pallet are also nice, the silver mine in particular. It's got a real howler of an ending that makes little sense, though. Billy shoots Dracula with his gun to no effect. However, when he throws his gun in Dracula's face, it knocks him flat on his back! With Dracula down, Billy drives a silver knife through his heart. As he does this, a bat flies out of the cave, then drops dead in mid-air. Mind you, Dracula's body is still on the cave floor; he didn't turn into a bat. So what exactly this is supposed to mean is unclear. In any case, Dracula turns into a skeleton, Betty wakes up from his spell, and a happy ending is had by all.

The film was not a hit when released to theaters and today survives mostly due to the notoriety of the concept.

FINAL WORD Not as exciting as the title makes it out to be, but definitely as campy as the title makes it sound.

JESSE JAMES MEETS FRANKENSTEIN'S DAUGHTER

(CIRCLE PRODUCTIONS INC.)
Release Date: April 10, 1966
Alternate Titles: *Jesse James vs. Frankenstein* (France) *Jesse James Meets Frankenstein* (working title)

Directed by: William Beaudine **Screenplay by:** Carl K. Hittleman **Makeup by:** Ted Coodley **Music by:** Raoul Kraushaar **Cast:** John Lupton (Jesse James) Narda Onyx (Dr. Maria Frankenstein) Estelita Rodriguez (Juanita Lopez) Cal Bolder (Hank Tracy/Igor) Jim Davis (Marshal MacPhee) Steven Geray (Dr. Rudolph Frankenstein) Rayford Barnes (Lonny Curry)

Spherical, Pathécolor, 83 Minutes

SYNOPSIS Jesse James, who has just faked his death, is riding across the country with his friend Hank. When Jesse is caught in an ambush staged by a jealous member of the Wild Bunch, Hank is mortally wounded while defending Jesse. The duo escapes and come across a friendly Mexican family. The daughter, Juanita, tells Jesse about a Dr. Frankenstein in her village who can help Hank. Jesse and Juanita take Hank to Dr. Maria Frankenstein, and she manages to save Hank. Dr. Frankenstein doesn't stop there, though. After sending Jesse off on a wild goose chase for medicine, in reality a trap, Dr. Frankenstein transplants an artificial brain into Hank and renames him Igor. Jesse escapes the trap set for him and rides back to Frankenstein's castle. There a confused Igor/Hank kills Frankenstein and then sets his sights on Jesse. A tearful Juanita shoots the monster, saving Jesse but killing Hank.

COMMENTARY Though *Billy the Kid versus Dracula* may sound like the more interesting feature of this strange Wild West/Horror double bill, it's actually this film that is the better of the two. And, ironically, one of the reasons that it is "better" is because it's actually worse. Whereas *Billy the Kid versus Dracula* was just boring, *Jesse James Meets Frankenstein's Daughter* gets into "so bad it's good" territory rather quickly. You know it's going to be that sort of film upon hearing the horrid Austrian accents of actors

Narda Onyx and Steven Geray respectively playing Maria and Rudolph Frankenstein. Then, moments later, we see one of Maria's patients wearing an odd, rainbow-colored helmet that looks incredibly out of place. The rest of the film is filled with awful fight choreography, timing, and bad acting in general.

But, on the good front, there's a lot more for both Western enthusiasts and horror fans to like in this movie. Maria Frankenstein has an interesting hacienda/castle hybrid, and the Mexican village at the foot of the castle has more of that old European village feel common to horror films. On the Western front, this film's portrayal of Jesse James is more accurate than that of Billy the Kid in the co-feature. While the actor playing Billy looked nothing like the real Kid, John Lupton at least passes for Jesse James. The outlaw even uses a historically accurate alias as Mr. Howard at one point. Jesse's penchant for stealing from the rich and giving to the poor is also used. All that said though, this should have been the film to star Billy the Kid. As the Kid spoke Spanish and had a soft spot for senoritas, two traits Jesse has here, the producers should have swapped them and had the Kid in this film instead.

In comparing the two film's monsters, it's tough to say who wins. While Dracula was fairly traditional in his appearance, and had the benefit of a past Dracula in the form of John Carradine, this film's monster is somewhat lacking. Said monster is basically just a bodybuilder who has a scar encircling his cranium. If it could be compared to any other Frankenstein monster, it's most similar to David Prowse's creature in *Horror of Frankenstein* (1970). This film certainly has a much better ending than its predecessor. It's not a happy one, but it's much more memorable as Juanita has to shoot the sympathetic character of Hank, who has become the monster. Nor do Jesse and Juanita stay together at the picture's end, and Jesse hits the trail.

FINAL WORD Though this is the superior picture of the two, *Billy the Kid versus Dracula* remains the better remembered of the duo. The filmmakers also should have struck to the original title, *Jesse James Meets Frankenstein*, since most people associated the word Frankenstein more so with the monster rather than the doctor anyways. Had they done so, perhaps the film would have been better remembered.

MUNSTER, GO HOME!

(UNIVERSAL)
Release Date: August 6, 1966
Alternate Titles: *Ghost Party* (Austria) *Frankenstein and the Counterfeiters* (Belgium) *The Monster as a Racer* (Finland) *The Return of Dracula* (Greece) *The Adorable Monsters* (Mexico) *The Frankenstein Family* (Germany) *Heritage of the Munster* (Spain)

Directed by: Earl Bellamy **Makeup by:** Albert Whitlock **Screenplay by:** Joe Connelly, Bob Mosher, George Tibbles & Earl Bellamy **Music by:** Jack Marshall **Cast:** Fred Gwynne (Herman Munster) Yvonne De Carlo (Lily Munster) Al Lewis (Grandpa) Butch Patrick (Eddie Munster) Debbie Watson (Marilyn Munster) Terry-Thomas (Freddie Munster) Hermione Gingold (Lady Effigie Munster) Robert Pine (Roger Moresby) John Carradine (Cruikshank) Bernard Fox (Squire Lester Moresby) Jeanne Arnold (Grace Munster) Maria Lennard (Millie) Diana Chesney (Mrs. Moresby)

Spherical, Technicolor, 96 Minutes

SYNOPSIS When Lord Munster of England passes away, out of spite for his family he bequeaths his title to nephew Herman, who lives in America, rather than son Freddie. Herman is the head of the American branch of the Munster family, which includes his vampire wife, Lilly, her vampire father, "Grandpa," plus Herman and Lilly's werewolf son, Eddie, and their beautiful niece, Marilyn. On their way to England via ocean liner, Marilyn begins a romance with an Englishman named Roger Moresby. When the Munsters arrive in England to claim their inheritance, the English Munsters do their best to run off their American relatives. Making matters more complicated, Marilyn learns that the Moresbys and the Munsters are mortal enemies, and Herman and Grandpa discover a money counterfeiting ring in the basement of the Munster Mansion. Herman tells his aunt Effigie about it, unaware she is in on the scheme. Aunt Effigie and her mysterious accomplice, known only as the Griffon, arrange for Herman to be killed in a local road race. The Griffon takes the place of Roger Moresby in the race, but the mysterious fiend's efforts are thwarted by the Munster family. The Griffon is unmasked as the family butler's daughter, and Roger and Marilyn reconcile before the Munsters head back home to America.

COMMENTARY In 1966, Universal's classic monster roster of Frankenstein's monster, Dracula, Dracula's daughter, and a werewolf returned to the big screen, and in color no less! Or, at least, in a manner of speaking, they did. The TV sitcom *The Munsters* premiered on September 24, 1964, though the germ of the idea was birthed back in the 1940s. The series was filmed in black and white as a way of lessening the production costs and also evoking the old Universal monster series. The show was very successful in the first season, but season 2 got beat in the ratings badly by the Adam West *Batman* series. The show was cancelled and ended its run on May 12, 1966. And how then, if the show was failing, did a theatrical film get produced? This was done solely to help sell the series into syndication overseas, where it had yet to be broadcast. The hope was that when theatergoers overseas saw the movie, the networks would be more likely to pick the series up. The same thing was done with *The Munster's* competitor via 1966's *Batman: The Movie*.

The resultant feature film is actually fantastic, and amongst its most ardent fans are none other than Rob Zombie. Only a scant bit of the film takes place at the Munster home, as this is essentially a vacation movie. A good deal of the first act takes place on the *United States*, a real ocean liner of the time. Among the better gags are Grandpa taking a portable laboratory with him and also accidentally turning himself into a wolf on the ship. Herman, meanwhile, is constantly mistaken by a drunkard for his wife, Emily. Whereas sometimes new characters can seem intrusive in an established franchise, the English branch of the Munsters family, while not monstrous physically, are quite macabre and funny. If anything, they seem more like the Adams Family. Though all of them are humorous, Terry Thomas's Freddie Munster, presented in a state of arrested development and often throwing fits while his sister Grace eggs him on, stands out the most.

Though the entirety of the film is solid, the ending race is still the best sequence. There's a lot to love in it between Herman racing around in the souped-up Drag-u-la (with a coffin for a body and organ pipes for the exhaust) and Lilly and Grandpa doing their best to intercept him. There's nothing quite like watching Lily and Grandpa speeding around in a motorcycle with a sidecar. When that gets wrecked, they switch to riding horses, and when that fails, Grandpa turns himself into a wolf. Think *It's A Mad, Mad,*

Mad World but with the Munster gang. Lily is also given a lot more to do during the ending than most female characters of the time would have. She even arrests the Griffon by posing as the chauffeur. If any character gets shortchanged, it's mostly Eddy, but being the youngest one of the bunch, it's forgivable. Marilyn, in particular, got a good romantic subplot with Roger Moresby. However, many fans were rightly irritated that the original Marilyn, Pat Priest, had been replaced by a brand new actress in the form of Debbie Watson.

Unfortunately, the film wasn't a hit at the box office despite being a solid comedy for the time. *The Munsters* wouldn't return until 1981 in the inferior TV movie *The Munster's Revenge.*

FINAL WORD Though it wasn't a hit in its day, the film is well-known and loved among monster fans today as one of the best monster mashup comedies of all time.

MAD MONSTER PARTY?

(RANKIN/BASS/EMBASSY PICTURES)
Release Date: March 8, 1967 (U.S.)
Alternate Titles: *Frankensteins Monster-Party* (West Germany)

Directed by: Jules Bass **Screenplay by:** Len Korobkin, Harvey Kurtzman & Arthur Rankin Jr. (story) **"Animagic" Technician:** Tad Mochinaga **Music by:** Maury Laws **Voice Cast:** Boris Karloff (Baron Boris von Frankenstein) Alan Swift (Felix Flanken/Count Dracula/Frankenstein's Monster/"Fang," the Werewolf/the Hunchback of Notre-Dame/the Invisible Man/Dr. Jekyll and Mr. Hyde/"It"/Yetch/Chef Mafia Machiavelli/Mr. Kronkite) Gale Garnett (Francesca) Phyllis Diller (the Monster's Mate)

Spherical, Eastmancolor, 95 Minutes

SYNOPSIS Experimenting in his castle on the Isle of Evil in the Caribbean, Baron Frankenstein discovers a destructive anti-matter formula. He decides to have one last big party, announcing his retirement to his monster friends (including the monster, his bride, Dracula, the Invisible Man, the Creature, and others). During the party, he will also announce his successor (secretly his nephew Felix Flanken). This doesn't sit well with his beautiful assistant Francesca, who feels she should be the successor, not Franken. During the party, she conspires with Count Dracula to kill Felix, though their attempts are unsuccessful. Eventually, Francesca falls in love with Felix at the same time that the monsters betray her. They, too, are after the Baron's new anti-matter formula. Things come to a head when 'It'—a gigantic ape—arrives on the island. Francesca and Felix escape via boat, while the Baron destroys himself, It, and the other monsters with his anti-matter formula.

COMMENTARY As stated earlier in this book, back in the 1940s Universal occasionally toyed with the notion of a true monster mash that would feature all of their monsters in one movie. In 1967, this finally came to pass, but not through Universal. Rankin/Bass, best remembered now as the creators of *Rudolph,* the Red-Nosed Reindeer and *Frosty the Snowman*, produced *Mad Monster Party?* At the time, Universal's old horror stable was quite popular again due to TV airings as well as spoofs like *The Munsters* and *The Adams Family*. Therefore Rankin/Bass decided to recreate the monsters via their "Animagic" stopmotion animation, overseen by Tadahito Mochinaga at MOM Productions in Japan.

All of the Universal monsters appear in some context, but many of them are redesigned for legal reasons. Boris Karloff headlines the cast playing Baron Frankenstein, the second time he had done so since *Frankenstein 1970* (1958). The figurine bears his likeness to a tee, only with a more squared head. Frankenstein's monster looks the most like its cinematic inspiration, being green and with a flat head. His bride, on the other hand, looks nothing like Elsa Lanchester, nor does she sport the famous electric hairdo. Instead she is made to resemble the actress voicing her, Phyllis Diller. Dracula is there too but looks nothing like either Bela Lugosi or Christopher Lee and if anything resembles Count Chocula (from the breakfast cereals). There is a werewolf, who is not called the Wolf Man and nor does he have a human form. (He is modeled after a gypsy in reference to Bela Lugosi's werewolf character in *The Wolf Man*, though.) There's a mummy that's differentiated from Kharis by way of a headpiece. Dr. Jekyll and Mr. Hyde are there too, but there having been no real significant adaptation of them from Universal, there was no fear of legal problems. The Invisible Man is present, wearing sunglasses and a fez which is a nice look for the character. The trickiest monster of the bunch to recreate was easily the Creature from the Black Lagoon, being a Universal creation 100%. Therefore, the character called "the Creature" in this film is basically a pink, bipedal fish of sorts that looks nothing like Universal's Creature. (Ultimately, the only classic monsters not present were the Phantom of the Opera and Dorian Gray.) Lastly, there is 'It'—basically King Kong. Actually, 'It' probably was King Kong in an early draft until it was presumably changed for legal reasons. (This is quite strange as Rankin/Bass had rights to Kong at this time. They produced the animated *The King Kong Show* in 1966, and the live-action movie, *King Kong Escapes* with Toho in Japan in 1967.) Further hitting home the fact that the monster is Kong is the fact that it's attacked by airplanes while perched atop the island.

There are fun new characters as well, particularly Francesca, easily the most interesting of the bunch. She starts off the story as a villain, plotting to do-in the Baron's heretofore unknown nephew, Felix Flanken. You see, the movie is a bit like a monster version of *Cat on a Hot Tin Roof*, wherein a family vies for a dying patriarch's inheritance. In this story's case, Baron Frankenstein is the patriarch who is retiring rather than dying, and all the monsters, Francesca included, are incensed that he plans to leave his latest invention (an anti-matter formula) to a normal human. By the film's end, Francesca has fallen in love with Felix and the two run away together. In a twist ending, Francesca tells Felix she can't marry him because she's actually a robot. Felix then answers that nobody's perfect, but has a glitch like a machine, implying he's also a robot!

Though you would think this was a Halloween TV special, this was one of Rankin/Bass's few theatrical productions. It's unknown just how successful it was (or wasn't), but either way it never achieved the fame that Rankin/Bass's holiday specials did. That said, it is a very fondly remembered film among "monster kids" today.

FINAL WORD If you love *Rudolph, the Red-Nosed Reindeer* and Universal's horror movies, then you'll probably love this as well.

FRANKENSTEIN
CREATED WOMAN

(HAMMER)

Release Date: March 15, 1967 (U.S.) June 18, 1967 (U.K.)
Alternate Titles: *And Frankenstein Created Woman* (South
America) *Frankenstein Captivated the Soul* (Finland)
Frankenstein's Bride (Greece) *Curse of the Frankensteins* (Italy)
Frankenstein As a Woman (Hungary) *Frankenstein: Revenge of
the Dead Beauty* (Japan) *The Beast Frankenstein* (Norway)
Frankenstein's Devil's Daughter (Sweden)

Directed by: Terence Fisher **Screenplay by:** Anthony Hinds (as
John Elder) **Special Effects by:** Les Bowie **Music by:** James
Bernard **Cast:** Peter Cushing (Baron Frankenstein) Susan
Denberg (Christina Cleve) Thorley Walters (Doctor Hertz) Robert
Morris (Hans) Duncan Lamont (Hans's father) Peter Blythe (Anton)
Barry Warren (Karl) Derek Fowlds (Johann) Alan MacNaughton
(Kleve)

Spherical, DeLuxe Color, 92 Minutes

SYNOPSIS Baron Frankenstein's newest experiments pertain to
how long the soul stays in the body after death. After successfully
determining that the soul doesn't leave the body for some time in
an experiment, Frankenstein sends his assistant Hans to the local
inn for champaign so that they can celebrate. While there, three
rich ruffians mock Hans's crippled girlfriend, Christina, and a
fight breaks out. Later that night, the three men return to the inn
and kill Christina's father. Hans is blamed for the murder and is
executed. Christina then commits suicide out of grief.
Frankenstein and his colleague, Hertz, harvest Hans's soul and
transplant it into Christina. Due to the Baron's advanced surgery,
Christina awakens as a vision of beauty, no longer deformed. But
soon, the spirit of Hans compels her to take revenge, and she kills
off the three ruffians one by one. Once her task is completed, she
commits suicide.

COMMENTARY Just as *Evil of Frankenstein* before it, Hammer's
next Frankenstein flick began under the title of *Fear of*

Frankenstein. However, the basis of the idea went back to 1958, when Hammer created a catchy title—but with no real story attached—called *And Then Frankenstein Created Woman.* The premise for Frankenstein #4 was inspired by two main concepts. First of all, *One Million Years B.C.* was in production, and supposedly Dick Zanuck, sensing a hit, wanted Hammer to sex up their Frankenstein picture with a pretty girl. The other major influence was a discarded storyline from the unmade *Tales of Frankenstein* TV series, which was to be about the Baron creating a beautiful girl named Lisa who lacked a soul. Due to *Evil of Frankenstein's* unimpressive grosses in the U.K., Hammer wasn't given much to invest in the film, and it had a modest budget of only £120-140,000 (depending on the source). They shot it on the leftover Cornish village sets from *Plague of the Zombies* and *The Reptile* between July 4ᵗʰ and August 12, 1966.

Although the Baron begins this film being "dead," no allusions are made to his previous adventure. Or, that is to say, the Baron isn't dead from the castle explosion at the end of *Evil of Frankenstein,* he's "dead" as part of an experiment he's conducting to determine how long it takes the soul to leave the body. Nor is the boy Hans meant to be the same Hans from the previous two films. It's simply a case of Hammer overusing the same names again and again (like Paul in the Dracula films). After two exciting horror scenes, the first being an execution and the second being the Baron's icy revival, the real story—that of Hans and Christina—begins. The plot was probably quite odd for audiences familiar with more traditional Frankenstein films, like *Evil.* Though it gets off to an exciting start, the long sequence at the inn might have been off putting for some audiences who expected something more akin to *Curse of Frankenstein* or *Evil of Frankenstein.* As was the case of the last film, the Baron is sometimes thrown into the background as the new, supporting characters take over. (This is in large part due to the treatments for *Tales of Frankenstein,* in which the Baron would often introduce the stories then fade into the background in favor of the guest stars.)

Furthermore, this was the first entry of the series to not contain a traditional "monster," because who could ever call Susan Denberg a monster? This trend would also carry over into the next sequel as well. As it is, the "monster," doesn't appear until an hour in. Just as he had done in *Dracula – Prince of Darkness,* director Terence Fisher spends the first hour setting up the characters so that the last thirty minutes is nothing but payoff. Again, it's the method of tension and release. The film does an excellent job of setting up the three rich men as thoroughly unlikable so that the audience can root for Christina when she kills them off one by one. It's actually rather odd that Johan is the first to die, as he was the ringleader, and should have been last. And yet, that said, Carl being the last one set to die is interesting, because Carl was the least detestable of the bunch. One can just almost feel some sympathy for Carl as the walls close in on him, and perhaps that was Fisher's intent as one wonders if Christina/Hans will really kill him.

As for the Baron, Frankenstein's heroic streak from the last film continues. It's difficult to tell whether the Baron is preserving Hans's soul out of compassion or because he just wants a soul for his experiment. Cushing's Frankenstein often teetered the line of outright villain and anti-hero in his films. Here he's settled into the mold of an anti-hero quite well, resurrecting Cristina and allowing Hans to get his revenge on the men who wronged him (even if Frankenstein selfishly uses the double tragedy to further his experiments). Anthony Hinds later said, "I enjoyed writing Frankenstein's more than Dracula's — he (Frankenstein) was witty."

Unlike previous Frankenstein films, critics were actually kind to *Frankenstein Created Woman* for a change. This didn't translate into box office gold, though, and the film basically made enough to break even and warrant a fifth Frankenstein feature.

FINAL WORD Though it may not be very Frankenstein-like, this film's tragic little love story between Hans and Christina might just be the best fairy tale/morality play that Hammer ever did.

THE MUMMY'S SHROUD

(HAMMER/20ᵀᴴ CENTURY FOX)
Release Date: March 15, 1967 (U.S.) June 18, 1967 (U.K.)
Alternate Titles: *Cursed Sarcophagus* (Brazil) *Revenge of the Mummy* (Finland) *In the Clutches of the Mummy* (France) *The Curse of the Mummy* (Greece/Germany) *Mummy Phantom Curse* (Japan) *The Mysterious Mummy* (Turkey)

Directed by: John Gilling **Special Effects by:** Les Bowie & George Partleton (makeup) **Screenplay by:** John Gilling based off of a story by Anthony Hinds **Music by:** Don Banks **Cast:** André Morell (Sir Basil Walden) David Buck (Paul Preston) Maggie Kimberly (Claire) John Phillips (Stanley Preston) Michael Ripper (Longbarrow) Richard Warner (Inspector Barrani) Elizabeth Sellars (Barbara Preston) Tim Barrett (Harry) Roger Delgado (Hasmid) Catherine Lacey (Haiti) Dickie Owen (Prem) Eddie Powell (the Mummy) Tim Turner (narrator)

Spherical, DeLuxe Color, 90 Minutes

SYNOPSIS In ancient Egypt, the young Pharoh Kah-to-bey must flee into the desert with his faithful guard, Prem. Kah-to-bey dies, and Prem buries him best that he can in a tomb in the desert. In 1920, the tomb is discovered by Sir Basil Walden, whose expedition is funded by wealthy industrialist Stanley Preston. When Kah-to-bey is reunited with the mummy of Prem in a Cairo museum, Prem is brought back to life to punish the people who disturbed the tomb of his master. Eventually four people, including Sir Basil and Stanley Preston, are killed. The final two survivors, Paul Preston and Claire, obtain the mummy's sacred shroud and utter the Words of Death, causing it to crumble into dust.

COMMENTARY Not only was *The Mummy's Shroud* the last Hammer film to be shot at Bray Studios, it was also the last of eleven pictures produced for 20ᵗʰ Century Fox. After having given the studio one Dracula and Frankenstein film, plus zombies and reptile people, Hammer decided to dust off the Mummy for their final film for the company. It was a quick production, with the script completed on September 6, 1966, and filming began less than a week later on September 12th.

The film is a slight improvement over the previous Mummy film, *Curse of the Mummy's Tomb*, but is naturally still inferior to the 1959 Hammer *Mummy*. Unlike those two films, which only had portions set in Egypt, this one is set entirely in Egypt like Universal's first two Mummy movies. The flashback that opens the film is by no means epic, but it's still well done and exciting. It is aided and abetted by Don Banks wonderful score, which was much better than the work he did on *Evil of Frankenstein*. The design for the Mummy is a nice departure from the previous two entries, and it possesses a memorable pair of blue eyes (shots of the eyes opening are among the film's most memorable visuals). The Mummy's rather unique look came from the fact that it was historically accurate for a change and was based upon a real mummy from the Roman era.

The Mummy's four murders are each fairly unique, and John Gilling's direction for the scenes is superb. For the first killing, Sir Basil sees the Mummy's reflection within a crystal ball before it grabs him from behind and then crushes his head (out of frame, of course). In the next death scene, the Mummy is revealed in the dark room of a photographer, who first sees its reflection in a photo tray. He fends off the Mummy with corrosive chemicals that do nothing to hinder it. The Mummy then pours the chemicals on the man, who begins to scream as the room catches fire. The third killing is a bit hard to watch because it happens to Michael Ripper's pitiful but likeable character Longbarrow (often touted as the best performance in the film, which it is). The poor man has just broken his glasses, and is unaware that the man standing in his doorway is one of the undead. The Mummy wraps Longbarrow in a bedsheet and then throws him through the window. The final killing is that of Stanley Preston. There's something of a fake out, as the audience is startled by a loud noise not caused by the Mummy—and then the Mummy suddenly appears behind Preston to kill him.

The final fight in the museum is nearly as good as the tussle in the study from the 1959 *Mummy* (and that scene in all likelihood inspired this one). Similar to how Cushing impaled the Mummy in his film with a spear, lead actor David Buck slices into the Mummy's dusty shoulder with an ax. The Mummy is also shot numerous times, and one can see dust expelled from its body with each bullet strike. Second to 1958's *Horror of Dracula*, this might be Les Bowie's most memorable disintegration scene as the Mummy clutches at its head as it turns to a dusty old skull. The hands are still moving and clasping at the quickly deteriorating body till the very last second.

Unfortunately, the film was not a big success. However, considering that it was the support feature for *Frankenstein Created Woman*, that's not really the film's fault. Nor was it kindly received by critics—not even the monster magazines of the time gave it high marks! As it was, this would turn out to be Hammer's final traditional Mummy movie.

FINAL WORD Though it wasn't well received at the time, *The Mummy's Shroud* has been reevaluated as one of Hammer's better efforts. It's certainly better than *Curse of the Mummy's Tomb*, and for that matter, most of Universal's Mummy sequels from the 1940s.

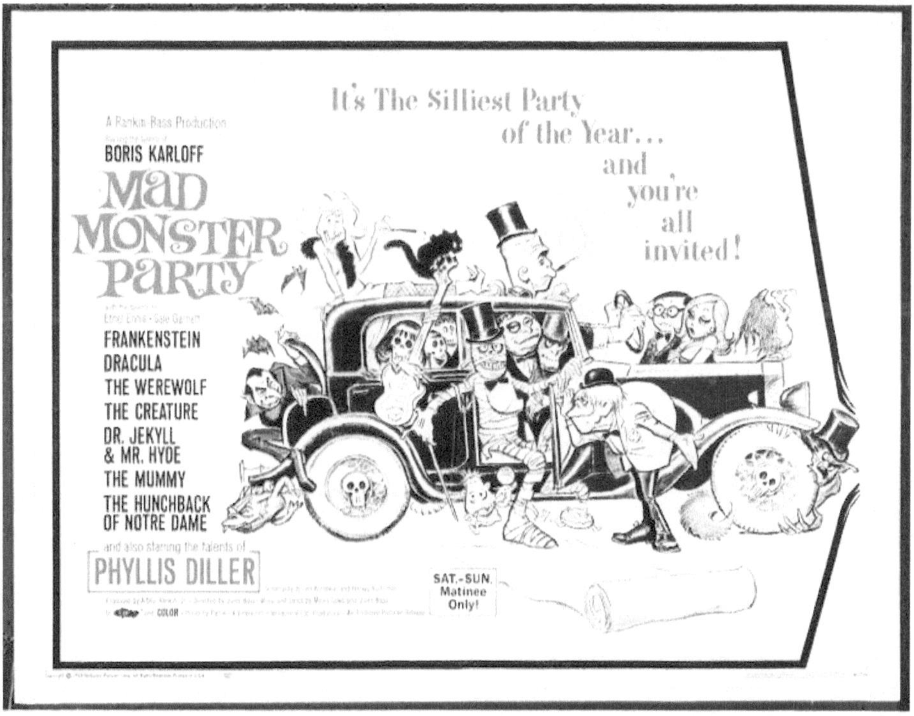

THE STRANGE CASE OF DR. JEKYLL AND MR. HYDE

(DAN CURTIS PRODUCTIONS)
Broadcast Date: January 7, 1968 (U.S.)
Alternate Titles: *Dr. Jekyll and Mr. Hyde* (Finland) *The Terrible Story of Dr. Jekyll and Mr. Hyde* (Spain)

Directed by: Charles Jarrott **Screenplay by:** Ian McLellan Hunter based upon the book by Robert Louis Stevenson **Makeup by:** Nicki Balch & Dick Smith **Music by:** Robert Cobert **Cast:** Jack Palance (Dr. Henry Jekyll/Mr. Edward Hyde) Denholm Elliott (Mr. George Devlin) Leo Genn (Dr. Lanyon) Torin Thatcher (Sir John Turnbull) Rex Sevenoaks (Dr. Wright) Gillie Fenwick (Poole) Elizabeth Cole (Hattie) Duncan Lamont (Sergeant Grimes) Paul Harding (Constable Johnson)

Academy Ratio, Color, 120 Minutes

SYNOPSIS In London in the year 1888, Dr. Henry Jekyll shocks his peers in the medical community by announcing that he plans an experiment to expose the duplicity of man's character. He does so without their support when they scoff at the moral implications of his experiment. His strange elixir turns him into his alter ego Mr. Hyde, who makes enemies and admirers alike on his first night out on the town. At Tessie O'Toole's Music Hall, a prostitute named Gwyneth becomes infatuated with Hyde and the two share a relationship of sorts, though it eventually turns violent. To cover for his alter ego, Jekyll lets on that Hyde is an employee of his, though his good friend George Devlin is suspicious of this and thinks Hyde is blackmailing Jekyll. Eventually, to his shock, Hyde reveals to Devlin that he and Jekyll are one and the same. Hyde convinces him to help Jekyll escape, and Devlin reluctantly agrees. However, Hyde eventually attempts to kill Devlin and so he shoots him, thus ending the existence of Hyde and Jekyll both.

COMMENTARY This production was organized by legendary TV horror producer Dan Curtis around the same time that he was developing *Dark Shadows*, the Gothic soap opera that would make him famous. (Fans will "recognize" the music from *Dark Shadows*

241

as this film's score. In fact, this score came first and was used on *Dark Shadows* later. Even the show's hit song for "Quentin's Theme" can be heard on this film's soundtrack.) Curtis's production of the Robert Louis Stevenson classic had a bit of a troubled start. It was originally to be written by Rod Serling (*Twilight Zone*) who backed out early, and so it was written instead by Ian McLellan Hunter. Jason Robards was initially cast in the title role, and the TV movie was to be shot in London. When that proved unfeasible, shooting was moved to New York. After the sets were constructed there was a technicians strike. Following that, the film moved to Canada, and some sources say that due to the strike Robards became unavailable. Whatever the reason Robards had to leave, it was a lucky accident, as Jack Palance might just be the best Mr. Hyde to ever grace the screen. His portrayal as Jekyll is wonderful too, but it's his satyr-like Hyde, with his exaggerated eyebrows that really steal the show. Rather than an outright monster as he was portrayed in some adaptations, this one had Hyde as a wild partier. And despite his ghoulish looks, his wild behavior even earns him several female admirers. Scenes of Hyde in action are spectacular, particularly one where he takes on a whole gang of men out for revenge on him.

The film does a good job of building anticipation for Hyde as we don't see Jekyll's first transformation. Essentially we're in the same boat as Jekyll when he wakes up, we don't know what happened exactly and we piece together the night before with him when he goes to a bar and hears of Hyde's wild deeds. The best bits come about during the end portion of the film, mainly in the form of Devlin finally learning the ugly truth of Jekyll and Hyde. The final scene finds Devlin wandering about the lecture hall where the picture started, Jekyll's initial remarks hanging heavy in the air as audial flashbacks of sorts. Eventually Hyde's voice breaks into Devlin's reminiscing and the final duel begins. Devlin shoots Hyde, who feigns his death throes only to pounce on Devlin in a truly chilling scene. Devlin is quick on the draw though, and shoots Hyde once more in midair ending his reign of terror.

The film was lauded by critics, who appraised it as not only the most faithful adaptation of the story so far, but also the best. It was also nominated for six Emmy's, two of them in a major category. Tessie O'Shea was nominated for Best Supporting Actress and the film itself was nominated for Outstanding Dramatic Program for 1967-1968 but lost to *Elizabeth, the Queen*. Today it is still considered the best Jekyll and Hyde adaptation amongst some scholars.

FINAL WORD It's quite a shame that this fine film was shot on videotape rather than film, as it's deteriorated badly over the years. Not to mention the fact that it's far too good for a simple video tape production and feels like it should be a cinematic production instead. Lastly, it's quite possibly the best Dr. Jekyll and Mr. Hyde screen adaptation ever.

DRACULA
HAS RISEN FROM THE GRAVE

(HAMMER)

Release Date: November 7, 1968 (U.K.) February 6, 1969 (U.S.)
Alternate Titles: *Dracula and the Women* (France) *Dracula Returns from the Grave* (Latin America) *Dracula, the Devil's Profile* (Brazil) *Bloodsucker Dracula* (Denmark) *Dracula's Return* (Germany/Japan/Poland) *Dracula's Lovers* (Italy) *The Sign of Dracula* (Portugal)

Directed by: Freddie Francis **Special Effects by:** Frank George **Screenplay by:** Anthony Hinds (as John Elder) **Music by:** James Bernard **Cast:** Christopher Lee (Dracula) Rupert Davies (Monsignor Ernst Muller) Veronica Carlson (Maria Muller) Ewan Hooper (Priest) Barbara Ewing (Zena) Barry Andrews (Paul) Marion Mathie (Anna Muller) Michael Ripper (Max)

Spherical, Technicolor, 92 Minutes

SYNOPSIS Upon inspecting a village church near Castle Dracula, the Monsignor decides to perform an exorcism on the castle. The village priest treks up the mountain with him but trips and falls along the way. His blood drips down an icy crevice until it reaches the frozen body of Dracula, who revives. Dracula enslaves the priest and demands he take him to the Monsignor, who lives in Keinenberg, to get revenge. There Dracula seduces the Monsignor's niece, Maria. When the Monsignor is mortally wounded while chasing after Dracula, he sends for Maria's atheist boyfriend, Paul, to help vanquish the vampire. The Monsignor dies and Paul teams with the priest, not knowing he's a servant of Dracula. The vampire king kidnaps Maria and takes her back to his castle, sealed shut with a cross. Maria tosses it into a ravine just as Paul shows up to rescue her. He and Dracula struggle, and the vampire falls into the ravine and is impaled on the crucifix. Paul crosses himself and the priest renounces Dracula's hold on him with a prayer.

COMMENTARY With the last film having been a huge hit in 1966, and with the British film industry in a bit of a lag the following year, in May of 1967, a meeting was held to propose another Dracula film. In fact, the film was greenlit before any type of story idea had even been pitched. All that mattered was that Lee would star in Dracula #3 (if one didn't count *Brides*, of course). However, it took some doing to get Lee, and Sir James Carreras literally had to call him on the phone and beg him to return for the sake of the Hammer staff. (Hammer was still refusing to pay Lee the salary that other studios were paying him for non-Dracula roles!) The film was supposed to go before cameras on March 18, 1968, but Terence Fisher was unable to meet the start date as he was recovering from an accident suffered in February. As such, future Oscar winning cinematographer Freddie Francis replaced him as director, and shooting began on April 22 and lasted until May 31st.

Because the movie had a larger £165,000 budget thanks to Warner Bros-Seven Arts, the film has undeniable production values, though many fans and critics consider it to be a little dull. Say what you will of the story, but the visuals, aided along by the music, are absolutely fantastic, especially the rooftop scenes with the filters. They make up some of the most striking imagery in the entire Hammer filmography. This version of Dracula also comes across better than the hissing boogeyman from the previous film, as Lee had dialogue this time around. Though he disliked the title very much, Lee did say that he liked the script in a letter for the Christopher Lee Club Bulletin for April-May of 1968. (However, during filming he described the script as "just adequate".) Lee was most vocal about disliking the removal of the stake scene, and also Dracula's method of demise at the climax. Lee respected the film's production values though and described Freddie Francis's direction as "more intelligent and less pedestrian" than Terence Fisher's.

In the absence of Van Helsing another holy man took his place in the form of Rupert Davies as a monsignor. However, Van Helsing would have been ill-suited for this film, and the family unit represented by the monsignor, his widowed sister-in-law and niece works quite well. Part of what makes the story engaging is Dracula's slow destruction of the family unit (a theme that would carry into the next film as well). Veronica Carlson, touted as Dracula's most beautiful victim, also makes for a more engaging, sympathetic female lead that Susan Farmer did in the previous outing as well. And, even though it had been only two years since the last Dracula, the series had been sexed up considerably in this outing. The direction of the scene where Dracula nuzzles Maria before biting her is excellent. Then Maria herself nuzzles and kisses Dracula's casket. This is also probably the film in which Michael Ripper truly cemented himself as such a loveable part of the Hammer staple. Yes, he had been in plenty of films, certainly. But his previous characters had always bordered on the meek and the pathetic. While we felt sympathy for his character in *The Mummy's Shroud* the previous year, he wasn't what I'd call a respectable character. His character of Max in *Grave* is downright adorable as the fatherly keeper of the inn who watches out for Paul, Xenia, and Maria. (It's no surprise that Christopher Lee once more or less said that Ripper was Hammer just as much as he was.)

The leading man, Paul, has an interesting arc in the film as an atheist. In an era where anti-religious sentiments were becoming more common place, it was actually surprising when at the film's ending Paul seems to have a change of heart. It's no surprise that the Catholic Church liked the Hammer brand. Some have argued that the religious aspect, more so than a reflection of the company's own beliefs, was played up in this entry because Hammer had become wise to just how popular their films were in predominantly Catholic territories like Spain and Italy. In any case, as the most religious of all of Hammer's films, this would have been a perfect film for Terence Fisher, a professed Christian. However, the visual flare given to the sometimes slow moving story by Francis cannot be understated.

Even the ending is heavily religious. In keeping with trying to find unique ways to do in Dracula, this time he falls from a ledge and is impaled by a golden cross. There's also a nice little payoff when the priest redeems his weak spirit by praying at the moment of Dracula's death, and Paul crosses himself, implying that he is now a believer in Heaven above. Though the priest's praying makes no sense in terms of the mythology established in previous films, in terms of this film by itself it works quite well. During filming of the bloody climax, the set received a visit from Sir Henry Floyd and others to present Hammer with the Queen's Award for Industry. The occasion was that between 1964 and 1967 Hammer had brought in £2,742,797 worth of earnings. Reminiscences from the set say it was a rather awkward affair as the nobles observed the gory scene being shot before them. (Peter Cushing also stopped by, for the record, so even if Van Helsing wasn't there to witness the Count's death, Cushing still was).

FINAL WORD Though many fans consider this film inferior to the two Draculas that preceded it, audiences of the time loved it. Not only did it break opening day records in Britain; it went on to become Hammer's highest grossing Dracula film ever.

FRANKENSTEIN
MUST BE DESTROYED

(HAMMER/WARNER BROS)
Release Date: June 8, 1969 (U.K.) February 11, 1970 (U.S.)
Alternate Titles: *Frankenstein Must Die* (Latin America/
Germany/Greece) *The Return of Frankenstein* (France) *Destroy Frankenstein!* (Italy) *Frankenstein Horror Biological Experiment* (Japan) *Baron Frankenstein* (Portugal) *The Brain of Frankenstein* (Spain) *Frankenstein Dead or Alive* (Sweden)

Directed by: Terence Fisher **Special Effects by:** Studio Creations Ltd. **Screenplay by:** Bert Batt (from an original story by Anthony Nelson Keys and Bert Batt) **Music by:** James Bernard **Cast:** Peter Cushing (Baron Frankenstein) Veronica Carlson (Anna) Freddie Jones (Professor Richter/Doctor Brandt) Simon Ward (Karl Holst) Thorley Walters (Inspector Frisch) Maxine Audley (Ella Brandt) George Pravda (Doctor Brandt)

Spherical, Technicolor, 101 Minutes

SYNOPSIS After his lab is raided by the police, Baron Frankenstein becomes a tenant at Anna Spangler's boarding house. As his luck would have it, Anna's boyfriend Karl is a doctor at an asylum where an old colleague of the Baron's is being held. Some time ago, Frankenstein and a Dr. Brandt had done some work together on preserving brains after death. While Frankenstein's experiments failed, Brandt's succeeded, but then he went mad. Frankenstein blackmails Anna and Karl into helping him break Dr. Brandt out of the asylum. The strain is too much on the doctor, and he dies. Frankenstein removes his brain and places it in the body of the recently killed Professor Richter. Not only that, in the process, Frankenstein also cures Brandt's insanity. However, Brandt escapes in his new body when Anna goes down into the cellar. In a rage, Frankenstein kills her and chases after Brandt, who has returned to his home. There his wife is horrified by the fact that he now inhabits a new body and she leaves. When Frankenstein arrives at his home, Brandt tricks the Baron into becoming trapped within a fire he sets inside the home.

COMMENTARY Despite *Frankenstein Created Woman's* not so dynamic performance at the box office, by October of 1967 Anthony Hinds had already started the first draft for Frankenstein #5. In February of 1968, Warner Bros had been secured as co-financers. However, when it came time to advance the script into its final stages, Hinds was too busy working on the Hammer Twentieth Century Fox TV series *Journey Into the Unknown.* Therefore Anthony Nelson Keys and an assistant director named Bert Batt did the final version of the script. The development for this project was a bit longer than was usual for Hammer, with it not going before cameras until January 13, 1969—nearly a full year after Batt and Keys began the script. Shooting in winter caused some problems, mainly when newly fallen snow caused continuity errors for location shooting, which resulted in the film going over schedule.

Compared to the last film, shot within the smaller Bray Studios, *Frankenstein Must Be Destroyed* feels downright epic by comparison with its lavish, expansive sets. For the first time in two films, Frankenstein is front and center again (probably because this one wasn't based upon an old *Tales of Frankenstein* treatment). The Baron's characterization is also very different in this entry compared to the previous two, and he's even more of a sociopath than he was in *Curse of Frankenstein.* In fact, this film presents the Hammer Frankenstein as dangerous as he's ever been, not just intellectually, but physically. The good doctor roughs up quite a few people throughout the course of the story. And what a start the movie gets off to, with the Baron, disguised in a fright mask, lopping off a man's head!

Like the last film, wherein the beautiful Susan Denberg was the "monster," this film too lacks a horrific creation. In this case, it's a simple case of brain transplanting from one human being to another, which had been done in the first two Hammer Frankensteins. Despite being repetitive, it still manages to feel fresh thanks to the attention given to the character of Dr. Brandt, plus the actor who played Brandt post-transplant, that being Freddie Francis. It's quite sad watching the poor man try to interact with his beloved wife in a new body that is foreign and unattractive to her. Despite not being a monster in the traditional sense, Brandt's final confrontation with the Baron is possibly the series best in terms of the creature vs. its creator. In this case, Brandt rigs a game with the Baron. The notes Frankenstein so badly desires are behind one of three doors within the house. Each time Frankenstein approaches one, Brandt throws a Molotov cocktail at the door. Arguably it's much more exciting than watching Cushing try to wrestle around a stuntman in bad makeup à la *Evil of Frankenstein*. Furthermore, the Baron was just an observer in the last film's climax which is just another reason why this film's ending is one of the series all-time best in terms of action and excitement.

In the absence of a traditional monster the film still manages to find ghoulish ways to please the audience. First and foremost is the aforementioned opening scene, with the Baron in his mask. Then there are scenes set in an asylum with a screaming woman who thinks she sees spiders on her arms. Best of all, perhaps, is the scene where a water main bursts open in the ground, right under the spot where Dr. Brandt's old body was buried. The corpse's arm then appears to become reanimated due to the spewing water. Because we feel sympathy for poor Anna, we feel great suspense for her as she struggles to hide the body.

And speaking of poor Anna, it was Warner Bros who insisted upon injecting more sex into the film. It's not certain whether it was Hammer or Warners who came up with the rape scene specifically, but no one involved on the film itself was happy about it. Though Frankenstein was no angel, in the past two films his image had been reformed into that of at least an anti-hero. This sequence regressed him back to a despicable villain. Ironically, Warners cut the scene out of the U.S. release when it was their fault to begin with! According to some sources, the film wasn't a hit in the U.S. either, and Warners were so disappointed in it that it more or less ended their production agreement. (Due to a long standing contract, Warners still had a say in their Dracula films, though). But, as usual, other sources to the contrary say that the film was more successful than the last in Britain and America both. Regardless of how big of a hit that it was or wasn't, critics of the time ironically criticized it for being too tame! How times had changed...

FINAL WORD All of Hammer's Frankenstein films are so well-done outside of one or two entries—looking at you *Evil* and *Horror*—it's tough to say which one is actually the best, but this one is certainly a contender.

COUNT DRACULA

(FILMAR COMPAGNIA CINEMATOGRAFICA)
Release Date: April 3, 1970 (West Germany) July 1973 (U.K.)
October 12, 1973 (U.S.)
Alternate Titles: *At Night, When Dracula Awakens*
(Germany/France) *Dracula - The Prince of Darkness* (Portugal)

Directed by: Jesús Franco **Screenplay by:** Augusto Finocchi, Jesús Franco & Erik Krohenke (story) based upon the book by Bram Stoker **Special Effects by:** Sergio Pagoni & Stuart Freeborn (makeup) **Music by:** Bruno Nicolai **Cast:** Christopher Lee (Count Dracula) Herbert Lom (Professor Van Helsing) Klaus Kinski (Renfield) Frederick Williams (Jonathan Harker) Maria Rohm (Mina Murray) Soledad Miranda (Lucy Westenra) Paul Muller (Dr. Seward) Jack Taylor (Quincey Morris)

Spherical, Eastmancolor, 96 Minutes

SYNOPSIS Jonathan Harker arrives in Transylvania to meet Count Dracula and arrange the sale of some property to him in England. Harker is horrified by an encounter with the Count's vampire brides and flees the castle in terror. He wakes up sometime later in the sanitarium of Professor Van Helsing in England. Around the same time, his fiancé Mina's friend Lucy dies a mysterious death only to rise again as a vampire. Van Helsing calls for Lucy's fiancé, Quincy Morris, and explains the situation to him. Van Helsing, Quincy, and Harker put Lucy out of her misery, and soon after Dracula targets Mina. The Count bites Mina, meaning she will become undead if Dracula isn't killed, and then leaves the country. Van Helsing instructs Morris and Harker to get to Castle Dracula first and ambush him, which they do by setting his casket on fire, destroying the vampire.

COMMENTARY Throughout the 1960s, Christopher Lee had lamented the fact that he'd never gotten to do a proper portrayal of Dracula that was faithful to the Stoker novel. The closest he had ever come was *Horror of Dracula*, which had deviated from the book due to restraints concerning budget and run time more than anything else. In 1970, Lee finally got the chance to do an

250

authentic version of *Dracula*, though not for Hammer. Produced by Harry Alan Towers, the resultant film was predominantly a Spanish production, shot in Spain and directed by famous Spanish director Jesús Franco. The movie was advertised as the most authentic adaptation of the Stoker novel, and in many ways it was, but that didn't make it a winner. Not by a long shot.

Though this film looks fabulous on paper, on film it's awkward and weak, most likely due to Franco's direction and a script that falters badly in the last act. (That, and the fact that Franco reportedly ran out of money towards the end of shooting.). So many of the scenes that Terence Fisher had directed with vigor in *Horror of Dracula* fall flat with Franco's direction in *Count Dracula*. Just compare Dracula's entrance into Lucy's room in *Horror* with this film, where Dracula chants Lucy's name until she comes outside to see him. It's not very dynamic by comparison. Lucy's staking also seems perfunctory more than anything else when compared to the version in *Horror*. And the climax, though semi-faithful to the book, is downright pitiful. Whereas both the book and *Horror* featured an exciting chase to the castle, here Jonathan Harker and Quincy Morris wait in ambush for the Count as he's transported to the castle by his gypsy servants with no sense of urgency. Once they run off the gypsies, the duo open the Count's casket and set him on fire, then unceremoniously dump him from the castle walls!

It's a shame the film turned out this way too, because the cast assembled was fantastic. The problem is the script doesn't seem sure of what it wants to do with the characters. Herbert Lom, a wonderful actor best remembered as Inspector Dreyfuss in the Pink Panther franchise, is excellent as Van Helsing. However, the character is quite enigmatic, and not in a good way. Lines like "I feel as though I know Dracula better than my own self even though I've never met him," leave one wondering if there were scenes explaining this that went unfilmed or were cut. Just what is Van Helsing trying to imply? Furthermore, he has only one scene with Lee's Dracula, and it would've been fun to see them interact more. (The fact that the actors weren't even in the same room together when the scene was filmed is painfully evident!) Klaus Kinski, in particular, is wasted as Renfield, a role he was perfect for under the right direction. This version of Renfield doesn't do much and can't compete with Dwight Frye's version from the 1931 film—and if anybody could have, it was probably Kinski. This version of Renfield isn't really even Dracula's servant. In fact, Dracula psychically influences him to commit suicide via a high jump that fails and Renfield survives. After this, Dracula then uses Renfield to strangle Mina when she goes to his cell to question him. This strangulation attempt also fails, and the next we see of Dracula, he's set Mina up with tickets to the opera so that he may go there and ambush her. He bites her but doesn't kill her, then abruptly decides to leave England for Transylvania. He doesn't even try to take Mina with him—not much suspense there. Renfield then begins babbling about the Count's journey, which doesn't make sense since the parameters of the relationship were never explained. And so Harker and Morris are off to Transylvania themselves. When we think Dracula is already gone, he shows up to share his one and only scene with Van Helsing, who wards him off with a flaming cross he's drawn on the floor. Then, a little later, Dracula is suddenly in the care of his gypsy servants. As stated already, the end positively falls apart from a narrative perspective.

All that said, there are things of interest in this adaptation for classic horror fans. The first act of the picture is its best and could be considered a quasi-remake of the 1930 *Dracula* with Lee in place of Bela Lugosi. We get to see Lee disguised as the mysterious coach driver who picks up Harker at Borgo Pass and later, he even utters the children of the night line, though his version isn't as good as Lugosi's. Whereas the Hammer Dracula only ever had one vampire bride in his castle, in this production scenes featuring Dracula's three brides might just be the best aspect of the film, as Franco depicts them as ghosts emerging from their crypts. And, most importantly, Lee does look good with the mustache and grey hair that is accurate to the book. His performance is also well done, he is Christopher Lee after all. But, for all Lee's complaining about silly sequels like *Dracula Has Risen from the Grave* and even *Dracula A.D. 1972*, the directors of those films still staged the action much more dynamically than Franco did for this film. Though Lee's performance received some praise, for the most part this production was justifiably panned.

FINAL WORD Due to the issues listed above this movie will be more of interest to horror film historians and completists as opposed to casual fans looking for a good adaptation of *Dracula*.

TASTE THE BLOOD OF DRACULA

(HAMMER/WARNER BROS)
Release Date: May 7, 1970 (U.K.) June 7, 1970 (U.S.)
Alternate Titles: *A Mass for Dracula* (France) *The Blood of Dracula* (Brazil) *Dracula, the Devil's Messenger* (Finland)

Directed by: Peter Sasdy **Screenplay by:** Anthony Hinds **Music by:** James Bernard **Cast:** Christopher Lee (Dracula) Linda Hayden (Alice Hargood) Anthony Corlan (Paul Paxton) Gwen Watford (Martha Hargood) Geoffrey Keen (William Hargood) Ralph Bates (Lord Courtley) Peter Sallis (Samuel Paxton) Isla Blair (Lucy Paxton) John Carson (Jonathan Secker) Martin Jarvis (Jeremy Secker) Roy Kinnear (Weller) Michael Ripper (Inspector Cobb) Russell Hunter (Felix)

Spherical, Technicolor, 95 Minutes

SYNOPSIS Three bored English aristocrats in the form of Hargood, Paxton, and Secker wish to spice up their lives with something different: namely an occult ceremony. They go to an occultist named Lord Courtley who takes advantage of the men's wealth to procure a very expensive item: the last remains of Count Dracula, collected by a merchant who just so happened to witness his demise years ago. Courtley performs the profane ritual in a desanctified church, encouraging the men to drink Dracula's blood from a goblet. They refuse to do so, and when Courtley does he begins to choke. Rather than help him, the three men kick Courtley's convulsing body until he dies. Later, when the men have left, Courtley is supernaturally transformed into Dracula himself. Through the men's children, the Count begins picking off the men one by one. Hargood is first by way of his daughter, Alice. Next comes Paxton through his daughter, Lucy. The last of the men, Secker, is smart enough to realize that a vampire is loose. Before he is killed by his own son, Jeremy, Secker leaves instructions to defeat the vampire to Paul, Alice's fiancé and Lucy's brother. Paul finds Lucy dead, but there's still time to save Alice. At sundown, just before Dracula awakens, Paul performs a ceremony that re-ordains the church, making it hallowed ground again. Dracula cannot stand on hallowed ground, and so drops dead freeing Alice from his influence.

COMMENTARY Ten years ago, in 1959, Hammer had begun work on a sequel to *Horror of Dracula,* which would not end up featuring the Count, though his name did appear in the finished film's title: *Brides of Dracula.* Ten years later, history was repeating itself. Having only just barely lured Christopher Lee back for *Dracula Has Risen from the Grave,* Hammer knew the chances of him returning—or at least returning cheaply—were slim to none. As such, Brian Lawrence decided to go the *Brides* route again by ordering another movie with only Dracula's name in the title. Remarkably, the first script is very close to the finished film. Lord Courtley performs the ritual (and makes the title literal), only he doesn't die and resurrect as Dracula—tasting the blood simply makes him a vampire himself. All of Dracula's scenes in the finished film were initially to be Courtley as the vampire controlling the three children. Lee returned due to the insistence of Warner Bros, who had signed an agreement on *Grave* with Hammer that gave them some creative control over their Dracula films. They simply wouldn't have a Dracula film without Dracula. Conflicting sources state different reasons for Lee's return, with some saying James Carreras begged him again like he had on *Grave,* while others say Hammer actually shelled out the money this time and Lee got paid three times what he received for *Grave.* If the latter is true, it's rather funny, because Lee has much less screen time in this film than he did in the former despite the pay increase.

And though Lee doesn't have much to do, *Taste the Blood of Dracula* is considered by many to be Lee's last great Dracula sequel. As it is, the story is quite engaging, and Peter Sasdy's direction is excellent. The production values are equal to if not greater than *Grave*'s. The elaborate church set where Dracula lurks about was so well constructed that it was re-used in three subsequent Hammer films, including *The Vampire Lovers, Horror of Frankenstein*, and *Scars of Dracula.* James Bernard's score is positively lovely, utilizing a romantic theme that would have been more appropriate in the previous film, but still does wonders here. The plot structure is a bit like *Frankenstein Created Woman* in that three aristocrats are stalked and killed for a past crime, in this case by Dracula for killing his servant. And as in that film, the most unlikable one gets it first. In fact, Geoffrey Keen's Hargood is so unlikable that you almost want to cheer when Alice whacks him

254

across the head with a shovel. Like the last film, religion is again in the forefront. While *Grave* had an atheist for a hero, this film too initially appears to have an anti-religious slant. After all, Hargood is an over-bearing negative stereotype of a religious hypocrite. Though he makes his family feel guilty for not being religious enough, in the shadows he cheats on his wife and takes part in the dark arts! As opposed to the hypocritical parents, it is the "sinful" children who end up being pure of heart. The picture's ending hinges heavily upon Catholicism. Though some have balked at the ending, the method of Dracula's demise is still unique. As Dracula is hanging out in a de-sanctified church, or unhallowed ground, the hero sets out to re-sanctify the church as a means of defeating the arch vampire—you have to admit that it is interesting and hadn't been done before. (Anthony Hinds said himself, "I gave extra thought to highly visual ways to do in the Count.") Upon performing the necessary ceremony, the grounds are again considered hallowed, and Dracula essentially drops dead on the spot. Some found this means of demise to be "funny," but the only thing funny about the ending was Dracula's rather poor aim when he was throwing pipe organs at the heroes!

Just as this is considered the last truly good Dracula film from Hammer, it was also the last one to generate significant grosses at the box office, notably more so in Britain than the U.S. The U.S. version notably trimmed five minutes from the runtime (mostly for scenes containing brief nude shots and over-the-top gore). This wasn't too bad, as the U.S. market still considered Dracula to be kid stuff and so wanted the film to be acceptable for younger audiences. What was insulting, though, was that *Taste* was made to be the support feature for *Trog*!

FINAL WORD Though the films that followed still have their fans and supporters, this is the last Hammer Dracula that fans unanimously consider to be good.

THE
VAMPIRE DOLL

(TOHO)
Release Date: July 4, 1970
Alternate Titles: *Fear of the Ghost House: Bloodsucking Doll*
(Japan) *The Night of the Vampire* (U.S.) *Legacy of Dracula*
(U.K. home video title)

Directed by: Michio Yamamoto **Special Effects by:** Teruyoshi Nakano **Screenplay by:** Ei Ogawa & Hiroshi Nagano **Music by:** Riichiro Manabe **Cast:** Yukiko Kobayashi (Yuko Nonomura), Kayo Matsuo (Keiko Sagawa), Akira Nakao (Hiroshi Takagi), Yoko Minakaze (Shidu Nomomura), Atsuo Nakamura (Kazuhiko Sagawa), Jun Usami (Dr. Yamaguchi), Kaku Takashina (Genzo)

Tohoscope, Eastmancolor, 71 Minutes

SYNOPSIS A young woman named Keiko goes in search of her missing brother, last seen at the estate of his dead fiancé Yuko which is now inhabited only by her somber mother and mute groundskeeper. There, she and her beau Hiroshi are menaced by a ghostly young woman until they finally realize it is the dead Yuko, hypnotized when she was at the point of death and now exists as a murderous vampire. In her final act of vengeance, Yuko kills the doctor—who had previously killed her mother's family in a homicidal rampage before raping her mother and siring Yuko—responsible for her hypnotic state.

COMMENTARY According to director Michio Yamamoto in *Monsters Are Attacking Tokyo*, he was at a party talking about how he would like to make a horror thriller like *The Birds*. This conversation was overheard by Toho producer Fumio Tanaka who subsequently tasked Yamamoto with doing a Japanese take on England's Hammer Studios' Dracula films. As it was, after Great Britain and America, Japan was the country where Hammer horror films grossed the most—in fact, Hammer sometimes shot extra footage just for the Japanese releases. Reluctant to imitate the Dracula films, Yamamoto decided to meet Tanaka in the middle and came up with a vampire story which took its inspiration from Edgar Allan Poe's short story *The Facts in the Case of M. Valdemar.*

The simply-plotted film, part haunted house mystery and part vampire movie, begins with the usual backdrop of a dark and stormy night. The audience is clued in to the film's contemporary setting in the first shot as glimpsed through a car's windshield with the wipers on. The modern setting was the only innovation Toho had on Hammer, who wouldn't try the same until they produced *Dracula A.D. 1972. Count Yorga, Vampire*, the original modern vamp-film, was only released in America one month before this film debuted in Japan, so it's doubtful it had any influence on Toho either. Unfortunately in Toho's case, the modern setting is a result of budgetary necessitation rather than creativity, and truthfully the story could have just as easily taken place in the 1800s.

The film does come up with some striking visuals headed up by the main set, a western-style estate adorned with European artwork, which is quite lavish. The most memorable aspect is the female vampire Yuko, who sets herself apart from other vampires with her reflective eyes (minus pupils) that appear silver in the moonlight and golden by candlelight. The character was effectively portrayed by Yukiko Kobayashi, one of Toho's "new faces" when she played the female lead in *Destroy All Monsters* (1968), and also appeared in *Space Amoeba* the same year as this film. In the film's only bloody scene, Yuko slashes the true villain's throat with a knife in which effects director Teruyoshi Nakano uses an extreme blood-spraying effect (an effect he would utilize again in 1974's *Godzilla vs. Mechagodzilla*). The film's most gruesome shot is when the heroine discovers her decayed dead brother sitting upright in a chair not unlike Norman Bates' mother in *Psycho* (likely this scene's direct inspiration as Yamamoto was a fan of Hitchcock). Some of the scares make no sense at all though, and at one point a mannequin—an inanimate decoy for the vampire's absent body—jumps out of a coffin with no explanation. However, this also denotes a rather large difference between Western and Eastern filmmaking, the latter of which is more focused on fun than logic.

If this author has one complaint about the film, it's the rather abrupt nature of the ending which is heavy on exposition in the form of a long sequence featuring the film's surprise villain (the hypnotist responsible for Yuko's vampiric condition) explaining everything to the two main characters.

257

Released during the summer (which is the ghost season in Japan rather than fall as in the west), the film was a moderate success. Known internationally as *The Vampire Doll*, this was the only entry of the trilogy not to be dubbed into English or get a U.S. television broadcast though it did receive some limited theatrical showings in Los Angeles and New York in subtitled format. It was followed by two sequels in 1971 and 1974, respectively.

FINAL WORD Fan opinion on this film is decidedly mixed, with some considering it the best of what was eventually dubbed "The Bloodthirsty Trilogy" and others the most boring. Either way, mutual fans of Hammer and Toho should give the film a chance.

THE VAMPIRE LOVERS

(HAMMER/AIP)

Release Date: October 4, 1970 (U.K.), October 22, 1970 (U.S.)
Alternate Titles: *The Passion of the Vampires* (Belgium) *Carmilla, Vampire of the Karnstein* (Brazil) *The Vampire-An Erotic Nightmare* (Finland) *Vampire Mistresses* (Greece)

Directed by: Roy Ward Baker **Makeup by:** Tom Smith **Screenplay by:** Tudor Gates, Harry Fine & Michael Style based on the novella by Sheridan Le Fanu **Music by:** Harry Robertson **Cast:** Ingrid Pitt (Marcilla/Carmilla) Madeline Smith (Emma Morton) George Cole (Roger Morton) Kate O'Mara (Mademoiselle Perrodot) Jon Finch (Carl Ebhardt) Peter Cushing (General Spielsdorf) Douglas Wilmer (Baron Hartog) Pippa Steel (Laura) Ferdy Mayne (the doctor) Dawn Addams (the Countess) John Forbes-Robertson (Man in Black)

Spherical, Technicolor, 91 Minutes

SYNOPSIS Many years ago, Baron Hartog exterminated a whole crypt of vampires at Karnstein Castle. But one vampire named Mircalla escaped. Years later, a beautiful young woman, Marcilla, becomes stranded at the estate of General Spielsdorf. Slowly, Spielsdorf's daughter, Laura, withers away and dies, while Marcilla disappears. A short time later, Marcilla, now called Carmilla, shows up at the estate of Roger Morton. Again pretending to be stranded, slowly she drains Mortan's daughter, Emma, of life. Eventually, Baron Hartog, General Spielsdorf, and Morton all connect in time to join forces and kill Carmilla.

COMMENTARY Looking for new material to adapt outside of the usual culprits of Dracula and Frankenstein, Hammer decided it would be controversial to produce a motion picture of *Carmilla*, the 1872 novella by Sheridan Le Fanu. The story, which predated Bram Stoker's *Dracula*, focused on a female vampire feeding on a beautiful young girl named Laura. Due to the exploitive nature of the content, Hammer managed to secure American International Pictures as a co-financer and distributer in the U.S.

Despite the fact that this is an exploitation film, *Vampire Lovers* has an odd fairy-tale quality to it that, when coupled with the

259

romantic score, gives it an almost innocent atmosphere—though innocent it certainly is not. The film starts out strong, and the pre-credits scene is classic Hammer at its best. (It feels more like an older Hammer film when compared to films released the same year like *Scars of Dracula* or *Horror of Frankenstein.*) In the scene, a vampire emerges from its tomb via a mist effect, then materializes into a shrouded wraith. Eventually it is revealed to be a beautiful young girl who is beheaded by Baron Hartog.

The film's plot structure is essentially a long, drawn out version of the Lucy Westerna portion of the *Dracula* novel. That is to say, a beautiful young girl withers away in bed as a vampire slowly feeds on her. Doctors puzzle over her condition until one night she finally expires. In this case, this happens twice. The film's first twenty minutes concern Carmilla feeding upon Pipa Steele's character until she dies (though whether or not she ever becomes a vampire isn't addressed). The rest of the film does the same with Madeline Smith's character, who is like Lucy in that she eventually spends a lot of time in bed, but also like Mina in that she is eventually saved. (It should be noted, though, that the *Carmilla* novella has scenes like this in it, it's just that audiences were more familiar with the Dracula mythos, hence my comparison to it rather than the relatively obscure source material.)

As it is, *The Vampire Lovers* really isn't one of Hammer's more exciting vampire films, and if anything seems content to rest on the shock value of its subject matter. That said, it's not bad by any means, it's just different when compared to Hammer's last non-Dracula vampire feature, which was *Kiss of the Vampire.* The ending of the film is a good example of this. It's not disappointing, but considering that the heroes merely follow Carmilla to her coffin and then behead her, it's also just a tad underwhelming. However, the fact that the Man in Black is glimpsed watching the heroes take away Carmilla's body lets us know to expect a sequel, which is unique for a Hammer production.

The cast is great, and Ingrid Pitt was easily the best of Hammer's Carmillas (in the two sequels she was recast). Peter Cushing is more of a guest star than a star, and only figured into the beginning and the ending really, though his scenes are certainly welcome. (On that note, he was apparently shoehorned into the film at the insistence of American International Pictures). Madeline Smith is the epitome of innocence as Emma Morton, and this is easily her most memorable Hammer performance. And, though he only appears briefly and we never hear him speak, John Forbes-Robertson's man of mystery has an excellent presence. The fact that we don't know who he is benefits the film rather than detracts from it. That the character also reappeared in the sequel was a nice continuity touch.

The film plays fast and loose with vampire mythology. Carmilla can appear in sunlight without being burnt to a crisp like Christopher Lee's Dracula (though she does state she prefers to stay out of it). In fact, it would almost appear that the Karnsteins sleep at night rather than during the day, as Baron Hartog is quoted as saying he spent "all night" destroying the vampires in their graves. If anything, just when the Karnsteins sleep is unclear. There are some odd, magical aspects to Carmilla, too. Again, unlike Lee's Dracula who needed a coach to travel long distances, Carmilla can apparently teleport like a ghost. She uses this strange ability twice in the film. Also, when she dies, we don't see her body decompose. Instead, like Dorian Gray, it is her portrait that turns into a vampiric skeleton!

Ultimately, AIP wasn't satisfied with *Vampire Lovers* because they considered it too risqué, and they weren't necessarily wrong. For the time it was a bit too much. As such, this proved to be the only Hammer AIP co-production even though the film managed to turn a profit.

FINAL WORD Easily the best of Hammer's Carmilla trilogy.

HORROR OF FRANKENSTEIN

(HAMMER/EMI)
Release Date: November 8, 1970 (U.K.) June 17, 1971 (U.S.)

Directed by: Jimmy Sangster **Screenplay by:** Jimmy Sangster &
Jeremy Burnham (based on characters created by Mary Shelley)
Special Effects by: Tom Smith (makeup) **Music by:** Malcolm
Williamson **Cast:** Ralph Bates (Victor Frankenstein) Veronica
Carlson (Elizabeth) Kate O'Mara (Alys) Dennis Price (graverobber)
Jon Finch (Lt. Henry Becker) Bernard Archard (Professor Heiss)
Graham James (Wilhelm Kassner) Joan Rice (graverobber's wife)
Stephen Turner (Stephan) Dave Prowse (the monster)

Spherical, Technicolor, 95 Minutes

SYNOPSIS A young and ruthless Victor Frankenstein sabotages
his father's hunting rifle so that he may die, and Victor may finally
go away to school. There he meets a kindred spirit in the form of
Wilhelm Kassner and brings him back home with him to begin an
experiment to revive the dead. Eventually Kassner objects to
Victor's macabre methods, and so Victor kills him as well. Victor
succeeds in creating and taming a man made from the dead.
However, his affairs spiral out of control as a childhood friend
named Elizabeth comes to live at his castle, and his maid, Alys,
blackmails him at the same time. Victor's creation escapes, and
chaos ensues. The monster is killed by way of accident, and Victor
narrowly avoids being exposed.

COMMENTARY Though some say Hammer produced this film as
a way of replacing Peter Cushing with the up-and-coming Ralph
Bates, this isn't entirely accurate. Hammer just happened to
receive something of a *Curse of Frankenstein* prequel/
reboot/remake script from a new screenwriter named Jeremy
Burnham. Most of the beats of *Curse* are present here: a dead
animal is revived, the Baron has a physical relationship with his
maid, he kills a brilliant scientist to possess his brain, and so on.
It was titled simply *Frankenstein* and as it was Cushing would
have been far too old to play the part. As Hammer liked the script,
they decided to simply recast Cushing and then they handed the

script over to trusty Jimmy Sangster, who agreed to rewrite it only if he could also direct. Hammer obliged, and Sangster rewrote the script with an eye towards comedy. However, though this film is often described as a "comedy," it is no more a comedy than one of Marvel's Avengers films. (It has humor, yes, but it is not an outright satire or spoof. The most far-out gag might be the grave robber who makes his wife dig the graves. But again, that gag is no more zany than something we might find in one of Marvel's films today.)

Obviously, the main thing to set this Frankenstein film apart from the others was the lack of Cushing's Frankenstein. As it is, Bates's portrayal of the character is quite good. While Cushing's Frankenstein had sociopathic tendencies throughout the series (the first film in particular), the later films made it hard to classify him as a full-on sociopath. Cushing's Baron seemed to care for Elizabeth, and he never would've murdered Paul outright like Bates's version killed Kassner. So, in that regard, Bates's Frankenstein is interesting in that he seems to be a full on sociopath, killing his father, his best friend, and his lover. He even allows another close childhood friend (who used to protect him from bullies no less) to take the blame for a kill that belonged to the monster! Something else the film has going for it is the relationship between Frankenstein and his monster. As opposed to the Cushing Frankenstein and all his creations, it is ironically this more sociopathic version of the Baron that seems to care for his creature. As the story progresses, he even manages to tame the monster.

As for the rest of the cast, Veronica Carlson returns for her second Frankenstein film, while Dave Prowse appears in his first Frankenstein film for Hammer (he had played the monster in 1967's *Casino Royale* and would play another monster in *Frankenstein and the Monster from Hell*). Kate O'Mara, from *Vampire Lovers,* also turns in a great performance as Alys. Actor Jon Finch, the heroic lead of *Vampire Lovers,* also turns up as a police inspector friend of Victor's, who eventually becomes suspicious of him. One thing Hammer never emulated from Universal's films was the Baron's relationship with an inquisitive police inspector à la *Son of Frankenstein,* so one could consider this film to have finally done that.

While most of the film is solid, the ending is a bit of a mess unfortunately. While the monster had been chained to the wall most of the film, suddenly he's no longer chained (we don't know how this happened) and he breaks through the door. He escapes the castle, randomly assaults a young girl (but doesn't kill her), then goes back to the castle. It almost seemed as though Sangster felt that the story had gone on long enough to make a feature film and now it needed to end. And on that note, though some may denote it as a "surprise ending," if anything, it's anticlimactic. There is no last great confrontation with the monster to make things exciting. As the Baron knows the police are coming, he has hidden the monster we know not where. The police arrive, and with them are the father and the little girl that the monster attacked earlier. As the police question Victor in the lab, the little girl pokes and prods at the equipment as children will do. When she activates the acid bath you just know that's where Victor hid his monster, and when all the party leaves, this is confirmed to be true. The Baron peers into the acid trough and looks sad as his monster's boots float to the surface. And that is how the film ends, with Bates's baron alive and well to await a sequel that would never come.

FINAL WORD Had the film been a success, Ralph Bates would've been a worthy successor to Cushing. Bates certainly fares better as a Frankenstein successor than he did as a Dracula replacement (or, that is to say, Lord Courtely would've been a pale substitute for Dracula). However, this film's lackluster ending didn't do anything to help it along, and it's no surprise that it wasn't well-received.

SCARS OF DRACULA

(HAMMER/EMI)
Release Date: November 8, 1970 (U.K.)
December 23, 1970 (U.S.)
Alternate Titles: *A Mass for Dracula* (France) *Count Dracula*
(Brazil) *Vampire Scars* (Finland) *Blood Exorcism: Resurrection of
Dracula* (Japan) *Fangs of Dracula* (Netherlands)
Dracula - Nights of Horror (West Germany)

Directed by: Roy Ward Baker **Screenplay by:** Anthony Hinds (as
John Elder) & Roy Ward Baker (uncredited) **Special Effects by:**
Roger Dicken **Music by:** James Bernard **Cast:** Christopher Lee
(Dracula) Dennis Waterman (Simon Carlson) Jenny Hanley (Sarah
Framsen) Christopher Matthews (Paul Carlson) Patrick Troughton
(Klove) Anouska Hempel (Tania) Michael Ripper (Landlord) Michael
Gwynn (The Priest) Wendy Hamilton (Julie)

Spherical, Technicolor, 91 Minutes

SYNOPSIS When a bed-hopping rapscallion named Paul goes on
the run from the law, he finds himself as a guest at Dracula's
castle. However, Paul's dalliance with Dracula's bride, Tania,
results in both of their deaths at the hands of the Count. Paul's
brother, Simon, and his friend, Sara, go to the castle looking for
him. They, too, become the guests of Dracula and his servant,
Klove, after which Dracula and Klove both set their sights on Sara.
However, out of compassion for Sara, Klove helps them escape and
then faces the wrath of his master. Simon returns to the castle to
resume his search for his brother, who he finds dead in Dracula's
tomb. Sara wanders back to the castle worried about Simon, who
is facing off with the Count atop the castle. Klove, too, tries to kill
Dracula but is instead killed himself. When all hope seems lost,
lightning strikes Dracula, destroying him.

COMMENTARY Ever see one of those movies within a movie that's
made to look cheap, clichéd, and exaggerated on purpose? (The
Godzilla movie being filmed that Pee Wee interrupts in *Pee-wee's
Big Adventure*, for instance.) Unfortunately, that's what many

265

scenes in *Scars of Dracula* are reminiscent of. This is best exemplified via the fake, wobbly bat prop, the cheap looking sets, and Christopher Lee's paler than usual makeup. Like *Evil of Frankenstein*, Hammer's most generic Frankenstein film, *Scars* is accused by many Hammer fans of having a typical Universal Horror feel to it (in large part due to the villagers storming the castle and the aforementioned fake bat). And what was the cause of the sudden drop in quality between this film and *Taste the Blood of Dracula*? It apparently wasn't the budget, as many sources claim it had the same £200,000 price tag. The real reason was probably that even though Warner Bros still had first refusal on Hammer's Dracula films in terms of distribution, the days of co-productions between the two studios were over. Hammer was now in bed with British-based EMI, who had requested a pair of Dracula and Frankenstein films for their first co-production. Though James Carreras ballyhooed the partnership as a positive thing (being that Hammer was now 100% British), in reality, it was the beginning of the end for Hammer.

Truth be told, it was too soon to produce yet another Dracula film after *Taste*, but Hammer pressed on anyways. Leery of whether or not Lee would return again, this film ended up being the first in the series to break continuity. The idea was that perhaps a new actor would be needed to replace Lee, and John Forbes Robertson, who had just turned in a short but memorable performance in *The Vampire Lovers*, was approached to play Dracula. Besides, Hammer had just produced *Horror of Frankenstein*, itself a remake of sorts, so perhaps it was time to do the same with Dracula? And, on top of all that, Roy Ward Baker was shocked to find that there wasn't actually a working script when he agreed to direct, just a rough draft straight out of Tony Hinds' notebook! So, Baker went back to Bram Stoker's novel to help flesh out the script.

Baker's utilization of the Stoker novel may have been what enticed Lee to return yet again to the role. Though Hammer never did a 100% faithful adaptation of the Stoker novel to Lee's chagrin, across all seven of their films they did incorporate various elements of the novel at least. While *Horror of Dracula* had followed the basic plot, *Prince of Darkness* had integrated the Renfield character, and *Taste* had finally brought the Count to London. *Scars*, it could be argued, took most of its inspiration from the early part of the novel set within Castle Dracula. Many of the film's more memorable scenes revolve in some way or another around Dracula's tomb, accessible only by climbing down the castle wall.

This famously allowed Hammer to film the scene from the Stoker novel where Dracula crawls up his castle wall. (And the scene didn't turn out half bad, even if it was uncharacteristic for Lee's version of the character.)

Just as *Horror of Frankenstein* was a remake of *Curse of Frankenstein*, portions of this film could be considered a remake of *Horror of Dracula*. The biggest callback is Dracula's bride, who comes to Paul and begs him to help her escape. (But this also being the looser 1970s, she also asks him to love her, and so he does, hopping right into bed with the vampire vixen.) In some ways, the film is also a quasi-remake of *Dracula – Prince of Darkness*, with much of the action revolving around a couple visiting the castle. Klove is also "back" from *Prince of Darkness* even though he died... though this film really seems to be a prequel... where Klove also dies (turning against his master at the film's climax). The ending is well done again in terms of how Dracula bites the dust. As in the last film, it's another case of the forces of good directly killing Dracula rather than the hero himself when lightning strikes the Count.

The film began shooting right after *Horror of Frankenstein* wrapped production on May 11, 1970, (coincidentally also only four days after *Taste the Blood of Dracula* hit theaters). It finished shooting on June 19th. Warner Bros passed on the film when it was offered to them, and in America it was distributed by American Continental where it was an abysmal failure. (However, this might've been due to the fact that Continental didn't have the resources to advertise the film like Warner Bros had done for the previous two films.) In Britain, the double bill of *Scars* and *Horror of Frankenstein* did respectable business when released in November, though it certainly didn't do as well as *Taste* had done there. In all likelihood, audiences had already had their fill of the Count that year.

FINAL WORD Though it's arguably the weakest of all the Hammer Draculas, it's still a Hammer Dracula movie starring Christopher Lee, and that always counts for something!

COUNTESS DRACULA

(HAMMER/RANK)

Release Date: January 31, 1971 (U.K.) October 11, 1972 (U.S.)
Alternate Titles: *Countess of Horror* (Germany) *600 Virgins for Dracula* (Greece) *Death Goes Hand in Hand with Virgins* (Italy) *I Am a Monster* (Sweden)

Directed by: Peter Sasdy **Screenplay by:** Jeremy Paul **Music by:** Harry Robertson **Special Effects by:** Bert Luxford & Tom Smith (Makeup) **Cast:** Ingrid Pitt (Countess Elisabeth Nadasdy) Nigel Green (Captain Dobi) Sandor Elès (Lt. Imre Toth) Maurice Denham (Grand Master Fabio) Patience Collier (Julie) Lesley-Anne Down (Countess Ilona Nadasdy)

Spherical, Eastmancolor, 93 Minutes

SYNOPSIS Upon the death of her husband, Countess Elisabeth Nadasdy is shocked when he divides his estate between herself and their daughter, Ilona, away at school. Not only that, he bequeaths a valuable stable of horses and property to the son of his best friend, Imre Toth. Elisabeth is immediately taken with the handsome Imre. During an accident with one of her maidservants, Elisabeth discovers that the blood of virgin girls rejuvenates her back to a youthful state. Elisabeth then begins murdering virginal young women to keep up her appearance. She then poses as her own daughter and begins a romance with Imre. Eventually Imre learns the ugly truth about the Countess, but is still forced to marry her under the charade that she is really Ilona. In front of the wedding goers, Elisabeth reverts to her elderly appearance to their horror. At the same time Ilona shows up, and Elisabeth, now insane, goes to kill her. Imre steps between them and falls victim to Elisabeth's blade. Elisabeth and all her accomplices are locked up in the tower, and she is given the new moniker of Countess Dracula.

COMMENTARY Back in the mid-1960s, Michael Carreras had toyed with a film based upon the legend of Countess Elizabeth Báthory. Infamously, the Countess had killed a number of virgin girls between 1602 and 1604 based on the belief that bathing in their blood would give her eternal youth. Oddly, Carreras's proposed film was titled *The Werewolf of Moravia* and slated for Peter Cushing! Obviously, that film never came to be, and when a film on Bathory was proposed again in 1970, it came not from Carreras, but from the future author of *The Truth About Dracula* (1972), Gabriel Ronay. With *The Vampire Lovers* having proved a hit, a movie called *Countess Dracula* seemed like another guaranteed success. Like that film, it would star Ingrid Pitt, which also meant that she'd bypass *The Vampire Lovers* sequel, *Lust for a Vampire*, in favor of this one. (It's unknown if Pitt didn't appear in *Lust for a Vampire* because she didn't want to—which some say was the case—or because Hammer wanted her for this film which was shot at the same time.)

As it turns out, Pitt does indeed dominate the proceedings as the Countess, whether it's in her aged, old crone guise or the vision of beauty that is her youthful form. Though the old crone makeup—which took four hours to apply and three hours to remove—isn't perfect, it's still pretty good. (To study for the part, Pitt observed her own elderly mother to imitate her voice and mannerisms to play the older version of her character.) However, fans of Hammer horror may find this a rather strange outing. As it is, there's not a great deal of horror or suspense in this film and it's really a gory period piece more than anything. And though we certainly do feel sorry for the Countess's innocent victims, none of the victims are significant characters that we can feel suspense for. Perhaps that's the problem, for a horror film to have true suspense one needs to have sympathetic characters to worry about. The main characters, the Countess and Dobie, are both villains. Among the sympathetic characters are Sandor Elès's Imre Tote and Leslie-Anne Down's Ilona. We know Imre is safe as the Countess won't kill him, or so we think, and Ilona we really don't know very well. Most of her scenes simply have her doing her best to escape a captor that's holding her hostage across the river per her mother's orders. Therefore, even though she is likable, we really haven't got enough emotional investment in her to truly worry when she gets locked up in the castle tower to serve as her mother's next victim.

However, all that said, the film is by no means bad, it just could have been better. Another positive that the film has going for it is that it was easily Hammer's most polished horror production in terms of the scope and the sets. Not only does it have an expansive exterior village, but the castle sets are larger than usual. The end wedding scene, in particular, is striking with its beautiful set and its more numerous than normal extras. Nor does the ending disappoint. It has a fairy tale quality to it—the Brothers Grim variety—as the beautiful Countess reverts back to her elderly, ugly self in front of her horrified subjects. At the same time, Ilona appears, and the mad Countess dashes off to try and stab her, though Imre suffers the blade instead. The film ends with the Countess and all those complicit in the killings locked up in the tower to await execution. Outside, one of the peasants utters the film's title when she calls her "Countess Dracula" for the first time.

The film, co-financed by Rank, was shot at Pinewood from July 27 to September 4, 1970. The movie was not a hit in either Britain or the U.S., where it was double-billed a year and a half later with *Vampire Circus* (which notably used the same exterior village).

FINAL WORD Even though she made only two notable horror films for Hammer, *Countess Dracula* arguably cemented Ingrid Pitt as Hammer's queen of horror.

LUST FOR A VAMPIRE

(HAMMER/EMI)

Release Date: January 17, 1971 (U.K.) September 2, 1971 (U.S.)
Alternate Titles: *To Love a Vampire* (U.S. TV title) *Young Virgins for a Vampire* (Belgium) *Thirst of the Vampire* (France) *Mircalla, the Immortal Lover* (Italy) *Fearful Bloodsucking Beauty* (Japan) *Coffin for a Vampire (Mexico)*

Directed by: Jimmy Sangster **Screenplay by:** Tudor Gates based off of characters created by Sheridan Le Fanu **Makeup by:** George Blackler **Music by:** Harry Robertson **Cast:** Yutte Stensgaard (Mircalla Herritzen/Carmilla Karnstein) Michael Johnson (Richard LeStrange) Ralph Bates (Giles Barton) Suzanna Leigh (Janet Playfair) Helen Christie (Miss Simpson) Barbara Jefford (Countess Herritzen) Mike Raven (Count Karnstein) Harvey Hall (Inspector Heinrich) Pippa Steel (Susan Pelley) Erik Chitty (Professor Herz) Jack Melford (bishop) Christopher Neame (Hans)

Spherical, Technicolor, 95 Minutes

SYNOPSIS Forty years since her last death, Carmilla Karnstein is revived yet again. She takes refuge at an all-girls finishing school. There she is the object of affection for both the headmaster, Giles Barton, and also the new English teacher, Richard LeStange. Barton, aware of Carmilla's vampiric origins, wishes to be her servant, but she kills him. LeStrange is also aware that Carmilla is a vampire, but he falls in love with her despite this. Eventually, an inspector comes to the school to investigate the death of one of the students. When the body is exhumed and shows two marks on the neck, the villagers become riled and storm Karnstein Castle. LeStrange tries to stop them, but a fire consumes the castle and kills Carmilla in the process.

COMMENTARY Considering that *The Vampire Lovers* came out in October of 1970, and *Lust for a Vampire* was released only four months later, this most likely means that Hammer was prepping this production before *Vampire Lovers* had even been released. In other words, Hammer had jumped the gun. Though profitable, *Vampire Lovers* was a bit too controversial due to the lesbian element, and so, for the provocatively titled *Lust for a Vampire,* that element was toned down a bit. Though Carmilla would certainly still prey upon young women, she would not fall in love with any of them.

Carmilla loose in an all-girls school seems like a no-brainer for a sequel. The twist on the formula, a good deviation in most sequels, occurs when Carmilla instead falls for the male lead. (Though, again, this mostly occurred due to the negative controversy surrounding the first film.) In yet another twist, it's Carmilla's roommate who tries to put the moves on her rather than the other way around. Ironically, this roommate who becomes Carmilla's first victim was played by Pippa Steele, Carmilla's first kill in *Vampire Lovers*. That same film's Harvey Hall is also brought back, this time as an inspector who ends up being tossed down a well. A few supporting characters from the previous film also returned but were recast. The mysterious Man in Black, previously played by John Forbes-Robertson, is revealed in this entry to be Count Karnstein himself and is played by DJ Mike Raven, who looks very Christopher Lee-ish. Nor does Dawn Adams return as the Countess and is replaced by Barbara Jefford. In any case, both characters get a good deal more screen time in this outing.

Lust for a Vampire was supposed to have two other returning cast members from *Vampire Lovers*: Ingrid Pitt and Peter Cushing. Pitt was naturally asked to reprise the role of Carmilla, but supposedly disliked the script and preferred to do *Countess Dracula* instead. As such, she was replaced by Swedish actress Yutte Stensgaard who wasn't quite as effective in the part. Cushing, on the other hand, was to play the bumbling Giles Barton. Though Cushing could have been hilarious in the role, he seemed a bit old to be lusting after nubile schoolgirls. (Had he appeared, he would've been in all three Karnstein films, giving them a sense of continuity.) Cushing, who wanted to spend more time with his ailing wife, was replaced by the much younger Ralph Bates, who gave the character a slightly different edge. Cushing wasn't the only one who left the project. Terence Fisher was the first choice for director, but he passed because he disliked the script. As a Christian, Fisher may have disapproved of the film's exploitive elements such as the opening resurrection sequence (which is a far cry from the one he staged in *Dracula-Prince of Darkness*), plus the rather ambiguous characters that lack a strong moral compass (notably, there are no characters like Father Shandor or Van Helsing to confront the vampires). Because he had just successfully helmed *Horror of Frankenstein*, Jimmy Sangster was asked to come direct. It was a decision that he would come to regret.

As it is, the film just isn't as good as the previous one. As stated before, the characters aren't as likable, mainly the male lead of Richard LeStrange who doesn't seem the least bit concerned that Carmilla is a vampire. All of a sudden, he's in love with her and that's that. The ending is also abrupt. Similar to the climactic portion of *Horror of Frankenstein*, it seemed like the script writer realized that they were approaching the 90-minute mark and it was time to wrap things up. As the villagers become more and more riled up over a dead girl (killed by Carmilla), a priest just happens to come into town. This pushes the villagers over the edge, and suddenly they are ready to storm Karnstein Castle.

And basically that's all that happens: the villagers storm the castle to kill the vampires. Although it was uninteresting in the sense that we'd seen that sort of thing play out in numerous Universal films, not to mention the recent *Scars of Dracula*, the chorus music at least instills the sequence with a grandiose feel. The problem is that there's little suspense generated by the story itself. Case in point, LeStrange is running around begging the villagers to cease their attack because he's in love with Carmilla. As such, it's unclear just who Sangster wants us to root for during the climax. We certainly can't root for LeStrange or the Karnsteins, and we have no emotional investment in the villagers whatsoever. Ultimately, the villagers set the castle on fire, LeStrange runs in, shares a final moment with Carmilla, and then the Count uses some sort of supernatural power to make her attack him. LeStrange pushes her away, and a flaming stake falls from the ceiling and impales her. Notably, Count Karnstein and the Countess are shown alive and well as the credits roll. And considering that the priest character kept going on and on about how fire wouldn't destroy the vampires, it was clear Hammer was keeping them alive so that the duo could resurrect Carmilla again in the next sequel (which ultimately didn't pan out that way).

FINAL WORD Easily the weakest of the Karnstein trilogy. However, with its somewhat troubled production and numerous casting changes, one has to wonder how it would've fared with Pitt, Cushing, and Fisher on board.

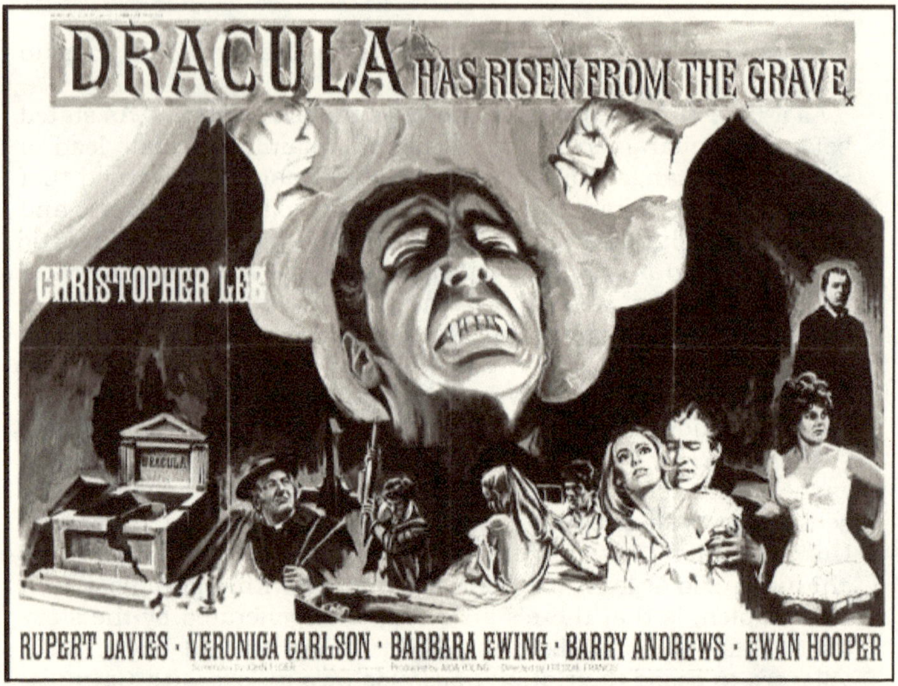
DRACULA HAS RISEN FROM THE GRAVE
CHRISTOPHER LEE
DRACULA
RUPERT DAVIES · VERONICA CARLSON · BARBARA EWING · BARRY ANDREWS · EWAN HOOPER

FRANKENSTEIN MUST BE DESTROYED!
THE SCREEN'S MOST FANTASTIC FIEND ...AND HAMMER SAY SO!
PETER CUSHING
SIMON WARD · FREDDIE JONES · VERONICA CARLSON · THORLEY WALTERS · MAXINE AUDLEY

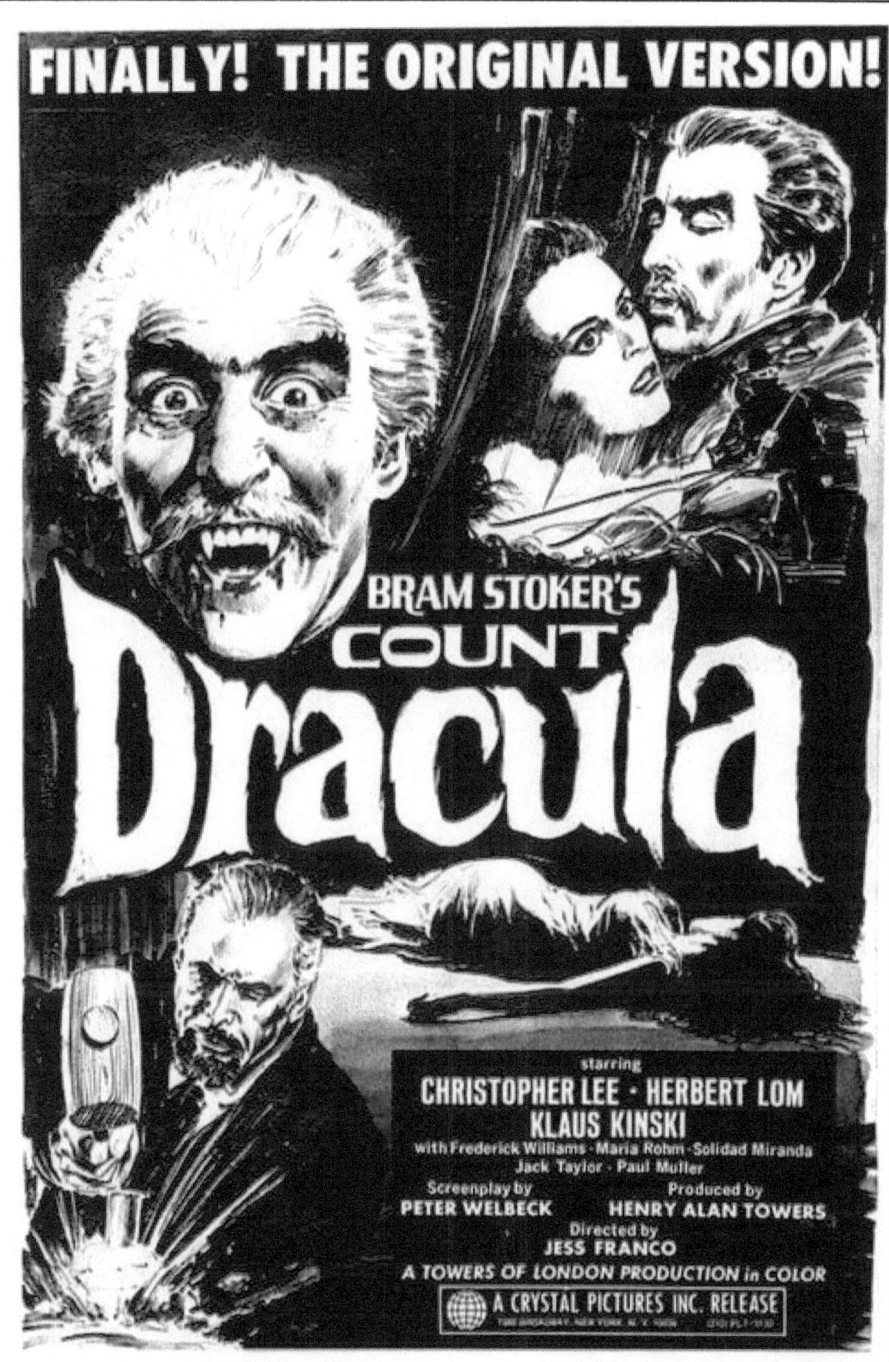

TERRORIFICO!!
DESALMADO!!
SANGUINARIO!!

AMABA...
PARA MATAR!

CHRISTOPHER LEE
JENNY HANLEY

LAS CICATRICES DE DRACULA

DIRECCION ROY WARD BAKER   UNA PRODUCCION HAMMER PARA ANGLO-EMI

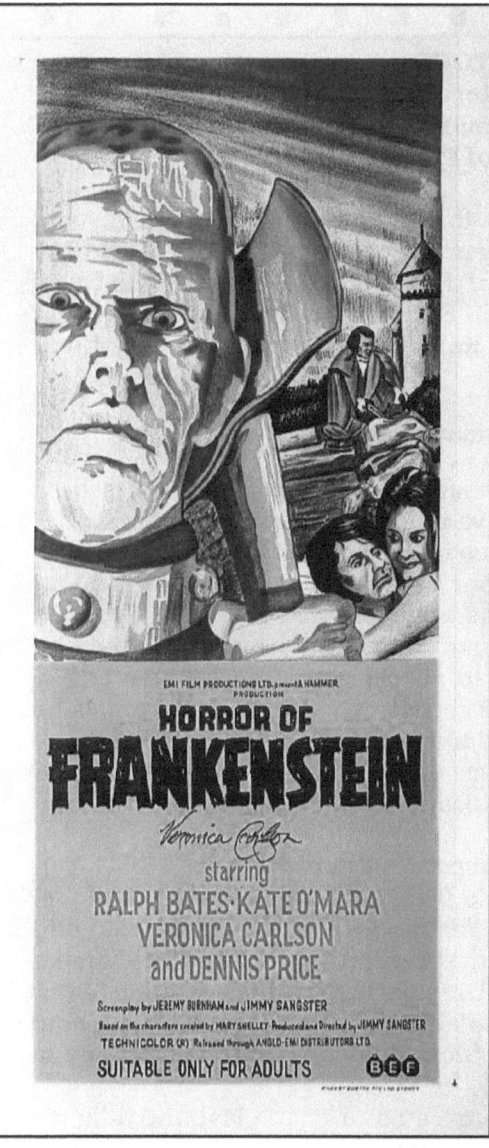

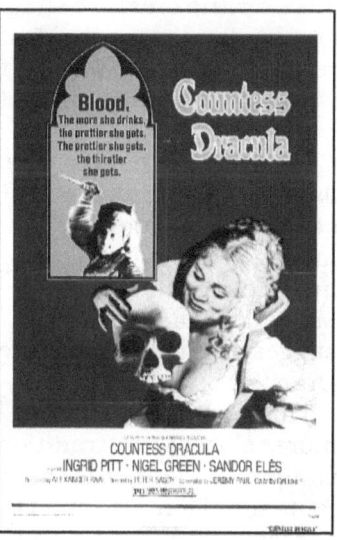

LAKE OF DRACULA

(TOHO)
Release Date: June 16, 1971
Alternate Titles: *Cursed House: Bloodsucking Eyes* (Japan)
The Lake of Dracula (U.S.)

Directed by: Michio Yamamoto **Special Effects by:** Teruyoshi Nakano **Screenplay by:** Ei Ogawa & Masaru Takesue **Music by:** Riichiro Manabe **Cast:** Midori Fujita (Akiko Kashiwagi), Choei Takahashi (Dr. Takashi Saeki), Sanae Emi (Natsuko Kashiwagi), Shin Kishida (The vampire), Kaku Takashina (Kyusaku), Shuji Otaki (The vampire's father)

Tohoscope, Eastmancolor, 82 Minutes

SYNOPSIS What a young woman named Akiko believes to be a vivid childhood dream about vampires comes back to haunt her when a real bloodsucker arrives in her small lakefront town. With her friends being vampirized one by one, Akiko fears her memory isn't merely a dream and turns to her fiancé Saeki, a doctor who doesn't believe in superstition, to confront the vampires. The duo eventually trails the vampire to an old gothic house where they discover the creature's father's corpse, whose notebook reveals he and his family are the descendants of Dracula. When the vampire returns, he and Saeki fight over Akiko, and the vampire is killed when he is impaled on a stair post.

COMMENTARY After *The Vampire Doll* proved to be a bit-hit in Japan, an enthusiastic Fumio Tanaka commissioned a sequel again to be helmed by Michio Yamamoto. Though Yamamoto had managed to avoid Dracula in the first film, this time Tanaka insisted the film feature a Dracula-like vampire. When actor Masumi Okada proved unavailable to play the role, Yamamoto suggested his longtime friend Shin Kishida, who reminded him of Dracula.

This movie is a marked improvement over the last and adheres more closely to traditional vampire myths. It contains four vampires lead by the imposing figure of Kishida, who makes for a fantastic Dracula (or Dracula-type as he plays an unnamed descendant of the Count). He too possesses the golden eyes seen

278

in the first film. Though in the next film he would be even more Dracula-like—complete with spooky old house—his restrained performance here is better without the cartoonish grunts and growls he would emit there. The vampire's origins are explained in yet another tedious info-dump of exposition in the last ten minutes of the picture. This vampire is a case of genetics, as the family is descended from Dracula himself, though this affliction apparently skips several generations. Further confusing the matter is the vampire's father, who, while obviously dead and stated not to be a vampire himself, inexplicably manages to return to life long enough to stop his monstrous son.

The climax seems to be inspired by both Hammer's 1958 *Horror of Dracula* and its 1968 sequel, *Dracula Has Risen from the Grave*. The male lead and Kishida wrestle endlessly atop a staircase until finally Kishida falls and is impaled by a stair post from behind. Nakano's version is bloodier and gooier, but nonetheless inferior to Hammer's—but only slightly. Kishida's disintegration is a near shot-for-shot mirror of Christopher Lee's death scene from 1958's *Horror of Dracula* that begins with a glimpse of Kishida's deflating hand, and then switches to him clawing at his face in a shot that goes on for just a bit too long. The source of the evil power keeping her "alive," Akiko's vampirized sister then drops dead.

On the production side, the film is well-directed by Yamamoto, and at one point Kishida's lack of reflection in a mirror makes for a particularly good scare. Due to the isolation of the film's lead female character (who everyone thinks is crazy), the scares in this entry are the most effective of the entire trilogy. The merits of Riichiro Manabe's weird scores were unusual for *Godzilla vs. Hedorah* and debatable at best for *Godzilla vs. Megalon,* but in this film, his odd instruments actually excel. Sections of his score here are evocative of Robert Cobert's *House of Dark Shadows* which came out in March of 1971 in Japan, three months before *Lake of Dracula*'s June release. The film was released to American television in 1980 as *The Lake of Dracula*, a moniker it successfully retained on home video. Oddly the climax—the film's main highlight—was severely edited for airing on television in a time when most of Hammer's horrors were shown uncut in terms of violence. As a result, this sequence was also missing from the U.S. home video release. To make matters worse, Kishida's vampire was dubbed with a thick European accent.

FINAL WORD Possibly the best of Yamamoto's Bloodthirsty Trilogy.

DR. JEKYLL AND SISTER HYDE

(HAMMER)

Release Date: October 17, 1971 (U.K.) April 1972 (U.S.)
Alternate Titles: *The Doctor & Sister Monster* (Brazil) *Return of Dr. Jekyll* (Finland) *Barbara, the Monster of London* (Italy) *Death Haunts the Night* (Mexico) *The Beauty and the Beast* (Portugal) *Dr. Jekyll* (Turkey) *Dr. Jekyll and Mistress Hyde* (working title)

Directed by: Roy Ward Baker **Screenplay by:** Brian Clemens
Music by: David Whitaker **Special Effects by:** Michael Collins
Cast: Ralph Bates (Dr. Henry Jekyll) Martine Beswick (Mrs. Edwina Hyde) Gerald Sim (Professor Robertson) Lewis Fiander (Howard Spencer) Susan Brodrick (Susan Spencer) Dorothy Alison (Mrs. Spencer) Ivor Dean (William Burke) Tony Calvin (William Hare)

Spherical, Technicolor, 97 Minutes

SYNOPSIS Dr. Henry Jekyll has the altruistic goal of curing all disease until he realizes that he won't live long enough to do so. In the name of the greater good, Jekyll begins harvesting female hormones from dead women to create an elixir for eternal youth. His experiment backfires and turns him into a woman, and when spotted by a neighbor, Jekyll claims that the woman is his sister, a widow by the name of Mrs. Hyde. Ironically, a brother and sister pair that live down the hall both begin to fall for Mrs. Hyde and Dr. Jekyll, respectively. Eventually, Jekyll begins murdering prostitutes in order to obtain more hormones, and when the police begin searching for the male killer, Jekyll continues the killings as the female Hyde. Eventually the police catch up to him and Jekyll escapes to the rooftop. Suddenly, Hyde takes control and the duo fall to their death. On the pavement, the brother and sister look on in horror at the remains, recognizable as both Jekyll and Hyde.

COMMENTARY Long before the female reboot craze of the 2010s, Hammer was at it with not only female-centric vampire and mummy movies, but even a female Hyde! However, this film wasn't born of social politics, but a simple joke that Brian Clemens cracked at lunch one day. He joked about Jekyll taking a potion and turning into a woman. The joke was on Clemens, as he was then asked to write that very idea! (Remember, *Frankenstein Meets the Wolf Man* was born the exact same way.) Carreras had already accepted the film before he'd even read the script, as evidenced by the fact that when Clemens went to his office to discuss the idea, Carreras already had the poster made up!

One of the first to be cast for the film was Ralph Bates, in his fourth Hammer film in a row. Though Bates had shone in *Taste the Blood of Dracula* and *Horror of Frankenstein*, he was naturally still in the shadows of Lee and Cushing. However, Bates could at least be considered the definitive Dr. Jekyll of Hammer, as his was easily the best. Though casting Martine Beswick in the role may have seemed like a no-brainer, Caroline Munro and Julie Ege were also supposedly considered for it. However, Beswick was the better option for three reasons. One: she could have passed for Ralph Bates's sister in real life. Two: she had experience in playing villains in past Hammer productions like *Prehistoric Women* (1967). Lastly, and most importantly, she would agree to nudity, which the other two wouldn't. (Bates himself wanted to play Sister Hyde and was thankfully denied, as this would have been comical more than anything else).

More so than the Robert Louis Stevenson story, *Sister Hyde* seems to owe more to Hammer's Frankenstein films. Dr. Jekyll is very much like Cushing's Baron in *Curse of Frankenstein*, willing to commit heinous acts in the name of what he considers the greater good. Also like that film, it begins with a flash forward and is narrated every so often by the doctor. Though he begins by paying off a worker in the morgue for bodies, also similar to *Curse*, Jekyll eventually relents to murdering women to obtain fresh samples. And, as in *Frankenstein Created Woman*, the story deals with a man in a woman's body. Or, at least, it initially does. In the first few transformations it would appear that Jekyll is still behind the wheel, so to speak, but as the film progresses Hyde becomes her own entity. Eventually, she and Jekyll begin to blur together, as evidenced by a scene where Jekyll reaches out to caress the face of a man whom Hyde is attracted to. One of the film's best scenes occurs when the dueling identities wrestle for control of the body. Jekyll throws a knife into his mirror, cracking it, and a moment later Hyde stands in front of it and delivers the famous line that it is she who is real, and that Jekyll will soon cease to exist.

Another nice touch is the brother and sister love interests, Howard and Susan, who live above Jekyll, with both of them becoming infatuated with the male and female counterparts of the doctor. This is where it becomes most evident that Hyde is her own entity, and not simply Jekyll in the body of a woman since Jekyll, as established, would not develop romantic feelings for Howard. Meanwhile, Jekyll himself has finally, reluctantly, come around to his feelings for Susan, knowing full well that Hyde wants to kill her.

Unfortunately, like *The Two Faces of Dr. Jekyll*, the film's ending feels a bit rushed and unsure of just what to do with itself. For starters, it's rather hard for Jekyll and Hyde to come to blows when they share the same body. And, the only man who figured out that they were one and the same was already seduced and killed by Hyde. As such, a bit of a *deus ex machina* plot device is used wherein a blind beggar is able to deduce that Jekyll is the real killer! As the mob marches on Jekyll's flat, he flees to the rooftops as the cops give chase. It isn't terribly exciting, but the score is excellent at least. A memorable shot has Jekyll hanging from a ledge in front of a stained-glass window. Through the distorted window, we see Jekyll turn into Hyde once more. In mid-transformation, they slip and fall, and the dead body on the ground is a combination of Jekyll and Hyde both.

Shot from February 22 to March 30, 1971, this was originally intended as Rank co-production but went to MGM/EMI instead. It was appropriately released on a double bill with *Blood from the Mummy's Tomb*, which AIP distributed in the U.S. market on the same double bill.

FINAL WORD Gimmicks aside, this is easily the best and most memorable of Hammer's three adaptations of *Dr. Jekyll and Mr. Hyde*.

BLOOD FROM THE MUMMY'S TOMB

(HAMMER)
Release Date: October 14, 1971 (U.K.) May 17, 1972 (U.S.)
Alternate Titles: *The Tomb of the Mummy* (Argentina) *The Mummy's Blood* (Canada) *The Blood Vault* (Iceland) *Exorcismus - Cleo, the Goddess of Love* (Italy) *Princess Terra's Tomb* (Japan) *The Blood of the Mummy* (Mexico) *The Blood Tomb* (Portugal)

Directed by: Seth Holt & Michael Carreras (uncredited) **Special Effects by:** Michael Collins **Screenplay by:** Christopher Wicking based upon the book by Bram Stoker **Music by:** Tristram Cary **Cast:** Valerie Leon (Margaret Fuchs/Queen Tera) Andrew Keir (Julian Fuchs) James Villiers (Corbeck) Mark Edwards (Tod Browning) Hugh Burden (Geoffrey Dandridge) George Coulouris (Berigan) Rosalie Crutchley (Helen Dickerson) Aubrey Morris (Doctor Putnam) David Markham (Doctor Burgess)

Spherical, Technicolor, 94 Minutes

SYNOPSIS On the same day that his expedition uncovers the lost tomb of Tera, the Queen of Darkness, in Egypt, Professor Fuchs's wife dies in childbirth in England. Years later, his adult daughter Margaret is identical to Queen Tera, perfectly preserved in Fuchs's basement. The professor gifts his daughter Tera's ring on her birthday, and from that point forward strange things begin to happen. Professor Fuchs suffers a heart attack, as does another member of the expedition when he sees Margaret wearing the ring. Members of the expedition, each of whom possesses a special relic connected to Tera, die mysterious deaths. Behind it all is Corbeck, another member of the expedition who wants to resurrect Tera via Margaret's life force. Corbeck performs the ritual to resurrect Tera, but is stopped by Fuchs when he realizes it will mean Margaret's death. Tera revives and stabs Fuchs, and is then stabbed herself by Margaret. In the supernatural chaos, the house collapses. Later, a woman wrapped entirely in bandages and described as the sole survivor is hauled away to the hospital.

COMMENTARY In early 1970, Hammer considered taking a fourth trip to the well with their Mummy franchise. Initially, it was to be a traditional Mummy film à la *The Mummy's Shroud*, to be written by Anthony Hinds and then co-written and directed by Jimmy Sangster. Perhaps realizing the Mummy movies really were just kid stuff, they dropped that aspect and decided to adapt Bram Stoker's *Jewel of the Seven Stars*. As that featured an Egyptian queen resurrected from the dead, that would allow Hammer a female take of sorts on the genre. (This idea was actually that of a former press agent, Howard Brandy, who convinced Hammer that a female mummy movie could be the way to go.) The film was given a healthy £200,000 budget and went before cameras with Peter Cushing as Professor Fuchs. However, Cushing shot only one day's worth of footage before he bowed out due to his beloved wife Helen passing away. Cushing was rapidly replaced by Andrew Kier (Father Shandor in *Dracula – Prince of Darkness*). The next to be replaced was director Seth Holt, who died during filming. Therefore Michael Carreras stepped in to shoot what ended up being his second Mummy movie for Hammer, having helmed *Curse of the Mummy's Tomb* in 1964.

Considering the production history, it's a marvel that *Blood from the Mummy's Tomb* turned out as good as it did. It was said that Carreras occasionally had trouble figuring out what Holt originally intended, but if one doesn't know this while watching the film it's not really apparent. Whereas, if you are aware of this production background, there might be a few scenes that seem disjointed stylistically but they don't detract from the film overall. Speaking of style, the movie has a surreal quality to it for several reasons. The flashback scenes, in particular, are much better than the ones from the last two Mummy pictures and have an unearthly dream-like quality to them. Unlike the daylight flashbacks of Hammer's other Mummy movies, these flashbacks take place exclusively at night, mostly as a way of showcasing the stars. (Stars are often seen in this film as a nod to the title of the novel *Jewel of the Seven Stars*.) Another thing that makes the film surreal is its setting, which appears to be the 1930s. However, the attitudes of the characters are so modern one would be forgiven in thinking it was set in the 1970s (Margaret spends the night at Tod's house, for instance, with her father's blessing). Furthermore, a few of the cars featured in the film are far more modern than anything pre-1950!

Despite not being a traditional Mummy movie, the formula is still the same: the desecrators of the tomb must all be killed. But, in place of a marauding mummy are three artifacts, each of which comes to life. The first is in the form of a cobra, which stalks a former member of the expedition who is now a patient in a mental ward. At first, the scene is quite effective. There's a chorus of screams in the ward from all the other inmates when, suddenly and curiously, it stops, causing the patient to be alarmed. He looks at the spot the statue occupied only to find it suddenly gone. We then see the statue moving via a shadow along the wall. (It's unfortunate that Hammer couldn't have animated the shadow to give it some fluidity.) A wind blows open the windows of his room until the snake strikes him. (The shot is unfortunate and silly and ruins an otherwise effective scene since they literally just jab the snake statue into the camera! If anything, it's reminiscent of a low budget episode of *Kolchak: The Night Stalker*.) The second killing is better, and has a spectral jackal stalking a man in a foggy alleyway. This time, Hammer used a real dog to cast the shadow along the wall, which is much better than the stiff snake they used earlier. The third and final killing has the expedition's lone female member being scratched to death by an invisible cat.

As stated before, these killings are an interesting departure from the usual mummy shenanigans. Furthermore, Hammer's female mummy works well decked out in her Egyptian garb (and would we really want to see Valeri Leon all covered up?). By bestowing Tera with the title of "Queen of Darkness," it almost seemed as though Hammer were trying to make her their female equivalent of their Prince of Darkness, Dracula. Though she hasn't one scene actually alive in the whole film until the very end, her presence is felt throughout thanks largely to dialogue since the characters are always talking about her. Overall, Tera stacks up nicely along with Hammer's other female "monsters" like Carmilla and Sister Hyde. The movie's final moments are spectacular and among Hammer's best twist endings. Though Tera had been devoid of bandages the entire film, she ends the story wrapped in bandages and on the way to the hospital!

FINAL WORD Later remade with Charlton Heston as *The Awakening* in 1980 with a higher budget, Hammer's version of Stoker's mummy story is still the favorite for many.

TWINS OF EVIL

(HAMMER)

Release Date: October 3, 1971 (U.K.) June 1972 (U.S.)
Alternate Titles: *Dracula's Daughters* (Latin America) *Dracula's Witch Hunt* (Denmark/Germany) *Twins of the Damned* (Finland) *Twins of Dracula* (Greece) *Dracula's Dripping Blood* (Japan) *Dracula and the Twins* (Spain)

Directed by: John Hough **Special Effects by:** Jack Mills **Screenplay by:** Tudor Gates **Music by:** Harry Robertson **Cast:** Mary Collinson (Maria Gellhorn) Madeleine Collinson (Frieda Gellhorn) Peter Cushing (Gustav Weil) Damien Thomas (Count Karnstein) David Warbeck (Anton Hoffer) Kathleen Byron (Katy Weil) Roy Stewart (Joachim) Isobel Black (Ingrid Hoffer) Katya Wyeth (Countess Mircalla Karnstein)

Spherical, Eastmancolor, 87 Minutes

SYNOPSIS A pair of orphaned teenaged twin girls, Maria and Frieda Gelhorn, have just arrived in the village of Karnstein to live with their aunt and uncle, Gustav and Katy Weil. Unfortunately for them, Uncle Gustav is a Puritan witch hunter, who has burned numerous women at the stake under false accusations. But, true evil does exist in the form of Count Karnstein, who after an arcane ceremony accidentally summons his ancestor Countess Mircalla Karnstein from the dead. She bites the Count, turning him into a vampire, before returning to the underworld. Frieda, the more rebellious of the two twins, makes her way to the castle to meet the Count, who makes her a vampire. When Frieda is caught red-handed by Gustav and his Puritan Brotherhood as she feeds in the woods, Frieda is jailed. As Frieda awaits execution, Count Karnstein kidnaps Maria and puts her in Frieda's place. Just as Maria is about to be burnt alive, an admirer named Anton comes to save her, proving she's not the vampire twin. Anton convinces the Brotherhood to finally march on Karnstein Castle. They do so, and Gustav beheads Frieda. But, when he makes a move to kill the Count he ends up killed himself. Anton throws a spear into Count Karnstein's heart and he dies.

COMMENTARY At the end of *Lust for a Vampire*, Mike Raven's Count Karnstein exits the film very much alive—a fact Hammer made sure to emphasize during the end credits. The plan was for Count Karnstein to be the primary villain of the third film, and he would be played by none other than Peter Cushing. The story was titled *Vampire Virgins* and focused heavily on a pair of vampire hunters. But then Hammer discovered twins Mary and Madelaine Collinson, who had become *Playboy's* first ever twin Playmates in October of 1970, and became infatuated with the idea of twin vampires. Hammer then contacted *Playboy* about them appearing in a film. And with that, *Vampire Virgins* was out, and *Twins of Evil* was in.

Though a Count Karnstein would serve as the central antagonist of the story, it was not the same Count from the previous entry. If anything his history is unclear, as he starts the film out as a normal human being, albeit one dabbling in the dark arts. One of his obscene rites summons Mircalla Karnstein from the dead, who sticks around just long enough to vampirize him and then disappear. (Supposedly Ingrid Pitt was offered to cameo as Mircalla but turned it down.)

While Cushing may not have gotten to play the villainous Count as planned for *Vampire Virgins*, he played a villain of an entirely different sort as it turned out. One could consider Cushing's Gustav Weil (pronounced "vile") to be a dark, misled version of Van Helsing, as Weil seems to seek out "evildoers" as a way of absolving his own sins. Therefore, Weil seeks out evil where there often is none, as though it's some kind of addiction for him. However, Cushing doesn't let the character become a one-note villain. In the third act he seems to finally question his morality. At the very end, when he beheads his vampiric niece, he at least seems remorseful and drapes his cloak across her dead body.

Speaking of the twins, they make for more of an interesting story ploy rather than intriguing characters in their own right. Maria, the good twin, isn't interesting enough on her own, while Frieda becomes downright unlikable as the story progresses. Though she has a few scenes where she displays affection for Maria, ultimately Frieda has no qualms about throwing her sister to the wolves by the film's end. The love story between Frieda and her suitor, Anton, is rather weak. Anton spends the film enamored with Frieda even though he ends the picture with Maria. It's not clear if he truly loves Maria, or if she's just a consolation prize for losing Frieda.

Though it's difficult to say whether or not *Twins of Evil* betters *The Vampire Lovers*—and it most certainly trumps *Lust for a Vampire*—it definitely stands out with the highest production values of the entire trilogy. Unlike the last two films, which were fairly stuffy and confined to interior sets, there are a great deal of scenes filmed outside on location, even a large village. (Of course, these are the same sets used for *Vampire Circus*, so it's no surprise.) The ending has a nice sense of urgency and excitement to it after Anton learns that the twins have switched places, and that it is the innocent Maria slated to be burned alive. From there it's not terribly different from *Lust for a Vampire*, as the villagers go off to storm Karnstein castle. The way in which it betters it, however, is in the character development. While the lead in *Lust* had been fairly one-dimensional, Anton sways the hypocritical and cowardly Brotherhood to finally face the real evil in their midst (they had been fearful of attacking Karnstein for political reasons). Anton is also interesting in that he's somewhat like Paul from *Dracula Has Risen from the Grave* in that he looks at good and evil both as though they are only fairytales. By the film's last act he comes around to the fact that they are not. In terms of action, there's nothing new or inventive. As stated earlier, Weil beheads Frieda and Count Karnstein takes a spear through the chest. When compared to more original vampire kills (the decapitation by crossbow in *Vampire Circus*, for example) in other Hammer pictures it's almost a let-down, but the high production values make it more exciting at least.

It's probably a safe bet that Hammer began production on this film before *Lust* saw its less than profitable release in theaters. Actually, the trilogy itself wasn't a flop so much as it didn't increase grosses over the recent Dracula movie, and the lesbian aspect of *Vampire Lovers* generated controversy that James Carreras disliked. And so he ordered Hammer to stick to making more traditional horror pictures from that point on.

FINAL WORD Though it's tough to say whether it's the best or second best of Hammer's Carmilla trilogy, *Twins of Evil* certainly has a lot of polish to it.

288

HANDS OF THE RIPPER

(HAMMER)
Release Date: October 17, 1971 (U.K.) July 13, 1972 (U.S.)
Alternate Titles: *Blood of the Ripper* (working title) *Jack the Ripper's Daughter* (French title)

Directed by: Peter Sasdy **Screenplay by:** Lewis Davidson & Edward Spencer Shew (story) **Special Effects by:** Cliff Culley **Music by:** Christopher Gunning **Cast:** Eric Porter (Dr. John Pritchard) Angharad Rees (Anna) Jane Merrow (Laura) Keith Bell (Michael Pritchard) Dora Bryan (Mrs. Golding) Derek Godfrey (Dysart) Marjorie Rhodes (Mrs. Bryant) Lynda Baron (Long Liz) Margaret Rawlings (Madame Bullard) Norman Bird (Police Inspector) Maijie Lawrence (Dolly)

Spherical, Eastmancolor, 85 Minutes

SYNOPSIS After he walks in on the scene of a murder where a seemingly harmless young girl, Anna, seems to be the culprit, Dr. John Pritchard takes the girl into his home for evaluation. Though Pritchard believes that she has a split personality, he doesn't know that Anna is the daughter of Jack the Ripper. At a young age she witnessed her father kill her mother, and anything that reminds her of the event triggers her to fall into a trance and kill. Acts of affection in particular trigger Anna, and the first victim is Pritchard's maid, Dolly. Though Pritchard is well aware of Anna's problem he keeps on studying her as more people die. Eventually Pritchard himself accidentally triggers Anna, and she stabs him, mortally wounding him. Still in a trance, Anna wanders outside and is taken out for the afternoon by Pritchard's soon to be daughter-in-law, Laura, who is blind. Laura takes Anna to St. Paul's Cathedral to gaze upon its beauty unaware of the danger she is in. The dying Pritchard follows them there, and shouts at Ann in the balcony to come to him as she begins to strangle Laura, who has triggered Anna with another act of affection. Anna snaps out of her trance thanks to Pritchard's voice and jumps to her death.

COMMENTARY In the same way that Hammer never made a straight adaptation of Dr. Jekyll and Mr. Hyde, nor did Hammer ever do a normal telling of the Jack the Ripper story. Instead, they did a female version of the character, and thankfully they didn't give the film a corny name like "Daughter of the Ripper." Despite what sounds like an exploitive premise, *Hands of the Ripper* is actually one of Hammer's finest films, in large part thanks to the direction of Peter Sasdy. The key difference between this film and Sasdy's last female-centric horror picture, *Countess Dracula*, is characterization and suspense. As noted before, *Countess Dracula* really didn't have any sympathetic characters to feel much suspense for, while this film does an excellent job of garnering sympathy for Anna and her victims alike.

As Anna suffers from either possession or a split personality (the film leads us on to think that either could be the case), the sweet girl is herself a victim of her father's horrid crimes. Her second victim, Dolly, in particular, is a very likable character who is more than happy to take in Anna. She doesn't show a hint of resentment towards the doctor for taking in a strange young girl, and is more than happy to make her feel at home. Therefore when Anna becomes triggered and slashes Dolly's throat, it's a very tragic scene. Later, Anna is taken to a psychic who sees the truth of her parentage in a chilling scene. She, too, is compassionate with Anna, but a simple kiss on the cheek triggers Anna to kill again. On the other end of the spectrum, one does not feel any sympathy for Anna's first victim, the fake psychic who had been exploiting Anna for many years as a prostitute. (This adds another touch of irony to the story, as Jack the Ripper killed prostitutes and his daughter is now one herself).

The killings themselves are all memorable (another problem remedied from *Countess Dracula*, in which they really were not). Two of them also offer surprise reveals. In the first, we are led to think that Anna has killed a man who slapped her (this is when she works as a prostitute for the fake psychic). When Dr. Pritchard rushes upstairs to see what happened, we at first don't realize that the fake psychic is dead, as she's standing upright. A few moments later, we see that she's been impaled by a poker and stuck to the door! Another surprise kill occurs when the real psychic leans in to give Anna a hug. There's been no indication of violence, and when the woman falls back with a knife in her stomach it's quite a shock.

The film is topped off by a superb ending, where the audience sympathy and the character relationships pay off in a major way.

290

This is because throughout the film Dr. Pritchard is himself never terribly sympathetic. His interest in Anna stems mostly from two desires. The first is to conduct a psychological experiment, and the second is the simple matter that Pritchard is attracted to Anna. At first, it would seem that the duo is heading towards a father-daughter relationship, but towards the end Pritchard's romantic feelings get the best of him and he kisses Anna. As he has not yet figured out that kissing triggers the girl, he's caught off guard when she shoves a sword through his abdomen. In a trance, Anna wanders off and finds herself alone with the film's most sympathetic character, Laura (the blind fiancé of Pritchard's son, Michael). As Laura, actress Jane Merrow easily steals the hearts of the audience right away, but oddly Professor Pritchard is not enthused by his son's engagement to a blind woman. However, after being stabbed, and knowing that Anna has left with his soon-to-be daughter-in-law, Professor Pritchard finally shows concern for Laura. And though he's in extreme physical pain, he uses his last hour on earth to save her from Anna. The film ends within the famous St. Paul's Cathedral, where Laura has taken Anna so that she may see how beautiful it is. In an attempt to save Laura, Pritchard calls to Anna from below, begging her to come to him. Though she comes close to attacking Laura, she eventually snaps out of her trance and jumps off of the balcony to her death, which is well done in slow-motion and accompanied by choir music.

This film was in many ways better than the film it accompanied, *Twins of Evil,* but *Hands of the Ripper* still played as the support feature of the two in the U.S. and U.K. alike.

FINAL WORD Though it's not terribly well remembered among casual horror fans, *Hands of the Ripper* is in fact one of the best films Hammer ever made.

LADY FRANKENSTEIN

(ALEXIA FILMS/CONDOR INTERNATIONAL)
Release Date: October 22, 1971 (Italy) October 1973 (U.S.)
Alternate Titles: *Daughter of Frankenstein* (Latin America)
Lady Frankenstein: Sex Addict (France)
Frankenstein's Daughter's Revenge (Japan)

Directed by: Mel Welles & Aureliano Luppi **Special Effects by:** Carlo Rambladi & Giuseppe Peruzzi (makeup) **Screenplay by:** Edward di Lorenzo & Dick Randall **Music by:** Alessandro Alessandroni **Cast:** Rosalba Neri (Tania Frankenstein) Joseph Cotten (Baron Frankenstein) Paul Muller (Dr. Charles Marshall) Peter Whiteman (the Creature) Marino Masé (Thomas Stack) Herbert Fux (the graverobber) Mickey Hargitay (Captain Harris) Renate Kasché (Julia Stack)

Spherical, Metrocolor, 99 Minutes

SYNOPSIS Having just graduated from medical school, Tania Frankenstein returns home to her father's estate. There Baron Frankenstein is experimenting with bringing the dead back to life with his colleague Dr. Charles Marshall. Tania wants in on her father's experiment, but he won't allow it. However, when the monster comes to life, it kills Baron Frankenstein. As the monster runs loose across the countryside, Tania and Charles embark on a new experiment. Tania, who knows Charles is in love with her, convinces him to let her transplant his brain into the body of the handsome young Thomas, who is mentally disabled. Reluctantly, Charles agrees and the experiment is a success. Not long after, the monster storms the castle with the villagers on its trail. The monster breaks into the lab. Charles and Tania manage to kill it, but soon the villagers set fire to the castle. As the lab burns, Charles and Tania make love, but at the last second he strangles Tania to death.

COMMENTARY Though Hammer produced a trilogy of female-centric vampire movies, plus female spins on Jack the Ripper, the Mummy, and Dr. Jekyll and Mr. Hyde, one thing Hammer never did was a female Frankenstein. Enter *Lady Frankenstein*, which is

292

often compared to Hammer's films, though really the similarities are only superficial. Yes, it's a gory, color Frankenstein film imbued with sex, but the resemblance ends there. The fact is that being an Italian production, this film has a great deal more sex and nudity than anything Hammer ever produced along with better production values and sets than the usual Hammer fare. However, had Hammer made the film it probably would have had better pacing, as this one moves rather slowly. This is partly the director's fault, and partly the writers. Even Joseph Cotton doesn't seem terribly enthused about his character and just phones it in. However, Rosalba Neri is excellent as Tania, and the film benefits greatly when she takes over the story after Cotton's Dr. Frankenstein dies at the hands of the monster.

On the note of the monster, its design is odd and makes it look more like an alien than a ghoul with its oversized brain cavity. The monster gets a few good scenes, but overall it just aimlessly wanders the countryside, interrupting trysts between lovers in the woods just for the sake of more nudity. Nor does the monster have any sympathetic traits at all, it's just a lumbering brute. The only thing interesting and unique about it is that the monster specifically targets the grave robbers who stole the parts to create it. How the monster knows who they are is difficult to discern, but it's interesting, nonetheless.

The idea of a female Dr. Frankenstein is explored better in this film than campy fare like *Jesse James Meets Frankenstein's Daughter* as well. That Tania uses her scientific powers for sexual purposes is rather interesting. In the story, Tania is quite attracted to the young and handsome Thomas, her father's mentally disabled stable boy. On an intellectual level, she's more attracted to Charles. So, she decides to combine the best of both worlds by transplanting Charles's brain into Thomas's body! That's not the only reason she does it though, she also wants to avenge her father's death by creating a second monster to destroy the first, which is another unique idea. Nor does the end confrontation between the two creatures disappoint. The choreography is good, plenty of lab equipment gets demolished and limbs get lopped off. The ending is interesting if not abrupt. As the castle burns, Tanya and Charles/Thomas make love amidst the fire. At the last moment, Charles/Thomas grabs Tanya by the throat and kills her! Though there had been some implication that he feared Tanya had no interest in him outside of being an experiment, the idea wasn't emphasized enough to make it clear why he finally kills her.

The Italian film had a heavy financial influence from the U.S. It was initially bankrolled by Harry Cushing, but just before shooting began a letter of credit was not accepted by the Italian banks. As such, $90,000 was put up by Roger Corman's New World Pictures and it was directed by famous voice actor and dubber Mell Welles. The film grossed 139,683,000 Italian lira when released in October of 1971, though it wouldn't be released in the U.S. until two years later.

FINAL WORD *Lady Frankenstein* may have its admirers, but it's ultimately one of those films you're more likely to enjoy for historical reasons as opposed to sheer entertainment value due to its rather slow pace.

VAMPIRE CIRCUS

(HAMMER)
Release Date: April 30, 1972 (U.K.)
Alternate Titles: *The Gypsy and the Vampire* (Chile)

Directed by: Robert Young **Screenplay by:** Jud Kinberg, George Baxt & Wilbur Stark **Special Effects by:** Les Bowie **Music by:** David Whitaker **Cast:** Adrienne Corri (Gypsy Woman) Laurence Payne (Professor Albert Müller) Thorley Walters (Burgermeister) Lynne Frederick (Dora Müller) John Moulder-Brown (Anton Kersh) Anthony Corlan (Emil) Domini Blythe (Anna Müller) Robert Tayman (Count Mitterhaus) Robin Sachs (Heinrich/male twin) Lalla Ward (Helga/female twin) Skip Martin (the dwarf) David Prowse (the Strongman)

Spherical, Color, 84 Minutes

SYNOPSIS Stetl, a small Serbian village, lives in mortal fear of Count Mitterhaus, a vampire, until one night the villagers storm his castle, kill him, and set it on fire. Before he dies, Mitterhaus curses the town and then instructs his servant, Anna, to find his cousin Emil who runs the Circus of Nights... Fifteen years later the town is ravaged by the plague, with no one allowed to enter or exit the village. Somehow a circus manages to make their way into the town to the delight of the depressed villagers. But it soon becomes apparent the circus is run by a disguised Anna and a group of vampires who also manage to succeed in resurrecting Count Mitterhaus. All the villagers band together, and though very few survive, they are able to kill the vampires and the reborn Mitterhaus.

COMMENTARY *Vampire Circus* begins with an ambitious—and lengthy—twelve-minute pre-credits sequence. In it, we get all the things you'd usually get at a vampire film's ending: the vampire is defeated and the castle is burned. But in *Vampire Circus*'s case, it's just the beginning. And unlike a similarly charged pre-credits scene for *Dracula A.D. 1972*, *Vampire Circus* doesn't disappoint in terms of what follows. Overall, it's a film full of fun ideas and twists on the mythos. For starters, while these vampires do still fear the cross, they are perfectly fine out in the daylight. Nor do they disintegrate when staked through the heart, also unusual. The vampire twins that can share each other's pain is also a unique idea. Apparently, they were carried over from an abandoned project to focus on vampire twins (unrelated to *Twins of Evil*, believe it or not).

Anthony Corlain, the hero from *Taste the Blood of Dracula*, has many of the best scenes as Emil, who can turn into a panther. Or maybe I should say the panther gets many of the best scenes. Emil, as the panther, stalking a poor family in the woods is one of the most horrific sequences Hammer ever put to film. In fact, there was significant debate as to just how extreme the gore should get in the film, and even by Hammer standards it was pretty extreme. Another excellent bit is the assault on the students' boarding house. A shot of Emil and his cohorts slowly approaching the building with evil intent seems like something out of a modern Quentin Tarantino film. The chaos that ensues when they get inside is also quite a show stopper. There's an excellent trick shot where actor Anthony Corlan's feet are filmed running up the stairs and seamlessly become those of a panther. We don't see the panther attack the students upstairs, but really we don't need to. Their screams are more than enough to feed the imagination. In the usual Hammer tradition, the means by which the head vampire is dispatched is innovative. The hero turns a crossbow into a crucifix. And then, when Count Mitterhaus falls to his knees, he hooks his neck through the crossbow, pulls the trigger, and the wire decapitates the Count!

It's remarkable that *Vampire Circus* turned out as well as it did, because according to reports, filming was shut down when it went over schedule by one week! Editor Peter Musgrave was then instructed to make a cohesive film out of what he was given. This information was quite surprising to me, as I feel the film is quite cohesive from a narrative perspective and feels "full" despite being unfinished. That said, there are a few lingering questions that the film doesn't address, such as who is the father of the twins, and is the gypsy woman really their mother? Likewise, some of the circus troupe would almost seem to have supernatural abilities even though they are not vampires. For instance, the gypsy woman is really Anna, only having shapeshifted somehow which isn't explained. Two of the dancers that seemed to have supernatural abilities are also later found dead, killed by the vampires for food, which was also odd. Perhaps these questions would have been answered somewhere within the un-shot scenes.

Vampire Circus came out at a time when Gothic horror was now passé. Foolish critics also trashed it, probably just thinking it was the vogue thing to do. The film, of course, was not a success upon release, but is highly regarded today.

FINAL WORD Though Hammer produced some pretty solid non-Dracula/Van Helsing vampire movies over the years, *Vampire Circus* is easily the best of the bunch.

BLACULA

(AIP)
Release Date: August 25, 1972 (U.S.)
Alternate Titles: *The Black Vampire* (France/Mexico) *Blacula, the Black Vampire* (Brazil) *Vampire Blacula* (Japan)

Directed by: William Crain **Screenplay by:** Joan Torres, Raymond Koenig & Richard Glouner **Special Effects by:** Roger George & Fred B. Phillips **Music by:** Gene Page **Cast:** William Marshall (Prince Mamuwalde/Blacula) Vonetta McGee (Tina Williams/Luva) Thalmus Rasulala (Dr. Gordon Thomas) Denise Nicholas (Michelle Williams) Gordon Pinsent (Lt. Jack Peters) Emily Yancy (Nancy) Lance Taylor Sr. (Swenson) Logan Field (Sergeant Barnes) Charles Macaulay (Count Dracula)

Spherical, Color, 93 Minutes

SYNOPSIS In 1780, Prince Mamuwalde and his wife, Luva, travel to Transylvania to seek the help of the distinguished Count Dracula in ending the slave trade. Instead, Dracula places the vampire curse on Mamuwalde and christens him Blacula. He kills Luva and leaves Blacula locked in a coffin. In 1972, the coffin is purchased as part of an estate sale by two interior decorators. When they open the coffin, the hungry Blacula feeds on them and turns them into vampires. While out perusing Los Angeles, Blacula sees a woman named Tina who is identical to Luva. Blacula begins a romance with Tina, but trouble arises in the form of her friend, Dr. Gordon Thomas, investigating a series of strange murders. Thomas believes the murders to be committed by a vampire, and the more he takes note of Mamuwalde's strange behavior he singles him out as the main culprit. Mamuwalde convinces Tina to go away with him, but she is shot by a police officer out to get Blacula. Mamuwalde gives Tina the kiss of the vampire to save her life, but she is later staked by accident when Thomas opens Blacula's coffin to kill him. Heartbroken, Mamuwalde walks into the bright sunlight and ends his existence.

COMMENTARY Sometime in the early 1970s, the exploitation masters at AIP decided to make a horror film aimed specifically at

African American audiences. Despite the film's exploitive title, it has a certain dignity to it, thanks in large part to lead actor William Marshall. As it turns out, the film's opening scenes and Blacula's backstory were created by Marshall. Initially, Blacula was just a regular man named Andrew Brown (a racist nod to the old Amos and Andy series). Marshall disliked the nod to Amos and Andy, citing it as an example of "ignorant, conniving stupidity that evolved in the United States to justify slavery." He suggested that Blacula be given a more regal backstory, where he is of royal blood similar to how Dracula is a nobleman.

And so, Andrew Brown became Prince Mamuwalde on a diplomatic mission to meet Count Dracula in Transylvania. He is there in the hope that Dracula can help him end the slave trade. (This film's portrayal of Dracula doesn't try to copy Christopher Lee or Bela Lugosi. Interestingly, this Count is bearded and nor does he walk around in a cape.) Instead of helping him, Dracula is incensed that Mamuwalde would ask such a thing of him. Dracula then turns on Mamuwalde and makes him a vampire. He locks him in a sealed room within a coffin. There with him is Luva, who eventually dies of starvation. All of this not only gives Mamuwalde a tragic backstory, it also makes him a hero turned villain of sorts. (Perhaps villain is a little harsh, as Mamuwalde was cursed in the midst of a noble cause. However, Mamuwalde also doesn't seem to show much remorse over his killings and seems to embrace his new existence as a vampire.)

Though it might seem like this movie borrows a common plot thread from *Dracula*—that being that the title vampire chases after the female lead because she resembles a lost love—that storyline was not present in Bram Stoker's *Dracula*. It was Richard Matheson two years later in his version of the tale that used that idea. So, in this regard, *Blacula* predates a common aspect of the more modern Dracula myth. Actually, Blacula may have been more inspired by Barnabas Collins than he was Dracula. Like Barnabas on *Dark Shadows*, Blacula is locked in a coffin for over a hundred years and upon being released is a somewhat sympathetic figure in spite of his feedings, which he can't really help. And, of course, the quest for his lost love is also like Barnabas and Josette on *Dark Shadows*. As for one last similarity, Barnabas too was cursed into his undead existence as an act of vengeance.

The screenwriters made a wise decision in setting this film in the present day rather than the Victorian era, though, like *Dracula A.D. 1972*, it has a prologue set hundreds of years before the main story which is a nice touch. This film came out the same year as *Dracula A.D. 1972* and handles its vampire in modern settings better than that film did. (It would be hard to imagine Lee's Dracula hanging out at the club like Marhall's Blacula.) And on that note, even though this film's title was a play on Dracula, this film was probably more so inspired by AIP's recent hit, *Count Yorga, Vampire* which also had a contemporary setting. That said, there are also nods to the old Universal films in that Blacula can turn into a bat and does so by animation just as in *Son of Dracula*.

Where the film more so resembles a typical Blaxploitation movie is when the murder mystery subplot comes into play, led by actor Thalmus Rasulala as Dr. Thomas (sort of this film's version of Van Helsing). Dr. Thomas's tenuous relationship with a white cop is similar to the character relationship in *Shaft* between the title character and a white cop. Dr. Thomas has an excellent scene where he digs up the grave of a man who he suspects was vampirized. Upon prying off the casket's lid, the undead man springs on him. It's probably the film's best scare, and it's most memorable scene in terms of vampires. The climax is also an interesting fusion of Blaxploitation crime thriller meets vampire movie. It takes place in a chemical plant with plenty of bullets flying. As stated in the synopsis, the bullets result in Tina's getting shot, which leads to her vampirism, which then leads to her being staked. Notably, Blacula isn't defeated by any of the protagonists, and ends his undead existence on his own terms, committing suicide by walking into the sunlight. (His disintegration scene is unique in that maggots crawl across his remains, though eventually he turns into a bleached skeleton.)

Blacula was met with its fair share of snide reviews naturally, but it was one of the top moneymakers for that year, and easily outperformed Hammer and Warner Bros' *Dracula A.D. 1972*.

FINAL WORD This progenerator of the Blaxploitation horror genre is more than just a gimmick or a catchy title, it's an excellent seventies horror film in its own right.

MAD, MAD, MAD MONSTERS

(RANKIN/BASS/FILMATION ASSOCIATES)
Broadcast Date: September 23, 1972 (U.S.)
Alternate Titles: *The Freaky Monster Show* (U.K. video title)

Directed by: Jules Bass & Arthur Rankin Jr. **Screenplay by:** William J. Keenan & Lou Silverstone **Animation by:** Mushi Studios **Music by:** Maury Laws **Voice Cast:** Bob McFadden (Baron Henry von Frankenstein) Allen Swift (Count Dracula/Igor/ the Monster/Claude the Invisible Man/Ghoul the Invisible Boy/ Boobula/Ron Chanley, the Werewolf/Dr. Jekyll and Mr. Hyde/ Rosebud the vulture/Harold/Harvey) Rhoda Mann (the Bride/ Nagatha the Invisible Woman/Wicked Witch of the East)

Academy Ratio, Color, 66 Minutes

SYNOPSIS When Baron Frankenstein decides to create a bride for his monster, he goes all out by securing a hotel in Transylvania for the wedding festivities, which will include a bachelor party. All the monsters—Dracula and his son, the Wolf Man, the Mummy, the Creature, and the Invisible Man and his family—arrive as planned, but there's one problem: Ygor is mad that the Baron won't create a bride for him as well. As such, Ygor sets out to sabotage the wedding.

COMMENTARY Many of you may not know that the beloved *Mad Monster Party?* (1967) received a sequel five years later in the form of this animated special. Unfortunately, it's just regular animation this time around, not Claymation or Stopmotion. It's also a bit sillier and more kid-oriented than the last entry, too.

Instead of a sequel—the island and all the monsters did explode—*Mad, Mad, Mad Monsters* is a prequel about the creation of the Bride. And as all prequels do, it wreaks some havoc with continuity. Baron Boris Frankenstein is now Baron Henry Frankenstein. Dracula and the Invisible Man now have kids (and a wife, Nagatha, in the latter's case), which seems more like sequel material than prequel. Also, the werewolf has a human form this time around, named Ron Chanley (Lon Chaney, get it?), and

301

similarly, the Invisible Man is referred to by his wife as Claude (as in Claude Rains). Lastly, there's a new character in the form of Ygor, who seems like he might be a version of Yetch from *Mad Monster Party?* (Something Ygor and Yetch both have in common is that they both are incensed that the Baron never made them a mate.) But, those are small quibbles for a children's film.

The film is peppered with amusing scenes, such as a mailman's efforts to deliver letters to each of the monsters. Then there's a dinner party where Nagatha berates the Invisible Man for using the wrong salad fork, while next to her, the Wolf Man gnaws on a drumstick. Then there's the bachelor party where the Wicked Witch of the East serves as entertainment! At only 44 minutes, the film manages to not wear out its welcome, but just barely in the case of adult viewers.

FINAL WORD Only recommended if you're an absolute fiend for *Mad Monster Party?*

DRACULA A.D. 1972

(HAMMER)
Release Date: September 28, 1972 (U.K.)
November 17, 1972 (U.S.)
Alternate Titles: *Dracula Chases Miniskirt Girls* (Austria/Brazil)
Dracula '73 (France/Spain) *The Vampire Hunts Hotpants*
(Denmark) *1972: Dracula Strikes Again!* (Italy)
Dracula '72 (Japan)

Directed by: Alan Gibson **Screenplay by:** Don Houghton **Special Effects by:** Les Bowie **Music by:** Michael Vickers **Cast:** Christopher Lee (Count Dracula) Peter Cushing (Professor Lawrence/Lorrimer Van Helsing) Stephanie Beacham (Jessica Van Helsing) Christopher Neame (Johnny Alucard) Michael Coles (Inspector Murray) William Ellis (Joe Mitchum) Philip Miller (Bob Tarrant) Marsha Hunt (Gaynor Keating) Michael Kitchen (Greg Fuller) Janet Key (Anna Bryant) Caroline Munro (Laura Jane Bellows)

Spherical, Eastmancolor, 96 Minutes

SYNOPSIS In the year 1872, Professor Van Helsing and Count Dracula fight a final battle in London's Hyde Park. Both die, but the Count's ashes are preserved by a follower. One hundred years later, the man's descendant, Johnny Alucard, performs an occult ceremony in a desanctified church to resurrect Dracula. Present among the thrill-seeking young people is none other than Jessica Van Helsing. The resurrected Dracula immediately sets his sights on her as a way of taking final revenge on the Van Helsing family. Jessica begins to suffer bizarre nightmares, which her grandfather, Lorrimer Van Helsing, takes note of. As several of Jessica's friends are found dead and drained of blood, Lorrimer fears a vampire may be about. When Jessica goes missing, Van Helsing confronts a now vampirized Johnny Alucard, who informs him Jessica is to be Dracula's bride. Lorrimer kills Alucard, and makes his way to the desanctified church where Dracula resides. There he destroys Dracula and saves his granddaughter.

303

COMMENTARY With *Scars of Dracula* turning in an unexciting performance at the box office, one might wonder how another Dracula even came about. The answer, oddly enough, was frozen rupees. Warner Bros had a frozen account in India that could only be utilized for an Indian production. When Hammer learned this, they wrote a Dracula sequel set in India! However, Warners eventually gave up on the rupees. They had taken note of *Count Yorga, Vampire's* success with a modern-day setting, and they wanted Hammer to try the same trick with Christopher Lee's Dracula. And so Warner Bros not only commissioned a modern-set Dracula film, but a modern-set sequel as well! And that is how *Dracula A.D. 1972* came about.

Say what you will of the film, but it gets off to one heck of a start. The very first shot, of leaves blowing gently across the ground, is accompanied by music with a wonderful sense of momentum. We can hear hoof beats and then a narrator breaks in explaining what we are seeing: Van Helsing and Dracula battling atop a runaway stagecoach. We don't know how they got there, and if anything, it seems like the exciting conclusion of another movie we have never seen. The choreography is quite good as the mortal foes fight atop the carriage until it finally crashes. Dracula, impaled on a broken wheel spoke, and Van Helsing then expire side by side. A sinister looking follower collects Dracula's ashes in a vile, and then buries that same vile next to Van Helsing's tombstone during his funeral. As the priest reads the well-known Bible verse about "He who believeth in Me shall never die," the music swells again, and the camera pans up from Van Helsing's now withered tombstone to a jet airliner streaking through the sky. It's an amazing way to kick off the film, and famous director Tim Burton cited this as his favorite Hammer Dracula in great part due to the exciting opening. The same is true of myself, as the exciting momentum of that opening scene stayed with me for the entire film. But the exciting opening was also something of a double-edged sword for others, as what followed arguably didn't live up to the wonderful pre-credits scene at all.

The film's story is essentially a repeat of *Taste the Blood of Dracula* (i.e., a youthful disciple revives Dracula on unhallowed ground in London which the Count then rarely leaves). Due to the weak storyline that we'd seen many times before by now, the film's merits come mainly from its production values and performances. Alan Gibson's direction has a certain sense of vigor to it that can't be denied. This is exemplified in many scenes, a notable one being Dracula's resurrection when the earth next to Van Helsing's grave begins to heave up and down. Finally a mist spews from the ground, and out of it appears the Count in an excellent shot. And though many people complain that all Dracula does is hang around the church, his scenes are still directed with great panache by Gibson. Thanks to the direction, Lee seems to give a more charged performance this time around and his scenes interacting with young Johnny Alucard are possibly his best. The duo have excellent chemistry together, and of all the Hammer Dracula's lackeys, Alucard is hands down the best. And, of course, it's great fun to finally see Peter Cushing return to the series as Van Helsing for the first time since *Brides of Dracula*. He too shares some excellent scenes with Christopher Neame's Alucard, notably a fight to the death between the two in Alucard's very mod apartment. All of these scenes are made all the better by Michael Vickers score, which is positively charged, even though it might have been off putting to fans of James Bernard.

As stated earlier, the film's ambitious opening hurts the ending to an extent. While it's great to see Van Helsing and Dracula face off again and share some dialogue, the choreography of the end fight isn't nearly as exciting as either the pre-credits scene or Van Helsing's tussle with Alucard. The means of dispatching Dracula are also rather subpar: Van Helsing throws Holy Water in his face, and the vampire falls into a trap of stakes in the ground planted by Van Helsing. When compared to the more exciting death scenes of *Horror*, *Prince of Darkness*, and even *Scars*, this one is a little underwhelming. And yet, all that said, thanks to the direction and music, the end battle still manages to be quite exciting, proving that good production values can certainly elevate a lackluster script.

The film had a healthy £220,000 budget and was shot from late September into early November of 1971. But, unfortunately, the film was dated before it even went before cameras, perhaps making the hip teen scenes more laughable at the time of release than they are even today, ironically enough. It's unknown if this was the reason why audiences didn't take to the film like they did the modern Yorga and Blacula films. However, as per their contract, Hammer had already begun work on the sequel.

FINAL WORD A divisive love it or hate it film, *Dracula A.D. 1972* is certainly interesting regardless of which of the two camps you may fall into.

FRANKENSTEIN

(DAN CURTIS PRODUCTIONS)
Broadcast Date: January 16, 1973 (U.S.)

Directed by: Glenn Jordan **Teleplay by:** Sam Hall & Dan Curtis based on the book by Mary Shelley **Makeup by:** Marvin G. Westmore and Michael Westmore **Music by:** Robert Cobert **Cast:** Robert Foxworth (Dr. Victor Frankenstein) Susan Strasberg (Elizabeth Lavenza) Bo Svenson (the Monster) Robert Gentry (Dr. Henry Clerval) Heidi Vaughn (Agatha DeLacey) Philip Bourneuf (Alphonse Frankenstein) Robert Gentry (Henri Clerval) Jon Lormer (Charles DeLacey) William Hansen (Professor Waldman) John Karlen (Otto Roget) Willie Aames (William Frankenstein)

Spherical, Color, 180 Minutes (TV version)
126 Minutes (home video version)

SYNOPSIS After returning home from the university, Victor Frankenstein creates a man out of corpses with his two assistants. In the act of stealing a heart for the creation, one assistant is shot and killed. Victor uses his heart to bring the monster life. Though good-hearted, the monster doesn't know his own strength and accidentally kills the other lab assistant, Otto. The monster escapes Victor's confinement to go live in the country. He takes shelter in an old abandoned house next to a small family. By observing them, the monster learns to speak. However, when he approaches them they react in fear and attack him. Soon after the monster encounters Victor's brother in the woods and accidentally kills him as well. Victor finds the monster, who demands that Victor create a mate for him. Victor agrees, but can't go through the operation and destroys the bride before she's brought to life. The monster vows to get revenge, and on Victor's wedding night to Elizabeth Lavenza, the monster kills her. Victor and the monster have a showdown in an abandoned village. Victor trips and falls, impaling himself on some ruins. The monster becomes frightened and distraught at seeing his master in death. Victor beseeches the monster to run away to the mountains and be free, but before he can some policeman arrive on the scene and shoot the monster dead.

COMMENTARY Just as Dan Curtis preceded his famous *Dark Shadows* with an adaptation of *The Strange Case of Dr. Jekyll and Mr. Hyde*, he also followed *Dark Shadows* with an adaptation of *Frankenstein*. Robert Cobert's music is used and *Shadows* star John Karlen even appears in an Ygor-type role. Thanks to the Robert Cobert library score and videotape, it feels like you're watching an episode of *Dark Shadows*, which is fine, but it's a shame the story couldn't have been shot on actual film.

As to unique little alterations that it makes, one of Frankenstein's assistants is shot while robbing a grave to procure a heart. Ironically, his heart is then put into the monster. Like *Frankenstein: The True Story* to come out later that year, this adaptation presents a more human, less frightening monster. The post-operation scenes are different from anything to come before them in that Frankenstein and his assistant have a peaceful, playful relationship with the monster, like new parents attending to their newborn. Things only take a dark turn when the monster accidentally kills Otto.

The entire cast is great, but it's Bo Svenson who stands out the most as the monster. His scenes observing a family in secret and learning to speak are quite touching and sad, especially when he sees his face in the mirror and understands that his appearance is frightening. The story makes another interesting variation here where instead of a blind man, the monster befriends a pretty blind girl. Victor is also given an adorable kid brother for the monster to kill—accidentally. The child befriends the monster and wants to help him. When the boy calls for help the monster tries to silence him and ends up suffocating him. Despite this, Frankenstein understands and still feels sorry for his creation, mending his arm, bloodied from a bullet wound. Instead, it's the monster who becomes hostile when he re-learns that Frankenstein is his creator. (Like a newborn, it had been so long since he had seen him that he had forgotten him.) The monster is angry because of his frightening appearance and demands that Frankenstein make him a mate. Begrudgingly, he agrees. Unfortunately the creation of the Bride is a non-event, with Victor deciding to end his new creation's life before it's even born, enraging the monster. Their conflict ends atmospherically in the foggy ruins of an abandoned village. Their final dying moments together make for some of the better interactions between Frankenstein and his creation. In his grief, the monster commits suicide by police, charging the law officers in hopes that they will shoot him. It's an interesting end for the monster to say the least.

The miniseries aired over two nights as part of ABC's Wide World of Mystery. Actually, the first half premiered on the same night as Curtis's much anticipated sequel to *The Night Stalker*, *The Night Strangler*, which somewhat overshadowed this film. Curtis's adaptation was further forgotten upon the bigger-budgeted, film-shot *Frankenstein: The True Story* which came out later that same year. All that said, critics at the time were kind to the adaptation with *The Los Angeles Times* describing it as "a handsome show, with huge, foreboding sets and a splendid array of special effects" and *Variety* praised it as "extraordinary entertainment."

FINAL WORD It's too bad that *Frankenstein* couldn't have been shot on film rather than videotape like Dan Curtis's production of *Dracula* that would come next. If it had, it might be better remembered and get more recognition today.

BRAM STOKER'S DRACULA

(DAN CURTIS PRODUCTIONS)

Broadcast Date: February 8, 1974 (U.S.)

Alternate Titles: *Dracula, the Last Romantic* (Argentina) *Dracula, the Dark Demon* (Brazil) *Dracula and his Vampire Women* (France) *The Black Demon* (Italy) *Dracula's Vampire* (Portugal) *Dan Curtis' Dracula* (home video)

Directed by: Dan Curtis **Teleplay by:** Richard Matheson based upon the book by Bram Stoker **Special Effects by:** Kit West **Music by:** Robert Cobert **Cast:** Jack Palance (Count Dracula/Vlad the Impaler) Simon Ward (Arthur Holmwood) Nigel Davenport (Abraham Van Helsing) Fiona Lewis (Lucy Westenra/Maria Tepes) Murray Brown (Jonathan Harker) Penelope Horner (Mina Murray) Pamela Brown (Mrs. Westenra)

Spherical, Color, 98 Minutes

SYNOPSIS When Jonathan Harker arrives at Castle Dracula to oversee a real estate deal, his host Count Dracula becomes obsessed with a photograph of his friend, Lucy Westerna, who looks exactly like the Count's long-dead wife. Harker is vampirized by Dracula's brides as the Count leaves for London to court Lucy, engaged to Arthur Holmwood. Dracula feeds on Lucy until she dies, despite the best efforts of Holmwood and vampire hunter Van Helsing. When Lucy rises again as a vampire, Van Helsing stakes her before Dracula can come to collect her. Upon seeing Lucy's staked body, he becomes enraged and sets his sights on Mina as an act of revenge. After making Mina drink of his blood, Dracula returns to Transylvania. Using Mina's psychic connection to the Count, Holmwood and Van Helsing follow him. At Castle Dracula they dispatch the vampire version of Harker, and then expose Dracula to sunlight. In Dracula's helpless state, Van Helsing drives a lance through his heart, ending the Count's reign of terror.

COMMENTARY In 1973, great television horror producer Dan Curtis finally adapted *Dracula*. I say finally because he had done not one, but two famous adaptations of vampires previous to this.

The best known was *Dark Shadows*, where Barnabas Collins essentially became the TV version of Dracula. Earlier in 1973 had also aired *The Nightstalker*, about a reporter pursuing a vampire through Las Vegas, which became the highest-rated TV movie of its time. Whereas Curtis's previous three horror adaptations of *Dr. Jekyll and Mr. Hyde*, *Dorian Gray* and *Frankenstein* had been filmed on videotape, his version of *Dracula* would be a much higher budgeted production, shot on film and made for British television. To that end it was even lensed on location in England and also caught some authentic exterior footage in Yugoslavia. Written and shot as a three hour masterpiece, CBS insisted that the film be edited down to a one night, two hour timeslot. Remarkably, that this version is much shorter than originally intended is not evident.

Story wise, the film is both a quasi-remake of *Horror of Dracula* and an antecedent to the 1994 *Bram Stoker's Dracula*. This is because it has elements unique to both of the aforementioned films. Like *Horror of Dracula*, it narrowed down the character count eliminating Renfield, Dr. Seward, and Quincy Morris as the Hammer film had done. Like the Jonathan Harker in *Horror*, this version is also vampirized early in the story and never returns to London. Arthur Holmwood is again the male lead paired with Van Helsing, with Lucy succumbing to Dracula first and then Mina. It even has the same ending of *Horror* to a degree, with Van Helsing ripping down the curtains to expose the Count to sunlight. There is no disintegration scene though, and we are left with the visual of Dracula impaled against a table standing on end. The camera then slowly pans to a painting on the wall of Vlad the Impaler, and an epigraph about Vlad is then scrolled over the painting in red letters for the final shot.

Vlad the Impaler is the big similarity that Curtis's version shares with Francis Ford Coppola's 1994 film. Writer Richard Matheson makes the case that Dracula and Vlad were the same person which had never been done before. The other bit from this film that Coppola copied, whether he meant to or not, was that Dracula was in pursuit of one of the girls because they resembled his long lost love. In the 1994 film it is Mina, but here it is Lucy. This was another interesting twist on the tale that this version delivered. Usually Lucy was just the warm up to Mina, so to speak. Here Lucy was Dracula's endgame. He intended for her to be his vampire bride forever. Upon finding her staked, he then seeks out Mina as a means of revenge, not love. On that note, the film also misses an opportunity to have the grieving Holmwood, who here was engaged to Lucy, to begin to fall for Mina. Though this is hinted at, it never occurs. Furthermore, Mina is probably this version's greatest casualty. There's not a great deal of suspense regarding her, and she doesn't figure into the climax. Whereas *Horror* had her as Dracula's prisoner at the end, here she's at home in bed when Arthur and Van Helsing storm Castle Dracula. We don't even learn her final fate, though it's presumable she returned to normal upon the Count's death.

As for other pluses, Jack Palance looks great as the Count. The only problem with Palance is that he's Jack Palance, so recognizable from numerous Westerns that seeing him as Dracula does take some getting used to (perhaps if you've never seen Palance before it's not so strange, though). Mostly he does an excellent job, though a few of his lines aren't delivered with quite the vigor that Christopher Lee did. Just compare Lee's utterance of the famous "You'd pit your brains against mine," line in *Dracula A.D. 1972* with Palance's version, which is a bit too subdued. However, Palance utters the line just before forcing Van Helsing and Holmwood to watch as Mina drinks blood from his chest! Not only was this a touch above Lee's version of the scene from *Dracula – Prince of Darkness*, it was also quite extreme for television at the time! Palance also has good physicality as Dracula, particularly in a scene where barges into a hotel, knocking men out of his way with aplomb and surviving a gory gunshot wound to the stomach. Palance's best scenes occur when he's grieving, either over Lucy's dead body or when he finds his caskets all burned by Van Helsing, after which he utters a truly chilling, unearthly scream. The production values are also superb, and though it might be strange to see Dracula's castle in such good condition (it's ornately decorated, clean, and well-lit for a change) it's just another way in which this version is distinct. Robert Cobert's score is also excellent, and immediately recognizable to fans of *Dark Shadows* and *The Night Stalker*.

The film's initial broadcast on October 12, 1973 was preempted by an address by President Richard Nixon in the U.S., and so CBS re-aired it in February of 1974. Today the film is regarded as one of the best adaptations of the novel, and certainly the best TV movie to do so (though, in some countries this was released theatrically). Today, to avoid confusion with the Francis Ford Coppola film, this one is now better known as *Dan Curtis' Dracula*.

FINAL WORD If you're a fan of Dan Curtis, then obviously this is a must-see. Even if you're not, it's still a must-see.

311

SCREAM, BLACULA, SCREAM

(AIP)

Release Date: June 27, 1973 (U.S.)

Alternate Titles: *Blacula, the Exorcist* (Greece) *Terror of Blacula* (Portugal) *Blacula II* (working title)

Directed by: Bob Kelljan **Screenplay by:** Joan Torres, Raymond Koenig & Maurice Jules **Special Effects by:** Jack DeBron **Music by:** Bill Marx **Cast:** William Marshall (Prince Mamuwalde/Blacula) Don Mitchell (Justin Carter) Pam Grier (Lisa Fortier) Michael Conrad (Lieutenant Dunlop) Richard Lawson (Willis Daniels) Janee Michelle (Gloria) Lynn Moody (Denny) Barbara Rhoades (Elaine) Bernie Hamilton (Ragman)

Spherical, Color, 96 Minutes

SYNOPSIS When voodoo queen Mama Loa dies, she decides to name Lisa Fortier as her voodoo successor rather than her son, Willis Daniels. Willis secures the bones of Prince Mamuwalde, AKA Blacula, and resurrects him to get revenge on Lisa. However, Blacula turns the tables on Willis, biting him and making him his vampire underling instead. Not long after at a party, Mamuwalde meets Lisa along with an African art collector (and ex-cop) named Justin Carter. At the party, Mamuwalde loses control of himself and bites one of Carter's friends. Carter investigates the death of his friend and begins to think a vampire is to blame. Carter manages to convince Lieutenant Dunlop of this, and together Carter and Dunlop storm Daniels' Mansion. At that moment, Lisa is conducting a ceremony to cleanse Mamuwalde of the vampire curse. The ceremony is interrupted by Carter, so it doesn't work. An enraged Blacula tears through the house, killing every policeman in sight. When he goes to bite Carter, Lisa stakes a voodoo doll of Blacula.

COMMENTARY Unfortunately, very little information exists on this sequel's preproduction history. The reason for the sequel was that *Blacula* was a hit, naturally, but in terms of story development, early ideas, etc., very little information exists. The only small nugget of pre-production information that I found stated that the film's final title was the result of a naming contest amongst AIP's employees.

Count Yorga, Vampire director Bob Kelljan took the directorial reins on this outing and reviews of the sequel, best exemplified by no less than Siskel and Ebert themselves, were definitely mixed. Ebert felt that it was an inferior sequel that he suspected was made in a hurry, while Siskel considered the sequel to be better than the original. Kevin Thomas of *The Los Angeles Times* agreed and wrote that the film was "far superior to the original, possessing much assured style as well as considerable humor." On the other end of the spectrum, Roger Greenspun of *The New York Times* argued that the film was "not, as the title might suggest, too much fun for anybody." Years later, the 1980 book *The Golden Turkey Awards* listed *Scream, Blacula, Scream* as the "Worst Blaxploitation Movie" of all time!

As it stands, *Scream, Blacula, Scream* by no means deserves the distinction given it by the Golden Turkey Awards, nor is it inferior to the original and is easily on par with it. There's plenty to enjoy in the film. It has a pretty good shot, accomplished via animation and live-action mixed, of Blacula turning into a bat. It's similar to the old Universal films, but done better. Not long after, we get a good sequence of Blacula walking down the street and taking in the modern setting. After passing up a prostitute's offer, her pimp accosts him, and Blacula slaps him through a glass window. Another great visual comes when Blacula bursts through some French doors accompanied by a thunder blast. He does so at just the right moment to save Pam Grier's character. Grier, famous for *Foxy Brown* and many others, is spectacular as the female lead and gives the film a memorable end by staking Balcula's voodoo doll through the heart rather than he himself.

Ultimately it wasn't the critics that kyboshed more sequels for Blacula, but the film's grosses, which were not up to par with the original's.

FINAL WORD On par with the original film despite what most critics said one way or the other. As such, it's too bad there were no more Blaculas, especially since this one's ending was somewhat ambiguous and we don't actually see Blacula decompose.

EXCELSIOR FILMS

DE HAND VAN DE MUMMIE

LA MOMIE SANGLANTE

ANDREW KEIR
VALERIE LEON
JAMES VILLIERS

REGIE
SETH HOLT
TECHNICOLOR

BLOOD FROM THE MUMMY'S TOMB

314

CONDOR INTERNATIONAL PRODUCTIONS presenta

LADY FRANKENSTEIN

con
JOSEPH COTTEN
ROSALBA NERI
PAUL MÜLLER
HERBERT FUX
PAUL WHITEMAN

RENATA KASHE • LORENZO TERZON • ADA POMETTI (c.s.c.) • ANDREA AURELI • GIANNI LOFFREDO • PIETRO MARTINOVICH • RICCARDO PIZZUTI • HERB ANDRESS • BALTIERO RISPOLI

E CON LA PARTECIPAZIONE STRAORDINARIA DI **MIKEY HARGITAY**   REGIA: **M. WELLS**   DISTRIBUZIONE ALEXIA CINEMATOGRAFICA   EASTMANCOLOR

315

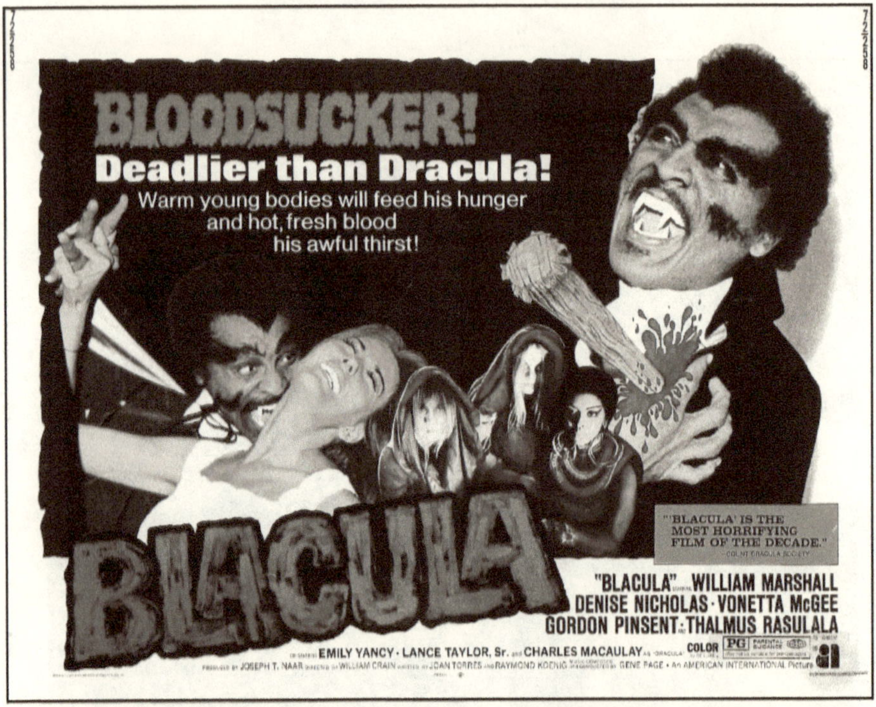

316

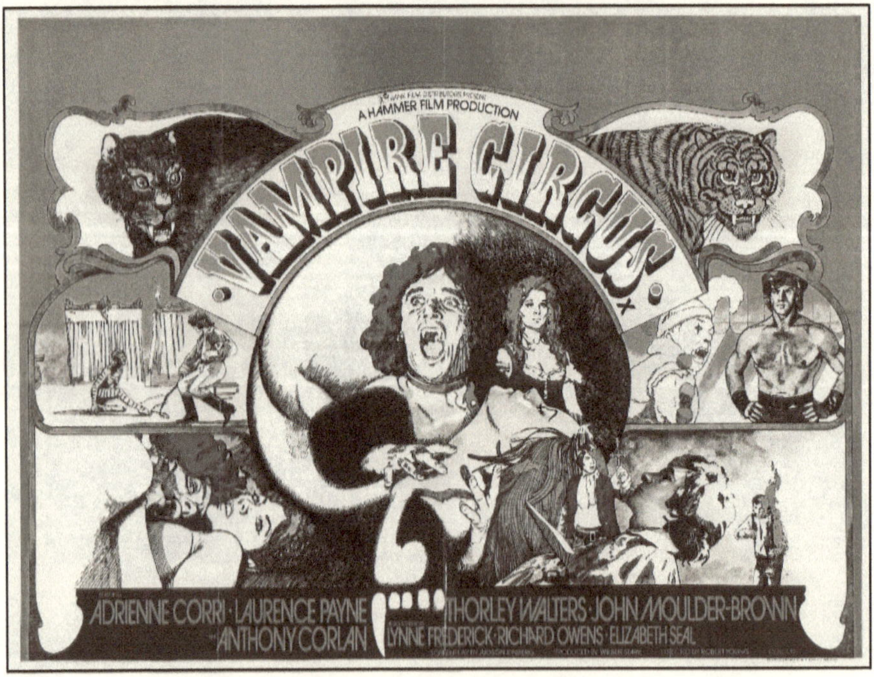

MAD, MAD, MONSTERS
The ABC Saturday Superstar Movie

JACK PALANCE
as Bram Stoker's
"DRACULA"

starring
SIMON WARD · NIGEL DAVENPORT · PAMELA BROWN · FIONA LEWIS · PENELOPE HORNER

Produced and Directed by DAN CURTIS   Written by RICHARD MATHESON   Eastmancolor   Distributed by EMI Film Distributors Limited   EMI

BLACKENSTEIN

(FRISCO PRODUCTIONS LTD)
Release Date: August 3, 1973 (U.S.)

Directed by: William A. Levey **Screenplay by:** Frank R. Saletri **Makeup by:** Gordon Freed **Music by:** Cardella Di Milo & Lou Frohman **Cast:** John Hart (Dr. Stein) Ivory Stone (Dr. Winifred Walker) Joe De Sue (Eddie Turner) Roosevelt Jackson (Malcomb) Andrea King (Eleanor) Nick Bolin (Bruno Stragor)

Spherical, Color, 87 Minutes

SYNOPSIS Eddie Turner is a Vietnam War veteran who has lost all of his limbs in the war. His fiancé, Dr. Winifred Walker, has Eddie transferred to an old colleague of hers, Dr. Stein, whose controversial research just might have what it takes to save Eddie. Dr. Stein grafts new arms and legs onto Eddie, but a jealous lab assistant with the hots for Winifred sabotages the experiment with a corrupted DNA solution. Therefore, Eddie begins to turn into a primitive brute monster that goes on a killing spree. The killing eventually leads the police to Dr. Stein's at the exact moment that the monster kills the doctor. The monster escapes into the night, and kills one last victim before it is torn to pieces by police dogs.

COMMENTARY Supposedly not long after *Blacula's* success, AIP themselves considered doing a movie called *Blackenstein*. For whatever reason they didn't and Frisco Productions made it instead. One has to wonder if the movie would have turned out better if AIP produced it. Although *Blacula* may have had a cheesy title, the movie itself wasn't all that cheesy and was easy to take seriously. *Blackenstein,* on the other hand, seems more like a spoof of *Blacula* focused on the Frankenstein legend. A big reason for this is the title character, who really can't hold a candle to Blacula in terms of character.

Hammer had more or less proved back in the late 1950s that Baron Frankenstein was a far more interesting character than his creation. The Universal films of the 1940s were, to some degree, kid stuff, which Hammer updated marvelously. This film returns the focus to the marauding monster with no real character traits.

Other studios at this time made their versions of the monsters unique by humanizing them (*Frankenstein: The True Story* and *Dan Curtis's Frankenstein*). The monster here really isn't enough to anchor the film and isn't interesting apart from its design. In fact, even before Eddie becomes the monster, his character isn't that interesting. If it had been, we might have felt more sympathy for him when he turns into a monster, but the fact of the matter is that his character is bland. If anything, the character's main reason to exist seems to be to produce an African American version of the Jack Pierce makeup. For many, the appeal of this movie will mostly lie in the monster's design, complete with a square afro meant to mimic the square head of Boris Karloff's monster. The monster's first kill is good, at least. Earlier, the story had established Eddie's male nurse as thoroughly unlikable and racist. Specifically, he even belittles Eddie for being an amputee! So, when Eddie becomes a monster, the first thing he does is escape back to the hospital, where he rips the orderly's arm right off.

On the other end of the spectrum, though, the monster's final victim, a random woman, has no characterization at all, sympathetic or otherwise. He chases her around a warehouse of some kind, kills her, and then the cops show up. Dobermans are set loose on the monster, and they tear off his grafted-on arms, making him armless yet again. Winifred is nowhere to be seen during this, but there is a tag scene of a minor detective comforting her, the implication being that they will probably get together later on.

Though critically panned, the film was apparently successful enough for people to at least talk about sequels, even though none of them ever got made. Among the proposed sequel titles were *The Fall of the House of Blackenstein* and *Black Frankenstein Meets the White Werewolf!* (*Blackenstein* was later rereleased as *The Return of Blackenstein,* which was not a sequel as the title would imply.)

FINAL WORD Unlike *Blacula,* which went beyond its catchy title, *Blackenstein's* historical merits only exist in the unique take on the makeup and the title and that's about it.

COUNT DRACULA AND HIS VAMPIRE BRIDE

(HAMMER)

Release Date: January 13, 1974 (U.K.) October 1978 (U.S.)
Alternate Titles: *Dracula Is Alive and Well and Living in London* (France/Finland) *The Diabolic Rituals of Dracula* (Belgium) *Dracula Thirsts for Fresh Blood* (Greece) *New Dracula Devil's Ceremony* (Japan) *The Rites of Dracula* (U.S. VHS release)

Directed by: Alan Gibson **Screenplay by:** Don Houghton **Special Effects by:** Les Bowie **Music by:** John Cacavas **Cast:** Christopher Lee (Count Dracula) Peter Cushing (Professor Lorrimer Van Helsing) Joana Lumley (Jessica Van Helsing) Michael Coles (Inspector Murray) Freddie Jones (Professor Julian Keeley) Barbara Yu Ling (Chin Yang) Richard Vernon (Mathews) Patrick Barr (Lord Carradine) Richard Mathews (Porter) (Peter)

Spherical, Technicolor, 87 Minutes

SYNOPSIS When an undercover agent exposes a strange plot involving government officials and the occult, Scotland Yard's Inspector Murray consults Lorrimer Van Helsing about it. One of the men in surveillance photos proves to be an old chum of Van Helsing's, Professor Keeley. Van Helsing pays him a visit and is shocked to learn that the man is developing a new, deadly strain of the bubonic plague. Van Helsing is attacked by a hired thug and rendered unconscious while Keeley is killed. Murray and Jessica Van Helsing investigate Pelham House, where the horrible ritual occurred and find a cellar full of vampires. When they tell Van Helsing of this he concludes that Dracula has returned. Jessica, Murray and his men stake out Pelham House, but are captured by snipers. Van Helsing visits the high-rise office complex owned by D.D. Denham, a man associated with Pelham House. Van Helsing meets Denham in his office, and figures out that Denham is really Dracula. The Count has his men subdue Van Helsing and he takes him to Pelham House. There he will make Jessica his vampire bride and will also unleash the plague upon the world. Dracula infects one of his followers, but luckily Inspector Murray has escaped and causes an electrical fire within the house. As the

320

infected man perishes in the flames, Murray rescues Jessica while Van Helsing chases Dracula outside. When Dracula becomes tangled in thorns, Van Helsing uses a fence post to stake him for the final time.

COMMENTARY Back in 1970, the *New York Times* had said to avoid *Scars of Dracula* as though it was the plague. Coincidentally, four years later, Dracula showed up bearing the plague itself! Though people probably often wonder why this film was produced considering *Dracula A.D. 1972* was not a hit, this was because Warner Bros was so certain that it would be a hit that they had contracted Hammer to produce two modern-day Draculas! That's also why the ever reluctant Christopher Lee returned yet again: he was under contract.

Though it has a more somber, laid-back feel to it when compared to the energetic *A.D. 1972*, this film does rectify the complaint regarding the previous film that Dracula didn't do anything. While here he still may not have many scenes, Dracula's function in the story's modern setting is handled better. For instance, rather than a castle or a desanctified church, Dracula now has both a mansion and a skyscraper to call home. Whereas in the old world, being of noble birth made one royalty, now, in addition to being a Count, Dracula is also wealthy and poses as an industrialist named D.D. Denham. Dracula also has something in this film that he didn't have in any of the old ones: a whole cellar full of vampire brides. (In the previous films, he stuck to only one vampire bride.)

There's plenty of exciting action in the film, and returning characters Inspector Murray and Jessica Van Helsing (now played by Joana Lumley as Stephanie Beacham was unavailable) are given more to do. Among their exciting sequences is an escape from the cellar of vampire brides, plus surviving a sniper's attack on them as they stake out the manor. Van Helsing's verbal sparring match with D.D. Denham in the office complex makes for one of the film's best scenes on the premise alone. Dracula, disguising his appearance via some bright lights and a Hungarian accent (a nod to Bela Lugosi), is undeniably cool. It's also the longest conversation ever had between Van Helsing and the Count during the entire series. The ending scene at Pelham House has some real stakes to it. Though the high-up officials that Dracula has been courting think that they will rule the world with him via the threat of the plague, they were unaware all along that the Count would not only unleash the plague but spread it through them, his own four horsemen of the apocalypse. (And with

Professor Keeley now dead, Van Helsing will serve as an unwilling replacement.) Just as the clock strikes midnight, Dracula causes the man holding the plague vile to break it in his own hands. The man immediately becomes infected and writhes in pain. Just as Dracula leans in to give Jessica the vampire's kiss, a fire breaks out thanks to Inspector Murray and all-out chaos ensues. It kicks Van Helsing's final confrontation with the Count up a notch. If the man infected with the plague makes it out of the mansion, then Dracula's plan will come to fruition. Not only does Van Helsing have to ward off Dracula amidst a raging fire, he also has to keep himself from being infected. It's most certainly an improvement over the last film's ending. It could even be argued that Dracula's decomposition scene is the second best in the series behind *Horror of Dracula*.

The idea of Dracula as a harbinger of the apocalypse was hinted at in *A.D. 1972's* shooting script, where Dracula was to proclaim "I am the apocalypse!" Lee refused to say the line, but the joke was on him as Dracula fulfilled that role in the next film. (One has to wonder if that was always writer Don Houghton's plan?) Even Lee admitted that the idea of Dracula wanting to finally die by denying himself victims via an extinction-level event was interesting. However, this ambitious storyline also would have been difficult to top had the series continued. (What would happen in the next film, Dracula gets the codes to all the nukes?) But no one needed to worry about that, as this was the last Lee and Cushing Dracula movie. As such, the series does go out with something of a bang with Van Helsing not only saving his granddaughter, but the whole world from Dracula's deadly grasp.

As stated earlier, this sequel, a Part II of sorts, was set into motion before Part I turned out to be a dud at the box office. As such, it should come as no surprise that this film was dead upon arrival. While it saw theatrical release in the U.K. right away, it wouldn't be released in the U.S. until nearly four years later with the rather generic title of *Count Dracula and his Vampire Bride*. Warner Bros, who had commissioned the film, washed their hands of it. Not only that, they even let it become one of the few Hammer films to lapse into public domain, though they have recently reacquired it.

FINAL WORD Marred only by a grotesque, exploitive opening sequence—which I also recommend that you skip—this film otherwise tops off Cushing and Lee's Dracula series with a rather unique ending.

322

FRANKENSTEIN
THE TRUE STORY

(UNIVERSAL TELEVISION)
Release Date: November 28-30, 1973
Alternate Titles: *Frankenstein* (France)

Directed by: Jack Smight **Teleplay by:** Don Bachardy & Christopher Isherwood based upon the novel by Mary Shelley **Special Effects by:** Roy Whybrow **Music by:** Gil Mellé **Cast:** Leonard Whiting (Dr. Victor Frankenstein) James Mason (Dr. Polidori) Michael Sarrazin (the Creature) David McCallum (Dr. Henry Clerval) Jane Seymour (Agatha/Prima) Nicola Pagett (Elizabeth Fanshawe) Michael Wilding (Sir Richard Fanshawe) Clarissa Kaye-Mason (Lady Fanshawe) Agnes Moorehead (Mrs. Blair) Margaret Leighton (Francoise DuVal) Ralph Richardson (Mr. Lacey)

Spherical, Technicolor, 185 Minutes (U.S. Mini-Series)/
115 Minutes (TV Movie)/ 123 Minutes (U.K. Theatrical Release)

SYNOPSIS Young Victor Frankenstein is bereaved over the death of his brother, and wishes he possessed the power to resurrect him. Along his travels he meets Henry Clerval, who has made progress reanimating dead tissue. Victor and Henry team up to create a perfect being from various dead bodies. When Henry dies unexpectedly, Victor takes over the experiment and transplants Henry's brain into that of their creation, Adam. The man is a perfect physical specimen when first brought to life, but as time progresses, his flesh begins to rot and deteriorate even though Adam is as strong as ever. Adam is so distraught over his ugly appearance that he tries to commit suicide by jumping off a cliff into the ocean. He survives and goes on to live nearby a family in the woods. He falls in love with the girl, Agatha, but she is run over by a stagecoach in trying to get away from him and dies. Adam then runs across a certain Dr. Polidori, who experiments with raising the dead like Frankenstein. Polidori takes Adam to Frankenstein and proposes that they make a mate for him. They do so, and she is a vision of beauty named Prima. However, she rejects Adam, who Polidori also considers inferior and wishes to see destroyed. Adam escapes being executed and kills Prima in a rage. Victor and his bride Elizabeth do their best to get away from Polidori and Adam by sailing away to America. However, Polidori and Adam have both boarded the ship as well. The entire crew abandons ship when Adam kills Polidori and Elizabeth. Adam takes he and Victor to the North Pole, where both are entombed in an icy avalanche.

COMMENTARY This lavish two-part mini-series was first broadcast on NBC in November of 1973 in two 90-minute installments. Ever since then, it has been shown as a 115-minute TV movie (the cuts are most apparent in the somewhat rushed beginning). The film certainly has the look and feel of Hammer horror, only much more lavish, with more elaborate sets, more extras, and more exterior photography. Otherwise, one might almost think Hammer had produced it. The film definitely has the unique angle that Hammer often took on their films at times. What makes this adaptation standout is that the "creature" begins the story as a handsome young man named Adam (for obvious reasons).

There is a darkly humorous scene where Victor and Henry go to the sight of a recent accident, where a group of young men were crushed in a cave-in. As they survey the corpses for the best usable body parts, they say things like, "Let's use Smith's hand and Burke's leg," etc. It sounds as though they are picking a roster for a baseball team. The creation scene differs greatly from both the original *Frankenstein* and *Curse of Frankenstein*. Though it doesn't have the excitement or buildup of those scenes, in an interesting departure, this version of Victor uses a powerful solar apparatus of some kind to give the monster life. (Solar power was apparently on the minds of scriptwriters at the time, as 1974's *The Man with the Golden Gun* featured a solar-powered McGuffin.)

The emotional core of the picture is easily Victor's loving relationship with his surrogate son/brother in the form of Adam, who is likable enough aside from seeming to be a bit vain. (He's fond of looking at himself in the mirror and cooing, "Beautiful.") This also shows how this film is the exact opposite of the old iterations of Frankenstein, where Boris Karloff's monster is enraged by his own reflection in *Bride of Frankenstein*. And unlike the hateful relationship that usually typifies Frankenstein and his monster, Adam genuinely loves his father figure. This could have been a commentary on society's obsession with looks. Whereas Karloff's monster was rejected for his ugly appearance, Adam is

324

immediately embraced. However, as Adam's looks go, he begins his path towards becoming a monster inside and out. Like Karloff's monster, his constant rejection by those around him eventually turns him violent.

Not only is this film a remake of *Frankenstein*, it is also a retelling of *Bride of Frankenstein*. It even features a version of Dr. Pretorius renamed Dr. Polidori. It's unknown if this was done for legal reasons regarding Universal, but Dr. Polidori was the real-life doctor of the Percy Shelley family. He was also the real author of *The Vampyre* (1819), which helped pave the way for *Dracula*. The character is played by the great James Mason (known to sci-fi fans for his starring roles in Jules Verne adaptations). Mason's character has some excellent dialogue that is very on the nose to the Pretorius character in *Bride*. And though even Mason can't hold a candle to Ernest Thesiger's version of Pretorius, it's still a grand portrayal. For modern audiences, he's even a little evocative of actor Christoph Waltz he puts on the charm. Overall, he gives the standout performance of the film.

The Polidori character has an odd Fu Man Chu quality to him in that both his servants are of Chinese descent, and Polidori himself dresses in Asian style robes. He and Victor's creation of the female monster makes for a wonderful scene, where the corpse is reanimated by a strange chemical bath. Probably given his anti-Biblical stance, Polidori chooses to name his creation Prima rather than Eve. And Prima is indeed a vision of beauty, introduced in a shot that is wonderfully lit and that features her hair flowing through the air.

Though it may all be coincidence, this film has several notable similarities to Hammer's *Revenge of Frankenstein* (1959). Though that film's "creature" was no Adonis like Adam in this film, Karl was at least a normal human being who gets monstrous looking as the picture progresses. It's the exact same thing here, as Adam slowly turns into a zombie with rotting flesh. Another similarity between the two pictures occurs when the monster attacks a recital towards the end. However, in this film's case, it's much more exciting. As Adam enters the dance/recital, the extras flee in horror. What happens next is more along the lines of what you'd expect in the 1994 *Mary Shelley's Frankenstein*, as Adam literally rips Prima's head off! Though it's not terribly bloody, not much is hidden from view and we do see it happen, which is pretty extreme for a TV movie in 1973.

The sequence has a great sense of momentum, and really should have led right into the ending. The ending that we do get is certainly epic, it's just that it interrupts the story flow at a high point where it really could have ended on a bang. Instead it stops and starts, with Victor and Elizabeth boarding a ship for America only to be unpleasantly surprised by Adam and Polidori. The scenes are well done and gruesome, with Adam stringing Polidori (strangely afraid of the lightning) to the ship's mast where he is struck by lightning and turned into a charred skeleton. This prompts the crew to abandon ship, leaving Victor and his creation alone after he kills Elizabeth (who wasn't a terribly likable character to begin with). And yet, in their final scenes on the Arctic ice, it doesn't seem as though Victor hates Adam. It would seem that he has a touch of a father's undying love for his son in spite of what he's done. As Victor shouts in an emotional outburst, it brings an avalanche down on the duo that both seem to welcome.

FINAL WORD Though it couldn't be said that this film is a classic on the level of either the 1931 *Frankenstein* or *Curse of Frankenstein*, it is technically speaking a better and more faithful (but still very unique) adaptation of Mary Shelley's novel.

CAPTAIN KRONOS
VAMPIRE HUNTER

(HAMMER)
Release Date: April 7, 1974 (U.S.) June 14, 1974 (U.S.)
Alternate Titles: *Vampire Hunter* (Japan) *Captain Kronos Against the Vampires* (France-alternate title)

Directed by: Brian Clemens **Screenplay by:** Brian Clemens **Makeup by:** Jimmy Evans **Music by:** Laurie Johnson **Cast:** Horst Janson (Captain Kronos) John Cater (Professor Hieronymus Grost) Caroline Munro (Carla) John Carson (Dr. Marcus) Shane Briant (Paul Durward) Lois Daine (Sara Durward) Wanda Ventham (Lady Durward) William Hobbs (Hagen Durward) Ian Hendry (Kerro) Paul Greenwood (Giles) Julian Holloway (voice of Captain Kronos)

Spherical, Color, 91 Minutes

SYNOPSIS At the insistence of his friend Dr. Marcus, the renowned vampire hunter Captain Kronos, along with his assistant, Professor Grost, come to Marcus's village to investigate a recent spate of strange deaths. In the cases, young girls are drained of their youth. Even Marcus himself is vampirized, and Kronos and Grost are only able to put him out of his misery with a steel cross. Eventually Grost deducts that someone within the wealthy Durward family is the vampire. Using their friend Carla as bait, it is revealed that the seemingly elderly Lady Durward is the vampire. In fact, she is a Karnstein and has even resurrected her dead husband, a great swordsman named Hagen. Kronos duels blade to blade with Hagen and kills the vampire with a special sword. Next, he kills Lady Durward and the vampires crumble to dust.

COMMENTARY After production on *Dr. Jekyll and Sister Hyde* ended, Michael Carreras asked Brian Clemens and Albert Fennell if they'd like to helm a vampire film for Hammer. Clemens wasn't excited about the idea until he took a little inspiration from Marvel Comics to make a superhero-type vampire hunter who was himself part vampire. At least, that's what Captain Kronos was in the initial inception, where Kronos would sleep in a golden coffin and have the ability to travel through time (Kronos means time in Greek). Eventually, these superpowers were done away with to simply make Kronos a bit like Van Helsing in *Brides of Dracula* in that he survived a vampire's bite. Other than that, he seems to have no special powers in the film. And what a wonderful little film it is, and one can only mourn that it produced no sequels. Hammer had hoped the film could become a series, and the possibilities were endless with matches planned between Kronos, Dracula, and maybe even Baron Frankenstein!

The film begins with a nice teaser sequence to set the main story in motion, where a young girl is drained of youth rather than blood. Immediately once this is established, we get a trumpeting good score accompanied by the giant K logo that's part of the Kronos name. The whole thing is almost Bond-like. And indeed, Kronos is like a vampire hunting James Bond, as evidenced between an exchange he has with Caroline Munro's Carla. When Kronos asks if Carla will be moving on soon, she says, "I'll stay, if you'll have me." He gives her a devious smirk and answers, "Oh, I'll have you." Further like the Bond series is Kronos's stable of professional vampire hunting hardware (his stakes are rather finely crafted compared to Van Helsing's). Professor Grost, it could be argued, is almost like the Q to Kronos's Bond.

Grost's spiel on the many different types of vampires and differing means of execution actually aides the Hammer continuity rather than hinder it. For instance, though a lesser vampire, Baron Meinster could turn into a bat while Dracula never did. Carmilla could exist in the daylight while Dracula couldn't, and so on. For that matter, Dr. Marcus turns himself into a bat at one point as well, though the other vampires never do so in the film. The method of how to kill the vampire is rather odd as well. Staking them through the heart doesn't work, nor does hanging. Only accidentally do they discover the means to kill Marcus when his crucifix necklace accidentally pierces his flesh. Grost then determines that only a steel cross can kill the vampire. (But, is it steel itself or specifically a steel cross? It's not entirely clear, but Grost forges the final weapon, "God's Blade," by melting a steel cross). Kronos's preparation for the final battle is also ingenious, as Gross marks Kronos's neck with the sign of the cross.

The film does a nice job of leading us in the wrong direction as to who the vampire is, with plenty of red herrings making it appear to be Lady Durward. While this fake-out does enable a nice surprise ending, it also hurts the film in a sense that we don't actually meet said villains until the very end of the movie. Since it's the first time that we and Kronos both meet them, there's no real buildup throughout the story. That said, the ensuing sword fight between Kronos and Hagen Durward is very well done and doesn't disappoint. Making it interesting from a visual perspective is the fact that all the onlookers are frozen still, hypnotized by Lady Durward. (Kronos uses a mirror on his special sword to turn her own powers against her, thus hypnotizing herself!)

In keeping with the premise that the Kronos series would have the vampire hunter face off against established properties, Lady Durward reveals herself to be a Karnstein. Technically she pronounces it Karstein, but we all know she means Karnstein. And the vampire does have Karnstein traits, as they often cloaked themselves within a shroud or hood, which is exactly what this vampire does throughout the picture.

Sadly, the film was not a hit when finally released in 1974 (it had been shot two years earlier in the spring of 1972), and the proposed Kronos series never materialized.

FINAL WORD Today regarded as one of Hammer's last great films, it's a shame the film didn't catch on at the time, as it would've been great fun to see the series continue.

FRANKENSTEIN AND THE MONSTER FROM HELL

(HAMMER)

Release Date: May 2, 1974 (U.K.) June 12, 1974 (U.S.)
Alternate Titles: *Frankenstein and Vampire Revenge* (Finland)
The Creature of Frankenstein (Italy) *Frankenstein vs. the Monster*
(Mexico)

Directed by: Terence Fisher **Screenplay by:** Anthony Hinds (as John Elder) **Special Effects by:** Les Bowie & Edie Knight **Music by:** James Bernard **Cast:** Peter Cushing (Baron Frankenstein) Shane Briant (Dr. Simon Helder) Madeline Smith (Sarah "Angel" Klauss) David Prowse (the monster) John Stratton (Asylum Director) Philip Voss (Ernst) Christopher Cunningham (Hans) Charles Lloyd-Pack (Professor Durendel) Patrick Troughton (bodysnatcher)

Spherical, Technicolor, 99 Minutes

SYNOPSIS When he's caught performing experiments similar to Baron Frankenstein, Dr. Simon Helder is sent to an asylum for the criminally insane. Upon arrival, he learns that none other than Baron Frankenstein, under the alias of Dr. Victor, runs the asylum. The Baron has faked his death and blackmailed the asylum director so that he has the run of the facility. There he has placed the brain of a genius, Professor Durendel, within the body of a Neolithic giant of a man. The Baron does so with the help of Simon, and also his mute assistant, Sara, called the "Angel" by the inmates. When the professor awakens in his new, horrific body, he is appalled. Eventually the professor's intelligence is suppressed by the primitive body, while the Baron comes up with a new plan for the monster to mate with Sara! Simon is horrified and tries to kill the monster before this can happen. But it escapes, runs afoul of the asylum, and kills the director before it is itself torn apart by the inmates.

COMMENTARY In 1972, Terence Fisher and Peter Cushing teamed up for what would be the former's final film and Cushing's last turn in the role that made him famous. Even Anthony Hinds was coerced out of retirement to write the script and provided a

330

great one at that. Though one couldn't call this a pastiche of all the past Hammer Frankensteins, it does certainly tip its hat to nearly all of them. As in *Revenge*, the Baron is now a doctor using an alias based upon his real name. While in that film he was Dr. Stein to the poor, here he is Dr. Victor to the insane. Likewise, Simon is a bit like Hans from *Revenge*, only more extreme in that he's already carrying out experiments similar to the Baron's. Actually, his first scenes establish him as being similar to the baron not only in his interests but in his charming yet condescending attitude. ("Is that smell coming from him or you?" he asks Patrick Troughton's grave digger character as they carry a corpse upstairs.) As for Sara, she might have been a nod to the mute, red-headed girl from *Evil of Frankenstein* (or, perhaps it's just coincidence). The monster is more or less created in the same way as the one from *Curse* in that its original body is upgraded with the hands of an artist and the brain of a genius. Only in this case, the brain actually works. As such, we get to see a road not taken from the first film, with the functioning brain of genius in the body of a monster. (The Neolithic-looking creature even solves complex mathematical equations on chalk board.) The monster is quite horrific looking, and in some fan circles even beats Christopher Lee's monster in popularity. It certainly fits the title (even though there's nothing supernatural about him) and looks a bit like the monster from the 1910 *Frankenstein* (in the proportions at least).

The professor's reaction to his new, grotesque body is also an expansion on what we'd seen with Professor Brandt in the previous film (at least he still looked human). The scenes of the professor in his horrific new form evoke quite a bit of sympathy, particularly when he picks up his old violin and then decides to crush it. When his body begins to reject the brain, this is a callback to Karl's new body rejecting his brain in *Revenge*. The titular monster's best scenes occur at the end, where he digs up the grave of his original body during a thunderstorm. After that, he goes and kills the director of the asylum. In the graphic scene, he stabs him in the neck with a broken shard of glass. This is actually the only person in the entire film that he kills. Finally, he himself is killed by the inmates of the asylum when they think he is going to attack their beloved "Angel" when he was going to do no such thing. The poor professor is then literally and gruesomely torn apart by the inmates.

Cushing gets several great moments in the film (even if his wig does make him look like Helen Hayes—that's his joke, by the way, as quipped in *Flesh and Blood*). He has two notable action scenes with his monster. In the first, he throws a beaker of noxious chemicals against the wall so that the fumes will knock the beast out. In a second encounter, he wraps his coat around a similar vile, smashes it against the wall so it will shatter, and then throws it over the monster's head. To do so, the Baron jumps from off a table and onto the monster's back. While it would seem that the Baron has resumed his anti-hero persona from films two, three, and four again, towards the end he takes a rather wicked turn. Even though he seems compassionate, he "accidentally" leaves one of his notes behind in a patient's cell that deems him incurable, knowing full well the man will kill himself when he reads it. Then there's the Baron's suggestion that the monster mate with Sara to produce a more perfect offspring, one that has the brains and the brawn of the monster! Simon naturally argues against this, which elicits a rather chilling response from the Baron. As he prepares to leave the asylum to get supplies, he threateningly puts his cane across Simon's shoulder and warns him not to do anything stupid while he is gone.

Ironically enough, though the Baron had died, or at least appeared to, in half of the films in the series, in this final entry he survives. The ending is open to interpretation, as it appears that the Baron has gone mad himself. (Our first indication that the Baron might be going mad occurs when he has a delayed but boisterous reaction to Simon's "he who sees" joke earlier.) It's an interesting note to end on for the character, that's for certain. Of course, had the film been a success, Hammer probably would have done another, but that wasn't the case.

The film was co-financed by the distributer, Paramount, with a budget of £137,000. It began shooting on September 18, 1972, and finished on October 27th at Elstree. Though it was shot before *Satanic Rites of Dracula*, it would not be released until after that film, and to very little fanfare at that. In the U.K. it was released via Joseph Levine's Avco Embassy Pictures on a double-bill with *Fists of Vengeance*, while in the U.S. it was distributed by Paramount on a more appropriate double-bill with *Captain Kronos: Vampire Hunter*. But, by 1974, *The Exorcist* had seen release, and Hammer's old offerings were now considered tame by comparison.

FINAL WORD Unlike Hammer's final Lee Dracula movie, most Hammer fans warmly regard Cushing's last Frankenstein film as being on par with the earlier entries.

LEGEND OF THE 7 GOLDEN VAMPIRES

(HAMMER/SHAW BROS/WARNER BROS)
Release Date: October 6, 1974 (U.K.) July 11, 1974 (China)
June 1979 (U.S.)
Alternate Titles: *The Seven Brothers Meet Dracula* (U.S.) *Dracula and the 7 Golden Vampires* (China) *The Seven Golden Vampires* (Latin America) *Dracula vs. 7 Vampires* (Japan) *Kung Fu Against the Seven Golden Vampires* (Spain)

Directed by: Roy Ward Baker **Screenplay by:** Don Houghton **Special Effects by:** Les Bowie **Music by:** James Bernard **Cast:** Peter Cushing (Professor Van Helsing) David Chiang (Hsi Ching/Hsi Tien-en) Robin Stewart (Leyland Van Helsing) Julie Ege (Vanessa Buren) Shih Szu (Mai Kwei) Chan Shen (Kah/Count Dracula's host) John Forbes-Robertson (Count Dracula) Lau Kar-wing (Hsi Kwei/archer) Huang Pei-Chih (Hsi Po-Kwei/spearman) Wang Chiang (Hsi San/twin swordsman) David de Keyser (voice of Count Dracula)

Panavision, Eastmancolor, 89 Minutes

SYNOPSIS In 1804, a traveler from China named Kah enters Castle Dracula and beseeches the Count to come back with him to China and help rule over the cult of the Seven Golden Vampires. Dracula takes on Kah's form, and 100 years later, Professor Van Helsing is doing a lecture tour in Chunking. There he is approached by Hsi Ching, plus his six brothers and their one sister, all of whom want the professor to help them rid their ancestral village of the vampires. Van Helsing agrees, and the expedition is financed by a wealthy socialite named Vanessa Buren. The group treks to the village, where they ward off the vampires and their zombie horde. In the battle, many of the brothers are killed, including Hsi and Vanessa. Their sister is abducted by the last surviving vampire and is chased back to its temple by Van Helsing and his son, Leyland. Leyland destroys the last vampire, and Kah transforms back into Dracula in front of Van Helsing, who kills him with a spear through the heart.

COMMENTARY *Legend of the Seven Golden Vampires* has such a zany premise, it sounds more like one of those mythical movies that was written but ultimately didn't get made. (Sort of like this film's own unproduced sequel, *Kali: Devil Bride of Dracula* set in India.) But *Legend* is no lost film. Not only was it produced, it was also quite good, and had the film seen a successful release in the U.S., it could've been the film to save Hammer. This movie began life because screenwriter Don Houghton had a family connection to the Shaw Brothers in Hong Kong through his father-in-law. Negotiations began in February of 1973, and the Shaws were open to a co-production with the famous Hammer and agreed to put up 50% of the budget on the condition that they got distribution rights through all of Asia. Hammer, on the other hand, put up 25% of the budget with Warner Bros investing the other 25%. As such, Hammer lost a little of their production clout, leaving most of it to the Shaws. Notably, the film was written without Dracula, who really wasn't needed from a story perspective. The Shaws felt differently and insisted that the character be included, and so he was shoehorned in (and poorly at that).

Christopher Lee wasn't even approached according to most sources, and had he appeared, he would have been wasted. As it is, even poor John Forbes-Robertson is wasted as he made for a decent Dracula. His first scene in Castle Dracula has him rise from his coffin Graf Orlok style and then glide down spectrally to meet Kah. It was rather well staged, all things considered (though Dracula's makeup is a bit extreme and silly). The real stars of the show are the titular seven golden vampires. In keeping with Captain Kronos's comment that there are as many different types of vampires as there are birds of prey, the seven golden vampires are unlike anything Hammer had produced before. Their faces are malformed and zombie-like, and each has distinctive clothing and hair colors, though all wear golden masks and have a golden bat around their belts. When these bats are ripped off, the vampires begin to deflate like a balloon, though we don't really know why. All that said, the real show-stealers are the vampire's zombie slaves, who can be defeated by punching their dusty hearts out. Scenes of them rising from the earth whenever Kah bangs a hellish gong are something else, and the film would be severely lacking without them, even if the zombies do only serve as fodder for the heroes.

Speaking of the heroes, Hammer fans should consider themselves extremely lucky that Peter Cushing returned for one last round as Van Helsing. Based on his lectures, this is clearly meant to be the same Van Helsing from *Horror* and *Brides*, both of which took place in the mid-1880s. As this film takes place twenty years later, Van Helsing has aged appropriately. (However, in typical Hammer sloppy continuity fashion, according to this film's pre-credit scene, Dracula has been in China since 1804!) Overall the film has the feel of an adventure/action movie more so than a horror film, and that's not a bad thing. In certain small ways, it's even a little comparable to *Indiana Jones and the Temple of Doom* in that Professor Van Helsing is chased out of China by a crime lord where he travels to a small village and fights a deranged cult. Though sometimes the film can get a little slow and *Lords of the Rings*-ish (what with all the trekking and camping) the ending brawl in the village is well worth the wait.

The film was supposed to begin shooting in September but didn't actually begin until October of 1973. Filming finished in December of that year, ahead of the nine-week schedule, but over budget. Encouragingly, Warner Bros was quite satisfied with the preview footage they had seen. Add to this the fact that *Enter the Dragon* had been a huge hit the previous year and you'd think that Warner Bros would waste no time in releasing the film. As it turned out, for reasons unknown, they abruptly shelved it. Had Warner Bros released the film, it likely would have been profitable due to the Kung Fu craze still at a high. And, had that happened, we likely would have seen Warners and Hammer produce *Kali: Devil Bride of Dracula*. As it was, *Legend* was a big hit in Singapore and most of Asia (that didn't help Hammer any, that was all Shaw profit there). The film even did decent in Britain, making it to #3 in its first week of release. After Warners passed, AIP picked up the film in 1976, and even constructed their own cut of it (including a small amount of new footage for the ending) that ran 84 minutes. Warner Bros then threw a monkey wrench into the plan, some say out of spite, and AIP dropped the film. As it turned out, *Legend* wouldn't be released in the U.S. until a full five years later, in part to ride the moderate hype wave surrounding the 1979 *Dracula*. It was poorly re-edited as *Seven Brothers Meet Dracula*, where conflicting sources state that it either did well or died a quiet death. Whether it was a hit or not in the States it was still too late. Hammer had already folded, and it was truly an end of an era.

FINAL WORD Love it or hate it, you can't deny the zany fun to be had during the end battle.

EVIL OF DRACULA

(TOHO)
Release Date: July 20, 1974
Japanese Title: *Bloodsucking Rose*

Directed by: Michio Yamamoto **Screenplay by:** Ei Ogawa & Masaru Takesue **Special Effects by:** Teruyoshi Nakano **Music by:** Riichiro Manabe **Cast:** Toshio Kurosawa (Professor Shiraki), Shin Kishida (The Principal), Mariko Mochizuki (Kumi Saijo), Kunie Tanaka (Dr. Shimomura), Mika Katsuragi (The Principal's Wife), Katsuhiko Sasaki (Professor Yoshi), Mio Ota (Yukiko Mitamura), Keiko Aramaki (Kyoko Hayashi), Tomoe Mari (Keiko Nonomiya)

Tohoscope, Eastmancolor, 83 Minutes

SYNOPSIS A new teacher, Shiraki, arriving at a secluded all-girls' school is surprised to learn the news that he will soon succeed the school's eccentric principal. Strange occurrences plague the school, with girls becoming pale and anemic until finally it is learned the current principal and his "dead" wife, both vampires, are to blame. Shiraki stabs the principal through the chest with a poker and kills him which causes the wife to expire as well.

COMMENTARY Though he had been offered a chance to direct a third vampire film hot off the success of *Lake of Dracula*, Michio Yamamoto was initially hesitant to do another. Producer Fumio Tanaka had also been transferred to Toho's TV department after that film's release, but by 1974, Tanaka had been moved back to the film division and production on a third vampire movie was pushed by Toho due to a recent crop of successful horror films in America.

Opinions on the finished film vary, with some calling it the best of the trilogy and others the worst. One thing is certain, the film has more gore than its predecessors, and in a first, nudity. It also has the most vampire content and serves as a hodgepodge of homage shots to Hammer's vampire films. Kishida (*not* portraying the same vampire as in the last film) is more Dracula-like than ever; his introduction is identical to Christopher Lee's charming walk down the staircase to meet Jonathan Harker in the 1958 *Horror of Dracula*. The antiquated European-style estate that

336

serves as the principal's home comes complete with a cellar, where his "dead" wife lies in state. The film's other major setting is an all-girls school dormitory inspired similar to *Lust for a Vampire* (1970) where see-through nightgowns and breasts abound. When Kishida appears to terrorize the girls, like Lee's victims began to do in the mid-1960s, they react with delight upon being bitten. Later in the film, bite marks are revealed to be closer to the breast than the neck (Kishida's character bites necks. The wife bites breasts, very much like Ingrid Pitt in *The Vampire Lovers*).

The first film had reoccurring imagery of dolls to back up its title; this film, not surprisingly, does the same with roses. Throughout the film, there is a white rose that slowly turns red as the vampires feed though the link is never explained. For once, the origin of the vampire is not confusing and is revealed midway through the story. A shipwrecked priest in Japan is forced to denounce his faith and spit on the cross. As punishment, God makes him wander aimlessly across the country, eventually having to suck his own blood to survive. To conceal his identity, he and his bride can take on the form of their victims. When this becomes known it explains an earlier scene between the new teacher and the principal wherein Kishida's dialogue, "You are my successor," takes on a new meaning. Though Kishida looks good in his black cloak with a scarf, he plays the vampire in an over the top fashion that descends the film into unintentional camp, a bad contrast in a story that strives for seriousness. Although *Lake of Dracula* utilized its contemporary setting well, this film, like the first, has no benefits from its modern placing. Manabe's score is a step down here, too. Though his compositions always carried their fair share of notoriety, in some instances, they can't even be called compositions but long stretches of annoying noises akin to a cat's screech.

The artfully done ending, in which the principal and his wife both crawl to one another in the midst of decomposing until finally their skeletal hands touch, was unscathed when it aired on American television in 1981 as *Evil of Dracula*. Unlike its two predecessors, *Evil of Dracula* was not a success at the Japanese box office, ending Toho's exploits with "Dracula."

FINAL WORD If you liked the previous two entries, you might think this one a bit too silly. Conversely, if you didn't like the other two because they didn't evoke Hammer enough, then this may be the one for you.

OLD DRACULA

(COLUMBIA)
Release Date: October 10, 1974 (U.K.)
Alternate Titles: *Old Dracula* (U.S.) *Vampira* (U.K.) *Vampire -
the Devil in the Teeth* (Finland) *Times are Tough for Dracula*
(France) *Mr. Vampire: Sleeping Beauty Coffin* (Japan)

Directed by: Clive Donner **Screenplay by:** Jeremy Lloyd **Makeup
by:** Philip Leakey **Music by:** David Whitaker **Cast:** David Niven
(Count Dracula) Teresa Graves (Vampira) Nicky Henson (Marc)
Jennie Linden (Angela) Linda Hayden (Helga) Bernard Bresslaw
(Pottinger) Andrea Allan (Eve) Veronica Carlson (Ritva) Minah Bird
(Rose)

Spherical, Color, 88 Minutes

SYNOPSIS In the 1970s, Dracula is alive and well and still living
in Transylvania. He's turned his castle into a tourist attraction
where his butler impersonates the Count for guests during the
day. At night, Dracula draws the guests' blood in secret via a
transfusion process so as not to bite them. He is also looking for a
special blood type that can revive his dormant wife, Vampira.
When a group of Playmates stays the night at the castle, Dracula
finally finds the right blood type among them. By mistake, all the
samples get mixed together. While the mixture does revive
Vampira, she awakens as an African American. Though Vampira
herself likes it, Dracula insists they track down the girl with the
right blood in hopes it will restore her to her original appearance.
Dracula and Vampira go to London where the playmates are
having a vampire-themed photoshoot. Dracula takes control over
the Dracula model, Marc, to collect blood samples from all the
girls. Eventually Dracula tracks down the right blood donor
through Marc and secures a sample at a vampire ball. However,
the blood has no effect on Vampira, and when she bites Dracula,
he turns black as well.

COMMENTARY Before *Love at First Bite* and even *Young
Frankenstein*, there was *Old Dracula*. Well, actually, first there was
Vampira, this film's original title when released in the U.K. in

October of 1974. In December of 1974 came *Young Frankenstein*, the massive success of which resulted in this film being renamed *Old Dracula* for its U.S. release in 1975. As such, the two films (which were sometimes double-billed) are often compared and many people (myself included for a time) assumed that *Old Dracula* was a rip-off of *Young Frankenstein*. And while *Old Dracula* may not be a rip-off of the aforementioned movie, it is inferior by comparison. It's not terrible exactly, and it does provide some very good laughs at times, but it has a lot of issues. As you can guess from the synopsis, some, but not all, of those issues stem from the race swap element of the plot. The other issues come from a lack of a clear-cut protagonist.

Case in point, the movie begins by presenting Dracula in a charming, non-lethal manner. After all, he does remove his victims' blood via syringe so as not to make them vampires. He's also quite likable thanks to David Niven's portrayal. However, what initially appears to be a light comedy becomes rather dark after Dracula bites a disgruntled worker, turns her into a vampire by accident, and then has her staked through the heart so he doesn't have to bother with her! Not exactly very likable for a protagonist. And then comes Dracula's subdued but still mortified reaction when his wife, Vampira, becomes black due to getting a transfusion from an African American playmate. It's not entirely clear if Dracula simply wants his wife to look the way she used to, or if he specifically has a problem with her now being black. Vampira herself—played by an African American actress so it's not blackface—is thrilled by the transformation, though, and seems quite pleased with her new look. It's only Dracula that has the problem with it. The rest of the story then hinges on Dracula trying to turn his black wife back to her original white.

I'm not one to go overboard on political correctness, especially with films produced in eras long ago, but even I had to ask: Was Dracula making fun of black culture, or was black culture making fun of Dracula? It's not entirely clear as the film goes on, with Vampira also taking on the slang and mannerisms of black women from the era. For that matter, for a while Vampira would appear to be our sympathetic hero. However, she too becomes a bit unlikable as the story progresses. By the end of the movie, both she and Dracula are villains outright. That leaves us with the human character, Marc, as the only true sympathetic hero figure of the film. And yet, in the final scene, where the vampires get away, it would seem as though we're supposed to be rooting for them and laughing at poor Marc, who, it appears, is about to be arrested.

Qualms with the film aside, there are still plenty of good gags in it and things to enjoy. The best one might be when Dracula and Vampira are on a commercial flight to London. A man (Freddie Jones, actually) asks Dracula, "Is this your first time?" Dracula responds, "No I've flown many times. Never by plane." Though it may not look like much on paper, Niven's delivery is impeccable. As for the inevitable comparisons to *Young Frankenstein*, as stated earlier, the comparisons are somewhat unfair since this film came first and was not actually a rip-off. It's also not similar to that film at all and is definitely a British comedy. And while *Young Frankenstein* set out to spoof the Universal films, *Old Dracula* draws more so from the Hammer films. (A few Hammer glamour girls appear like Linda Hayden and Veronica Carlson.) I'm not sure how well the film did at the box office, and today it's not terribly well-remembered, though it does have its admirers.

FINAL WORD There are so many good gags in this film's first thirty minutes at Castle Dracula, that it's a shame they couldn't have been put to better use in a better movie. If anything, this film had the potential to be a precursor of sorts to the dark vampire comedy franchise *What We Do in the Shadows*. However, *Old Dracula* unfortunately lacks the tonal consistency of that franchise, where the vampires are presented as the morally reprehensible but hilarious protagonists that they are.

YOUNG FRANKENSTEIN

(TWENTIETH CENTRUY FOX)
Release Date: December 15, 1974
Alternate Titles: *Frankenstein Junior*

Directed by: Mel Brooks **Screenplay by:** Gene Wilder and Mel Brooks based on the characters created by Mary Shelley **Special Effects by:** Henry Millar Jr. & Hal Millar **Music by:** John Morris **Cast:** Gene Wilder (Dr. Frederick Frankenstein) Peter Boyle (The Monster) Marty Feldman (Igor) Cloris Leachman (Frau Blücher) Teri Garr (Inga) Kenneth Mars (Inspector Kemp) Madeline Kahn (Elizabeth)

Spherical, Black and White, 106 Minutes

SYNOPSIS Upon inheriting his grandfather's estate, Frederick Frankenstein heads off for Transylvania. At his grandfather's castle he meets Ygor, the hunchback; Inga, his beautiful lab assistant; and Frau Blücher, secretly his dead grandfather's girlfriend. It doesn't take long for Frederick to get the itch to create life. Frederick transplants what he thinks is the brain of a genius into the dead body of a giant criminal, only the brain is really an abnormal specimen swapped by Ygor. The monster is brought to life and escapes soon after. Frederick, Ygor, and Inga manage to capture the monster with Frederick appealing to the poor creature's softer side, thus taming him. Frederick and the monster put on a live stage show that ends in disaster and the monster goes on another rampage. At the same time that Frederick has began an affair with Inga, Frederick's fiancé Elizabeth arrives at the castle. Elizabeth never suspects the affair, but ends up getting abducted by the monster, who she ends up falling in love with. Frederick and co. recapture the monster one more time and perform a brain fluid transplant that somehow makes the monster intelligent. The villagers decide to let the monster and his creator be. Frederick then marries Inga, while the monster marries Elizabeth.

COMMENTARY During the shooting of *Blazing Saddles*, Gene Wilder pitched the idea to Mel Brooks of doing a Frankenstein movie. Brooks said, "Not another! We've had the son of, the cousin of, the brother-in-law. We don't need another Frankenstein." However, Wilder changed Brooks's mind when he pitched him the idea of Dr. Frankenstein's grandson wanting nothing to do with the family name. (In fact, it's slyly alluded to in a throwaway line at a village meeting that this is a sequel to *The Ghost of Frankenstein*.) Brooks and Wilder wrote the script over several nights until they pitched it to Columbia, who wouldn't agree to the budget, and so the project was taken to 20th Century Fox. The rest is history.

Young Frankenstein is a pastiche, naturally. It pays tribute to the first three films in the series more than the rest. For instance, you've got the little girl with the flowers, the old blind man, the one-armed sergeant and the creation scene. One could argue the final "brain transfer" scene was evocative of the later entries like *Ghost of Frankenstein* and *Abbott and Costello Meet Frankenstein* as well. The only scene that's not inspired by any of the Frankenstein films is the big song and dance number, which I would guess was a spoof on Carl Denham's showcase of King Kong. Another way in which this movie is a pastiche is the setting. The story is set in Transylvania while most of the Frankenstein films took place in villages such as Vasaria and even one named Frankenstein in *Son of Frankenstein*. On that note, more so than any of the others, this film pulls from that one. Wilder's Frederick is more so modeled on Basil Rathbone's Wolf Frankenstein than it is Colin Clive's Henry Frankenstein. Also on the note of *Son*, Ygor is also a pastiche of sorts. He is nothing like Bela Lugosi's Ygor that appears in *Son*, and is really more like Fritz the hunchbacked assistant from *Frankenstein* played by Dwight Frye. However, in the public consciousness, Ygor was the name of the hunchback character just as Transylvania was the main setting.

All of the main characters are extremely funny, there's not a stinker in the bunch. All of them also correspond to characters central to the Universal Frankenstein mythos. As already stated, Frederick and Ygor are modeled after Wolf and Fritz, while Frau Blücher is probably inspired by Una O'Connor's character from *Bride of Frankenstein*. Elizabeth serves as an amalgamation of the fiancé character from the original and the Bride from the sequel. Inspector Kemp is inspired by Lionel Atwill's character from *Son*. Lastly, Inga seems to be the only one not inspired by a Universal character. If anything, I might argue that she was inspired by the sexy Frankenstein maid/concubines from Hammer's

Frankenstein films. (Specifically I'm referring to *Curse of Frankenstein* and *Horror of Frankenstein*.)

Young Frankenstein largely succeeds because it plays it straight and treats itself very seriously, just like the movies on which it was modeled. It lets the audience decide what it thinks is funny and doesn't point out to the audience what it thinks should be funny, as many unsuccessful comedies do. Not only does the cast play it straight, but so too very importantly, does the score. If one were to listen to the score by itself, one would think that it was the score from an old Universal horror film. To take it a step further, if one were to watch the opening credits, set against a matte painting of Castle Frankenstein, without knowing what this film was, they probably would assume that it was a Universal horror from the forties (if they didn't recognize all the big name comedy actors, that is). The last triumph of *Young Frankenstein* is the fact that it actually manages to pull off a touching ending in the form of the monster's impassioned speech. And like any great comedy, it gets in one last great payoff/laugh via the honeymoon sequence.

FINAL WORD Is it possible that *Young Frankenstein* eclipses the very classic films that it's spoofing? Possibly. Either way, it's a true classic on par with very films that inspired it.

LEGEND OF THE WEREWOLF

(TYBURN)

Release Date: April 1975 (U.K.)

Alternate Titles: *Return of the Werewolf* (Argentina) *Plague of the Werewolves* (West Germany) *The Werewolf* (Mexico)

Directed by: Freddie Francis **Screenplay by:** Anthony Hinds (as John Elder) **Music by:** Harry Robertson **Special Effects by:** Charles Staffell, Jimmy Evans (makeup) & Graham Freeborn (makeup) **Cast:** Peter Cushing (Professor Paul) David Rintoul (Etoile) Lynn Dalby (Christine) Ron Moody (Zookeeper) Hugh Griffith (Maestro Pamponi) Roy Castle (Photographer) Stefan Gryff (Inspector Max Gerard) Renee Houston (Chou-Chou) Marjorie Yates (Madame Tellier)

Spherical, Eastmancolor, 85 Minutes

SYNOPSIS Etoile is a young, orphaned boy raised by wolves. He is civilized somewhat when he's taken in by a family of circus performers where he's exhibited as the wild wolf boy. He grows into manhood peacefully until one night a wolf's howl causes him to transform. He kills one of the family and then runs away to Paris. He finds work at a zoo, and becomes enamored with a girl who lunches there every day named Christine. Unaware that Christine is a prostitute, when he finds out, it proves too much for him and he begins transforming into a werewolf regularly. Professor Paul, a medical doctor for the police, takes a special interest in the case and figures out that most of the victims are the clientele of the brothel where Christine works. Eventually, Paul figures out that it is a werewolf, and crafts a silver bullet. Paul confronts the werewolf Etoile in the sewers, but does so peacefully and almost gets him to revert to human form with the help of Christine. At the last second, Etoule is shot by a policeman who took the silver bullet. Etoule changes from beast to man and then dies.

COMMENTARY If one were to miss the opening credit line for Tyburn, one could be forgiven in thinking that this is a slightly off-kilter Hammer film. After all, it was written by the great John Elder (still Anthony Hinds's penname after all these years), was directed by Freddie Francis (*Evil of Frankenstein*, *Dracula Has Risen from the Grave*), and stars Peter Cushing. There's even a small role for Michael Ripper to top it all off. One could also be forgiven in thinking this is some kind of sequel to *Curse of the Werewolf* as the makeup is nearly identical. But Hammer it is not, and Tyburn was a short lived imitator who came about in the mid-1970s. It produced a few horror films and some Sherlock Holmes pictures until it became defunct in the 1980s. And why did Tyburn think it would be a good idea to replicate Hammer's old gothic thrillers when they were no longer popular? The reason for that was probably Tyburn's founder, Kevin Francis, son of Freddie. Kevin had long loved Hammer films, had worked on *Dracula Has Risen from the Grave* with his father, and had even written his own sequel to that film, *Dracula's Feast of Blood*. Though Hammer didn't use it, they did use ideas from it in *Taste the Blood of Dracula*, resulting in a paycheck to Kevin only after he pointed this out to Hammer. As such, Kevin wanted to make his own horror films (in fact, another attempt at *Dracula's Feast of Blood* was among Tyburn's cancelled productions).

Legend of the Werewolf is a quasi-remake of *Curse of the Werewolf* (also written by Hinds) only set in Paris. And, though *Curse* was a licensed adaptation of *Werewolf of Paris*, that story is not credited anywhere in *Legend's* production background (probably to avoid purchasing the screen rights). Among the similarities to *Curse* is the fact that the young boy is born on Christmas Day (however, this is a common facet of werewolf lore in general and was not unique to *Curse*). Otherwise, the main similarities stem from the great resemblance in the makeup. Odder still, *Legend* has a great deal of similarities to Robert Florey's unfilmed *Wolf Man* movie for Universal pitched to them in 1931, before *Werewolf of Paris* was even published. That story had a boy briefly raised by wolves, which causes the lycanthropy same as in this film. A notable subplot had the young man falling in love with a woman, unaware that she is a prostitute. When he sees her with a client he flies into a rage and attacks him. Both of those story aspects occur in *Legend*. It's enough to make me speculate that at one point Hinds might have seen Florey's old draft (which was possible since Hammer made a deal to remake films from Universal's library).

On the note of story development, it is said that the characters of both Professor Paul and the photographer didn't actually appear in the first draft, and unfortunately it shows as Cushing's character seems a bit removed from the rest. In the absence of screen time, Cushing narrates the picture and doesn't show up in person until around 30 minutes in. But any film appearance by Cushing is always welcome, and in this one he plays the rather lighthearted, humorous Professor Paul who eventually ferrets out the truth of the werewolf. Many of his scenes feel like filler, though. For instance, when Paul goes to the brothel to ask the Madame to come to the morgue to identify her clients, she refuses. This results in a subplot where Paul procures a photographer to photograph the bodies, which he then takes back to the brothel. Notably during this time we lose track of Etoile as well, making the story feel a bit disjointed.

This is probably the main problem with the film, while many Hammer fans want to like it, it's just not that good overall in terms of its pacing. Etoile is a likeable sympathetic character for the first half—though he's certainly no Oliver Reed—but in the second half the film emphasizes Cushing's character more, which seems to be a mistake in hindsight as Etoile, the film's emotional center, fades into the background. But, if nothing else, the werewolf makeup is excellent and makes for a scarier, 1970s version of the design from *Curse*. The killings are gorier, too (there are many shots of Etoile's bloodstained teeth). The final confrontation in the sewer is atmospheric thanks to the set, but is still relatively uninteresting and lacks the suspense and emotional impact from the climax of *Curse*.

The film began shooting at Pinewood Studios in the late summer of 1974 and would see theatrical release in Britain via Rank in the spring of 1975. It didn't see a wide theatrical release in other countries though, notably the U.S. Today, the film even lacks a substantial DVD release.

FINAL WORD Even though it's not great, if you've seen every film in the Hammer catalogue and need a quick fix, this flick is still more than welcome.

Frankenstein

The True Story

starring

JAMES MASON LEONARD WHITING

DAVID McCALLUM JANE SEYMOUR

NICOLA PAGETT & MICHAEL SARRAZIN as THE CREATURE

Guest Stars MICHAEL WILDING CLARISSA KAYE AGNES MOOREHEAD

MARGARET LEIGHTON RALPH RICHARDSON JOHN GIELGUD TOM BAKER

Produced by HUNT STOMBERG JR. Screenplay by CHRISTOPHER ISHERWOOD and DON BACHARDY
From the Classic Novel by MARY W. SHELLEY Music by GIL MELLE Directed by JACK SMIGHT
A UNIVERSAL PICTURE   TECHNICOLOR ® DISTRIBUTED BY CINEMA INTERNATIONAL

THE
ONLY MAN
ALIVE
FEARED
BY THE
WALKING
DEAD.

PARAMOUNT PICTURES presents
A Hammer Production

CAPTAIN
KRONOS:
VAMPIRE
HUNTER

Produced by ALBERT FENNELL BRIAN CLEMENS Written and directed by BRIAN CLEMENS
R   Prints by Movielab In Color   A Paramount Picture

His brain came from a genius.
His body came from a killer.
His soul came from hell!

Your blood will run cold
when the monster rises.

Paramount Pictures presents
A Hammer Production

FRANKENSTEIN
AND THE
MONSTER FROM
HELL

starring
Peter Cushing Shane Briant Screenplay by John Elder
Produced by Roy Skeggs Directed by Terence Fisher Prints by Movielab
In Color   A Paramount Picture

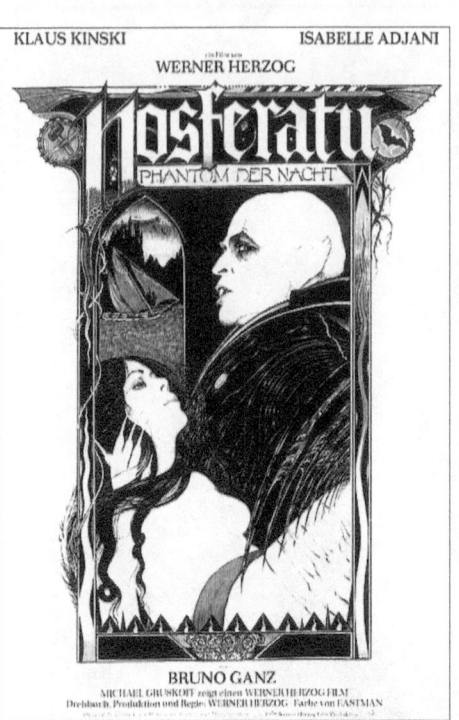

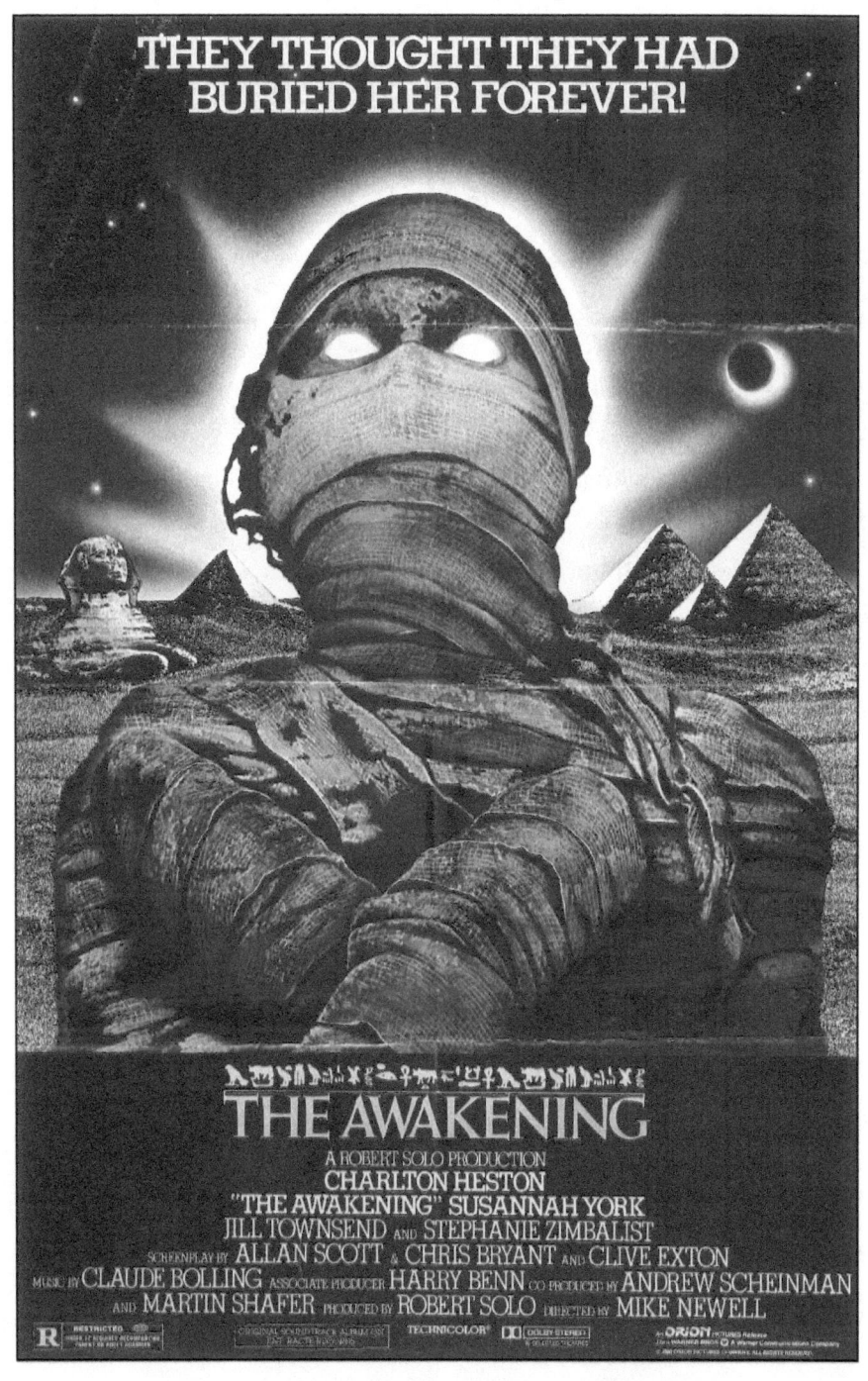

THEY THOUGHT THEY HAD BURIED HER FOREVER!

THE AWAKENING

A ROBERT SOLO PRODUCTION
CHARLTON HESTON
"THE AWAKENING" SUSANNAH YORK
JILL TOWNSEND AND STEPHANIE ZIMBALIST
SCREENPLAY BY ALLAN SCOTT & CHRIS BRYANT AND CLIVE EXTON
MUSIC BY CLAUDE BOLLING ASSOCIATE PRODUCER HARRY BENN CO-PRODUCED BY ANDREW SCHEINMAN
AND MARTIN SHAFER PRODUCED BY ROBERT SOLO DIRECTED BY MIKE NEWELL

351

COUNT DRACULA

(BBC)
Broadcast Date: December 22, 1977 (U.K.)
March 1, 1978 (U.S.)

Directed by: Philip Saville **Screenplay by:** Gerald Savory based on the book by Bram Stoker **Music by:** Kenyon Emrys-Roberts **Cast:** Louis Jourdan (Count Dracula) Frank Finlay (Professor Van Helsing) Susan Penhaligon (Lucy Westenra) Judi Bowker (Mina Westenra) Jack Shepherd (Renfield) Mark Burns (Dr. John Seward) Bosco Hogan (Jonathan Harker) Richard Barnes (Quincey P. Holmwood)

Spherical, Color, 150 Minutes

SYNOPSIS Jonathan Harker travels to Dracula's castle in Transylvania to finalize the Count's purchase of Carfax Abbey in England. Although charming at first, Harker realizes that Dracula is a vampire. Harker tries and fails to kill him before fleeing the castle. Dracula travels to England where he begins draining the life out of Lucy Westerna, the sister of Harker's fiancé, Mina. After Lucy's death and Harker's return, Harker and Lucy's fiancé, Quincy Morris, team up with Abraham Van Helsing to destroy the vampires. Though they are successful in ending Lucy's undead existence, Dracula gets away after vampirizing Mina. Van Helsing and Mina track Dracula back to Transylvania while Quincy and Harker take an alternate route to the castle. There, Dracula is staked through the heart ending his reign of terror.

COMMENTARY Despite the Hammer films having run their course, the late 1970s saw a revival of interest in Dracula. One of the first production entities to hop on the bandwagon was the BBC, which produced this elaborate mini-series which is nearly on par with the 1973 Dan Curtis adaptation. What this version has of interest above all the others is the actor playing Dracula in the form of future Bond villain Louis Jordan (*Octopussy*). Jordan is positively superb as Dracula. Even though he may not be as much of a lady-killer as either Christopher Lee in his younger days or Frank Langela, who would play the Count two years later, he's undeniably suave and well-suited to the role.

The BBC's *Count Dracula* is very faithful to the novel, but like all onscreen adaptations inevitably do, it does alter the story. Lucy and Mina are made to be sisters, and instead of eliminating Quincy Morris as usual, he's combined with Arthur Holmwood to become Quincy Holmwood. (That said, he's more Morris than Holmwood as he retains his Texan accent.) The film even contains the scene often not included of Van Helsing and Mina camping in the woods of Transylvania and warding off Dracula's brides with communion wafers. (This scene was planned for an early version of *Dracula's Daughter*, for instance, before it was discarded.) Dracula's famous crawl down the castle wall is included as well. The shot is well done, and Jordan does mimic the mannerisms of a crawling bat quite well except for that it also makes the visual look just a tad silly. This adaptation also uses some then-new video effects that cheapen and date the picture badly. (They are used whenever Dracula does something supernatural.) Furthermore, the scenes at Dracula's castle and the scenes back in England appeared to have been shot on different film stock. The Transylvania scenes are of very high quality, while the London scenes look a little closer to videotape at times. As for other odds and ends, this film's version of Van Helsing, though accurate to the novel, seems more akin to something from a Mel Brooks spoof with his thick accent. And the last interesting innovation of note that this version has is the scene of a near-death Lucy in bed, which seemed to have been inspired by *The Exorcist!*

Reaction to the miniseries was mostly positive, and it first aired over two nights on the BBC in late December of 1977. In the U.S. it was shown in three parts as part of PBS's Great Performances in March of 1978.

FINAL WORD If you're looking for a faithful 1970s adaptation of *Dracula*, this one is similar to *Bram Stoker's Dracula* from 1973. If watched back-to-back, you would essentially be watching the same storyline with different actors. The only advantage this one really has over the Dan Curtis version is Louis Jordan's excellent performance as the Count.

NOSFERATU THE VAMPYRE

(WERNER HERZOG FILMPRODUKTION)
Release Date: February 25, 1979 (Germany)
October 19, 1979 (U.S.)
Alternate Titles: *Nosferatu: Phantom of the Night* (original title)

Directed by: Werner Herzog **Screenplay by:** Werner Herzog
Special Effects by: Cornelius Siegel **Music by:** Popol Vuh **Cast:**
Klaus Kinski (Count Dracula) Isabelle Adjani (Lucy Harker) Bruno
Ganz (Jonathan Harker) Roland Topor (Renfield) Walter Ladengast
(Dr. Van Helsing) Carsten Bodinus (Schrader) Martje Grohmann
(Mina)

Spherical, Eastmancolor, 107 Minutes

SYNOPSIS Jonathan Harker is a real estate agent living in
Wismar, Germany. Renfield, his boss, sends him on a job to
Transylvania to sell property to a Count Dracula. The demonic
looking Count behaves oddly around Harker, and immediately
becomes infatuated with a portrait of Harker's wife, Lucy. Dracula
puts the bite on Harker, then locks him in the castle as he departs
for Germany via the ship *Demeter*. Dracula kills the entire crew,
and when the ship arrives at port he also unleashes a horde of
disease ridden rats. While many in the town succumb to the
plague, Harker manages to escape the castle and make his way
back to Wismar, where he reunites with Lucy. However, he is very
pale and stricken with amnesia. Dracula tries to seduce Lucy, but
she wards him off. As the town slowly dies, Lucy reads that the
only way to defeat the vampire is by a maiden who is pure of heart
luring him into the sunlight. Lucy decides to sacrifice herself,
luring Dracula to her, and then keeping him in her bedroom until
dawn where the sunlight strikes him down. However, though
Dracula is dead, Harker is now himself a vampire who sets out to
continue the Count's legacy of terror.

COMMENTARY In the late 1970s, since its initial release over fifty
years ago, *Nosferatu: A Symphony of Horror* had grown into not
only a cult film, but also a highly respected silent film.

354

Furthermore, Dracula had lapsed into the public domain in the 1960s (remember, Nosferatu was banned due to copyright infringement). German director Werner Herzog was among the old film's admirers, and considered it the best German made silent film of all time. And, while that version had renamed many of the characters, his version could retain the names of Count Dracula, Jonathan Harker, and so on. There was enough interest in the film that 20th Century Fox even got on board and requested that Herzog shoot an English language version side by side with the German version. (The two versions are exactly the same and the only difference is the spoken language, there are no scenes unique to one or the other.)

Up to a point, the film is nearly a shot-for-shot remake of the original, but not quite as there are still plenty of differences. The most notable one is that Dracula's victims, namely Harker, do turn into vampires after being bitten unlike the first film where they just died. And, as in the first film, much of the action takes place in Transylvania and on board the *Demeter*. (However, we never do get a recreation of the iconic shots of Dracula stalking the deck of the ship.) Though this film may not be able to beat the original's photography, one thing it does ostensibly better is the portion set in Wismar. In the original, the Wismar portion seems brief when compared to the film's preceding acts, but more time is spent there in this version. The effects of the plague, and the way that it's depicted is much better in this version. Particularly artsy and interesting is the scene where the town has an outdoor "last supper" for the survivors among rat infested streets!

Whereas Klaus Kinski was wasted as Renfield in *Count Dracula* (1970), here he's positively riveting as Count Dracula himself. Not only does he look amazing, he also imbues the character with a degree of sympathy—quite a feat considering how evil he looks. In one of the film's best scenes, the Count laments to Lucy the fact that he can never die. Like the 1979 *Dracula*, to be released a few months later, this adaptation makes Lucy the central female character rather than Mina. As in the original film, Lucy is the heroine of the film rather than Harker or Van Helsing. In this case, she's even more proactive than she was in the 1922 version, finding Dracula's lair and placing communion wafers in his coffin. Even though Kinki's Dracula is ugly as can be, Lucy's seduction scene is sexualized a great deal. However, she and Kinski's Dracula don't have the connection that Jack Palance's Dracula had to Mina in the Dan Curtis version or the soon to be released Frank Langela film.

Dracula's death is almost a non-event. Once the sunlight hits him, he falls over. There's no burning flesh or disintegration. And, whereas Van Helsing did nothing in the 1922 film, he pops up here to stake Dracula. The staking undermines Lucy's sacrifice, as we were led to believe Dracula would be dead and gone once the sunlight struck him, why then did he also need to be staked? Did Lucy not really have to die? It's a bit messy and is made all the more odd by the fact that the staking takes place off-screen! Also, like many horror films of the 1970s, good doesn't definitively triumph over evil. In this case, poor Van Helsing is arrested, and then the seemingly catatonic Harker finally rouses to life. He is now pale and sports the same rat teeth as his deceased master. Once Van Helsing is taken away, Harker departs, claiming that he has work to do. The film's last shot is a haunting one, set to effective choir music, as Harker rides his horse across a desert under a cloudy sky. (This at least makes up for Dracula's rather lackluster demise.)

Despite being a remake in an era where remakes could often be ill-received (the 1976 *King Kong*, for example), the reception to this film was and still is overwhelmingly positive. (In fact, the movie made it to many "Must See" lists by respected critics over the years.) The film was also a moderate success when released, more so in Germany than the U.S., though.

FINAL WORD A classic in its own right, this film can make for an interesting companion piece to either the original 1922 *Nosferatu*, or the 1979 Frank Langela *Dracula*, of which this film is the exact opposite in many ways despite telling similar stories with the same characters.

LOVE AT FIRST BITE

(AIP)

Release Date: April 6, 1979

Alternate Titles: *Dracula Sucks* (working title) *Dracula: Love at First Bite* (Argentina) *Dracula in New York* (Greece) *Dracula Goes to the City* (Japan) *Love at First Bite: Dracula's Loves* (Mexico) *Hotel Drakula* (Yugoslavia)

Directed by: Stan Dragoti **Screenplay by:** Robert Kaufman & Mark Gindes **Music by:** Charles Bernstein **Cast:** George Hamilton (Count Vladimir Dracula) Susan Saint James (Cindy Sondheim) Richard Benjamin (Dr. Jeffrey Rosenberg/Van Helsing) Dick Shawn (Lieutenant Ferguson) Arte Johnson (Renfield)

Spherical, Color, 96 Minutes

SYNOPSIS When Dracula is more or less evicted from his castle by the Transylvanian government, he and his manservant Renfield travel to New York. There Dracula seeks out a model, Cindy Sondheim, who he believes to be the reincarnation of Mina Harker. As Dracula navigates the strange new world of New York City, he eventually manages to woo Cindy. Just as the relationship begins to cement itself with Cindy falling for the Count, competition emerges in the form of her psychologist/sometimes boyfriend Dr. Rosenberg, a descendant of Van Helsing. Dracula survives numerous attempts on his life by Rosenberg, and eventually has to rescue Cindy from his grasp. Rosenberg and an NYC police Lieutenant chase Dracula and Cindy to the airport. Although Dracula and Cindy miss their flight, Dracula turns Cindy into a vampire and both fly off into the moonlight as bats.

COMMENTARY Similar to *Curse of the Undead*, this project's inspiration came about due to some simple poolside shenanigans. George Hamilton was doing an impersonation of Bela Lugosi's Dracula for screenwriter Robert Kaufman and keeping him in stitches. Before long, the duo were musing about what would happen if Dracula visited modern day New York. Kaufman began writing a screenplay on just that, with Dracula based on Hamilton's impressions. The script came about at a very fortuitous time when Dracula was becoming quite popular again. In fact, there were no less than four major Dracula movies in production in 1979. If not for that, perhaps this film would have been financed by a major studio. Instead, it was an independent production and the money for it was put up by Melvin Simon, a shopping-mall developer.

Like *Young Frankenstein*, this one parodies the old Universal Draculas as opposed to Hammer's more recent movies. Case in point, the hilarious first line of the film is, "Children of the night, shut up!" Along those same lines, Renfield is also a major character in the film. Though it's not clear if this is the same Renfield from the Stoker novel who somehow survived into the 1970s, it's an interesting upgrade for the character who serves as Dracula's servant in his castle in Transylvania. Dracula's interactions with Renfield bring to mind the *What We Do in the Shadows* franchise with the vampires and the familiars. Actually, one has to wonder if this film helped to inspire that well-loved franchise, as Hamilton's portrayal of the Count and the comedy in general is quite similar to that series.

Among the better gags are Dracula riding a horse and carriage in New York traffic. When Dracula first meets Cindy and offers to give her eternal life, she thinks he's an insurance salesman. Another great line comes when Renfield opens a refrigerator at a modern blood bank and Dracula says, "Only in America. Plastic, disposable bodies. It's like a supermarket." *Love at First Bite* also has a commercial airliner scene like in *Old Dracula*. This one is funnier though, with Dracula in his coffin in the baggage hull. Inside his lighted coffin he's reading up on American slang to kill time, while Renfield laments that there's no live food on the menu. Just when the story almost seems to lag, a romantic rival in the form of Van Helsing's great grandson, Dr. Rosenberg, is thrown into the mix. A dinner between Cindy, Rosenberg, and Dracula makes for a funny recreation of Dracula and Van Helsing's first meeting from the 1931 film. It has all the familiar bits, mirror slap included, and concludes with a hilarious bit where they both try to hypnotize each other. On that note, Van Helsing could have been a simple one-note villain, but he's actually quite funny. He even gets one of the last laughs of the film when he finds Dracula's discarded cape at the airport and takes to wearing it.

As stated in the opening paragraph, this film was released smack dab in the middle of a Dracula revival. As such, it was a huge hit, so much so that it actually ended up hurting the straight adaptations to follow, notably Frank Langella's excellent *Dracula*.

Furthermore, *Love at First Bite* was so successful that it remained one of the highest grossing independent movies of all time for many years.

FINAL WORD One of the best "classic monster" comedies of all time, second only to *Young Frankenstein*.

DRACULA

(THE MIRISCH CORPORATION/UNIVERSAL)
Release Date: July 13, 1979
Alternate Titles: *Dracula – A Love Story* (Austria) *Dracula 80*
(Canada) *Count Dracula: Escape from the Carpathians* (Greece)
Dracula 79 (Japan/Germany)

Directed by: John Badham **Screenplay by:** W.D. Richter based upon the play adapted from Bram Stoker's Dracula by Hamilton Deane, John L. Balderston & Garrett Fort **Special Effects by:** Roy Arbogast **Music by:** John Williams **Cast:** Frank Langella (Count Dracula) Kate Nelligan (Lucy Seward) Trevor Eve (Jonathan Harker) Laurence Olivier (Professor Abraham Van Helsing) Donald Pleasence (Dr. Jack Seward) Jan Francis (Mina Van Helsing) Tony Haygarth (Milo Renfield)

Panavision, Technicolor, 109 Minutes

SYNOPSIS On a stormy night in 1913, the ship *Demeter* crashes ashore in Whitby, England. The only survivor is Count Dracula, who has recently purchased the large estate Carfax Abbey. Dracula dines with his neighbors, the family of Dr. Seward, who owns and runs an adjoining asylum. With Seward are his daughter Lucy Seward, her boyfriend Johnathon Harker, and Lucy Van Helsing. Both women are attracted to the Count, who returns in the night to feed on Mina, who dies the next morning. Dr. Seward sends for Mina's father, Abraham Van Helsing, to come at once. By the time he arrives, Mina has risen as a vampire, and Dracula has begun courting Lucy while Jonathan is away on business. Seward and Van Helsing find Mina and destroy her while Lucy begins to turn into one of the undead as well. Lucy runs away with Dracula of her own free will and the two book passage on a ship bound for Romania. Harker and Van Helsing are in hot pursuit and commandeer a boat to intercept the larger ship. On board, they confront Dracula, and though Van Helsing is killed, the vampire king is expelled via sunlight. Lucy, free of his vampiric hold, still smiles when she sees his cape blow away in the wind, hinting the Count may yet live...

COMMENTARY Between classics like *Dracula* (1931), *Horror of Dracula* (1958) and *Bram Stoker's Dracula* (1994), this excellent adaptation of the Stoker story from 1979 is often forgotten. Unlike Hammer, which provided their own unique take on the vampire, and also unlike attempts to adapt the book by Dan Curtis and Jesús Franco in the early 1970s, this late seventies version is an actual remake of the 1931 *Dracula*. This is because it was based upon the same stage play by Garrett Fort that the 1931 version was adapted from. Not only that, like Bela Lugosi before him, new Dracula Frank Langela had been playing the Count on Broadway in a revived version of the play. (Langela was even nominated for a Tony for the part). The play was then optioned for a movie by the Mirisch Corporation with the blessing of Universal, which would distribute just as they had done with the original.

Though it's quite similar to the 1931 version, like all the adaptations before it, this one mixes up the characters and events for various reasons. The opening scenes in Transylvania are done away with entirely, starting the film with the stormy voyage of the *Demeter* in a very effective scene. Though we don't know what exactly has transpired, the sailors are riled enough to try and toss Dracula's crate overboard into the stormy sea. A hand bursts from the crate and tears out the sailor's throat—quite an entrance for the Count, who next turns into a wolf. In England, similar to the 1931 *Dracula*, much of the action takes place between Seward's asylum, his home, and Carfax Abbey, which has essentially supplanted Castle Dracula. Here Carfax Abbey looks very much like a big budget 1970s version of the castle set, cobwebs and all, from the 1931 original. As in that version, Arthur Holmwood and Quincy Morris are absent and only Jonathon Harker remains. To simplify the character relations, Lucy is made to be Seward's daughter as opposed to Mina, who is made to be Van Helsing's daughter in this iteration. What's more, Mina plays second fiddle to Lucy instead of the other way around. (When asked why the switch was made, W.D. Richter didn't remember and speculated that perhaps he simply liked Lucy's name better for the female lead!)

As for Langela, he wisely chose not to try and evoke Christopher Lee or Bela Lugosi and carved out his own unique performance as the Count. In the past, when actors like Jack Palance and Lee tried to say the lines made famous by Lugosi, they fell somewhat flat, but Langela does much better with them. Most all of them are quoted from "I don't drink wine" to the "children of the night line," which has been altered to state "what sad music they make." One scene that might have been best left un-recreated was the breaking of the mirror bit with Van Helsing, which seemed a bit silly and over the top for Langela's Dracula. (He throws an object into Van Helsing's large mirror on the wall and then does his usual bit about hating mirrors.) But, other than a few minor nitpicks—Langela makes some cartoonish grunts and growls every now and then—he has some superb moments as Dracula. He gets a visually stunning scene with Renfield, where he takes flight in his human form before turning into a bat. There are several shots of Langela's Dracula crawling down the face of a building, specifically down to Mina's room, where he hangs upside down like a bat while clawing open the window. Another wild scene has him execute Renfield by twisting his neck until his head is backwards!

As excellent as the film is, there are still a few quibbles and questions. As for questions, though Mina looks terrifying in her vampire form (she's chalky white like a corpse and has pitch black eyes like a bat), why doesn't Dracula look like this when he feeds? For that matter, why is Mina staked through the heart and killed, in the undead sense, only to later still be alive, necessitating that her heart be cut out and removed? And, why does it work on Dracula when Van Helsing uses the cross, but not when Harker does it? (When he does it, Dracula grabs the cross and it bursts into flame.)

As for quibbles, even though Langela's Dracula is excellent, Laurence Olivier's version of Van Helsing is one of the weakest and most uninteresting portrayals of the character ever. (In Olivier's defense, he was quite ill during production, though.) Unfortunately, Donald Pleasance turned down the part when it was offered to him because he felt it was too similar to Dr. Loomis from the *Halloween* movies. While Pleasance was correct about the similarity, that's exactly the reason why he would've made an excellent Van Helsing! Instead, he chose to play Dr. Seward, who is also a rather uninteresting character (he almost seems less concerned with his daughter's wellbeing than Van Helsing does!). Kate Nelligan is excellent as Lucy, at least, and creates a more independent version of the character than was seen in the past. Like Wynona Rider's version of Mina in the 1994 film, this Lucy seems to truly fall in love with the Count and regret his defeat at the end. However, with all that said (and with no disrespect to the cast), the real star of this movie might just be composer John Williams, because his score is positively fantastic throughout. (One of his cues even foreshadows the more famous Darth Vader theme from 1980's *The Empire Strikes Back* while in other sections certain bits foreshadow his score for *Raiders of the Lost Ark*.) His score is so invaluable to the film one has to wonder how it might've turned out without it.

The film deserved a better reception than it got with audiences. While most critics praised it, audiences didn't flock to the film and it was only a moderate success. Some have attributed this to the fact that three Dracula films were released in 1979, and this one was beaten to theaters by the spoof *Love at First Bite*, a hit which may have made audiences take the Count less seriously.

FINAL WORD This might just be the best Dracula film of the 1970s, barely beating out Dan Curtis's Dracula with its slick production values, excellent performances, sets, music, and direction.

THE AWAKENING

(EMI)
Release Date: October 31, 1980
Alternate Titles: *Death in the Valley of the Pharaohs* (Argentina)
Reincarnation (Brazil) *The Secret of the Mummy* (Denmark)
The Queen's Curse (Finland) *The Curse of the Valley of the Kings*
(France) *The Awakening of the Pharaohs* (Greece)
Pyramid 1980 (Japan) *The Curse* (Mexico)
The Awakening of the Sphinx (West Germany)

Directed by: Mike Newell **Screenplay by:** Chris Bryant, Allan Scott & Clive Exton based upon the book by Bram Stoker **Special Effects by:** John Stears **Music by:** Claude Bolling **Cast:** Charlton Heston (Matthew Corbeck) Stephanie Zimbalist (Margaret Corbeck) Susannah York (Jane Turner) Jill Townsend (Anne Corbeck) Patrick Drury (Paul Whittier)

Spherical, Technicolor, 101 Minutes

SYNOPSIS In 1961, British archeologist Matthew Corbeck is in Egypt in search of the tomb of an ancient Egyptian queen who has no name. Along with Corbeck is his pregnant wife, Anne, and his assistant, Jane. Anne feels neglected between Corbeck's search for the unnamed queen and his assistant Jane. Eventually, Corbeck finds the accursed tomb of the evil queen, who they learn is named Kara. At the moment that Corbeck breaks into Kara's tomb, Anne goes into labor. Corbeck successfully excavates the tomb and Anne gives birth to a baby girl, who they name Margaret. Eighteen years later, Corbeck and Anne are divorced, and Corbeck has married Jane. Margaret comes to visit her estranged father at the same time that he is recruited to investigate Kara's mummy, which has suddenly begun to deteriorate. Margaret begins to exhibit strange personality changes and Corbeck believes that Kara is trying to possess his daughter. Corbeck decides to fulfill an ancient prophecy to resurrect Kara's body, thinking that by doing so she will stop trying to possess Margaret, who has fallen into a coma. When Corbeck performs the ritual, Margaret awakens as Kara and kills him.

COMMENTARY I have no idea what prompted this second theatrical adaptation of *Jewel of the Seven Stars,* but I have a feeling that it was *The Omen* franchise, the most recent entry of which was *Damien: Omen II* (1978). And indeed, this movie is basically *Blood from the Mummy's Tomb* by way of *The Omen.* (Rather ironic considering that star Charlton Heston turned down the Gregory Peck part in *The Omen.*) The fundamental concept of a child possessed by an ancient evil is there, of course, but the similarities go further than that. For instance, *The Omen* had zoo animals going berserk at the sight of Damien, while here an animal in Central Park reacts to Margaret with great hostility.

In *Blood from the Mummy's Tomb,* all of the killings were uniquely linked to cursed artifacts. Each artifact would in some way come back to life to kill a certain member of the expedition. Here, the deaths are mostly freak accidents à la *The Omen,* but not nearly as clever. Case in point, an obelisk falls on a man as its being hoisted down from a desert precipice. Later, another man is nearly run over by a truck (this also happened in *Omen II,* but they still did it better). There are two scenes where the killings are linked to cursed objects, again an Anubis statue and a snake effigy. Despite the higher budget, the scenes are nearly identical in their handling with the inanimate snake being hurled at the camera at one point. The first of these deaths is Jane's and is decent enough. The second death is of Margaret's love interest and is curiously bungled in the editing as what happens isn't really clear. On that note, the director even described the final cut's edit as "miserable".

As to what *The Awakening* does better than *Blood from the Mummy's Tomb,* there's not much. The budget is higher, which allowed for more on-location filming in Egypt. However, the nicer sets and locales can't make up for the slower pacing. The only big improvement on *Blood* is the handling of Margaret's birth. The direction is excellent as Heston opens the tomb and his wife begins to have labor pains. It also has a great booby-trapped tomb which was ahead of its time, as *Raiders of the Lost Ark* was still one year away. It's only other improvement, which is debatable, is that it does feature an actual mummy as opposed to *Blood,* which had Tera inexplicably well preserved.

FINAL WORD It's easy to see why most people forget about *The Awakening* when compared to the better-remembered *Blood from the Mummy's Tomb.* Even though the latter had a smaller budget, it had a lot more charm.

TRIVIA

DR. JEKYLL AND MR. HYDE (1912)

Though many sources list Harry Benham as the sole actor who played Mr. Hyde, in reality the character was mostly played by Harry Benham. This was revealed in an interview with Benham in the October 1963 issue of *Famous Monsters of Filmland*.

DRACULA (1931)

The film is unscored, which though not uncommon back then, gives the film a strange air today. At the time, studios felt that music playing in scene might confuse the viewer.

Original releases had the film ending with an epilogue with actor Edward Van Sloan, who had played Van Helsing, telling the audience what they have just seen. This makes sense, as Van Helsing tells Harker and Mina that he is going to remain in the cellar a bit longer when they announce they are leaving. It's not lost though, as a clip of it appeared in the 1999 documentary *The Road to Dracula*.

Allegedly Better Davis was considered for the part of Mina.

Edward Van Sloan, like Lugosi, also came from the stage play.

Some prints of the film may have been tinted green to give them a more eerie look.

One of the early treatments still had the film ending with the heroes chasing Dracula back to his castle.

The original cut of the film was supposedly too scary, and so it was re-edited to tone it down much to Todd Browning's disappointment. Supposedly this lost original cut was 84 minutes long, or ten minutes longer. Among one of the cut scenes was likely Van Helsing's tracking of Lucy. With Harker, he would have watched the undead Lucy stroll into a mausoleum. Van Helsing would have followed her inside, but we would not have seen the staking. It's possible that this scene wasn't even shot, but it is in

366

the shooting script. Another scene that went unfilmed for sure was that of Dracula attacking Reinfeld, as studio executives feared it would imply a homosexual relationship between the two!

THE MUMMY
There was a very expensive sequence showing Anckesenamun throughout the ages being reincarnated. One even involved actress Zita Johann working with lions!

THE INVISIBLE MAN
When Boris Karloff was passed on by James Whale for the project, he also briefly considered Colin Clive for the role.

One discarded screenplay had the title character as an alien from Mars trying to take over Earth.

Leading lady Gloria Stuart would famously go on to be nominated for an Oscar for Best Supporting Actress at the age of 88 for *Titanic* (1998).

BRIDE OF FRANKENSTEIN
Some of Henry Frankenstein's inactivity in this film is due to Colin Clive having broken a leg shortly before filming began.

Karloff was actually against making the monster speak. This also meant that he was unable to remove his partial bridgework that he had done to give the monster sunken cheeks in the first film. Therefore, the monster has a fuller face in this film.

Elsa Lanchester's famous hiss as the Bride was inspired by the hissing swans in Regent's Park, London.

Bela Lugosi was considered for the role of Doctor Pretorius, though a few sources also imply he was also considered to replace Colin Clive as Dr. Frankenstein! Claude Rains was also offered the role of Dr. Pretorius but was unavailable.

MARK OF THE VAMPIRE
Elements of *London After Midnight* seemed to be inspired by *Dracula*. Right after its release, Universal courted Lon Chaney to play Dracula. He died before filming began and was replaced by Bela Lugosi, who played his vampire part in this film, a remake of *London After Midnight*.

This film's writer, Guy Endore, also wrote *Werewolf of Paris*.

Bela Lugosi missed out on appearing in *Werewolf of London* due to this film.

Browning didn't reveal to the cast the film's twist ending until late into the production. Bela Lugosi was not happy that he hadn't been playing a real vampire!

WEREWOLF OF LONDON

Before this film was greenlit, Universal was indeed considering *The Wolf Man*, to star Boris Karloff and be directed by Robert Florey.

Bela Lugosi was originally cast as Dr. Yogami, the werewolf who bites Glendon. Ironically, Lugosi would play the werewolf who infects Larry Talbot in *The Wolf Man* (1941).

The howl is a combination of Henry Hull's voice mixed with that of a wolf.

There was a deleted scene where one of the man-eating plants almost eats a young boy, but he is saved by Glendon at the last second.

DRACULA'S DAUGHTER

Some have claimed that *Carmilla* influenced the story. This is uncertain, but Stoker actually acknowledged the *Carmilla* story in "Dracula's Guest" in that the female vampire is from Styria, where the Karnsteins hail from.

SON OF FRANKENSTEIN

The film was shot on a larger than usual budget of $500,000. At one point, they considered shooting it in color, but Karloff's makeup didn't look too good in color. It's a good thing too, as this film, like so many other universal chillers, makes excellent use of shadows within the confines of black and white. Visually speaking the house's obtuse architecture is also particularly striking in black and white.

The film begins a plot device that would be used in every Frankenstein sequel thereafter: restoring the monster to its full capacity.

At over 100 minutes long, this is the lengthiest Universal horror film.

Supposedly one of Christopher Lee's favorite horror films.

On November 23, 1938, Karloff's birthday, the crew duped Karloff into thinking that they were filming a scene of him crawling up a ladder into Wolf's lab. To Karloff's shock, when Basil Rathbone stepped aside, he found a birthday cake waiting for him. Filming was suspended and they celebrated the great actor's 51st birthday. That same day, his wife Dorothy gave birth to his only child, Sara Jane.

Some sources say that Universal intentionally aimed for Friday the 13th for the film's release day to make it seem spookier.

THE INVISIBLE MAN RETURNS
According to Vincent Price, Director Joe May only spoke German, so the German-speaking Price was one of the few on set that was able to communicate with him properly.

THE MUMMY'S HAND
Supposedly during the initial theatrical release, certain scary scenes were tinted green.

THE WOLF MAN
Bela Lugosi's werewolf form was played by Chaney's own German Shephard, which often cameo in his films. Speaking of Bela Lugosi as Bela, though the role wasn't a monumental one for him, it did technically mean that Lugosi also played a werewolf, just not in makeup. As such, one can argue that just like Chaney Jr., Lugosi has also therefore played three of Universal's classic monsters as Dracula, the Frankenstein monster, and maybe not the Wolf Man himself, but at least the werewolf that made the Wolf Man. (Coincidentally, Lugosi was supposed to play the same function in *Werewolf of London* but didn't). However, since Lugosi didn't really wear the makeup itself, that still makes Chaney Jr. the king of the Universal monster roster, having also played the Mummy. And unlike the other actors, Chaney was the only one of his brethren to play the character he originated exclusively (no one else played the Wolf Man until Benicio Del Torro in the 2010 remake).

GHOST OF FRANKENSTEIN
When Janet Ann Gallow's mother died in 1946, Chaney offered to adopt her and her brother but her father retained custody. (Gallows played the little girl who befriends the monster.)

Towards the end of the day Chaney would often be drunk.

THE MUMMY'S TOMB
Future Frankenstein Glenn Strange appears as a farmer holding his horse at bay as Kharis walks by.

The last film was set in 1940. This one takes place 30 years later, but still obviously takes place in the 1940s and even references World War II!

INVISIBLE AGENT
Supposedly there was to be a scene of the titular character kicking Hitler in the pants according to the pressbook. If the scene was ever filmed or seriously considered is unknown.

PHANTOM OF THE OPERA
Filmed on same sound stage as the original *Phantom*.

Allegedly, comedic versions of the film were also considered to star either the Three Stooges or Abbott and Costello!

SON OF DRACULA
Lon Chaney Jr.'s father was the original choice for the title role in the 1931 *Dracula* before he died.

Supposedly Louise Allbritton secretly got into her coffin naked as a joke, so as to shock her fellow cast members when they opened the casket.

Alan Curtis was the original actor cast as Frank, and it's possible he may have even shot a few scenes. Whatever the case, the actor had to bow out after injuring his knee.

According to the script, the character's full name is Anthony Alucard!

Count Alucard was allegedly supposed to appear in *Abbott and Costello Meet Frankenstein* alongside his father, but this seems unlikely.

From a story perspective, *Son of Dracula* almost feels like we are walking in on a movie already in progress. That is to say, there's a lot of backstory right up front, with characters abuzz about a mysterious Hungarian Count invited to the plantation. As it turns out, the first six pages of the script went unfilmed, which might have given the opening a less rushed feel.

THE INVISIBLE MAN'S REVENGE
The heroic German Shepherd, Grey Shadow, was the grandson of silent era dog-star Strongheart.

Stills exist indicating that the backstory involving the Herricks and Griffin in Africa were actually filmed. The still shows the Herricks looking down at an unconscious Griffin on a riverbank, implying they really did leave him for dead!

THE MUMMY'S GHOST
Lon Chaney Jr. punched through real glass in the scene where Kharis breaks into the Scripps Museum. The propman had forgotten to replace the real glass with breakaway glass. A shard of glass flew out and cut Chaney on the chin, so when Kharis is seen to bleed, that was really Chaney's blood.

According to interviews with director Reginald Le Borg, he wasn't the first pick to direct the film, and replaced someone (he can't recall the name) who had become injured and couldn't shoot the picture.

According to actor William Phipps, Lon Chaney Jr. had a vodka flask hidden within his mummy bandages. A concealed tube ran from the flask to Chaney's lips, so that he could sip on it all day during filming!

HOUSE OF FRANKENSTEIN
Had a very healthy $354,000 budget and 30-day shooting schedule from April 4, to May 8, 1944.

The final scenes shot were the Dracula scenes even though they make up the first portion of the film.

Naish and Chaney reteamed for *Dracula vs. Frankenstein* in 1971, where Naish plays a scientist and Chaney his henchman.

There are conflicting reports as to why Bela Lugosi didn't reprise the Dracula role. Some sources say Universal didn't want him after the rough shoot on *Frankenstein Meets the Wolf Man*, while others say Lugosi was unavailable, ironically enough because he took over the role recently vacated by Boris Karloff in *Arsenic and Old Lace* (albeit with a different production company).

John Carradine told *Fangoria* magazine that, "When they asked me to play Dracula, I said yes, if you let me make him up and play him the way Bram Stoker described him—as an elderly, distinguished gentleman with a drooping mustache. [Universal] didn't like a big mustache, so I had to trim it and make it a very clipped, British mustache. It wasn't really in character."

THE MUMMY'S CURSE
Actress Virginia Christine naturally felt panicked whenever Chaney was scripted to carry her around as he was often drunk. She was relieved when Chaney was replaced by his stunt double for the scenes.

HOUSE OF DRACULA
Lon Chaney Jr. felt sorry for Glenn Strange, cold and in the mud for the scene where the monster was discovered. Chaney shared his Scotch with him to help keep him warm. By the time the day was over Strange was so drunk he could barely change back into his street clothes and go home.

At first Bela Lugosi was announced as playing Dracula, but for reasons unknown Carradine reprised the role again.

The Wolf Man doesn't kill anyone in this film because the Breen Office stipulated that if the Wolf Man killed he'd have to die, and the producers wanted a happy ending where Talbot lived for a change.

Due to stock footage, four different actors appear as the Frankenstein Monster. Boris Karloff appears via *Bride of Frankenstein* (1935) and Lon Chaney Jr. and his stunt double, Eddie Parker, appear as the Monster via *Ghost of Frankenstein* (1942).

Lionel Atwill died from lung cancer a few months after the film was released on April 22, 1946.

ABBOTT AND COSTELLO MEET FRANKENSTEIN
Boris Karloff was asked to play the monster again, and though he wouldn't do that he was nice enough to agree to do publicity for the film itself.

During shooting Glenn Strange became injured and was unable to perform, and so for that one day Lon Chaney Jr. reprised the role of the monster for the first time since *Ghost of Frankenstein*.

ABBOTT AND COSTELLO MEET THE INVISIBLE MAN
This film has an official continuity tie to *The Invisible Man* in that it references Dr. Jack Griffin both visually and by name as the inventor of the serum. Claud Rains photo hangs on the wall of Dr. Gray's lab, even though Grey refers to him as John rather than Jack (though Jack can be a nickname for John).

DRACULA IN ISTANBUL
Because no fog machines were on hand to generate the fog for the graveyard scenes, all the stagehands smoked and puffed cigarettes offscreen to make the fog!

ABBOTT AND COSTELLO MEET THE MUMMY
Eddie Parker, who played Klaris, was Lon Chaney Jr.'s stunt double as Kharis.

The comedy duo were named "Pete Patterson" and "Freddie Franklin" in the script and are identified as such in the closing credits, but they used their real names during shooting.

Though this was the least likable Mummy design, it was used for the 1986 Universal-licensed Classic Movie Monsters series from Imperial Toys.

REVENGE OF THE CREATURE
Off all the sea predators in the tank with the real actors, it was a sea turtle who tried to bite off the creature's toe! Obviously, the turtle was not afraid.

Clint Eastwood makes his screen debut as a lab technician.

CURSE OF FRANKENSTEIN

The first shot in the movie, that of the priest riding up the mountain road, was the first footage shot for the film. After that came the scenes of Victor in his cell. This meant that the first scenes and last scenes were shot back to back, and the middle portion with the monster was done after.

The young Elizabeth in the flashback is played by none other than Hazel Court's daughter, Sally Walsh.

Bernard Bresslaw might've been cast as the monster if not for the fact that Lee was only two pounds cheaper!

Supposedly Patrick Troughton had a small role as a mortuary attendant (his name is credited in some early publicity material as such) but his scenes were cut from the finished film. Troughton would later appear as the gravedigger in *Frankenstein and the Monster from Hell* (1974).

I WAS A TEENAGE WEREWOLF

Roger Corman changed the title of his upcoming caveman movie from *The Prehistoric World* to *Teenage Caveman* because of this film.

Jack Nicholson turned down the lead role in this film. Years later he went on to play a werewolf in *Wolf* (1994).

The original title for AIP's *Attack of the Puppet People* (1958) was *I Was a Teenage Doll* thanks to this film's success.

I WAS A TEENAGE FRANKENSTEIN

Herman Cohen toyed with one more similar title in the form of *I Was a Teenage Gorilla*, which eventually transformed into *Konga* (1961).

Herman Cohen told Tom Weaver that the alligator they used for the movie was the same one that had been used to "dispose" of the bodies of victims killed by serial killer Joe Ball from a small town outside San Antonio!

HORROR OF DRACULA

For years fans talked about a "lost" Japanese cut of the film, which included an even more grotesque, extended version of the disintegration scene. The disintegration scene had extended shots of Dracula's legs and arms beginning to turn to dust. In the normal version, we see his leg begin to deflate, so to speak, but in the extended version, his pant leg begins to roll up exposing his charred flesh. The same is true of the shot of his hand. The real gem of the bunch shows Christopher Lee in grotesque makeup, clawing the skin off of his face as he utters a terrible groan! There's also a short shot Van Helsing reacting to this in disgust. In 2010, a writer/cartoonist named Simon Rowson, who lived in Japan, managed to track down the lost footage, which has since been restored.

First time ever that Dracula wore fangs

FRANKENSTEIN 1970
Frankenstein's Castle, *Frankenstein 1960*, and *Frankenstein 2000* were alternate titles considered during production.

Strangely, the sound made by Dr. Frankenstein's body disposal machine was considered too horrific by the Breen Office and so the original grinding sound was replaced with the flushing of a toilet! As such, this is believed to be the first time a toilet flush can be heard in a film.

REVENGE OF FRANKENSTEIN
The film began shooting at Bray only a few days after *Horror of Dracula* had wrapped.

Though Hammer had been afraid of tropes unique to the Universal films, in this one they gave Frankenstein a hunchbacked assistant. Perhaps the fact that Universal was working with Hammer now played into the equation, or maybe it's because Columbia's TV branch had broadcast rights to *Frankenstein* (1931).

BRIDES OF DRACULA
Yvonne Monlaur was almost cast as Domino in *Thunderball* (1965).

The film's novelization follows the version of the script where Van Helsing summons vampire bats to destroy Meinster. It also has an added storyline where Van Helsing and Marianne fall in love (complete with a sex scene!).

PHANTOM OF THE OPERA
Ironically, or perhaps deliberately, the tune that Herbert Lom plays as the Phantom is the exact same music he played as Captain Nemo in *Mysterious Island* (1961).

KISS OF THE VAMPIRE
The TV version, called *Kiss of Evil*, more or less removed the best scenes from the ending. If you saw that version of the film, you only saw the horde of bats circling the castle, you would not see them attacking the vampire horde. Furthermore, to make up for missing time, new scenes were specially shot for the TV version.

Anthony Hinds envisioned a publicity gimmick for the climax where paper bats would be released confetti-style over the audience in the theater!

EVIL OF FRANKENSTEIN
The mask hanging on the wall behind the Baron when he orders a meal at the tavern was one of the ones worn by the vampires in *Kiss of the Vampire*.

Cushing did his own stunts in the fiery climax. He and Kiwi Kingston both received third-degree burns.

To create the right sound effects, Peter Cushing cut into some cabbage during the operation scenes.

Kiwi Kingston was a wrestler and would sometimes have wrestling matches in the evenings and then come to work beat up the next day.

THE GORGON
Facemasks were handed out at theaters for those who feared looking upon the Gorgon as a gimmick.

CURSE OF THE MUMMY'S TOMB
Originally, the idea for this film was much more ambitious, and was to see the mummy of a 20-foot-tall giant unearthed.

Perhaps it's just a coincidence, but this film is set around the same time as *The Gorgon*, in the very early 20th Century as opposed to the mid-19th Century as so many Hammers were.

The exterior shot of the ocean liner is actually in black and white (but tinted to look as though it's in color) and is from the film *A Night to Remember* (1958).

DRACULA – PRINCE OF DARKNESS
Peter Cushing was replaced on this film by Andrew Kier, who would also replace him again on *Blood from the Mummy's Tomb*.

While in this film they played a married couple, in *Rasputin: The Mad Monk* (1966), Francis Matthews and Suzan Farmer played siblings.

Eddie Powell (Lee's stunt double) became trapped underwater during the ice scene and nearly drowned!

The flashback to *Horror of Dracula* was added in post-production when the film came up a few minutes short of the desired runtime. This mistake cost Hammer, as they had to pay Universal for the footage ($25,000 to be exact) and also had to pay Peter Cushing (they paid for a new roof on his house directly).

Father Shandor was well liked enough that in the 1970s he got his own comic series in *House of Hammer Magazine* (there was even talk of a film adaptation!).

There are, of course, some plot holes in the film. For starters, why did Klove wait ten years for some random travelers to come along rather than abducting a local to resurrect his master? Why did Hammer set the film ten years after the original for that matter? This ten year jump also limited future sequels to the very late 1890s.

JESSE JAMES MEETS FRANKENSTEIN'S DAUGHTER
As was the case in *Young Frankenstein* (1974), the lab equipment in this film was provided by Ken Strickfaden and presents a rare instance of the equipment being shot in color.

FRANKENSTEIN CREATED WOMAN
In keeping with the sex appeal angle of that same year's *One Million Years B.C.*, Hammer did a famous photoshoot of Cushing and Susan Denberg. None of the stills are even remotely close to what happens in the film. They feature Denberg in a bandaged,

mummy-like bikini as Frankenstein examines her. They were great advertising in any case.

This was almost the first sequel to *Curse of Frankenstein*, or at least the title was. One of the earliest pitches alongside *Blood of Frankenstein* was *And then Frankenstein Created Woman*, a play on the title *And Then God Created Woman*. By 1965/6, that title was no longer as fresh as it once was, but somebody clearly fancied it and so it was used for Frankenstein #4.

According to the script, this movie takes place in 1895.

Although it's not evident in the finished film, the three men are the sons of characters we see in the film, including the judge that sentences Hans and the Police Chief who heads up the murder trial.

Rather than *The Mummy's Shroud*, *Slave Girls* (AKA *Prehistoric Women*) was also considered as a double-bill mate. This would have been interesting in that both were Hammer Glamour Pictures as opposed to *Shroud*, which was not.

THE MUMMY'S SHROUD
Tony Hinds treatment was called *Shroud of the Mummy*.

Dickie Owen, who played the bandaged mummy in the last film plays Prem here. Eddy Powell played the Mummy.

Peter Cushing does not narrate the film, as is erroneously reported. Tim Turner is the narrator.

The disintegration scene took one week to set up, film, and get right.

Originally, John Richardson (Tumak in *One Million Years B.C.*) was the first choice for Paul Preston.

FRANKENSTEIN MUST BE DESTROYED
Roger Moore came by during filming of the rape scene and more or less offered his condolences as an actor to Cushing and Carlson for having to film a distasteful scene that they both disagreed with.

Veronica Carlson turned down the chance to appear as one of Blofeld's beauties in *On Her Majesty's Secret Service* to do this film.

Bert Batt took a bus to Anthony Nelson Keys house to show him the script, only he left the script on the bus! Keys and Batt then boarded Keys' car and had to chase down the bus so that the script wasn't lost for good.

When it came time to film the brain transplant scene, there was no brain on set! Therefore Christopher Neame ran to a butcher shop and bought three sheeps' brains, which were sewed together into one. Then, when the producer arrived on set midway and found everyone in a panic, he revealed there had been a prop brain in his office all along!

Batt's script was too short to meet feature-length requirements, and so new scenes of Thorley Walter's investigator were dreamed up. Ironically, it ended up being the longest of Hammer's Frankenstein films at 100 minutes.

There's an odd pattern in the Frankenstein films. At the end of every odd numbered entry, he "dies" or at least appears to, while at the end of every even numbered entry, he lives.

Veronica Carlson's first scene was her death scene.

COUNT DRACULA
Supposedly Klaus Kinski ate real flies as Renfield!

Christopher Lee and Herbert Lom never shot scenes together, but were merely edited into the same scene together.

Was the first film to accurately depict Dracula as Stoker wrote him.

Vincent Price was Franco's first choice for the role of Van Helsing, but Price was contractually committed to AIP at the time. His second choice was Dennis Price, who was also unavailable.

SCARS OF DRACULA
Michael Ripper was given another large role, in fact the biggest role he'd ever had in a Dracula film. The character is a less likable, bitter version of the one he played in *Dracula Has Risen from the*

Grave. As it turned out, it was his last Gothic horror for Hammer (his last appearance for them was in a comedy).

Once again, a prominent character is named Paul (when asked why the frequency of this name, Hinds said because it was easy to type!)

Final major production of Anthony Hinds.

Lee still had a bad back during filming, which was partially why Dracula didn't open the door himself while carrying Hanley. It was decided that Dracula would never be shown entering or exiting a room. He would simply be there already. He would not open doors, they would open for him instead.

Jenny Hanley was unaware that she'd be dubbed.

According to *Hammer Complete*, the treatment for this film was written by Anthony Hinds before *Taste the Blood of Dracula* and was used as the sequel to that film instead.

THE VAMPIRE LOVERS
Madeline Smith would later go on to marry David Buck from *The Mummy's Shroud*.

In some interviews, Madeline Smith implied she was led to believe that the nude scenes would only appear in the Japanese release!

AIP's displeasure with their working relationship with Hammer led to the cancelation of a proposed co-production of *Dante's Inferno*.

COUNTESS DRACULA
Despite Ingrid Pitt's excellent turn in the role, director Peter Sasdy had wanted Diana Rigg for the part. To add insult to injury, it was also Sasdy who decided to have Pitt dubbed, which infuriated both she and James Carreras. However, when Carreras ordered her voice be reinstated, it was learned Sasdy had thrown out the voice tracks!

LUST FOR A VAMPIRE
After this film was scripted *The Vampire Virgins* (aka *The Vampire Hunters*). Rather than Carmilla, the Count Karnstein seen in this

film was to be the main villain. He was to be played by neither Mike Raven nor Christopher Lee, but Peter Cushing for once!

The Japanese title, *Fearful Bloodsucking Beauty*, is quite similar to the titles of Toho's Hammer-inspired vampire movies: *Fear of the Ghost House: The Bloodsucking Doll* (1970) and *The Bloodsucking Eyes* (1971).

BLOOD FROM THE MUMMY'S TOMB
Helen Dickerson is played by Rosalie Crutchley, who played the old crone in that same year's Hammer caveman movie, *Creatures the World Forgot*.

Margaret's boyfriend is named Tod Browning in a nod to the director of *Dracula* (1930).

TWINS OF EVIL
Kate O'Mara (*The Vampire Lovers, Horror of Frankenstein*) was considered as one of the titular twins but Hammer couldn't find an actress who resembled her enough to play the sister.

HANDS OF THE RIPPER
Aida Young's final film for Hammer.

Was filmed on leftover sets from *The Private Life of Sherlock Holmes* (1970).

Hammer wasn't allowed to shoot within St. Paul's Cathedral, and so Aida Young had stills taken of the interior, which were then used by the special effects crew to superimpose as backgrounds.

In 1950, before they got into the horror game, Hammer had produced a Jack the Ripper related movie called *Room to Let*.

DRACULA A.D. 1972
Before signing Stoneground, Rod Stewart's band was to appear in the film!

This film and *Taste the Blood of Dracula* had the same double-bill mates, only reversed. In the U.S., *Taste the Blood of Dracula* was released with *Trog*, while in Britain *Dracula A.D. 1972* was released with *Trog*. In the U.S., *A.D.* was double-billed with *Crescendo*, which had been the double bill with *Taste* in the U.K.

Though Lee often claims he refused to speak the dialogue written for him in *Dracula – Prince of Darkness*, it was actually this film. Lee revised lines like "I am the apocalypse" to become "You would play your brains against mine, against me who has commanded nations?" from Stoker's novel.

BRAM STOKER'S DRACULA
In interviews, Dan Curtis joked that he had ripped himself off by inserting the love story between Barnabas Collins and Josette into his version of *Dracula*, with the titular character in love with Lucy, who resembles a past love.

In 1994 CBS re-aired the film to take advantage of the hype surrounding Francis Ford Coppola's *Bram Stoker's Dracula* (1994).

After his portrayal here, Jack Palance was supposedly offered the role of Dracula in other productions, which he turned down.

Before Palance had even played Dracula, Marvel Comics based their version of the Count for *Tomb of Dracula* on Palance's appearance!

BLACULA
The prologue originally took place in 1815 rather than 1870.

In 1972, William Marshall was given an award for his performance by The Academy of Science Fiction, Fantasy and Horror Films (at one point known as The Count Dracula Society).

COUNT DRACULA AND HIS VAMPIRE BRIDE
It was Lee's idea to give D.D. Denham an accent not dissimilar to Bela Lugosi so that it would throw off the audience, and they might wonder where Dracula was, and if this was even him?

In Don Houghton's original script, Dracula had the ability to shapeshift into D.D. Denham. This presumably was a means of cutting down on Lee's shooting time. Houghton reused the idea in *Legend of the 7 Golden Vampires*.

Many fans have taken note of the film's final moment, where Van Helsing picks up Dracula's silver ring and stares at it. Denis Meikle, author of *A History of Horrors: The Rise and Fall of the*

House of Hammer, has an interesting theory on that. Meikle thinks that Don Houghton was planning to use the ring as a key plot point in potential sequels without Lee.

FRANKENSTEIN THE TRUE STORY

There was a prologue that was meant to open this story in a similar manner to *Bride of Frankenstein*. It would have seen Nicola Pagett as Mary Shelley, Leonard Whiting as Percy Shelley, David McCallum as Lord Byron, and James Mason as Polidori, who was the real author of *The Vampyre* (1819). Elsewhere, IMDB claims that the original broadcast featured a prologue with James Mason visiting the grave of Mary Shelley.

The film's writers, Christopher Isherwood and Don Bachardy, were so disappointed in this adaptation that they made sure to publish their original version of the teleplay.

Writers Christopher Isherwood and Don Bachardy pushed for Jon Voight be cast as Victor Frankenstein, and for John Boorman to direct.

OLD DRACULA

Ironically enough, this film was distributed by Columbia, who wouldn't agree to put up enough money to make *Young Frankenstein* the way that Mel Brooks wanted to.

YOUNG FRANKENSTEIN

The lab equipment was the original props used in *Frankenstein* in 1931 created by Ken Strickfaden. Brooks found that Strickfaden had preserved the equipment in his garage. Brooks offered to give him screen credit for use of the props, which he didn't receive in the original film, and he agreed. (You probably already knew that, but hey, I had to include it!)

The "shifting hump" gag was thought up by Marty Feldman, who switched it during filming until the cast and crew finally noticed and decided to integrate the joke into the film.

Gene Hackman, who played the Blind Man, ad-libbed the "I was gonna make espresso," line and everyone busted out laughing. Hackman was never able to repeat it without laughing himself, and so the original take was the only option, hence why it fades to black so quickly.

FRANKENSTEIN AND THE MONSTER FROM HELL

Caroline Munro was offered the role of Sara.

Shane Briant disliked the "plastic-y" look of the monster. To his horror, Dave Prowse asked him what he thought of the makeup. Briant looked it over and found the one thing that he liked. "The feet are fantastic!" he said. "They're mine," Prowse replied.

This was Prowse's second turn as the monster, but his first time playing the monster opposite Peter Cushing. Three years later, the two actors would share scenes again in *Star Wars* (1977).

As usual, the time period doesn't add up with continuity. While *Frankenstein Must Be Destroyed* looked like it was set in the early 1900s, this one looks like it's set in the 1850s!

CAPTAIN KRONOS: VAMPIRE HUNTER

As was done in *Twins of Evil*, Ingrid Pitt was supposedly offered the role of Lady Durward/Karnstein. However, this bit of trivia could simply be a mix-up in regards to *Twins of Evil*.

LEGEND OF THE 7 GOLDEN VAMPIRES

As a promotional giveaway in Britain, matchboxes filled with sand labeled "vampire dust" were given away.

While shooting in Hong Kong, Robin Stewart and Julie Ege went to a nightclub where they ran into her former co-star from *On Her Majesty's Secret Service*: James Bond himself George Lazenby. He was there filming *The Man from Hong Kong*.

Supposedly second-unit director Chang Cheh added scenes that led to the Asian version of the film to run 110 minutes.

Eva Reuber-Staier was considered for Julie Ege's part.

Michael Carreras prepared a cut of the movie that removed Dracula altogether, but it made the film too short.

NOSFERATU THE VAMPYRE

Klaus Kinski was a royal terror to work with, according to director Werner Herzog, who supposedly said that the hordes of rats were better behaved!

Kinski wanted to give an overblown performance as Dracula, while Herzog wanted it subdued. To work around this, he would provoke Kinski into an outburst or meltdown, so that when it came time to shoot the scene, Kinski was so exhausted that he gave the desired, subdued performance.

DRACULA

Though the Dracula play of the 1920s/30s had been performed straight, the one in the 1970s was meant to be campy (though it was quite popular). Despite this, the film played it straight (the only nod to the play's camp origins being when Dracula looks directly into the camera at one point as he crawls down a wall).

The scene between Dracula and Van Helsing, where the former breaks a mirror, was a late addition. Frank Langela played the scene more in the vein of his theater performance, which had to be a bit "overblown" to reach the audience. When Langela realized what he had done he asked if they could reshoot the scene and they did.

As odd as this may sound, Universal had hopes for a sequel to *Dracula*. The reason we know this boils down to two aspects of the climax. For starters, it is said that Van Helsing was killed so that Laurence Olivier would not have to return as Van Helsing in a sequel. (He didn't want to, and apparently nobody else did either. Not only was he expensive at $750,000, his performance wasn't exactly dynamic.) Second, the reason Dracula's cape flutters around in the wind with a mind of its own was to hint to the audience that the Count wasn't really dead. Unfortunately, the film's mediocre grosses crushed any hopes of a sequel.

The director wanted to shoot the movie in black and white, which Universal wouldn't allow. As a compromise, years later for the film's Laserdisc release, he watered down and muted the colors, giving the film a greyish look. The full color version was lost until recent years when it was restored.

THE AWAKENING

Ahmed Osman, who plays Yussef in this version, also played a character in *Blood from the Mummy's Tomb*.

Supposedly there is an alternate ending of Queen Kara's giant shadow leering over London for the British version.

BIBLIOGRAPHY

Articles

Blaine, Richard. "Terence Fisher—A Few Bytes from *The Brides of Dracula*." *Little Shoppe of Horrors* #14.

Hallenbeck, Bruce G. "The Making of the Hammer Classic *Blood from the Mummy's Tomb*." *Little Shoppe of Horrors* #24.

------------------------------ "*Scars of Dracula*." *Little Shoppe of Horrors* #13 (Kindle Edition).

Kelley, Bill. "Peter Cushing on *The Brides of Dracula*." *Little Shoppe of Horrors* #14.

Kinsey, Wayne. "Interview with John Forbes Robertson." *Little Shoppe of Horrors* #32 (Kindle Edition).

Koetting, Christopher. "John Elder, Christopher Lee and TASTE THE BLOOD OF DRACULA." *Little Shoppe of Horrors* #13.

Meikle, Dennis. "Anthony Hinds: The Man Who Made the Monsters." *Little Shoppe of Horrors* #32.

----------------------"Remembering 1959: Michael Carreras in Conversation with Dennis Meikle." *Little Shoppe of Horrors* #24.

Books

Fellner, Chris. *The Encyclopedia of Hammer Films*. Rowman & Littlefield Publishers, 2019.

Feramisco, Thomas M. *The Mummy Unwrapped: Scenes Left on Universal's Cutting Room Floor*. McFarland & Company, 2007.

Hearn, Marcus. *The Hammer Vault: Treasures From the Archive of Hammer Films*. Titan Books, 2016.

Jacobs, Stephen. *Boris Karloff: More Than a Monster: The Authorized Biography*. Tomahawk Press, 2011.

Kinsey, Wayne & Tom Johnson and Joyce Broughton. *The Peter Cushing Scrapbook*. Peveril Publishing, 2013.

Kinsey, Wayne. *The Legend of the 7 Golden Vampires Scrapbook*. Peveril Publishing, 2020.

Maxford, Howard. *Hammer Complete: The Films, the Personnel, the Company*. McFarland & Company, 2018.

Pierson, Jim. *Produced and Directed by Dan Curtis*. Pomegranate Press, 2004.

Rhodes, Gary D. & Tom Weaver. *Dracula's Daughter*. BearManor Media, 2017.

Riley, Philip J. (Ed.). *Horror of Dracula*. BearManor Media, 2013.

----------------------- *House of Frankenstein (Universal Filmscript Series, Vol. 6)*. Magicimage Filmbooks, 2019.

Riley, Philip J. (Ed.) & Gregory Wm. Mank. *Frankenstein Meets the Wolf Man: (Universal Filmscript Series, Vol. 5)*. Magicimage Filmbooks, 2019.

----------------------- *The Wolf Man (Universal Filmscripts Series Classic Horror Films, Vol. 12)*. BearManor Media, 2020.

Sangster, Jimmy. *Inside Hammer: Behind the Scenes at the Legendary Film Studio*. Reynolds & Hearn, 2001.

Weaver, Tom & Michael Brunas. *Universal Horrors: The Studio's Classic Films, 1931-1946, 2d ed.* McFarland & Company, 2017.

Weaver, Tom & David Schecter and Steve Kronenberg. *The Creature Chronicles: Exploring the Black Lagoon Trilogy*. McFarland & Company, 2018.

Other Sources
www.classic-monsters.com Classic Monsters is the ultimate horror movie website, with horror movie information, profiles of classic monsters and horror film star biographies.

About the Author

John LeMay is the Rondo Award nominated author of such film histories as *The Big Book of Japanese Giant Monster Movies: The Lost Films; Kong Unmade: The Lost Films of Skull Island; Jaws Unmade: The Lost Sequels, Prequels, Remakes and Rip-Offs* and *Classic Monsters Unmade: The Lost Films of Dracula, Frankenstein, the Mummy and Other Monsters*. LeMay also writes on Fortean subjects such as cryptozoology and U.F.O.logy in the *Cowboys & Saurians* series and *The Real Cowboys & Aliens* series with Noe Torres. LeMay is also the editor and publisher of *The Lost Films Fanzine* and a contributor to magazines *G-Fan, Mad Scientist, Xenorama,* and *Cinema Retro*.

THE BICEP BOOKS CATALOGUE

The following titles are available for purchase on Amazon.com, and are available to bookstores at a wholesale discount via Ingram Content Group (ISBNs of available editions listed for this purpose)

THE BIG BOOK OF JAPANESE GIANT MONSTER MOVIES SERIES

The third edition of the book that started it all! Reviews over 100 tokusatsu films between 1954 and 1988. All the Godzilla, Gamera, and Daimajin movies made during the Showa era are covered plus lesser known fare like *Invisible Man vs. The Human Fly* (1957) and *Conflagration* (1975). Softcover (380 pp/5.83" X 8.27") Suggested Retail: $19.99 SBN:978-1-7341546-4-1

This third edition reviews over 75 tokusatsu films between 1989 and 2019. All the Godzilla, Gamera, and Ultraman movies made during the Heisei era are covered plus independent films like *Reigo, King of the Sea Monsters* (2005), *Demeking, the Sea Monster* (2009) and *Attack of the Giant Teacher* (2019)! Softcover (260 pp/5.83" X 8.27") Suggested Retail: $19.99 ISBN: 978-1- 7347816-4-9

This second edition of the Rondo Award nominated book covers un-produced scripts like *Bride of Godzilla* (1955), partially shot movies like *Giant Horde Beast Nezura* (1963), and banned films like *Prophecies of Nostradamus* (1974), plus hundreds of other lost productions. Softcover/hard-cover (470pp. /7" X 10") Suggested Retail: $24.99 (sc)/$39.95(hc)ISBN: 978-1-73 41546-0-3 (hc)

This sequel to *The Lost Films* covers the non-giant monster unmade movie scripts from Japan such as *Frankenstein vs. the Human Vapor* (1963), *After Japan Sinks* (1974-76), plus lost movies like *Fearful Attack of the Flying Saucers* (1956) and *Venus Flytrap* (1968). Hardcover (200 pp/5.83" X 8.27")/Softcover (216 pp/ 5.5" X 8.5") Suggested Retail: $9.99 (sc)/$24.99(hc)   ISBN:978-1- 7341546 -3-4 (hc)

This companion book to *The Lost Films* charts the development of all the prominent Japanese monster movies including discarded screenplays, story ideas, and deleted scenes. Also includes bios for writers like Shinichi Sekizawa, Niisan Takahashi and many others. Comprehensive script listing and appendices as well. Hardcover/Softcover (370 pp./ 6"X9") Suggested Retail: $16.95(sc)/$34.99(hc)ISBN: 978-1-7341546-5-8 (hc)

Examines the differences between the U.S. and Japanese versions of over 50 different tokusatsu films like *Gojira* (1954)/*Godzilla, King of the Monsters!* (1956), *Gamera* (1965)/*Gammera, the Invincible* (1966), *Submersion of Japan* (1973)/*Tidal Wave* (1973), and many, many more! Softcover (540 pp./ 6"X9") Suggested Retail: $22.99(sc)   ISBN: 978-1- 953221-77-3

This second volume examines the differences between the European and Japanese versions of tokusatsu films including the infamous "Cozzilla" colorized version of *Godzilla, King of the Monsters!* from 1977, plus rarities like *Terremoto 10 Grado*, the Italian cut of *Legend of Dinosaurs*. The book also examines the condensed Champion Matsuri edits of Toho's effects films. Coming 2022.

Throughout the 1960s and 1970s the Italian film industry cranked out over 600 "Spaghetti Westerns" and for every *Fistful of Dollars* were a dozen pale imitations, some of them hilarious. Many of these lesser known Spaghettis are available in bargain bin DVD packs and stream for free online. If ever you've wondered which are worth your time and which aren't, this is the book for you. Softcover (160pp./5.06" X 7.8") Suggested Retail: $9.99

389

THE BICEP BOOKS CATALOGUE

CLASSIC MONSTERS SERIES

Kong Unmade explores unproduced scripts like *King Kong vs. Frankenstein* (1958), unfinished films like *The Lost Island* (1934), and lost movies like *King Kong Appears in Edo* (1938). As a bonus, all the Kong rip-offs like *Konga* (1961) and *Queen Kong* (1976) are reviewed. Hardcover (350 pp/5.83" X 8.27")/Softcover (376 pp/ 5.5" X 8.5") Suggested Retail: $24.99 (hc)/$19.99(sc) ISBN: 978-1-7341546-2-7(hc)

Jaws Unmade explores unproduced scripts like *Jaws 3, People 0* (1979), abandoned ideas like a Quint prequel, and even aborted sequels to Jaws inspired movies like *Orca Part II*. As a bonus, all the Jaws rip-offs like *Grizzly* (1976) and *Tentacles* (1977) are reviewed. Hardcover (316 pp/5.83" X 8.27")/Softcover (340 pp/5.5" X 8.5") Suggested Retail: $29.99 (hc)/$17.95(sc) ISBN: 978-1-7344730-1-8

Classic Monsters Unmade covers lost and unmade films starring Dracula, Frankenstein, the Mummy and more monsters. Reviews unmade scripts like *The Return of Frankenstein* (1934) and *Wolf Man vs. Dracula* (1944). It also examines lost films of the silent era such as *The Were-wolf* (1913) and *Drakula's Death* (1923). Softcover/Hardcover(428pp/5.83"X8.27") Suggested Retail: $22.99(sc)/$27.99(hc)ISBN:978-1-953221-85-8(hc)

Volume 2 explores the Hammer era and beyond, from unmade versions of *Brides of Dracula* (called *Disciple of Dracula*) to remakes of *Creature from the Black Lagoon*. Completely unmade films like *Kali: Devil Bride of Dracula* (1975) and *Godzilla vs. Frankenstein* (1964) are covered along with lost completed films like *Batman Fights Dracula* (1967) and *Black the Ripper* (1974). Coming Fall 2021.

NOSTALGIA

Written in the same spirit as *The Big Book of Japanese Giant Monster Movies*, this tome reviews all the classic Universal and Hammer horrors to star Dracula, Frankenstein, the Gillman and the rest along with obscure flicks like *The New Invisible Man* (1958), *Billy the Kid versus Dracula* (1966), *Blackenstein* (1973) and *Legend of the Werewolf* (1974). Coming 2021.

Written at an intermediate reading level for the kid in all of us, these picture books will take you back to your youth. In the spirit of the old Ian Thorne books are covered *Nabonga* (1944), *White Pongo* (1945) and more! Hardcover/Softcover (44 pp/7.5" X 9.25") Suggested Retail: $17.95(hc)/$9.99(sc) ISBN: 978-1-7341546-9-6 (hc) 978-1-7344730-5-6 (sc)

Written at an intermediate reading level for the kid in all of us, these picture books will take you back to your youth. In the spirit of the old Ian Thorne books are covered *The Lost World* (1925), *The Land That Time Forgot* (1975) and more! Hardcover/Softcover (44 pp/7.5" X 9.25") Suggested Retail: $17.95 (hc)/$9.99(sc) ISBN: 978-1-7344730-6-3 (hc) 978-1-7344730-7-0 (sc)

Written at an intermediate reading level for the kid in all of us, these picture books will take you back to your youth. In the spirit of the old Ian Thorne books are covered *Them!* (1954), *Empire of the Ants* (1977) and more! Hardcover/Softcover (44 pp/7.5" X 9.25") Suggested Retail: $17.95(hc)/$9.99(sc) ISBN: 978-1-7347816-3-2 (hc) 978-1-7347816-2-5 (sc)

THE BICEP BOOKS CATALOGUE

CRYPTOZOOLOGY/COWBOYS & SAURIANS

Cowboys & Saurians: Prehistoric Beasts as Seen by the Pioneers explores dinosaur sightings from the pioneer period via real newspaper reports from the time. Well-known cases like the Tombstone Thunderbird are covered along with more obscure cases like the Crosswicks Monster and more. Softcover (357 pp/5.06" X 7.8") Suggested Retail: $19.95 ISBN: 978-1-7341546-1-0

Cowboys & Saurians: Ice Age zeroes in on snowbound saurians like the Ceratosaurus of the Arctic Circle and a Tyrannosaurus of the Tundra, as well as sightings of Ice Age megafauna like mammoths, glyptodonts, Sarkastodons and Sabertoothed tigers. Tales of a land that time forgot in the Arctic are also covered. Softcover (264 pp/5.06" X 7.8") Suggested Retail: $14.99 ISBN: 978-1-7341546-7-2

Southerners & Saurians takes the series formula of exploring newspaper accounts of monsters in the pioneer period with an eye to the Old South. In addition to dinosaurs are covered Lizardmen, Frogmen, giant leeches and mosquitoes, and the Dingocroc, which might be an alien rather than a prehistoric survivor. Softcover (202 pp/5.06" X 7.8") Suggested Retail: $13.99 ISBN: 978-1-7344730-4-9

Cowboys & Saurians South of the Border explores the saurians of Central and South America, like the Patagonian Plesiosaurus that was really an lemisch, plus tales of the Neo-Mylodon, a menacing monster from underground called the Minhocao, Glyptodonts, and even Bolivia's three-headed dinosaur! Softcover (412 pp/ 5.06"X7.8") Suggested Retail: $17.95 ISBN: 978-1-953221-73-5

UFOLOGY/THE REAL COWBOYS & ALIENS IN CONJUNCTION WITH ROSWELL BOOKS

The Real Cowboys and Aliens: Early American UFOs explores UFO sightings in the USA between the years 1800-1864. Stories of encounters sometimes involved famous figures in U.S. history such as Lewis and Clark, and Thomas Jefferson.Hardcover (242pp/6" X 9") Softcover (262 pp/5.06" X 7.8") Suggested Retail: $24.99 (hc)/$15.95(sc) ISBN: 978-1-7341546-8-9\(hc)/978-1-7344 730-8-7(sc)

The second entry in the series, *Old West UFOs*, covers reports spanning the years 1865-1895. Includes tales of Men in Black, Reptilians, Spring-Heeled Jack, Sasquatch from space, and other alien beings, in addition to the UFOs and airships. Hardcover (276 pp/6" X 9") Softcover (308 pp/5.06" X 7.8") Suggested Retail: $29.95 (hc)/$17.95(sc) ISBN: 978-1-7344730-0-1 (hc)/ 978-1-73447 30-2-5 (sc)

The third entry in the series, *The Coming of the Airships*, encompasses a short time frame with an incredibly high concentration of airship sightings between 1896-1899. The famous Aurora, Texas, UFO crash of 1897 is covered in depth along with many others. Hardcover (196 pp/6" X 9") Softcover (222 pp/5.06" X 7.8") Suggested Retail: $24.99 (hc)/$15.95(sc) ISBN: 978-1-7347816 -1-8 (hc)/978-1-7347816-0-1(sc)

Early 20th Century UFOs kicks off a new series that investigates UFO sightings of the early 1900s. Includes tales of UFOs sighted over the *Titanic* as it sunk, Nikola Tesla receiving messages from the stars, an alien being found encased in ice, and a possible virus from outer space!Hardcover (196 pp/6" X 9") Softcover (222 pp/5.06" X 7.8") Suggested Retail: $27.99 (hc)/$16.95(sc) ISBN: 978-1-7347816-1-8 (hc)/978-1-73478 16-0-1(sc)

391

LOST FILMS FANZINE BACK ISSUES

THE LOST FILMS FANZINE VOL.1

ISSUE #1 SPRING 2020 The lost Italian cut of *Legend of Dinosaurs and Monster Birds* called *Terremoto 10 Grado*, plus *Bride of Dr. Phibes* script, *Good Luck! Godzilla*, the King Kong remake that became a car comm ercial, Bollywood's lost *Jaws* rip-off, Top Ten Best Fan Made Godzilla trailers plus an interview with Scott David Lister. 60 pages. Three variant covers/editions (premium color/basic color/ b&w)

ISSUE #2 SUMMER 2020 How 1935's *The Capture of Tarzan* became 1936's *Tarzan Escapes*, the Orca sequels that weren't, Baragon in Bollywood's *One Million B.C.*, unmade *Kolchak: The Night Stalker* movies, *The Norliss Tapes*, *Superman V: The New Movie*, why there were no *Curse of the Pink Panther* sequels, *Moonlight Mask: The Movie.* 64 pages. Two covers/ editions (basic color/b&w)

ISSUE #3 FALL 2020 Blob sequels both forgotten and unproduced, *Horror of Dracula* uncut, *Franken-stein Meets the Wolfman* and talks, myths of the lost *King Kong* Spider-Pit sequence debunked, the *Carnosaur* novel vs. the movies, *Terror in the Streets* 50th anniversary, *Bride of Godzilla* 55th Unniversary, Lee Powers sketchbook. 100 pages. Two covers/editions (basic color/b&w)

ISSUE #4 WINTER 2020/21 *Diamonds Are Forever's* first draft with Goldfinger, *Disciple of Dracula* into *Brides of Dracula, War of the Worlds* That Weren't Part II, *Day the Earth Stood Still II* by Ray Bradbury, *Deathwish 6, Atomic War Bride, What Am I Doing in the Middle of a Revolution?, Spring Dream in the Old Capital* and more. 70 pages. Two covers/editions (basic color/b&w)

THE LOST FILMS FANZINE VOL.2

ISSUE #5 SPRING 2021 The lost films and projects of ape suit performer Charles Gemora, plus *Superman Reborn, Teenage Mutant Ninja Turtles IV: The Next Mutation, Mikado Zombie,* NBC's *Big Stuffed Dog,* King Ghidorah flies solo, *Grizzly II* reviewed, and War of the Worlds That Weren't concludes with a musical. Plus Blu-Ray reviews, news, and letters. 66 pages. Two covers/editions (basic co-lor/ b&w)

ISSUE #6 SUMMER 2021 Peter Sellers *Romance of the Pink Panther,* Akira Kurosawa's *Song of the Horse, Kali - Devil Bride of Dracula,* Jack Black as Green Lantern, *Ladybug, Ladybug, The Lost Atlantis,* Japan's lost superhero Hiyo Man, and *Lord of Light,* the CIA's covert movie that inspired 2012's *Argo.* Plus news, Blu-Ray reviews, and letters. 72 pages. Two covers/editions (basic color/b&w)

ISSUE #7 FALL 2021 *Hiero's Journey,* Don Bragg in *Tarzan and the Jewels of Opar,* DC's *Lobo* movie, Lee Powers Scrapbook returns, Blake Matthew's uncovers *The Big Boss Part II* (1976), Matthew B. Lamont searches for lost Three Stooges, and an ape called Kong in 1927's *Isle of Sunken Gold.* Plus news, and letters. 72 pages. Two covers/editions (basic color /b&w)

ISSUE #8 WINTER 2021/22 The Bicep Books Story, Steve Reeves unmade third Hercules movie, Stan Hyde unveils the *Fate of Dr. Phibes,* Forgotten Saturday Supercade, sequels to *The Good, the Bad and the Ugly* that weren't, the 45th anniversary of Luigi Cozzi's "Cozzilla". Plus news, Blu-Ray reviews, and letters. 72 pages. Two covers/editions (basic color/b&w)

MOVIE MILESTONES BACK ISSUES

MOVIE MILESTONES VOL. 1   VOL.2

ISSUE #1 AUGUST 2020 Debut issue celebrating 80 years of *One Million B.C.* (1940), and an early 55th Anniversary for *One Million Years B.C.* (1966). Abandoned ideas, casting changes, and deleted scenes are covered, plus, a mini-B.C. stock-footage filmography and much more! 54 pages. Three collectible covers/editions (premium color/basic color/b&w)

ISSUE #2 OCTOBER 2020 Celebrates the joint 50th Anniversaries of *When Dinosaurs Ruled the Earth* (1970) and *Creatures the World Forgot* (1971). Also includes looks at *Prehistoric Women* (1967), *When Women Had Tails* (1970), and *Caveman* (1981), plus unmade films like *When the World Cracked Open.* 72 pages. Three collectible covers/editions (premium color/basic color/b&w)

ISSUE #3 WINTER 2021 Japanese 'Panic Movies' like *The Last War* (1961), *Submersion of Japan* (1973), and *Bullet Train* (1975) are covered on celebrated author Sakyo Komatsu's 90th birthday. The famous banned Toho film *Prophecies of Nostradamus* (1974) are also covered. 124 pages. Three collectible covers/editions (premium color/basic color/ b&w)

ISSUE #4 SPRING 2021 This issue celebrates the joint 60th Anniversaries of *Gorgo, Reptilicus* and *Konga* examining unmade sequels like *Reptilicus 2,* and other related lost projects like *Kuru Island* and *The Volcano Monsters.* Also explores the Gorgo, Konga and Reptilicus comic books from Charlton. 72 pages. Three collectible covers/editions (premium color/basic color/b&w)

MOVIE MILESTONES VOL. 2   VOL.3 COMING SOON

ISSUE #5 SUMMER 2021 *Godzilla vs. the Sea Monster* gets the spotlight, with an emphasis on its original version *King Kong vs. Ebirah,* plus information on *The King Kong Show* which inspired it, plus Jun Fukuda's tangentially related-ed spy series *100 Shot/100 Killed.* 72 pages. Three collectible covers/editions (premium color /basic color/b&w)

ISSUE #6 FALL 2021 Monster Westerns of the 1950s and 1960s are spotlighted in the form of *Teenage Monster, The Curse of the Undead, Billy the Kid Versus Dracula, Jesse James Meets Frankenstein's Daughter,* and Bela Lugosi's unmade *The Ghoul Goes West.* 50 pages. Special Black and White exclusive!

ISSUE #7 WINTER 2022 This issue is all about Shaft on the 50th Anniversary of *Shaft's Big Score* (1972). Original versions of the films, unmade sequels, plus books in the series never adapted to film will be explored.

ISSUE #8 SPRING 2022 *Godzilla vs. Gigan* turns 50 and this issue is here to celebrate with its many unmade versions, like *Godzilla vs. the Space Monsters* and *Return of King Ghidorah,* plus *The Mysterians* 65th anniversary and *Daigoro vs. Goliath's* 50th.

The year is 1950, and old timers connected to the outlaw Billy the Kid are popping up dead in the sleepy town of Fort Sumner, New Mexico. It's up to the local sheriff, Hondo Dumez, to figure out why. Matters become complicated upon the news that a man claiming to be a surviving Billy the Kid is about to meet with the current governor of New Mexico. Added to the mystery are whispers of a secretive organization known as the Santa Fe Ring and rumors of something called a Skinwalker haunting the area. As the case twists and turns its way from the haunted halls of Dorsey Mansion to the ice caves of the Malpais, Dumez won't just need all the help he can get to solve the greatest mystery of the Southwest, he'll be lucky to survive the investigation at all.